The Life and Crimes of John Morrissey

Bare-Knuckle Boxing Champion, New York Gangster,
Irish American Politician

I0125373

Kenneth Bridgham

**WIN BY
KO**

Win By KO Publications
IOWA CITY

The Life and Crimes of John Morrissey

Kenneth Bridgham

(ISBN-13): 978-1-949783-02-5

(softcover: 50# acid-free alkaline paper)

Includes footnotes, index, and bibliography

© 2020 by Kenneth Bridgham. All Rights Reserved.

No part of this book may be reproduced, or transmitted in any form or by any means, graphic, electronic or mechanical, including photocopying, recording, taping, or by any information storage retrieval system without the written permission of Kenneth Bridgham or Win By KO Publications.

Cover design by Christian Baldo ©

Manufactured in the United States of America.

Win By KO Publications

Iowa City, Iowa

winbykopublications.com

To Mom and Dad, thanks...for everything.

To Kenny, my best bud. I'm so proud of you.

Contents

Acknowledgements

The first people to thank are the friends, family, teachers, and professors who have been supportive of my writing, and in particular this book, over the years. Big or small, whether it was your encouragement, inspiration, patience, help, or sacrifice, it means a great deal to me. This book is as much yours as it is mine. However, there are a few individuals who have provided support or inspiration worthy of extra recognition, and I would like to take the time to acknowledge their contributions now.

My mother Ann Bridgham took my sister and I to the library every week, and had us writing book reports and taking classes on a wide array of topics through the summers. She has a love for learning and experiencing new things, and has supported and encouraged my desire to be a writer all along

My father Kenneth Everett Bridgham has been obsessed with one branch of history or another as long as I can remember, and it is from him that I inherited my own obsessiveness, which kept me going in researching ever more information about John Morrissey. His encouragement and honest assessments have made him my most valuable consultant in writing this book. As such, he endured several drafts throughout its several years of creation, always providing encouraging and constructive feedback.

I would like to thank John Seidling. I always had a passing interest in boxing since I first saw a *Rocky* movie as a kid, but it was John who got me watching the sport when I was a teenager, introduced me to fellow boxing fans, and really kicked off my true interest in the sport. This book would not exist had it not been for all those nights watching great fights and debating boxing.

Thank you also to Christian Baldo, whose talent produced the design for the cover of the book you hold in your hand.

Finally, Adam Pollack, owner of Win By KO Publications, is more than that. As a boxing writer and historian, Mr. Pollack's series of biographies on the heavyweight champions of the gloved era of boxing set a new standard for exhaustive research and uncovering vivid details about boxing matches that happened before the age of film and television. His dedication to truth over myth raised the bar for all boxing historians, a bar I hope I have touched with this book. Mr. Pollack has been nothing but encouraging and helpful as my publisher, his advice, eye for detail, and constructive criticism helping to make the final draft of this book something of which I am very proud.

Prologue: The Man on the Train

A mighty train engine eased itself to a stop at the Bergen, New Jersey station like an exhausted pugilist stomping back to his corner for a brief respite between rounds. This was one of many stops along the brand-new New York Central Railroad's route from New York City to Buffalo. Among those waiting on the platform were two young men, their friendship with one another as obvious to their fellow travelers as their inebriation. Those forced to wait along with them for the train's arrival were by now clearly embarrassed by their drunken behavior and uncouth language. Once the train pulled in, the crowd waited to see which car these two would board first, before entering cars as far removed from them as possible. Traveling with that pair for the several hours to Buffalo was simply too much for any decent person to endure.

When the two obnoxious friends stepped into their chosen car, they found it mostly full. The only two open seats together were across from a small boy and two ladies, one of them obviously the child's mother. The drunks took the open seats and, paying little attention to their company, proceeded to continue the bawdy conversation they had begun on the platform. The train got under way. As is often the case when two intoxicated people begin telling jokes, each profane curse word was topped by one even worse. The cursing had the two women visibly shaken now, the mother covering her fascinated son's ears.

Sitting separately but within earshot was another young man. In his early twenties, he was the biggest man in the car. His bristly black hair and goatee and dark eyes added to his intimidating appearance. His muscular frame stretched the fabric of a poor man's suit. He had been quiet for the entire ride since boarding in New York City, but he was now shifting in his seat, flexing his hands and clenching his jaw, struggling to hold his tongue at hearing the behavior of the other two men in public. The language itself did not bother him; he had personally heard and said much worse all his life. It was the fact that these men clearly had no regard for the sensitivity of their company that had him struggling to maintain his composure. Finally, one of the two drunks uttered something completely beyond the bounds of decency, and all in earshot cringed at the vulgarity. The man from New York City had heard enough. He got to his feet. With a deep breath, he made a last effort to keep his temper in check as he made his way over to the offensive duo.

Putting on as friendly of a tone as he could muster, the big man said to the drunks, "Come, boys, let's go in the smoking car and have a good cigar." Their reply was as vulgar as the rest of their conversation. At this, the big man took the lone open seat beside the women and the boy, across from the pair of troublemakers. With anger storming underneath his furrowed brow, the man leaned forward and, in a hushed but insistent tone, asked the drunks to lower their voices. This time, neither man bothered to even reply, but instead one of them began to tell the other a story with such explicit and lurid details as to be a direct challenge to the man in front of them, who interrupted the story by demanding they both stop talking at once.

"Mind your own business," the storyteller replied dismissively.

"My business," shot back the black-haired stranger, rising to his feet once more, "is to protect ladies from insult, and if either of you says another improper word, I will pitch you both out of the cars."

The two men shot out of their seats. Now he had their attention. One of them sent a drunken punch fumbling through the air. The big man's natural fighting instincts easily dodged it and, before either of his opponents could react, he had grasped them both around their coat collars and smashed their skulls against each other. The knees of both men buckled, and they tumbled into his massive arms.

At this, the conductor appeared to investigate the news of trouble on his train. As soon as he stepped inside the car, someone shouted for him to open the door behind him. Seeing the two culprits caught up in the grip of the burly, black-haired fellow, he did just that. Once the door was open, the stranger first tossed one man and then dragged the other into the adjoining car. The passengers there sat in awed silence as they watched him beat, kick, and drag the pair through their car too. Someone stood up and opened the door to the next car, the smoking car. Here the big man dropped the stunned drunks on the floor and departed back through the intermediary car to his own, where he quietly took his seat for the remainder of the ride to Buffalo.[1]

The name of the powerful young man on board the train that day in the early 1850s would have been unknown to his grateful fellow passengers then, but he would very soon become one of the most famous men in America. He was an Irish immigrant named John Morrissey, and the incident on the train illustrates many qualities that would direct the course of his unique life. He was obviously good with his fists. He had a notoriously violent temper and an especially short fuse when it came to men who abused women. He was a restless and fearless traveler, who by this time in his life had already made the journey from the Irish countryside to industrial Troy, New York, and then to the swelling metropolis of New York City itself, and had also stowed away on a boat to California, lured by the 1849 Gold Rush. That journey west would be the first of many

[1] *Ogdensburg Journal*, November 12, 1877; *Sporting Life*, March 28, 1860

endeavors during which John Morrissey's eventful life intersected closely with important events in American history.

———

Morrissey's life would encapsulate the inextricable web of American sporting culture, street crime, local and national politics, and high finance that spread throughout nineteenth century New York more than that of any other man of his time. He was an undefeated bareknuckle prize-fighter widely recognized as the national champion. He was a feared gangster and mob boss before either term was coined, rumored leader of the Dead Rabbits street gang, and alleged conspirator in one of the most publicized American murders of the mid-nineteenth century. He was the millionaire operator of some of the world's most opulent gambling halls and the founder of the Saratoga thoroughbred racecourse. He was a leader of New York's corrupt Tammany Hall political organization, a U.S. congressman, and a New York state senator. He married one of the most beautiful women in New York. He counted among his friends and allies pimps, madams, and thieves, as well as railroad tycoon Cornelius Vanderbilt, presidential candidates Horace Greeley and Samuel Tilden, and President Andrew Johnson, while pursuing rivalries with the likes of boxers Yankee Sullivan and John Heenan, feared streetfighter Bill "The Butcher" Poole, corrupt politicians William "Boss" Tweed and "Honest" John Kelly, as well as Wall Street magnate "Diamond" Jim Fisk. Perhaps most importantly, he rose to a level of wealth and power unprecedented for Irish Americans to that point in the nation's history. During his lifetime, some admired him as a paragon of American ingenuity and capitalism, others as a heroic model of masculinity, and by others still as a worthless, drunken brute indicative of all that was wrong in the country. Each description is an over-simplification of a short life defined by ambition, conflict, and change.

1.

Immigrant

John Morrissey was born the first child of Timothy and Julia Morrissey on February 12, 1831 in Templemore, County Tipperary, Ireland, "famous for the fighting propensities of its peasants." Tipperary was home to more than 402,000 people at the time. Geographically, it is the country's largest landlocked county, resting at the heart of the island's southern end. Templemore itself lay toward the northern end of the county and was perhaps most famous then for being the site of McCan Barracks, a military base constructed in 1809. Between its parish and its town, Templemore itself was home to 4,983 people in 1831. It was, according to one late nineteenth century writer, "in the centre of a fertile country, richly planted and most picturesquely diversified.... No town in the county can compare with it in the beauty of the approaches." Like most rural towns, it served primarily as a marketplace for the many local farmers, complete with a Market House built in 1816. Templemore was also the site of several fairs said to be "among the best in Ireland." A Protestant church, erected in 1790, served as a center for local religious and social life.[2]

As beautiful as Templemore may have been to the naked eye, things were becoming increasingly dismal for the common people who lived there by the year of John Morrissey's birth. Tim had been a child during the Irish Rebellion of 1798, but he had seen first-hand the British crown's brutal and bloody repression of the Irish afterward, a memory that would prove painful for him to discuss in adulthood. The potato blight that would send huge masses of people into Canada and the United States was still years away, but already signs of trouble were evident. A typhus epidemic had struck Ireland between 1816 and 1819, killing tens of thousands of people, most of them from the lower class to which the Morrisseys belonged (though one source reports the family as being of an "old and respected stock – a sturdy class of yeomen"). More recently, a mysterious crop failure had struck Ireland in the early 1830s, which made the already challenging task of finding food and money in one of Ireland's most populous counties even more difficult. As is often the case when essential resources are scarce, civil unrest was also becoming more frequent throughout the county.[3]

---

[2] *New York Times*, October 23, 1858; "Return of Population of Counties of Ireland, 1831," archive.org, accessed 9/16/2016; "Census of Population of Ireland, 1831: Comparative Abstract, 1821 and 1831," archive.org, accessed 9/16/2016; Bassett, 347
[3] *Irish American*, October 9, 1875

Fleeing these conditions, the Morrisseys left Ireland in August of 1832, when John was only about eighteen months old, taking a boat from Belfast to the United States and arriving in New York Harbor in September. From there, like many Irish of the time, they moved on to Canada, settling for a brief period in Quebec. However, employment for Tim proved scarce, and he relocated his family once again, this time to Troy, New York in the United States of America, a town on the banks of the Hudson River, close to Albany. John was somewhere between three and five years old when the family arrived in Troy.[4]

Close in proximity to the recently completed Erie Canal, Troy had only just incorporated as a city in 1816. A humble port located between Vermont and New York City, it had been a modest agricultural village for most of its history. However, a growing iron industry was now in evidence, giving families like the Morrisseys hope of plentiful work opportunities to come. That other families from Tipperary had settled in Troy made the transition easier. This was where John Morrissey would grow up.

In his later life, reporters interviewed Morrissey about his humble beginnings on multiple occasions. In none of these did he even make mention of his parents. Whether this was because the reporters simply did not ask or because he wanted to avoid portraying himself as anything but American, or because he somehow resented his parents for something about his upbringing cannot be known, but it nonetheless seems a peculiar choice.

Perhaps his avoidance of his parents as a topic for discussion stems from stories that both Tim and Julia were alcoholics. Hardly the ideal motherly figure, Julia would eventually become well-known throughout Troy as "a woman of unsteady habits [who] has probably engrossed the attention of the Troy magistrates more than any other person." At least one source describes Tim as a heavy drinker in later years. Most likely, neither addiction developed until after the family arrived in America. Such was the case for many Irish people who had been unable to afford alcoholic beverages at home. For them, the availability of affordable liquor and beer in the United States was a true cultural shock. Nineteenth century Irish politician John Maguire, in his book *The Irish in America*, noticed that Americans of all backgrounds used alcohol much more prevalently than did the people of Ireland. "Invitations are universal, as to rank and station, time and place, hour and circumstance," he observed, "they literally rain upon you." Putting the matter more plainly, one nineteenth century Irishman in New York City wrote home warning his family that any "person that does not think to mind himself let him stop at home for the whiskey is so cheap that it encourages the Irish fool to take it." The reputations of both of his parents as alcoholics, the fact that John would be

---

[4] *New York Times*, May 2, 1878; *Daily Albany Argus*, May 10, 1875; *Chicago Daily Tribune*, May 2, 1878; Bouyea, 16 (e-book); Kofoed, 19

kicked out of the family home as a young man, that he had little contact with his several sisters as an adult, and that he rarely spoke of his parents when remembering his early years all suggests a dysfunctional home life for the Morrisseys in Troy. At any rate, young John would grow up to emulate the drinking habits exhibited by his parents and many of the other adults who populated his community.[5]

Though he would have grown up relatively insulated among fellow Irish immigrants, John Morrissey doubtless encountered anti-immigrant and anti-Irish prejudice from a young age. His parents had witnessed the mistreatment of the Irish by the English in their native land, and Tim, "a stern, uncompromising nationalist," was said to be particularly sensitive to the topic; given his passion on the subject, it is likely that he passed along stories of the struggles in Ireland to his boy. Troy had itself been the scene of a violent anti-Irish St. Patrick's Day riot in 1835, when John was barely out of toddlerhood. Though hatred for the Irish was not as fervent in America as in England, the prejudice was still ever-present. Because they came from a culture that was more openly emotional than their English neighbors, an America still clinging to vestiges of conservative puritanism perceived their emotionality as rude and crude. One 1836 schoolbook on geography went so far as to describe all Irish as "ignorant, vain, and superstitious." Other less scholarly descriptions described them as "bog-trotters" and "niggers turned inside-out." They spoke English and had white skin, which gave them an advantage over some other ethnicities, but their customs (particularly the Catholics) and their tell-tale brogue clearly separated them from natural-born Americans. The wealthy considered them a drunken, alien rabble of little to no value except as cheap labor, while the working classes, including fellow immigrants, saw them as unwanted competition.[6]

It was amid this atmosphere of family dysfunction, alcoholism, poverty, and prejudice that John Morrissey would learn how to interact with the world and his fellow man, and those lessons would become the foundation for a life of violence, adventure, and ambition.

[5] Kofoed, 109; *New York Times*, March 19, 1860; *Daily Empire*, March 22, 1860; Maguire, 283; Anbinder, 136, quoting Pat McGowan
[6] Isenberg, 22, 41; Redmond, 53; *Irish American*, October 9, 1875

2.

Chief Devil

Like most adult male Irish immigrants, Tim Morrissey worked whatever menial labor jobs were available to him, mostly in the lumber trade, earning around one dollar a day. Over the next several years, while her husband toiled in the mills, factories, and boats of Troy, Julia would give birth to six more children, all of them girls.

By the time he reached his teens, John was already noticeably bigger than most boys his age and had earned a reputation as a ruffian who rarely heeded authority. According to one source, his father, "remarkable for his herculean strength," was known to be something of a fighter back in Ireland, and it was from his father that John was supposed to have inherited his fistic abilities. By John's own admission, he attended only one year of school and "learned more mischief than letters." He would not learn to read or write until adulthood. He was an unruly youth, known for using his fists and causing havoc in the streets. Even his future wife had no illusions about her beloved husband's unsavory beginnings. Having known him since childhood, she later described him as "a ragged little boy about Troy, barefooted and belligerent, always looking for a fight." John ran with street gangs almost from the time he could run at all, eventually forming his own clique, the Down Town Gang, to battle older rivals Jack O'Rourke and John Mackey and their Up Town Gang. Clearly a troublemaker who loved a good brawl, John quickly established himself as the "chief devil" (his own words) of the Down Town toughs.[7]

Among those running the Troy streets at this time was another bruiser whose size eclipsed even Morrissey's. John Heenan was three years Morrissey's junior, yet towered over all the other boys — and most of the men — they knew. The Morrissey and Heenan families had both hailed from Templemore and had arrived in the United States and Troy at about the same time, the Morrisseys eventually settling on the east side of town, while the Heenans lived in West Troy. If they had not already been close in Ireland, the two clans became quick friends in America. Unlike John Morrissey, John Heenan had been born on American soil. The head of the Heenan family was also named Tim, and he worked as a foreman at the Watervliet Arsenal just outside of town. Unfortunately, the two Tims had a falling out over the results of a cock fight when the two Johns were still boys. It seems Tim Morrissey's bird had won, and he had gloated too

[7] Kofoed, 21; *New York Times*, May 2, 1878; *Wilson County Citizen*, October 8, 1875; *Danville Express*, May 8, 1878; *New York Tribune*, March 10, 1855; *Manawatu Times*, February 7, 1888; *Irish American*, October 9, 1875

much for Tim Heenan's taste. The escalating feud between the fathers would seep into the relationship between their sons, who would bear a lifelong grudge toward one another. Though they would fight at each other's side in the gang, their alliance likely had more to do with their mutual hatred of the Up Town Gang than any friendship with each other. Perhaps, too, each already recognized in the other the physical prowess and ambition that would one day make them two of the most notorious American men of their generation, and they decided it best to keep the other as a begrudging ally rather than an enemy. At any rate, if any other gang existed in the sphere of Morrissey's Down Town Gang, they didn't do so for long. A young tough like Heenan would have probably had the choice of either joining the Down Town Gang or joining no gang at all, which may have appeared to be the more dangerous proposition, even for a boy of Heenan's build.

———

When John Morrissey was twelve, his family moved to the East side of the Hudson River, settling on Ferry Street. The hope was that Tim would find more work there. John left school a year after the move to join his father in the labor force, finding employment in Orr's wallpaper factory for $1.25 every sixty-hour work week. He spent his days brushing paint across pieces of cloth, onto which a printer would then press wood-cut blocks, which were in turn used to transfer the paint onto wallpaper. Somehow the undisciplined ruffian stuck around for at least a year of this mind-numbing work before he found other employment.

Not surprisingly, the promise of doubling his pay enticed him to leave Orr's and sign on for the more strenuous work of removing heavy and still hot metal bars from the forge at what would later be known as the Burden Iron Mills. By that time, the iron works industry was quickly becoming the foundation of Troy's economy. During the nineteenth century, the south side of the city was home to the four largest iron mills in the United States, all of them constructed along the Hudson. The original building had been built in 1809 and expanded upon in 1813, after the Troy Iron and Nail Factory Company bought it. By 1822, Henry Burden had arrived from Albany and stepped in as superintendent. An 1824 newspaper account estimated that the mill was then producing up to a thousand tons of iron in a year. Burden developed several innovative patents, particularly one for mass producing horseshoes, which brought his company a great profit through developing the United States federal government as a client. The superintendent would slowly buy up stocks in the company until he was able to transform it into H. Burden & Sons in 1864. At these mills, the teenage Morrissey's size and strength made him a valuable commodity, earning him a reputation for being able to handle a grown man's duties.[8]

---

[8] *New York Times*, May 2, 1878 and July 7, 1885; www.rootsweb.ancestry.com; Weise, 43 - 46

He eventually left the iron works too, having secured nine dollars a week working in the molding room at the Johnson, Cox & Co. stove factory. During the winter months, when the stove making business was slow, the company put John to work on making bomb shells for the U.S. Army to use in the Mexican War. John must have been proud of this job as, years later, when famed journalist Benjamin Perley Poore interviewed him and asked for his occupation, John replied, "On the whole, for my boy's sake, put it down molder, as I worked at that business in a Troy stove foundry before I went to New York." Twentieth century Morrissey biographer Jack Kofoed records that John Heenan also worked at the stove factory, while a *New York Times* article says that Morrissey and Heenan worked in the same shop at the Burden Mills. [9]

In no more than a couple of years, young Morrissey had worked three separate jobs and, through opportunism and hard work, went from making just over a dollar a week to making nine dollars a week, exemplifying the restlessness, ambition, greed, and physical prowess that would all be hallmarks of his adult personality. The hard labor jobs were developing his body as well. He was already a large young man for his time, but this work was now lining his skeleton with taught muscle that would intimidate the many enemies John would develop over the coming lifetime.

———

A trouble-making denizen of the streets like John Morrissey had no difficulty finding opportunities to put his newly muscle-bound body to the test. The moments he did not spend doing manual labor he spent in malicious violence. Quick-tempered and "built like a young bull," Morrissey regularly found himself in arguments with co-workers and rival gang members on the job site, in the streets, or in the saloon. If the arguments came to blows, which often happened, it would be imperative that John have friends as well as enemies. He made sure to cultivate friendships with co-workers who knew how to handle themselves with their fists. The street wars between his Down Town ruffians and those of Jack O'Rourke's Up Town Gang became "incessant and very annoying to the respectable citizens of Troy." On one such occasion in 1848, the teenager found himself in the street alone, surrounded by a crowd of Up Towners that included O'Rourke himself. A clearly inebriated O'Rourke set upon the younger man right away, but his cronies pulled him off Morrissey, fearing that their drunken leader would be badly beaten. As his opponents argued amongst themselves, John made his exit, cursing himself for being caught off guard and promising himself that it would not happen again.

Just a few days had passed when the men again ran into each other in Lawrence's Saloon on River Street. This time, a large contingent of

[9] *New York Times*, May 2, 1878 and July 7, 1885

Downtowners accompanied John, as they had every night since his previous encounter with O'Rourke. O'Rourke's own supporters were once again at his side. The entourages proved unneeded; Morrissey and O'Rourke tore into each other at first sight, without their cronies needing to lift a finger. As O'Rourke's men had feared, Morrissey badly punished his older rival and emerged victorious. Embarrassed by their man's defeat at the hands of a teenager, eight members (some sources report nine) of the Up Town Gang would challenge John to fist fights one after another in the coming days. When all eight met the same fate as their leader, Morrissey's reputation as the most fearsome brawler in Troy was secure.[10]

By the winter of 1847, word of the teenager's fistic abilities reached the ears of Alexander Hamilton (no relation to the Founding Father), the overlord of Troy's most successful prostitution ring. One source says Hamilton first heard of young Morrissey from a bragging Tim Morrissey, John's father. Hamilton's various brothels had earned a reputation for unruliness that was beginning to scare away patrons and take a toll on the whoremaster's finances. He had been in search of a rough and intimidating fellow who could prevent bloodshed in his establishments and summoned Morrissey to visit him in the upstairs office of a saloon he ran. To prove his qualifications at the job interview, the sixteen-year-old picked out from among the crowd at the bar one Bibber M'Geehan, a two-hundred-pound dockworker notorious locally for gouging out the eyes and biting off the noses of men who riled his temper. Utilizing a few choice words, John picked a fight with the older man and then proceeded to relieve him of his consciousness with a single blow, lift him over his shoulders and toss him out through the front door into the street. Delighted at his discovery, Hamilton offered John twenty dollars a week. Before the boss had shelled out the first twenty, peace had returned to the brothels of Troy. According to Jack Kofoed, John always split his pay with his mother, spending his own half quickly enough that his pockets were empty by the time Hamilton paid him the next twenty.[11]

Hamilton was on hand to witness another of John's violent displays following a baseball game where the hot-tempered and viciously competitive youth wound up in an argument with a rival player named Malachi Brennan, better known to the locals as "the bully of Albany." The two men fell into impromptu fisticuffs that lasted an hour in length, during which "both boys displayed great pluck and endurance." When his new employee emerged the victor, Hamilton was again impressed. He suggested to John that he think of pursuing prize fighting seriously. A thrilling idea planted in his mind, John nonetheless returned to Hamilton's saloon, continuing to pour whiskey and bust heads through to the next summer.

---

[10] *Danville Express*, May 9, 1878; *New York Times*, May 2, 1878
[11] Fox, 33; Kofoed, 26-29

John's unruly behavior and notorious reputation had him in trouble with the law on numerous occasions. Decades later, an enemy would hand John's Troy rap sheet over to a reporter for the *New York Tribune*. It showed that in December 1848, the Troy police indicted a young Morrissey for assault with the intent to kill. April 1849 proved particularly troublesome. He was first tried for burglary and then sentenced to 60 days in prison for assault and battery. These events may have led to Tim and Julia kicking John out of their home, as John later remembered being homeless in this period, sleeping on a park bench or in "the meanest lodging-houses" when not in jail.[12]

———

Though many streetwise seventeen-year-olds would have been perfectly content with his reputation as the most feared tough in Troy and earning a tidy sum in the process, John Morrissey was already showing clear signs of the restless ambition that would come to define his entire life. Like most other Troy youths, he had long dreamed of success in New York City. However, the difference between John and the others was his fearless self-confidence. While the other boys daydreamed, John acted. He was not working for Hamilton long before he was already plotting how to succeed at his next venture.

John knew his spending habits would never allow him to save up enough cash to finance a move to the big city, and he never fooled himself into thinking he could curb those habits. So, he hit upon another idea. Troy lay about 150 miles north of New York City along the Hudson River. There were always riverboats shuttling up and down the Hudson, boats that could find use for a strapping young man such as himself. Dreams of adventure and wealth pushing him on, John payed a visit to the Troy docks and inquired of employment with Levi Smith, Captain of a local riverboat, *Empire*. Tim Morrissey had worked for a time under Captain Smith when the family had first moved to Troy and was proud of the fact; thus, Smith was the first Captain to whom John went looking for work. Smith took him on as a deckhand, paying him fifteen dollars a month, a salary supplemented by anywhere from fifty to a hundred in tips. "I was a river-boy," Morrissey himself later described, "handling baggage and running for passengers, and very ambitious with very little opportunity." John had been at work for Hamilton for six months when he took his leave to work aboard the steamship. Upset at losing his best henchman, the whoremaster offered a pay raise to thirty dollars a week but Morrissey, excited by the opportunities presented by his new job, turned him down.[13]

[12] *New York Tribune*, November 2, 1877; *Memphis Daily Appeal*, April 19, 1871
[13] *New York Times*, May 2, 1878; *Chicago Daily Tribune*, August 1, 1874; *Daily Albany Argus*, May 10, 1875

John's unruly and restless nature continued to get the better of him and he later remembered being "kicked ashore 'most every day from the boat." Yet he was also ambitious, wanting more than the life of labor that his father had endured. Travelling up and down the Hudson presented that opportunity for excitement and money. It allowed him the opportunity to sneak away whenever the boat docked in New York City. He thrilled at the sights and sounds of the exciting metropolis, doubtless spending considerable time carousing through the saloons, theaters, and gambling dens of the notorious Five Points and waterfront neighborhoods, as well as taking in the carnival atmosphere of the Bowery, "the most interesting street in the city."[14]

Working for Captain Smith also gave John the opportunity to make better friends with Susannah Smith – Susan or Susie for short – the Captain's teenage daughter, whom John had known since childhood. What Levi Smith, not just a river boat captain but also a modestly successful businessman, thought of Susan talking with some Irish ruffian four years older than herself has not been recorded, but for John it was a rare opportunity to converse and learn from a person who lived on a higher rung on the social ladder. The Smiths were by no means wealthy, but the Captain was no day laborer. He made enough money to ensure that his family lived comfortably, and the Smiths raised young Susan to attend school and church dutifully and display good manners. To the son of working-class alcoholic immigrants, the Smith household was a different world entirely. If John harbored any romantic fantasies for the boss' daughter, they would have seemed impossible at the time. His ambition had a practicality which told him to look elsewhere for money, respect, and romance.[15]

By now John had developed into a full-grown man, standing just short of six feet in height and weighing more than 170 pounds. He had long been interested in athletics, with at least one source saying he was an "apt ball player." But his favorite sport was without a doubt boxing. "I looked around me, very poor and illiterate" he later told an interviewer, "and asked what I could do best of anything to get on. There was nothing I could think of but to fight, and I had to think of that."[16]

[14] *New York Sun*, May 2, 1878; *Chicago Daily Tribune*, August 1, 1874
[15] *Chicago Daily Tribune*, August 1, 1874; Haswell, 354
[16] *New York Sun*, May 2, 1878; *Chicago Daily Tribune*, August 1, 1874

3.

Manly and Courageous Contest

On Wednesday, February 7, 1849, Alexander Hamilton, the vice lord of Troy and until recently John Morrissey's employer, was among a select crowd of other notorious characters who gathered to watch a boxing match between the two best prize fighters on American soil. Hamilton had traveled roughly three hundred miles from Troy to arrive at a secluded beach on Still Pond Creek in Maryland, where men had marked out a ring in the snow with posts tied around with rope. The two combatants were to be native born Tom Hyer and an Irishman calling himself Yankee Sullivan. The men bitterly detested one another and made their mutual hatred known in the newspapers which had covered their rivalry with great financial rewards; for the grudge between the American and the Irishman had sparked the interest of the American populace like no other boxing match previous.

Indeed, until very recently, boxing had been all but ignored by Americans in general, mention of it popping up only sporadically in newspapers and magazines prior to the 1830s. Fist-fighting for pay and entertainment existed only as a cultural oddity imported from England, where Londoners first revived it from its Ancient Greek origins with serious intentions in the prior century. Many Brits adored boxing, some commending the refined science of self-defense while others were fascinated by the primitiveness of its violence. Members of the royal family and others within the British nobility had patronized boxing for decades. The public increasingly referred to these extremely upper-class men who enjoyed gambling, sport, and gaudy living as "the fancy." They invented various rules for the fighters to follow, such as not hitting a man when he was down, no punching the groin, and other rudimentary guidelines for behavior that helped the well-to-do spectators feel less squeamish about watching two men tear each other apart. In 1838, these rules were collected and catalogued into what were known as the London Prize Ring Rules, which, revised and refined through the years, would become the agreed upon standard for boxing matches for most of the rest of the nineteenth century. The heroes of the English ring became idols of the common man, lauded as champions, their backgrounds and ring exploits recited in widely read publications like *The Sporting Magazine* and *Bell's Life in London*. British immigrants, merchants, sailors, and soldiers who read those magazines avidly were the first to bring the sport to American shores.

Despite the London Prize Ring Rules, boxing in the nineteenth century was a far cry from the gloved and regulated sport practiced today. Boxers used gloves only for sparring and "scientific exhibitions." Any prize fight that took place while the participants wore gloves of any kind would not be taken seriously by anyone. Rounds had no time limit, ending only when a fighter fell to the ground. After this, the referee gave both fighters thirty seconds to make it back to a line marked at the ring's center, called "the scratch." If one did not make the scratch, the referee declared his opponent victor. All serious prize fights of this period were to the finish. While rules existed, grappling, wrestling, rabbit punching, and kidney punching were encouraged rather than outlawed. Technically, head-butting, ear tearing, tripping, low blows, choking, eye-gouging, biting, and hair pulling were all illegal, but still widely practiced. A boxer was well advised to enter the ring with his head shaven to avoid having his hair pulled. He might also wear shoes with spiked soles, ostensibly to provide firm footing in the sod, but also good for raking against an opponent's shins.

A fighter typically entered the ring with two corner men, called "seconds." One would kneel in his man's corner, with one leg up to serve as a stool for the fighter. The other man stood, offering encouragement and instruction. There were two sets of ropes making up the ring. The inner circle was where the fighters, the referee, and seconds went about their business. Each fighter also selected a judge or umpire, typically a trusted friend. Umpires were allowed inside the outer set of ropes and it was their job to make sure that no foul was committed against the man who selected them. If an umpire cried foul and the other umpire disagreed, it was up to the referee, a neutral party agreed to by both fighters, to decide the truth of the matter. Everyone else was supposed to stay on the outside of the second set of ropes, a rule which proved difficult to enforce. Overzealous and sometimes armed spectators often made their way across both barriers with violent intentions.

No time limit and no gloves meant that boxers also fought differently than they do today, out of necessity. Combination and haymaker punching were rare, and participants usually fought in an exceedingly defensive posture. The lack of gloves meant that most boxers had less than a half-dozen prize fights in their lifetimes, due to the damage done to their bare hands. Historian Alan Lloyd, in describing a famous nineteenth century bout in England, gives an accurate account of the manner of the era's best prize fights:

> With no system of scoring, no limit to the rounds involved, the contest became a battle of attrition with exhaustion playing an increasing role. Neither man boxed for a knock-out. Both knew that, while the half-minute count curtailed the chances of a *coup de grace*, big punching invited knuckle injury, a disastrous circumstance in the ring. Instead, the pugilists went for soft targets, chiseling at nerves, heart and kidneys, 'rabbit' punching, holding-and-hitting.

They also hugged and threw the opponent, 'accidentally' falling on him.[17]

Just as in England, evidence of the practice of organized boxing in America dates as far back as the early eighteenth century, but it did not catch on with the public at large as swiftly as it did across the proverbial pond. America's puritanical beginnings put a high moral value on self-restraint and hard work, allowing little understanding for frivolous recreation and leisure, let alone bloodletting for entertainment. In the almost entirely agricultural America of the colonial period, a man might enjoy the sport of hunting or fishing, but the practical purpose of these pursuits was the measure of their true importance. The first prominent American fighters did not appear until the early nineteenth century. These were Bill Richmond and Tom Molineaux, both African Americans (and, legend has it, freed slaves) who pursued their careers in England to get the big fights and big money not available stateside. Tradition points to the 1816 brawl between Jacob Hyer, a butcher by trade, and sailor Tom Beasley, two "very large and powerful first class men," as the first important match on American soil. However, they seem to have fought over personal differences rather than money; thus, the match was not truly a prize fight. Though boxing fans would fondly remember the Hyer-Beasley bout (which ended in a draw) for decades to come, it did not ignite any lasting, widespread interest in the sport.[18]

The first boxers to generate enduring mainstream notoriety for boxing in America were successful English pugilists who crossed the Atlantic in the 1830s, during John Morrissey's childhood. By this time, boxing had become a difficult profession to pursue in England. Where once boxers had enjoyed royal patronage and status as national icons, a series of high-profile fixed fights and ring deaths in the preceding years had lost the sport many fans and supporters. Worse yet, a wave of religious evangelism and moral rectitude was swiftly overtaking the popular conscience, soon to find a symbol in the young Queen Victoria. The troubles culminated with the Gaming Act of 1845, which outlawed boxing and several other unsavory entertainments. Though men continued to practice the sport, mainstream British society now shunned boxers as scandalous characters, fights were clandestine events, and money became increasingly scarce in pugilistic circles. To many English boxers, fighting in the relatively lawless United States, which was experiencing an influx in the immigration of working-class Englishmen and Irishmen (the people who most avidly followed boxing) in these same years, now seemed an attractive proposition.

When James Burke of London killed a man in the ring and narrowly avoided jail time, he fled to American shores as much out of necessity as anything else. Partially deaf and burdened with a resulting speech

[17] Lloyd, 16
[18] Timony, 29; Isenberg, 44

impediment, Burke was a natural entertainer who played the role of the buffoon in the ring and out, going so far as to wear clownish makeup and "cavort like a large child." The English took to calling him Deaf Burke or The Deaf 'Un. But Burke was a talented and dangerous fist fighter recognized in some circles as the Champion of England. When, in 1833, opponent Simon Byrne died following more than three hours of fighting, Burke and his corner man faced manslaughter charges. A coroner later testified that Byrne's remains showed signs of a "former disease in the lungs" which could have contributed to his death, resulting in an acquittal for the defendants. They could not, however, avoid the public scandal, which proved disastrous for Burke's career in England. With popular taste for boxing already on the wane, finding opponents and financial backers had been difficult. Byrne's death made it impossible. After three years of inactivity, Burke sailed for America.[19]

Burke's notoriety in the States was as much due to further scandal as it was to skill. A match with one Sam O'Rourke in New Orleans on May 5, 1837 ended in chaos when, claiming a foul on Burke's part, the pro-O'Rourke mob cut the ropes to the ring and pandemonium ensued. Breaking free of the assault, Burke bolted from the scene on the nearest horse and made haste for the North. The bout and its inglorious ending received prominent coverage in several major newspapers. Though commentators decried the event as morally degrading and exemplary of foreign wickedness, there was no such thing as bad press, even in the nineteenth century.

The scandal only generated more public interest in Burke's second U.S. bout, in New York against a man named Tom O'Connell. At least three hundred spectators from America's growing sporting culture turned up, including fans from as far away as Baltimore. Burke demolished his adversary and again major newspapers were forced to reluctantly contend with the public's slowly increasing appetite for boxing news. "Although we regret and detest such exhibitions," complained the *New York Herald*, "our duty as chroniclers compels us to make public what otherwise we should bury in oblivion." Still, even the *Herald* recognized that there might be something more than brutality in boxing. "The British people are particularly fond of this exhibition," the writer editorialized, "and there are some good consequences attending it.... With all its disadvantages, therefore, and demoralizing tendency, it may be doubted whether the spirit emanating from it may not be productive of benefit among the lower classes." To the less scrupulous *Spirit of the Times*, started just a few years earlier as one of America's first sporting magazines and decried as "obscene" by moralists, the fight was "what the prize ring out to be – an exhibition of manly and courageous contest." Burke's name did not just appear in national newspapers and magazines, he was now a big enough cultural figure to be name-dropped by Captain Ahab in Herman Melville's

[19] Lloyd, 7; *Atlas*, July 14, 1833

1851 novel *Moby-Dick*. Having thrown the first blow for boxing's notoriety in America, James Burke eventually returned to England, losing that country's championship by disqualification to William "Bendigo" Thompson in 1839.[20]

Though the practice of and attention to the sport was clearly on the rise in America, that did not mean that a man could yet expect to make a living from pugilism. The great majority of boxing matches still took place as amateur recreation rather than as a professional pursuit. Burke and O'Rourke joined two men named Ned Hammond and George Kensett as probably the only boxers in America during the 1820s and 1830s who even tried to make a living primarily through boxing. Most of the country's boxers were either first- or second-generation Irish immigrants. Those men who took part in public boxing exhibitions earned their true living in other, less exhibitionist trades such as butchery, carpentry, and blacksmithing. Only a very few men successfully made money as boxing instructors. None outside of the professionals previously mentioned attained any notoriety beyond their own hometowns. Middle class Americans still abhorred pugilism as barbaric – especially if done for pay – and would continue to do so for generations to come.[21]

———

Enter the man who would be known alternately as James Ambrose, Frank Ambrose, Jim Sullivan, Frank Murray, Frank Martin, and, most famously, Yankee Sullivan. Indeed, Sullivan used so many sobriquets that even the best researched sources differ as to his birth name, some giving Frank Ambrose and others James Ambrose. The dates given for his birth range from 1807 to 1813, but most sources agree that the location was Brandon, near County Cork, in Ireland. Whatever his real name and origin, he would be the next nationally known boxing star in America and would eventually become a despised nemesis of John Morrissey.

The surviving accounts of Sullivan's life as a criminal jack-of-all-trades explain his need for so many false identities. According to legend, Sullivan was a part-time pugilist and full-time crook in his native land before the authorities shipped him off to Botany Bay, Australia in 1837. His crime was apparently theft or, according to some sources, the murder of his wife. Two years later he escaped as a stowaway on a ship bound for America, and from there made his way to England, where he resumed his boxing career and first began using the name Yankee as a reference to his brief foray stateside. After he proclaimed himself the champion middleweight of England, rumors that the police had finally discerned his true identity forced Sullivan to flee back across the Atlantic, where he settled in the predominantly Irish Five Points neighborhood of New York.

[20] Lloyd, 9, quoting *New York Herald*; Gorn, 45, quoting *Spirit of the Times*; Browne, 69
[21] Gorn, 45

Once in New York, Sullivan opened a saloon called the Sawdust House at 9 Chatham Street in the Bowery district and found work as a "shoulder hitter," the period's term for thugs who did the bidding of politicians. In a memorable description of the phrase, the *New York Times* once described shoulder hitters as "fellows who are trained to hit deadly blows 'straight from the shoulder;' who can fell an ox if they like; and who are especially to be feared when they bring their 'maulers' into play upon the human face divine…. In physical development, they are a splendid set of fellows – all muscle and no flesh." Sullivan became one of the most feared members of the Spartans, a band of toughs who worked for Mike Walsh, a radical within the Democratic Party ranks who pushed for working man's rights. When he wasn't running with the Spartans, Sullivan cracked heads in support of Matthew T. Brennan, an influential saloon keeper who also acted as the foreman of one of the neighborhood's several fire companies. Sullivan would often switch allegiances between the various political factions of the Five Points but remained a feared New York gangster into the early 1850s, regardless of which side he was on.[22]

His reputation as a fearsome streetfighter quickly and brutally established after his arrival, Sullivan wasted no time in notifying the city sporting circles that he was willing to face the best boxers America had to offer. Englishman Vincent Hammond and native-born American Thomas Secor were both conquered. The Secor contest drew 2,000 spectators, probably more than any previous prize fight on American soil, tripling the highest turn out for a Deaf Burke fight. His victories galvanized the sporting public and, as no one could think of a credible American fighter to best him, some Americans regarded him as the nation's first national boxing champion. He was "the adored hero and champion of all the Celts" in particular. "The largest cities and the largest states seemed not large enough for expressing the delight of Sullivan's enthusiastic admirers," alleged one effusive account. A few years later, one of the first published histories of boxing in the United States said that Sullivan "was looked up to on all sides, not only as a personage to be revered, but an oracle whose opinion was infallible and without appeal on the subjects connected with the Prize Ring."[23]

Like many sporting men, Sullivan was a drinker and, according to the *New York Times*, not a very good one. "Drink made Sullivan insane," claimed the newspaper. "When overcome by liquor, he was furious against everybody, never distinguishing friend from foe." However, even the *Times* admitted that "there was some good feeling, much overlaid by rascality and very difficult to be discerned." Sullivan also began the tradition of American boxing champions flaunting their money. Another early source

---

[22] *Daily Alta California*, January 22, 1856, quoting *New York Times*; Anbinder, 156, 159
[23] *Frank Leslie's Illustrated Newspaper*, May 12, 1860; Gorn, 71, quoting *American Fistiana*; Timony, 1; Fox, 7

who knew Sullivan personally gave an account of Sullivan's memorable look and dandy style as it contributed to his fame:

> Anyone who ever saw Jim Sullivan once could never forget him, and in every city he visited he became a conspicuous object of peculiar interest. His close-cropped, bullet-like head, not unlike the head of a ram, except the horns; fierce, glaring gray eyes; high cheek bones, flat face; reddish-brown hair, prominent ears and thick neck, made him the beau-ideal of a fighter. His close-fitting, bottle-green velvet cutaway coat, tight-legged corderoys [sic], high cut vest, spotted scarf and cluster diamond pin, protruding shirt collar and straight broad-brimmed plug hat, were decidedly Sullivan-like. He carried very little flesh, had a jaunty, springy, devil-may-care air, and when not in liquor was a clever sort of man, with an open heart for those not always too worthy.... [Sullivan] was never so happy as when he had on the mittens.[24]

In 1842, Sullivan narrowly avoided jail time for manslaughter after he acted as a second in a match that proved lethal for one of the combatants. It seems likely his work as a shoulder hitter earned him a pardon from newly elected Governor William C. Bouck. Bouck's lone provision, according to one source, was that Sullivan promise to engage in no more prize fights.

Not that there were any fights to be made. As would be the case for many famous boxers to follow him, Sullivan was as despised by some as much as others admired him. The ring death of 1842, the first known to take place on American soil, sparked a firestorm of indignation from prominent social and religious figures in New York and elsewhere. That Sullivan had escaped conviction only exacerbated the animosity a large portion of America held for him. Moral crusaders once again pushed boxing, and with it Sullivan, to the underground, the sport disappearing from the general public's attention for a period of five years.

Not until 1847, when Sullivan returned to the ring to face English import Robert Caunt, brother to England's champion Ben Caunt, did boxing once again grab headlines. Governor Bouck had by that point been out of office for more than three years and America's most famous boxer felt no further obligation to keep his promise. The Irish versus Anglo-Saxon angle, accentuated by periodicals printing public challenges between the fighters, polarized public opinion. Seven hundred men gathered in Harper's Ferry, Virginia on May 11, many of them hoping Caunt would whip the Irishman. They were disappointed when Sullivan won in just twelve minutes. Despite the lackluster result, the build-up had generated enough interest for the results to make their way into newspapers as far off as Milwaukee. Having won the then enormous stake of $1,000 in defeating Caunt, the public presumed that Sullivan's days as a prize fighter were

---

[24] James, *Sullivan*, 21; *New York Times*, June 30, 1856

behind him, unless someone could organize a fight between him and the other famous fighter of the day, a young New Yorker whose violent past rivaled Sullivan's own.[25]

Tom Hyer was the son of Jacob Hyer, whose 1816 draw with Tom Beasley was still spoken of fondly anywhere boxing fans gathered. Tom had been born on New Years' Day in 1819, making him twenty-eight years old at the time of Sullivan's set-to with Caunt. The press and his contemporaries described him as "one of the finest looking men of modern times," "the American Achilles," "the perfect picture of manly beauty and strength," and "beautifully modeled." George Walling, a one-time Chief of Police in New York, would later remember of Hyer: "Quiet, sober, he made a specialty of playing the gentleman, but could be very dangerous if you rubbed his fur the wrong way." Robert Roosevelt (uncle to the yet to be born President Theodore Roosevelt) knew Hyer personally and later remembered him as well-dressed, modest, and "not wholly unheard of in respectable circles." Like his father before him, Hyer worked as a butcher, a trade practiced almost exclusively by native-born Americans and one that frequently led to some less than savory social and political connections. In his youth, he was arrested five times for "rioting." Apparently not yet practiced at playing the gentleman, at seventeen Hyer participated in the vandalism of a grocer business, the "attack" of three whorehouses, and the gang rape of a prostitute, all in a single evening. Another assault on a brothel occurred in 1838, Hyer leaving a badly beaten prostitute in his wake. Prior to 1841, he had been a novice to true prize fights but already enjoyed an established reputation in sporting circles as "a tall and powerful young man, of some six feet two in height, who had already gained considerable pugilistic fame in the chance encounters he had from time to time met with in the streets." It was in 1841 that Tom proved his value in an organized fight when he defeated John McCleester in a 101 round marathon fight held on the banks of the Hudson. McCleester had been a friend of Sullivan's (Sullivan served as his second for the fight) and regarded as a formidable boxer in his own right. Nativist sports had grown tired of the "lads from the land of potatoes" bragging about Sullivan's dominance of American fighters, and they now saw in Hyer their deliverance.[26]

Debate over the results of a hypothetical match between Sullivan and Hyer was the talk of the sporting community for years, but with neither man doing anything inside the ropes between 1842 and Sullivan's return against Caunt in 1847, the chance of a true fight seemed slim. Then, on a spring night in 1848, a chance encounter between the two men, both inebriated, at a Broadway restaurant laid the blood-soaked foundation for a long-awaited contest. To the astonishment of many, Hyer rendered the "theretofore invincible" Sullivan unconscious. Hyer was loading his pistol

---

[25] Gorn, 83
[26] Stott, 123; Sutton, 138; Duane, 7, introduction by John Boessenecker; Timony, 1; Fox, 8; Lewis, 46, 51; *Frank Leslie's Illustrated Newspaper*, May 12, 1860

to administer the coup de grace when Walling, then just a policeman on the beat, interrupted the affair and hauled him away. The senseless Sullivan's astonished friends carried him out of the restaurant. The news traveled quickly through sporting establishments throughout the city. Hyer was followed for days by "crowds which concentrated from all quarters of the town to catch a glance, while parading from one drinking house to another, of the man who had whipped Yankee Sullivan." Meanwhile, the friends of the two combatants seemed headed for full-on gang warfare, Sullivan's supporters claiming that their man was too drunk and that Hyer, apparently less intoxicated, took unfair advantage. When, on June 2, Sullivan posted an advertisement in the *New York Herald* challenging Hyer to settle the issue in the ring ("I can 'flax him out' without any exertion"), and Hyer followed with his own ad agreeing ("Mr. Sullivan will find me always much readier to meet him anywhere than in the newspapers"), followers of both parties were jubilant.[27]

Backers of the fight guaranteed Sullivan and Hyer $5,000 each, an unprecedented sum in the history of the American prize ring to that point. That Sullivan had earned a record payday of $1,000 just a year earlier speaks to the rapidly growing public interest in boxing that Sullivan and Hyer generated. Again, the ethnicities of the combatants played a large part in the nation's fascination. The Irish and some other nationalities of immigrants tended to support Sullivan while native born Americans, particularly those concerned over the influx in foreign arrivals in recent years, held high hopes for Hyer. Some showed their patriotic hopes for his success by nicknaming him Young America. "Also," Walling later mused, "while Hyer was a singularly handsome man, Sullivan was as ugly as the seven deadly sins." Public interest in the fight surpassed all previous boxing matches combined, with sporting magazines reporting on the histories, physiques, and training of both principals. More reputable rags sold papers by debating the moral implications of pugilism's rising hold over the public imagination. For the first time ever, Americans of all levels of society were all discussing "The Great $10,000 Fight."[28]

To avoid harassment from do-gooders and law enforcement, the fight's organizers kept the exact location and time of the fight a secret until the previous day. The site, selected by Sullivan, was to be Poole's Island in Chesapeake Bay, Maryland. Organizers notified the *Spirit of the Times* to publish instructions for fans to gather in Baltimore on February 6, where they could catch steamers to the undisclosed scene of the fight. The local authorities promised to keep the bout from taking place. "Stimulated rather than deterred by the police activity," thousands of sporting men descended upon the city that day and began boarding the boats chartered to take them to the fight. Despite the secrecy about the fight's location, police were able

[27] Timony, 2; *National Police Gazette*, July 3, 1880; James, *Hyer*, 7, quoting *New York Herald*; *Lewis, 48*
[28] Fox, 19; Lewis, 46

to stop many of the ships from departing and commandeered one to pursue the combatants themselves. Both fighters and their parties narrowly avoided arrest and agreed to find an alternate location to pitch the ring. They and the hundred or so men who traveled with them settled on Still Pond Creek, a snowy field overlooking the Chesapeake. Among the hundred was John Morrissey's former employer, Alexander Hamilton of Troy.[29]

The fight began at twenty minutes past four in the afternoon. Though Sullivan had yet to lose a prize fight and was by far the more experienced fighter, Hyer held every physical advantage; youth, height, weight, and reach were all significantly on his side. From the start of the bout, the Irishman had trouble working his way inside of his opponent's longer arms. When he did finally get to the target, Hyer threw him to the ground, ending the first round. Sullivan redoubled his efforts in the second round but, after some fierce exchanges of blows, Hyer threw him again. By now Sullivan's face was a bloody mask. Each man fought hard through the next few rounds, but it was always Sullivan who went down at each round's close. Shirtless, and wanting to keep warm in the winter air, neither fighter took the allotted thirty seconds rest between rounds. By the eighth, Sullivan was clearly exhausted, but Hyer's face showed that he too was taking damage; his right eye was badly swollen. Before the ninth, Hyer's seconds lanced the hematoma to make it easier for their man to see, and the blood streamed down to the American's chest by the start of the ninth. Sullivan having been the aggressor to this point, the fighters switched roles from the ninth on, with the fresher Hyer now pursuing his fading foe. Sullivan's punches now seemed ineffectual and he was having more difficulty defending himself. The rounds were passing faster now, as Sullivan hit the ground with more frequency, sometimes from throws, other times from punches. Slow to rise for the start of the sixteenth, Sullivan made it to the scratch, but his arms quivered with pain and fatigue. He could not get his hands up to shield himself from Hyer's blows, nor could he counter. After a brief skirmish against the ropes, Hyer again threw his man to the ground and fell upon him. Edward James, an early chronicler of the American prize ring, describes what occurred next: "When he was taken off, Sullivan was found to be entirely exhausted, and when lifted up reeled half round and staggered backward toward the ropes. The fight was done." While Sullivan's friends carried him out of the ring, the new champion wrapped himself up in a coat to shield his sweat-covered body from the cold and began his trip back to New York for celebration. The fight had lasted a mere seventeen minutes and eighteen seconds.[30]

---

[29] Gorn, 91; Gipe, "run, Sullivan! Run!"; Kofoed, 37
[30] James, *Hyer*, 18

4.

Five Points

The one-sided nature of the fight between Yankee Sullivan and Tom Hyer did nothing to lessen the notoriety that continued to surround the event, even after its conclusion. Prominent newspapers and public figures continued to write and talk about the fight. Hyer's victory naturally elated his fans, and upon his return to New York, they followed and cheered him from one saloon to another. For the next several years, he would remain, in the estimation of a friend, "one of the best-known men in the country." Sullivan fans, meanwhile, were inconsolable. Though they lamented the Irishman's defeat, they continued to admire him for his courage in facing the bigger, younger man, and his drinking establishment on Chatham Street experienced a boom in business.[31]

Men and women who admired neither fighter and detested boxing in general were the most upset of all. One New York paper reported, "Through this vast community… nothing has been heard or talked of for several days past but the fight between Hyer and Sullivan… the only exceptions to the general prevalence of this excitement were the rigidly righteous, the pious, the saints, the puritans, or those who had no time to spare from their private rogueries or pious prayers, to public matters." Other papers marveled that so many people would "debase themselves" by cheering for prizefighters or condemned the crowds of sports fans as "painful and humiliating." Former New York mayor Phillip Hone lamented the *New York Herald's* coverage of the event as "disgraceful" and "disgusting." Everyone had something to say, and America's urban centers buzzed with sports talk like never before. "The excitement throughout the country was intense, and in Philadelphia and Baltimore, the anxiety to learn the result was as great as that in New York," reported the popular sporting rag the *Clipper* years later. For an entire generation, the fight would continue to hold almost mythic status. Fifteen years after its conclusion, *The Clipper* believed that the events of that day had "become as familiar as the Declaration of Independence." In his autobiography, Theodore Roosevelt remembered that his first boxing instructor kept illustrations of the fight on the walls of his gym. Those who had seen the fight and those who wished they had, traded and kept souvenirs, early example of sports memorabilia as a phenomenon.[32]

---

[31] Duane, 74; Fox, 24
[32] Gorn, 94-96; Anbinder, 206, *New York Clipper*, October 15, 1853

Alexander Hamilton, having been one of the lucky one hundred men to see the match firsthand, was not immune to the hysteria that continued to surround the fight. A native-born American himself, he was a Hyer man and, overjoyed at the result, decided to extend his vacation from Troy with a stop-over in New York City so that he might join the new champion in celebration. Having long ago cultivated the necessary connections to the city's sporting culture, he knew exactly where to go to find Hyer. One of the new champion's favorite watering holes was the Americus Club at 28 Park Row, a bastion for nativist ruffians in the Five Points neighborhood. The club's proprietor was the most feared Five Pointer of the age, Captain Isaiah Rynders, "a knife fighter and political weathercock." As for Hyer, the police picked him up in Philadelphia while he was en route back to New York, pending news of the extent of the hospitalized Yankee Sullivan's injuries. It was not long before news that Sullivan's injuries were not life threatening arrived, and the authorities let Hyer go to continue his journey. When the fighter arrived in New York, he began a hard-drinking tour of known establishments for "old sports," of which the Americus was one of many. Thus, Hamilton did indeed find Hyer celebrating there, along with Rynders and "as fine a collection of murderous malcontents as could be imagined." Bill "the Butcher" Poole, Tom Burns, Charley Duane, and "One Eye" Daly were just some of the noted Five Points shoulder hitters, killers, and pugs milling about the hero who had finally bested the "Irish braggart."[33]

There are two differing stories of Hamilton's experience in the Americus. One, recounted by the imaginative (and thus often unreliable) biographer Jack Kofoed, states that, sitting amongst this cohort of criminals, Hamilton, "a boastful little pigeon by nature," remarked that he knew of a better fighter than any man in the room, Hyer included. He proceeded to describe to them young John Morrissey from Troy. The very idea that an unknown teenage deckhand from upstate could handle himself against any two-fisted man from the streets of the Five Points, much less Hyer, sent those who heard Hamilton's boast into hysterics. Charley Duane, a colorful Irish boxer in Rynders' coterie and a devotee of Hyer, spoke for the group when he said, "There ain't a man in the place couldn't murder that farmer of yours. Just send him down and I will agree to bite off his ears." Hamilton said no more of Morrissey for the rest of his stay in New York.[34]

An 1878 article from the *New York Sun* tells a tale similar to Kofoed's and may have been his source for an otherwise invented conversation. According to the *Sun*, Hamilton told Duane that Morrissey could best him in a fight and even promised to arrange the match, an offer that received only a dismissive laugh from Duane. However, the *New York Herald* records that Hamilton's stay at the Americus was far less pleasant. This

---

[33] Kofoed, 37-38; James, *Hyer*, p. 7, quoting *New York Herald*
[34] Kofoed, 38

paper records that the crowd dealt Hamilton a vicious beating after he insinuated that Morrissey could beat Duane. All of these stories appeared in print years after the actual events took place. It is possible that none of them are correct, but it does seem something must have happened, and none of the parties directly involved ever went on record about the incident.[35]

Neither did John Morrissey, who was back in Troy eagerly awaiting Hamilton's return at the time. Though he now worked for Captain Smith, he remained on good terms with his former employer. A follower of boxing, Morrissey had been "thoroughly aroused" by the Hyer-Sullivan bout. He wanted every detail of Hamilton's first-hand account. Upon his return, Hamilton was happy to oblige and related the tale of his trip to the Americus Club, whatever its nature might have been. Whether Kofoed's story or that published in the *Herald's* is true, neither would have pleased the hot-headed young fighter.

John had by this time made several excursions to New York City, thanks to his job aboard a riverboat, but he had always returned home. The excitement generated by the Hyer-Sullivan fight, his own lust for notoriety and money, and finally Hamilton's news of what occurred at the Americus, now settled the young man's mind to stay in New York the next time Captain Smith's boat made the trip.

When interviewed years later about the impetus for his decision to move, Morrissey made no mention of Hamilton or Duane. His recollection speaks more to a desire for glory over vengeance. "I had read of Hyer and Sullivan, and the great pugilists in New York," he reminisced, "and one day I took my bundle and came to the city, determined to get a fight out of them." The explanation seems over-simplified, perhaps an effort by the adult Morrissey, wealthy and important, to paint a less malicious picture of himself for the masses. It could also be evidence of an aging man's nostalgia getting the better of him. This was no naïve innocent who traveled to New York on a whim. John Morrissey was a man of lofty ambitions, often bloody-minded ones. Thus, the assertion of the *New York Herald* that John came to New York "to avenge the injuries of his employer" is very likely as true, if not more so, as that put forth by the man himself.[36]

————

In the Fall of 1849, during one of the riverboat's trips to New York City, eighteen-year-old John Morrissey disembarked one night without any intention of returning to the boat. During the trip, John had run into trouble by fighting and beating a fellow crew member who had insulted

[35] *New York Sun*, May 2, 1878; *New York Herald*, October 22, 1858 and May 2, 1878
[36] *Chicago Daily Tribune*, August 1, 1874

him. Once the boat docked, John decided to leave his deckhand job and head straight for the Americus Club. From the Hudson River docks, he would have walked directly East into Manhattan, probably passing the prosperous residential and commercial establishments on Church St. and Broadway before entering the city's Sixth Ward, at the heart of which was the Five Points neighborhood, its "festering nucleus," and one of the most notorious slums in the world.[37]

Several years earlier, a very different kind of newcomer ventured into these streets and wrote down his observations in a book he later published as the travelogue *American Notes for General Circulation.* England's Charles Dickens would arrive in Boston for his 1842 tour of the United States and visit not only New York, but Lowell, Philadelphia, Richmond, St. Louis, and Washington, D.C. His long section on New York City gives a thorough description of the colors, sounds, smells, and people of the swelling city. The city's diversity enchanted him, and he marveled at the positivity and incessant bustle of most New Yorkers. However, what Dickens saw and recorded in the Five Points struck both he and his readers as both dangerously thrilling and socially unconscionable. He wrote:

> This is the place: these narrow ways, diverging to the right and left, and reeking everywhere with dirt and filth…. Debauchery has made the very houses prematurely old. See how the rotten beams are tumbling down, and how the patched and broken windows seem to scowl dimly, like eyes that have been hurt in drunken frays….
>
> What place is this, to which the squalid street conducts us? A kind of square of leprous houses…. [Inside,] Where dogs would howl to lie, women, and men, and boys slink off to sleep, forcing the dislodged rats to move away in quest of better lodgings.
>
> Here too are lanes and alleys, paved with mud knee-deep: underground chambers, where they dance and game… ruined houses, open to the street, whence, through wide gaps in the walls, other ruins loom upon the eye, as though the world of vice and misery had nothing else to show: hideous tenements which take their name from robbery and murder: all that is loathsome, drooping, and decayed is here.[38]

Dickens would also venture into the largest building in the Five Points, the Tombs. Morrissey may have passed this monstrous edifice as he neared the epicenter of the Sixth Ward. Constructed just a few years prior to Dickens' visit and about a decade before Morrissey's arrival, the New York City Halls of Justice and House of Detention took up an entire city block between Elm, Leonard, Centre, and Franklin Streets. Feared for the dismal conditions inside, the city used it primarily to detain prisoners before their

---

[37] *New York Sun,* May 2, 1878; Browne, 273
[38] Dickens, 211 - 216

sentencing to the prisons at Blackwell's Island or Sing Sing. Dickens described it as "a dismal-fronted pile of bastard Egyptian, like an enchanter's palace in a melo-drama!" This references the rumor that Ancient Egyptian tomb architecture had inspired the Tombs architects who designed the building, a rumor that helped establish the house's common name. However, the darkness and unsanitary conditions Dickens found inside gives a likely reason why the building's nickname stuck for good.[39]

The land on which the Tombs and the rickety tenements of the Five Points stood was artificial, having filled in a literal cesspool of a pond which had previously existed there. During the colonial era, this part of Manhattan had been home to various factories and businesses considered too repulsive for one reason or another to be inside of the residential sections of the city. Tanneries, buildings which produced a repugnant stench, had been in operation for years on the pond before city workers filled it with dirt from the leveled Bunker Hill in 1813. Following this, most of the industries which relied upon water, like the tanneries, departed, and the resulting abandoned buildings and open land created a boom in real estate speculation and development in the Collect, as the area was then known. In its earliest years, the growing neighborhood was known for the many small businesses which leased shops in newly constructed two-story wooden buildings. However, the draining of the original pond had not been thorough enough, and during the 1820s the land under these buildings became increasingly sodden and soft, causing the knee-deep mud through which Dickens would later wade. The foundations of many buildings began to sink, become unbalanced or flooded. Demand for Collect real estate plummeted. Almost simultaneously, immigration to the City began to spike, and landlords learned they could make more money by subdividing the rooms of their now abandoned buildings into ever-smaller apartments and renting them cheaply to the impoverished new arrivals, as well as to the city's many African Americans, who remained always in systematic poverty.

With financial desperation comes crime, including prostitution. By 1830, the neighborhood had surpassed the waterfront as the area of the city where the most prostitutes plied their trade. The immorality, dangers, and disease with which the decent folks of New York associated prostitutes sealed the neighborhood's reputation as a detestable slum, a degradation which would only get worse with time.

Nineteenth century New York journalist Junius Henri Browne would later say the first thing anyone who arrived in the Five Points noticed was children running amok "in every street, before every house and shop, and at every corner; children of all ages and color, though the general hue inclines dirt." These children were, according to Browne, "the offspring of vice... unkempt, unwashed, unrestrained." He noted the mixes of races and

---

[39] Dickens, 199; Browne, 529

nationalities (making particular notice of African-Americans, Germans, Italians, English, and "mulattos"), the hard-staring, humorless faces, and the vulgar language and behavior of the men, women and children who lived there. "Everybody drinks, even the children," he noticed, noting a rumor that there was a "groggery" for every one hundred adult males in the neighborhood. When you visit the Five Points, said Browne, "Your senses ache, and your gorge rises, at the scenes and objects before you.... But if, like a young student in the dissecting-room, you have come to see and learn, you will stay your flying feet." John Morrissey was there to see and learn, but also to do some damage.[40]

The Five Points got its name because it was the confluence of Orange Street, Cross Street, Anthony Street, and Little Water Street, the corners of these intersections creating five sharp points in Paradise Square, the center of neighborhood life. As he passed through Paradise Square, John Morrisey could see the country's most infamous tenement building, the Old Brewery, a four-story structure which had stood since the colonial days, when it was a beer factory on the old Collect pond. It was, decried the *National Police Gazette*, "the wickedest house on the wickedest street that ever existed in New York, yes, and in all the country and possibly all the world." This blight upon the city's reputation was a dilapidated, crowded, and violent living quarters where the city's most desperate souls could squeeze in for shelter, provided they could scrounge up the rent of just under two dollars per month. Though urban legends have greatly exaggerated the level of bloodshed and disease that permeated the Old Brewery (Some of the less scholarly histories of the neighborhood describe scenes that would have Hieronymus Bosch shuddering with disgust), it was indeed a very dangerous place and was actively avoided by all who did not absolutely have to enter, police included. Violence was the norm and lack of hygiene tragic. The denizens of the Brewery were not against burying the corpses of victims and other recently deceased people in the walls and floorboards, the stench of which emanated from the building. The Old Brewery eventually became something of an early New York tourist attraction for the slumming well-to-do, but few sightseers ever dared to step over the threshold of that crumbling, stinking, shadowy edifice. Indeed, there is no record of the tough and adventurous John Morrissey ever setting foot inside the Old Brewery in his life, despite its being at the very center of the neighborhood in which he resided for years.[41]

Continuing his journey from the docks and past the Old Brewery, John would have had to weave through the crowds of people carousing the saloons and whorehouses and ignore the whispers and gestures of prostitutes from windows and doorways, including those inside of the Old Brewery. Naïve out-of-towners lured inside by the call of a prostitute would very often find themselves waking up on the floor sometime later

[40] Browne, 274
[41] Anbinder, 67, quoting *National Police Gazette*; English, 18-19

with a sore head and empty pockets. Having spent a good deal of time working in whorehouses, John knew the tricks of that trade well enough to keep clear of those doorways. He likely strode two blocks northeast along Cross Street, passing the Zion Episcopal Church on his left, and turned right to go one block south on Mott to arrive in Chatham Square, which marked the border between the Sixth and Fourth Wards. There, standing at 28 Park Row, he found the Americus Club.[42]

In 1849, the Americus Club was at the center of Sixth Ward politics as the gathering place for prominent "shoulder hitters" employed by the city's Native American Party. Many of these men, like Tom Hyer, were accomplished boxers as well, and it was a famous hangout for "sporting" men. While no thorough description of what the Americus looked like survives, saloons were more than commonplace in the Five Points and historian Tyler Anbinder gives a general description of a typical Five Points saloon of this period as "a long, narrow open space, with a long bar running down one wall and an empty floor opposite it to accommodate the crowds that might visit at lunchtime and in the evening. Sawdust covered the floors to sop up spit tobacco juice and spilt beer, and a large stove stood at the center of the room to provide warmth during the winter.... [Saloons] lacked seats primarily because there was no space for them." Finally, Anbinder points out that "the New York saloon was an overwhelmingly male domain," and such was certainly the case for the Americus.

John stopped in front of the infamous haunt for nativist goons. He had just abandoned a steady job and walked halfway across Manhattan to come to this place, witnessing one of the world's most impoverished and dangerous slums as he did so. Evidence of filth, crime, poverty, and sickness had been plain to every one of his five senses. These kinds of dangers would be enough to understandably turn away many men and women. John Morrissey himself had grown up in poverty and was no stranger to violence, but Troy's slums were middle class neighborhoods compared to the depraved streets of the Five Points. Still, the young man had not thought to go back. As would be the case throughout his life, where most would have been convinced of certain peril, John Morrissey saw opportunity for himself. This, he thought, is where he would finally become somebody. He took a deep breath, gripped his bundle of clothes tight, and moved for the door of the Americus Club.

---

[42] Anbinder, 67, quoting *National Police Gazette*

5.

Becoming "Old Smoke"

The unknown Irish immigrant burst into the barroom full of nativist thugs looking for Charley Duane, the notorious shoulder hitter and prize fighter who had either insulted or assaulted Alexander Hamilton earlier that year. He immediately cast his eyes about the room and observed some of the most terrible men of a terrible community, men with cauliflower ears, or ears missing entirely, others with noses or a great many teeth missing. Many of the faces he saw were marked with scars of all kinds, telling of encounters with blades, teeth, fists, and other weapons. The room grew silent as the youngster entered. This was the kind of place where an unknown face was either a potential spy or a potential victim. These were men who knew how to size up other men as to just how dangerous they could be. This outsider, obviously Irish, just as obviously young, and clearly new to town, with nothing but his pathetic bundle clutched in his hands, looked to be all victim, delivering himself naïvely to their very door. He was big and moved like he knew how to handle himself, yes, but he was clearly out of his element and in over his head.

Careful not to betray any sign of regret at the brash move he had just made, Morrissey scanned the crowd for Duane. He found no one matching Hamilton's description of Duane in evidence. Duane had gone off to see a horse race. However, as a young fight fan, John certainly recognized Tom Hyer in attendance from newspaper illustrations, as well as the lord of the club himself, the feared Isaiah Rynders. Perhaps a bit surprised that a man of Rynders' fearsome reputation was significantly smaller than himself, John went directly to Rynders himself. Sobered by the presence of so many dangerous men about him, Morrissey addressed the older man in an uncharacteristically polite tone. "Mr. Rynders, I've come down here from Troy to fight. I've got no money, but I will fight for reputation. I will fight Mr. Hyer, or you, or anybody you can pick out." As Morrissey himself put it years later, "there were numerous responses in the affirmative." A crowd that included Rynders, Hyer, Bill "the Butcher" Poole, Tom Burns, Mike Murray, and others set upon the stranger with fists, feet, chairs, clubs, bottles, and other weapons near at hand. John tried to fight his way out of the club, but Rynders crashed down a spittoon behind his ear, sending him to the floor unconscious.[43]

---

[43] Asbury, *Gangs*, p. 83; *Chicago Daily Tribune*, August 1, 1874; *New York Herald*, May 2, 1878

John awoke in the best bedroom above the saloon. One can only imagine his astonishment to learn that it had been Rynders, the very man who had rendered him senseless, that had saved him from further beating and now oversaw his recovery. For three days, Rynders allowed the bloody, bruised, swollen, and sometimes delirious Irishman to convalesce in that room, paying a doctor to visit. Later, Charley Duane returned to the club from his gambling sojourn and, having been told of the young Irishman who came in looking for him, went up for a visit. He found a young man with two black eyes and his head wrapped in bandages lying asleep in bed. Charley was unimpressed and told Rynders he could certainly best the Irishman in a fight, to which the Captain replied, "Well, all the gang tried it. They pounded him with pitchers and clubs until they were exhausted, and he never squealed. If you want to tackle us on the same terms you'll never have a better chance." No account of Duane accepting the Captain's offer exists.[44]

Once John had recovered sufficiently to leave, Rynders offered Morrissey work as part of his coterie of thugs. Isaiah Rynders was arguably the most vehemently anti-immigrant gang leader in New York at the time, as well as the dominant boss of the Sixth Ward. At face value, that he would offer work to an immigrant Irishman who had invaded his place of business and threatened him just days earlier seems entirely out of character. But clues to Rynders' decision lie in his own adventurous past. Like John Morrissey, he was an ambitious opportunist who knew how to use his talents, as unsavory as they might be. By the time John met him, Rynders "bore the scars from numerous fights with bowie knives, pistols, and one red-hot poker." The gutsy nobody who entered one of the most dangerous places in the city looking for a fight may very well have reminded Isaiah Rynders of his younger self. [45]

Like Morrissey, Rynders (whose real name was Sawyer Renners) hailed from a town on the Hudson, close to Albany. Only about five miles separated Rynders' home of Waterford from Morrissey's in Troy. He shared Morrissey's Irish heritage, but Rynders, twenty-seven years Morrissey's senior, was a native born American, a fact of which he was very proud. Unlike Morrissey, he had been studious in his youth and into adulthood adored the work of Shakespeare, memorizing long passages of the bard's work, which he enjoyed reciting before others. He apparently abstained from alcohol all his life, an accomplishment to which Morrissey did not aspire. Nevertheless, their histories share remarkable details, as well as a common ambitiousness and restlessness of spirit. As a young man, Rynders found work as a deck hand with the ships that traveled along the Hudson and by the tender age of twenty-one was already captaining his

[44] *New York Sun*, May 2, 1878
[45] Cliff, 196

own little boat, which shuttled produce and other goods between upstate towns and New York City. His time aboard the sloops became a defining part of the Rynders legend, as most people would henceforth refer to him as Captain Rynders until his death. Those who knew him best used the nickname Ike.

At some point in his twenties, Rynders ventured with a brother to the South, where he became a noted gambler and all-around "sporting man." In 1832, following a knife duel in Mississippi, he fled murder charges to South Carolina, finding work there as the manager of a stable of racehorses owned by General Wade Hampton I. He also began to take an interest in Southern politics. A steadfast Jacksonian Democrat, he inspired locals with his passionate speeches in support of states' rights, memorable for his "mixture of terrible profanity and liberal quotations from the Scriptures and Shakespeare." Though he had put together a considerable savings from his various ventures, Rynders' finances were threatened by the death of General Hampton and his subsequent unemployment in 1835, followed by a national economic crisis two years later.[46]

His finances dwindling, Ike made his way to New York City and the Five Points, where he quickly became one of the neighborhood's most visible "sporting men" and election-riggers. He first aligned himself with Tammany Hall, the organization that controlled the Democratic Party in New York, Rynders passionately supporting Martin Van Buren's failed bid for the U.S. Presidency in 1840. Unlike many of the bullies with which he surrounded himself, Rynders was not a physically big man, nor was he particularly good with his fists. He built his political success not on brawn but on charismatic leadership, winning over friends, and his willingness to resort to knives to settle matters in the event he was not able to make friends. Writer and physician Thomas Low Nichols, who knew Rynders, described him as "cool and enterprising in his manners, and fluent and audacious in his speech." Nichols remembered that the Captain could often be found "dealing at a faro table, or presiding over one of those suppers of oysters, canvas-back ducks, and champagne, with which the gamblers of New York nightly regale their friends and customers." In this way, Rynders assured himself a place in the minds and hearts of his fellow members of the sporting fraternity. He cleverly set up shop in a place called Sweeny's House of Refreshment on Ann Street, "a thoroughfare much frequented by volunteer firemen." Through much of the nineteenth century, New York City firemen were noted for their passionate and sometimes violent involvement in city politics. Here Rynders would cultivate a hearty, rowdy constituency molded to his ambitions.[47]

Having achieved his version of success in New York, Rynders founded his own political club and saloon at 25 Chatham in 1844, which he dubbed

---

[46] *New York Times*, January 24, 1885
[47] Anbinder, 143; Nichols, 317; Asbury, *Gangs*, p. 39

the Empire Club. The place quickly became "a powerful democratic organisation [sic], and held its own against clubs of the opposite party." From this base, Rynders would organize various Five Points street gangs like the Plug Uglies and the Roach Guard into his personal, streetwise army. According to the *New York Times*, the Empire Club brought thousands of men under Rynders' sway (many of them Irish immigrants) and became "the leading spirit of the [1844 James K. Polk] campaign" against Henry Clay.[48]

The Polk and Clay election year was a particularly viscous one. Rynders made it the Club's mission to disrupt all Whig and abolitionist gatherings in the city. Ballot stuffing was also a favorite tactic. After the results were in and published, the final tally would have amused a keen-eyed newspaper reader. A total of 55,086 New York ballots had been cast between the two nominees; there were only approximately 45,000 people who could legally vote living in the city. The thirty-six New York electoral votes that went Polk's way won the election for him, a fact which secured Rynders' status as the most politically valued gang leader in New York State.[49]

Over the next several years, Rynders was the dominant voice at all Tammany Hall meetings which he attended, using his small army of thugs to force the direction of the city's Democratic Party with unprecedented success. His Tammany friends even secured him a lucrative and mostly symbolic position in the New York Customs House, and he would later win a post as U.S. Marshal. When the *New York Express* published articles criticizing his power over Tammany and his violent life, Rynders personally lead a gang of toughs into the newspaper's office and openly threatened the lives of every employee present. Then, in the late 1840s, the Captain suddenly did an about face, abandoning his Tammany allies and taking up the nativist cause. He supported the anti-Catholic, anti-immigrant Native American Party, a party then rising in the political landscape, its members called "Know-Nothings" because of the secrecy with which they went about their activities. Disapproving of the Democratic Party's perceived courting of the Irish and just as upset by the abolitionist influences within the Whig Party, the Native Americans fancied themselves protectors of the interests of those they saw as "true" Americans, namely native-born white males of Protestant faith. To reflect this change, Rynders renamed the Empire Club the Americus. His reasons for the complete reversal of his politics have never been fully explained, but the Irish thugs who had once populated the Empire Club were replaced at the Americus by nativist bullies like Tom Hyer, Charley Duane (an Irishman, yes, but apparently one with no qualms about working against his own kind), and Bill Poole.[50]

In 1849, just a few months prior to John Morrissey's arrival, Rynders' infamy spread from the state to the national level when his name appeared

---

[48] *New York Times*, January 24, 1885; Stanway, 105

[49] Nichols, 317; *New York Times*, January 24, 1885; Ackerman, 21; Anbinder, 144

[50] Stanway, 107, quoting *New York Express*

in newspapers across the country as one of the instigators of the Astor Place Riot. He was an admirer of the Philadelphia-born Shakespearean actor Edwin Forrest, one of the most successful stage performers in New York. Forrest's chief rival was William Macready, of English extraction, the animosity between the two being the talk of dramatic circles in both countries. On May 7, Rynders and some of his friends incited a mob to heckle and threaten Macready from the stage of the Astor Place Opera House in Manhattan on Lafayette Street. Three days later, persuaded by admirers like Washington Irving and John Jacob Astor, Macready made a return appearance, ignoring evidence that the situation was even more dangerous. Someone passed around and posted handbills with inflammatory calls to action throughout the city. In Irish sections, they called for a show of force against the spoiled upper class; in others, the message was to defend America from foreign influence, represented by an Englishman taking the stage. That night a much larger mob, composed of between ten and fifteen thousand people, both native and Irish, most of them working class men, surrounded the theater. People of the time would long remember what followed as "one of the most serious disturbances which has ever occurred in New York."[51]

From outside, the rioters used street cobblestones to bombard the police detail and the building's windows. As the police withdrew, members of the crowd began ramming the theater door. Some of the protestors had bought tickets and were already inside when the show started. As police struggled to arrest these infiltrators, Macready left the stage and skulked out of the building in disguise, headed for his room at the New York Hotel. Failing to gain control of the situation, the police sent for the Army's Seventh Regiment, which took its positions at 9:15 p.m. The crowd did not relent, badly injuring several soldiers. At this, the commanding officer gave the order to open fire. Future Chief of Police George Walling was a police officer there and remembered "The first volley was aimed over the heads of the crowd. Many of the bullets struck the wall of Mrs. Langdon's house… and many innocent persons [inside], taking no part in the riotous proceedings… fell to the ground, wounded by the spent bullets." Reassured by their leaders that the soldiers were firing blanks, the mob refused to leave. The militia next shot several volleys directly into the mob. "Scores lay on the ground, writhing with pain, Terror-stricken" recalled Walling. "The cowardly rioters rushed from the scene, trampling upon the prostrate forms of those who had fallen." Twenty seconds after the first shot hit the crowd, eighteen people were dead, all innocent bystanders, policemen, or members of the militia. More than 150 others lay wounded, four of whom would later die from their wounds.[52]

Though the worst had passed, the turmoil was not over. A crowd gathered for several days outside of the New York Hotel, demanding that

[51] Walling, 44
[52] Walling, 44-46; Burrows, 764

the staff or authorities produce Macready for hanging, unaware that the actor had already left town, never to return. A third uprising occurred on May 11, but dispersed peacefully at the sight of Army reinforcements, including troops and artillery placed strategically along Broadway and the Bowery. Officer Walling received the assignment of tracking down the source of the handbills that had led to the hostility. His sources led him to the Americus, though no one owned up to their creation. Months later, Walling confronted Rynders about it face-to-face. Rynders blamed it all on "a big red-headed Irishman." In his memoirs, Walling admitted he had no hard evidence of Rynders' involvement, "but I shall always believe that he was one of those who incited the trouble." So did the rest of the city. Historians and newspapers writers would continue to refer to Rynders as the "principal instigator" of the Astor Place Riot until his dying day and beyond.[53]

Thus, when John Morrissey found himself offered a position in the gang run by Captain Rynders, he had a precarious decision to consider. To have the city's most feared gang leader offer him membership must have made him proud. He came to New York looking for trouble, but also to make a name for himself. After just a few days in town, he had certainly found the former and now Rynders presented him with an opportunity for the latter. Service to Rynders meant being put on a fast track within ward politics and immediate credibility in the "sporting" community. But Rynders was also one of the men who had just beaten him senseless, not to mention one of the city's most famous anti-Irish gang leaders. Would Morrissey be willing to betray his own countrymen as Charley Duane had done? As an Irishman, John would also have to consider if Rynders could keep nativist cut-throats like Bill "the Butcher" Poole from mounting another potentially fatal attack. Then again, John had to consider his very immediate future. Still weak and woozy, he was currently locked in an upstairs room with the notorious knife fighter himself. What would happen to him if he dared refuse the offer?

For the moment, John agreed to serve the Captain, pending his full recovery. After three days, he was able to get out of bed on his own, but he remained in poor condition. He would later remember that the beating "made my head sore for three weeks." Rynders gave his new protégé money to return to Troy, ostensibly to fully recover, contingent on the promise that Morrissey would come back to New York and work for him. How long John spent back in Troy is not known. One source reports his stay there to be only a few weeks, while another claims John spent an entire year in Troy before returning to New York City. What John did in that time is not clear, though at least one source suggests he may have helped Rynders expand his interests into Troy. Walling remembered that, prior to setting up permanent residence in New York, Morrissey "kept a veritable 'rum hole' in Troy, then the favorite resort of gamblers, thieves and

[53] Asbury, *Gangs*, 40 – 41; Walling, 47

dissolute persons of the lowest grade." Historian Herbert Asbury also notes that John ran a saloon "for a few months." If this is true, then Morrissey, who would not have had the capital to buy such a place, must have had financial backers in the enterprise. As to whether Morrissey was operating the establishment in the interests of Isaiah Rynders, or whether this was one of the places in which Morrissey had previously worked under Alexander Hamilton's employ, neither Walling nor Asbury offers any clues.[54]

———

John was certainly back in New York by the summer of 1850, fully recovered from his first aborted trip. Most secondary sources say that he immediately reported to Rynders, who took him under his wing as a protégé. Some others say he refused to work for the nativist cause. An 1855 article from *The New York Daily Tribune* stated that John did work for the Captain, but only after Rynders returned to the pro-Tammany fold and once again renamed his place the Empire Club. In later life, Morrissey himself disputed that he ever worked with Rynders or his men, insisting that, after the beating at the Americus, "I laid for them individually. Said I: 'Gentlemen, I will lick your crowd and make you acknowledge me, if it takes me years.'" Whether on the orders of Rynders or not, John spent next several months on the New York docks, working as a thief and immigrant runner.[55]

Immigrant runners functioned as intermediaries between the city's political bosses and the newly arrived Irish immigrants, who had been coming to the United States by the thousands for the past several years. Life had been harsh for working class men and women in Ireland for decades prior to the devastation caused by a fungus that infected and then annihilated the vital Irish potato crops between 1845 and 1849. The potato was always the basis and usually the sole component of every meal in the daily life of the average Irish person, with an adult male laborer devouring as much as fourteen pounds of potato in a single day. Far from an exaggeration, fourteen pounds was considered by some to be "hardly sufficient." One Irishman estimated that his family of two adults and three children consumed thirty-five pounds of potato each day. When the fungus ruined the crops for years on end, the resultant disease and famine compounded the troubles already present due to overpopulation and poverty. Labor came to a standstill, corpses piled up in the streets (Over one million Irish had died from issues related to the blight by 1850), and any commoner who could escape the island did so. Some large land owners, their estates populated by thousands of tenants who could neither work nor pay rent, paid to ship them off to Canada and the United States,

[54] *Chicago Daily Tribune*, August 1, 1874; Walling, 375; Asbury, *Sucker's*, 362
[55] *New York Daily Tribune*, March 10, 1855; *Chicago Daily Tribune*, August 1, 1874

looking to avoid the newly passed laws that made landowners partly responsible for feeding those starving on their estates. Canada and the U.S. were tempting enough destinations for the starving, not only because anywhere seemed better than Ireland, but also because both countries had large English-speaking populations, as well as already considerable Irish populations. England, though closer, was famous for its longstanding hostility toward Irish immigrants.[56]

The people who were crammed into the boats sailing from Ireland to the New World hoping for salvation often found surviving the journey as difficult, if not more so, than enduring the potato blight. Crossing the North Atlantic safely required clothing very few of those who boarded the ships would have owned. Many wore nothing but tattered rags, without shoes. Food was poorly preserved, strictly rationed, and sorely lacking in nutritional variety. Sickness spread quickly in close quarters with little in the way of medical supplies present. One New York reporter described a group of recent arrivals from the crossing as having no purpose in America but "to find a grave." This too was no exaggeration. Of those who managed to survive the journey, many arrived so weakened that they collapsed on the dock and died in a city hospital. An entire section of one of the city hospitals was allegedly called the Landsdowne Ward, after the emigrants from the Landsdowne estate who packed the place and "who left it commonly in their coffins."[57]

Between 1840 and 1859, more than four million immigrants came to the United States, forty percent of them of Irish extraction. Three quarters of them came through New York at an average of 157,000 annually. In the year 1854 alone, 319,000 immigrants settled in Manhattan, which was more than the entire population of New York City in 1840. By 1855, immigrants outnumbered native-born New Yorkers, with Irish-born immigrants representing 28% of the population. The rare man who survived the blight and the cross-Atlantic passage with enough strength to work needed to find shelter and employment fast. It was not only the new country which was a change for him. The vast majority of those leaving Ireland had grown up on and worked on farms; they had never seen a city of New York's size and population and were entirely unfamiliar with urban life. As a stranger in a foreign land and frightening new environment, an Irish immigrant knew that he or she could also use directions, friendship, protection, and advice. It was an immigrant runner's job to provide all of this and earn the gratitude and trust of the desperate people filing out of the ships and onto the New York docks. The runner would greet the immigrant with directions to grocers, saloons, brothels, and tenement apartments for rent, as well as give advice on how to get quickly naturalized through a corrupt local judge, and on who to vote for once made a citizen. He would tell the immigrant to seek out a specific local political boss who could further assist

---

[56] Anbinder, 55-61; Isenberg, 17
[57] Anbinder, 64-65

with finding work and a place to stay. For these services, runners collected fees from the merchants, madams, and politicos they promoted, not to mention whatever cash they could finagle out of their gullible prey. In John Morrissey's case, he received pay from the keeper of a boarding house on Cherry Street, to which he sent the immigrants he approached.[58]

In the first half of the nineteenth century, most immigrants that came to New York did so via the docks on the eastern shore of Manhattan. This area was once some of the prime real estate in the city, the locale for homes owned by George Washington and John Hancock. But the early nineteenth century influx of immigration to the United States through the wharves prompted the hasty exodus of the well-to-do. Mansions gave way to tenements, saloons, dance halls, and whorehouses. It was not long before the East River docks became known as one of the most crime-ridden areas of the country, home to gangs like the Daybreak Boys, Slaughter Housers, Short Tails, and others. Historian Herbert Asbury, writing in the twentieth century, described what an outsider who ventured into New York's Fourth Ward could expect:

> No human life was safe, and a well-dressed man venturing into the district was commonly set upon and murdered or robbed, or both, before he had gone a block. If the gangsters could not lure a prospective victim into a dive, they followed him until he passed beneath an appointed window, from which a woman dumped a bucket of ashes upon his head. As he gasped and choked, the thugs rushed him into a cellar, where they killed him and stripped the clothing from his back, afterward casting his naked body upon the sidewalk.[59]

The Fourth Ward lay just to the east and south of the Sixth, which was home to Rynders and the Five Points. But the mayhem on the city wharves was even bloodier than that of the notorious Five Points. According to Asbury, the criminals of the Five Points "were primarily brawlers and street fighters." By contrast, those of the waterfront "were killers and robbers first of all." A journalist writing in the 1860s said that in the Fourth Ward low class gambling dens prevailed, run by "desperate characters... with dirty cards and bloated faces, prepared for burglary and murder, but preferring the easier task of swindling." The most popular haunt for the bad men of the Fourth was Kit Burns' Sportsmen's Hall, well-attended for the animal fights (dogs, rats, raccoons, chickens) put on there. Another dive, appropriately called the Hole-In-The-Wall featured less organized carnage of the human kind. According to Asbury, city officials condemned the place after seven murders occurred there inside of two months. Piracy, too, was a lucrative racket on the docks. In 1850, New York City Chief of Police George W. Matsell estimated the number of pirates active in the

---

[58] Burrows, 737; Kofoed, 56-57; Asbury, *Sucker's Progress*, 362; Adler, 94 (e-book)
[59] Asbury, *Gangs*, 45

Fourth Ward alone to be between four and five hundred, comprising fifty separate gangs. These men prowled the East River at night aboard small boats and, upon spotting a poorly guarded ship, made off with its cargo beneath the cover of darkness. Crime, murder, depravity, pestilence, and poverty dominated the Fourth Ward. This was where John Morrissey went to work.[60]

He was partnered alternately with George "One Eyed" Daly, one of Rynders' cronies, and Orville "Awful" Gardner, a part-time prize-fighter and all-around low life. An acquaintance from this period said that John Morrissey the immigrant runner was "powerfully built, strong as an ox, and seemed to be afraid of no one." By day, John worked as one of the above-described immigrant runners. By night, he was something of a pirate, though without a boat, hijacking merchandise and cargo from the docks and docked ships. It's not surprising that, years later, when describing life on the docks to a reporter, a wealthy Morrissey left out these details. He was but an honest dockworker, he insisted. In fact, from Morrissey's perspective, it was he who was exploited and abused. "I was a poor river rat and could barely pick up my food," John explained, "but I kept on the wharves, unloading steamers, working with 'longshoremen, and getting beaten so often that I was hardly ever right well."[61]

He was honest about the beatings. John was not on the docks long before he and Gardner ran afoul of an armed gang of immigrant runners that included Tom Burns and Mike Murray, two of the men who had ganged up on John in the Americus. This crew operated out of the Battery on the southern tip of Manhattan, and did not appreciate Morrissey's return to New York, nor his encroachment on the docks considered their territory. As the *New York Herald* tells it, Morrissey, in typical fashion, tore into the enemy before they could make a move. Having felled two of the men surrounding him, he checked on Gardner to find that his partner had escaped the fight by climbing up the riggings of the boat. "There never was a chipmunk that climbed a tree faster than he climbed that masthead," John later mused. But what was happening on the deck in that moment was far from a joke. John was surrounded and "had his head pretty well swelled and hammered out of shape before he got ashore." Though they would remain friends through the years to come, Morrissey never again worked on the docks with Awful Gardner. Gardner's name continued to pop up in the newspapers for everything from public drunkenness to prize-fighting throughout the 1840s and 1850s. In one boxing match, he bit his opponent's ear off and had to flee the ring to avoid arrest. By the end of the 1850s, Gardner found God, gave up drink, and became a renowned teetotaler, the founder of a temperance society called the Dashaways, until he was committed to an insane asylum in 1889.[62]

[60] Asbury, *Gangs*, 47 & 57; Browne, 250
[61] Breen, 526; *Chicago Daily Tribune*, August 1, 1874
[62] *New York Herald*, May 2, 1878; *Richmond Enquirer*, October 18, 1853

The dock fight with Burns and Murray was the second time that John had survived a brutal beating from a group of armed men that might have killed another man, a fact which helped spread his reputation for toughness. "John never seemed to know when he was licked," one man who had been in a tussle with the young Morrissey later recalled, "and just as you got tired of thumping him he kind of got his second wind, and then you might as well tackle the devil as try to make any headway against him." Just how very rugged the young man was became clear not so long after his encounter with Burns and Murray. John had begun to associate with a local madam named Kate Ridgely, "a shapely and voluptuous young woman, who owned one of the most expensive bagnios in New York" at 74 Duane Street. Prostitution ran rampant in nineteenth century New York, particularly in the Sixth Ward. Historian Tyler Anbinder gives a well-researched account of just how prevalent prostitution was in the Five Points alone during the antebellum years:

> Bordellos operated in thirty-three of the thirty-five dwellings on Anthony Street between Centre and the Five Points intersection at some point during the 1840s and '50s. Brothel proprietors were likewise prosecuted in twelve of the fifteen houses on Cross Street between the Five Points intersection and Mulberry, and in thirteen of the seventeen residences on Orange Street from the Five Points intersection to Leonard Street.[63]

That Anbinder's research speaks of the prosecution of the men and women who ran whorehouses in the Five Points does not mean that authorities strictly enforced laws against the vice. In the Sixth Ward, like in much of the rest of the city, the world's oldest profession thrived with the collusion, and frequently the patronage, of the legal authorities. Most of the legal punishment meted out to pimps, madams, and prostitutes amounted to slaps on the wrist. Police rarely made arrests for prostitution, unless a related crime or disturbance of the peace occurred, compelling them to do so. Only repeat offenders, those who robbed their clients, or those prostituting young children were likely to receive jail terms of more than a few days. A great many women in the Five Points engaged in prostitution at some point in their lives, usually in times of extreme financial distress or to support alcohol addiction.

Kate Ridgely, however, was a lifelong professional. She was part of the first generation of women to operate bordellos in New York. Until mid-century, men dominated prostitution proprietorship; those women who did run them did so in partnership with husbands. Though competitors, the new generation of independent madams created a network to assist with

[63] Asbury, *Sucker's Progress*, 362, quoting *New York Daily Tribune*; Kofoed, 57; Anbinder, 208; Fox, 36

legal troubles, referring clientele, and rotating employees. At least thirty-five such women ran brothels for a period of four years or more in the 1850s, and Kate was one of the most successful.[64]

John Morrissey was no stranger to prostitutes; he had worked in Alexander Hamilton's brothels as a bartender and bouncer in Troy. He took a liking to Kate, and apparently the feeling was mutual, because she spurned the affections of her prior lover, a young hulk named Tom McCann, "the hero of many bar-room fights and the terror of the gamblers," who also happened to be a particularly fearsome friend of Tom Hyer. Enraged with jealousy, McCann gathered a group of friends and caught up with Morrissey at Sandy Lawrence's pistol gallery at the St. Charles Hotel, on the corner of Broadway and Leonard Street. a rectangular establishment about thirty feet wide and seventy long, which included a bar for drinking and another for oysters. Yankee Sullivan, Tom Hyer, and Bill Poole were frequent customers at Lawrence's. After an exchange of insults, the men fell into a wrestling match, with McCann, the bigger man, initially gaining the upper hand. He shoved Morrissey backward into a stove, which tipped over, pouring hot coals onto the floor. McCann then tackled John so that his back fell onto the still burning coals. As McCann held him down, the stench of John's burning clothes and flesh spread through the room. Despite continued blows from his adversary, which had him "pommeled almost into a jelly," Morrissey refused to surrender and, seeing this, some present grabbed buckets of water, pouring them over the men and the coals. The resulting smoke and steam blinded and choked McCann, and John seized the advantage. He "bucked and pounded McCann into insensibility." According to one source, Tom Hyer was on hand to witness this scrap and, seeing his friend beaten, insisted that Morrissey fight him at once. Exhausted, scalded, and only standing with the aid of friends, John understandably declined, but he promised to give Hyer the same treatment his friend received the next time they met. McCann spent several weeks in bed recovering from his injuries, but bore his conqueror no ill will upon re-emerging, and it said he and Morrissey became friends afterward.[65]

Word of mouth spread through the streets about the Irishman whose back had smoked with fire as he won a brutal fist fight. From then on, the fight with McCann became one of the most storied moments of John Morrissey's life, and his admirers reverently referred to him as Old Smoke.

John's reputation as a near-invincible tough impressed the various Democratic politicos of the Sixth and Fourth Wards, who began to provide him with more work as an immigrant runner and as hired muscle. This of course also made him a target for his counterparts on the nativist side. Tom Hyer remained resentful of the rising status of "that blower from

[64] Gilfoyle, 73

[65] *Spirit of Democracy*, April 27, 1870; *New York Sun*, May 2, 1878; *New York Herald*, May 2, 1878; *Sunday Star*, September 19, 1926

Troy." Not long after his pummeling of McCann, John came very close to achieving his long-standing goal of a fight with the champion when they encountered each other at the corner of Canal Street and Broadway. The resulting argument saw both men removing their shirts in preparation for an impromptu showdown when, to the disappointment of the quickly gathering crowd, the police arrived and prevented the fight by arresting both men. According to Morrissey, he thereafter made it known to the sporting community that he was ready and willing to face Hyer in a prize-fight, but the champion had "lost his moral force" and insisted that he was retired.[66]

———

Exactly where Morrissey lived at this point in his life is not known for sure. One source reports that by 1850 he had taken up residence on Cherry Street, which ran the length of Manhattan near the East River, a few blocks over from the Five Points. He wasn't yet making any considerable amount of money, so he may have shacked up with Kate Ridgely. Unless she or another New York friend (like gambling impresario John Petrie) provided board, John would have likely lived, along with so many other Irish, in one of the many dilapidated tenements in the Five Points. Horribly overcrowded but affordable to most, these rooms could be in anything from two-story apartment buildings to makeshift lean-to's, to re-purposed factories like the Old Brewery. Windows and beds were scarce, fires were frequent, robberies and homicide not unusual, and disease ever-present.[67]

When Morrissey wasn't plying his trade on the docks or enjoying the company of Kate Ridgely, he held court behind a faro table at John Petrie's saloon at Church Street behind the city hospital, on the other side of Broadway from the Five Points. Petrie and Morrissey would become good friends and drinking companions, and he later remembered Morrissey as a man "whose passion for fighting was so great that he often came in at night with both hands full of negro wool, trophies of fights in the vicinity." We can assume the reference to "negro wool" to be a racist reference to the texture of the hair of African Americans. Democratic politicians and the shoulder hitters who worked for them were proudly anti-abolitionist and generally against anything benefitting African Americans, who found support mainly from Whigs. Free blacks were the chief rivals of German and Irish immigrants for employment and social standing in New York, and those immigrants made up a hefty portion of the Democratic constituency in the city. That John spent his days and nights fighting or attacking black men on the docks and in the streets is therefore not surprising. His nightly

[66] Breen, 526; *Chicago Daily Tribune*, August 1, 1874
[67] English, 15

entrances bearing evidence of these encounters would have been something the other patrons of Petrie's saloon would have admired and cheered. [68]

It was at Petrie's that John most likely learned the skills needed to run a successful gambling house and learned the then prevalent card game known as faro. Popular belief falsely held that the game originated in ancient Egypt, despite its actual origins in late eighteenth-century Venice. In faro, players placed bets on what card the dealer would pull next from the top of the deck. A bastardized version of it became the most popular card game in the United States in the nineteenth century, adored by gambling and sporting men across the country.

Men like Rynders and Petrie valued Morrissey as trustworthy muscle, and his fellow streetfighters feared his pugnacity in a battle. Soon enough, word spread beyond the sporting world into other social circles of the city of the hot-tempered and rugged young man from Troy. The decidedly upper-class Robert Roosevelt, uncle to President Theodore Roosevelt and an active politician himself, knew Morrissey and remembered him as "particularly constituted. He had in him more of the bulldog than any man I ever met. Always honest, he was sometimes wrong; but, right or wrong, he fought and hung on. Men stopped him now and then but no one ever conquered him. The possibility of surrender had been left out of his makeup. When sober, he was as quiet and as much the gentleman as [Tom] Hyer. Drunk or drinking, he was first-class company to avoid." Many who knew Morrissey during his early years in New York would echo Roosevelt's observations of the young street fighter's resilience, tenacity, and drunkenness.[69]

John's pride at the respect his fellow sporting men and gangsters afforded him was bittersweet. By winter, he had become bored and disheartened. Dealing cards, intimidating immigrants, being Kate Ridgely's kept man, and partaking in regular street brawls was far from the glory he had sought when he first invaded the Americus the previous year. It was only a slight improvement from tossing drunks from Alexander Hamilton's saloons or swabbing the decks of a riverboat. He was frustrated by his inability to get a fight with Tom Hyer, Yankee Sullivan, or Charley Duane. He had endured the serious injuries he had taken in the Americus and on the docks, as well as against Tom McCann, with scant reward. John Morrissey was again on the search for a new direction to achieve the wealth and notoriety he so badly desired. That direction presented itself with thrilling news from California.

[68] *New York Sun*, May 2, 1878
[69] Lewis, 52

6.

The Journey West

In 1848, James Marshall knew nothing about John Morrissey, and Morrissey knew nothing about him. But what happened to Marshall in January of that year would change John Morrissey's life as it would those of countless other Americans in the coming years. Marshall was a farmer and carpenter originally from New Jersey who had made his way westward during the previous decade, first spending several years in the Midwest until a bout with malaria forced him to seek recovery first in Oregon Territory and finally in California. Settling in Sutter's Fort (later called Sacramento), he found work as a carpenter for Johann Sutter himself. Sutter, a Swiss immigrant, had become a citizen of Mexico. Impressed by lies about military service in the Swiss Guard, Mexican officials granted him 48,827 acres in California. Not long after going to work on Sutter's land, Marshall purchased his own plot along Butte Creek with Sutter's financial assistance and began farming and ranching. Service in the military during the Mexican War forced Marshall to abandon his ranch, resulting in the loss and theft of much of his livestock and financial savings. Looking for work, he took a post as the manager of a Sutter sawmill in the Cullomah Valley. Marshall himself describes what happened not long after the mill went into operation:

> While we were in the habit at night of turning the water through the tail race we had dug for the purpose of widening and deepening the race, I used to go down in the morning to see what had been done by the water through the night, and about half past seven o' clock on or about the 19th of January... I went down as usual, and after shutting off the water from the race I stepped into it, near the lower end, and there, upon the rock, about six inches beneath the surface of the water, I DISCOVERED THE GOLD. I was entirely alone at the time. I picked up one bright, yet malleable; I then tried it between two rocks, and found that it could be beaten into a different shape, but not broken. I then collected four or five pieces and went up... with the pieces in my hand and said, "I have found it."[70]

Since arriving in California, white men had heard various legends about a treasure trove of gold hidden somewhere in the mountains. By the nineteenth century, most adults who heard the tales, particularly those who had been born in the East, were more than skeptical about the possibility.

---

[70] http://malakoff.com/marshall.htm, accessed 4/26/2020

Marshall tried to keep his discovery of 23 karat gold in the Cullomah Valley a secret among the Sutter family and his employees at the mill. He and Sutter feared that word of the strike would cause the land to be overrun by prospectors. Sutter's right to the land was tenuous, based on a lease drawn up with the Native Americans who inhabited the valley. California's governor had refused to officially recognize Sutter's lease, meaning that he and Marshall would have a difficult time preventing others from staking claims in the valley. But the men could not keep the word from getting out, originating from close relatives of some of the mill workers and quickly spreading east to spark "one of the most far-reaching events in US history."[71]

As word of the discovery of Gold spread through the surrounding region, it produced little excitement, and little had changed in the Valley by the arrival of Spring. Skepticism prevailed among locals as to whether Marshall had truly discovered gold or not, and if he did, how much of it really was there to be found. Samuel Brennan, the publisher of the *California Star*, decided to investigate the story that May and returned to the nearby town of Coloma carrying a bottle of gold dust and crying "Gold! Gold! Gold from the American River!" Within days of Brennan's confirmation, seventy-five percent of San Francisco's men (total population 500) had left town for the hills. Thousands of out-of-towners soon replaced them. A little-known port town prior to Marshall's discovery, San Francisco was suddenly and unexpectedly on its way to becoming a bustling, mercantile city.[72]

By summer, most of the country had heard the news, and the federal government wanted confirmation. Governor Richard Mason and his staff came to the area to investigate and compiled a report to President Polk of the great success men were having at finding gold. On December 5, Polk addressed Congress, telling them, "The accounts of the abundance of gold in that territory are of such an extraordinary character as would scarcely command belief were they not corroborated by the authentic reports of officers in the public service." Newspapers too were now confirming the rumors for the public, often embellishing them with sensationalist reports of the ease with which gold could be found. The Gold Rush was on. [73]

On November 17, 1851, *The New York Times* published its first accounts of "unusually large" amounts of gold men were finding in California, reprinted from the *San Francisco Herald*. "The yield of gold is at present extraordinary, and the prospects are that an increase is to be expected far more than a decrease dreaded," the paper reported. "[The riverbeds, riverbanks, and mining shafts are] only waiting the advent of the rain to give forth their golden produce." The news had New York men of all ages

[71] Grayson, 7
[72] Grayson, 24
[73] http://www.malakoff.com/goldcountry/tcgcintr.htm, accessed 4/20/2020

and backgrounds leaving their families, abandoning their jobs, deserting the Army, and heading west with "gold fever." [74]

———

Many of John Morrissey's fellow sporting men and street characters from in and around New York's Five Points neighborhood were among those to depart for the West. Yankee Sullivan left his saloon at 82 ½ Chatham in the care of his brother-in-law and caught a train for San Francisco as early as 1850. John's fellow gang member from back in Troy, John Heenan, now seventeen, set out for California in 1851. There he would find work swinging a sledgehammer for the Pacific Mail Steamship Company in Benicia, a town just northeast of San Francisco. Tom Hyer and Charley Duane went to California too. All of these men worked at times as shoulder hitters for local politicians and became nearly as notorious for their violence in the West as they had been in New York, in the cases of Sullivan and Duane, even more so. None struck it rich in the gold mines.

John was not immune to the gold fever that had infected his associates. He was as intrigued by the promise of easy money and a new beginning as his sporting brethren had been, and his interest was even more piqued when Sullivan, Hyer, and Duane all beat it west. For more than a year now, John had been chasing after these men, futilely trying to convince any one of them to face him in a boxing match. "As long as I was poor nobody would do me the favor to fight me in the ring," he remembered years later, "and I finally went to California in the mining times to make a stake." If he couldn't get them to commit to a fight in New York, perhaps earning some fast money in the mines would allow him to garner a big fight out West. [75]

Daniel "Dad" Cunningham, who worked with Morrissey at John Petrie's place in Manhattan, was also looking to make his way to California. If John Morrissey can be said to have had a best friend in his early life, outside of his wife, that man would probably be Cunningham, who was once described as "a very small but exceedingly spunky specimen of rowdyism." His name routinely appears alongside Morrissey's in newspaper articles, and the pair were partners in various ventures and adventures throughout Morrissey's early adulthood. [76]

At just five feet, four inches tall and weighing less than one hundred pounds, Cunningham looked diminutive next to his bruiser friend. Born in New York City, he apprenticed under his father as a cooper but proved a restless youth prone to trouble. He and Morrissey had met while working at Orr's wallpaper in Troy. Despite his small stature, he became known on the streets as a fearless scrapper, always armed with a weapon and prone to

[74] *New York Times*, November 17, 1851
[75] *Chicago Daily Tribune*, August 1, 1874
[76] *Brooklyn Daily Eagle*, March 22, 1858

fits of violent rage, though he showed an almost gentle loyalty to Morrissey. "He cherishes a deep regard for Morrissey," one *New York Times* writer would later observe, in a rare newspaper account of a personal relationship between street-level criminals, "takes him home when he is beside himself with liquor, lies down on the sofa to keep him from going out again till he is thoroughly sober, and exercises a kind of fraternal protection over him." In 1849, Morrissey and Cunningham decided to throw in together for their California adventure.[77]

What follows is the thrilling and quite possibly invented account of the perilous westward journey of John Morrissey and Dad Cunningham, as related by the *Times* on the day after John Morrissey's death (and subsequently recounted in various publications). The two men could pool between them just thirteen dollars. With no tickets available at anything close to that price, the friends stowed away on a Pacific Mail steamer leaving New York, not to be discovered until the ship was three days out of port. Finding them without tickets, members of the ship's staff brought them before a Captain Schenck who, hearing that they intended to mine for gold in San Francisco, decided not to allow them to leave the ship. He ordered them put to work at shoveling coal to earn their keep and that they stay on board for the return journey back to New York. However, when the ship temporarily weighed anchor off the shores of Chagres, Panama, the men escaped while a visiting party of locals distracted the captain and crew.[78]

Buying two tickets on a steamer going up the Chagres River to the town of Gorgona, they disembarked there and walked thirty-six miles the rest of the way to Panama City, where they intended to either buy passage on another boat to San Francisco or stow away. When they got there, they found neither was possible. Between them they now had just five dollars and tickets to San Francisco, probably inflated by the Gold Rush, began at $1,200 each. Armed guards patrolled the docks and boats for the expressed purpose of preventing stowaways. Their only chance, figured the two experienced sporting men, was to step into the city's many gambling establishments and risk it all. After six weeks of monte and faro, Morrissey and Cunningham had accumulated a $700 profit. However, they were now growing impatient to leave, dreaming of greater fortunes elsewhere. One night, hearing that the steamer *SS Panama* was headed to California in two days and that the price of two tickets was $2,500, the friends pressed their good luck by agreeing that they would take the entire $700 into the gaming parlors and put it all on the line that night. By the end of the night they were both flat broke.[79]

[77] *Daily National Era*, May 26, 1854, quoting *New York Times;* Troy Weekly Times, March 27, 1858
[78] *New York* Times, May 2, 1878
[79] *New York Times*, May 2, 1878

Now desperate, they decided to risk death in trying to stow away upon the boat, which was anchored two miles from shore and patrolled by guards. Under cover of night, they stole a small boat and rowed their way out toward the *Panama*. However, when a guard spotted them and opened fire with his musket, they aborted their mission and returned the stolen boat. Knowing the vessel would leave the next night, Morrissey and Cunningham remained undaunted. That night, they seized on an opportunity to stow away on a less secure smaller boat which was to deliver a final shipment of freight out to the larger vessel. They hid amongst the cargo lifted onto the steamer and, once placed on deck, immediately mixed themselves inconspicuously amongst the ship's paying passengers.

When the ship was two days out to sea, Morrissey and Cunningham were again discovered and brought before the ship's commander, a Captain Hudson. Hudson ordered them both put in leg irons until such time as the ship reached Acapulco, where he intended to leave them to their own resources. The prisoners once again profited from good luck, at least for them. The ship was very crowded, and rations had grown short. As a result, the crew received very little to eat and were forced to sleep mostly on deck. As time passed, they became at first irritated and finally mutinous, stealing the remaining rations and threatening to take control of the ship. Needing men to help maintain his command, Hudson turned to Morrissey and asked if he could fight. "Well," the prisoner answered, "I guess that's a kind of trade with me. I'm somewhat [experienced] at fighting." With no alternative, the Captain ordered the pair released and gave each of them a cutlass and two pistols each. Keeping their word, the pair joined the defensive line of Hudson's supporters as the mutineers approached. The attackers stopped, stunned to see that the stowaways had joined the Captain's side. Morrissey called out, "Cold steel and hot lead for them as endeavor to pass this line," and none approached closer. Following a tense period where the leaders of the mutiny conferred amongst themselves, they sued for peace from the Captain, who granted it only on the condition of total surrender. After promising the troublemakers that he would see to their complaints, Hudson rewarded Morrissey and Cunningham with first class passenger status, a state room to share, and free passage to their intended destination.[80]

When the ship did arrive at the San Francisco docks, Morrissey and Cunningham disembarked and John met up with some friends in town who fronted him enough cash to pay back Captain Hudson for the travel and accommodations. The Captain refused the money, thankful to them for their aiding him in maintaining order on his ship. Morrissey and Cunningham instead pocketed the cash, agreeing to use it to stake their future in California.[81]

---

[80] *New York Times*, May 2, 1878
[81] *New York Times*, May 2, 1878

Much about the *Times'* account of the journey seems like a sensationalist adventure invented by a reporter to entertain his readership and lend heroism to the Morrissey story. Jack Kofoed, Morrissey's twentieth century biographer, showed no compunction against printing any unverifiable legend about the man and yet he mentions none of the adventure described above. He states simply, "The friends arrived in San Francisco during the winter rains," a statement which contradicts the *Times'* assertion that the *SS Panama* arrived in San Francisco in the autumn of 1850. The *Times'* timeline does seem a bit off, as Morrissey was still working as a shoulder hitter on the New York docks as late as the summer of 1850, and research shows that a one-way trip from New York to San Francisco took more than six weeks. Considering that Morrissey and Cunningham had an extended layover in Panama, their trip must have taken longer than that. The *Sun* says that Morrissey was still working at Petrie's saloon in the winter and that he did not leave for San Francisco until early 1851. However, *The Sun* does give a similar account to the one printed by the other newspaper and printed on the same day, with some of the details changed. They also throw in an intriguing afterward: "The captain afterward became very poor, and even as late last summer [1877] wrote Morrissey for money. Morrissey at various times sent him sums aggregating thousands of dollars." Talking to a reporter for the *Chicago Tribune* about his early years in 1874, Morrissey himself made no mention of stowing away on steamers but neither did he give any account of how he got to California.[82]

There is only circumstantial evidence to verify the *Times'* tale. A review of California newspapers from 1850 to 1851 shows that the Pacific Mail Steamship company had begun, not surprisingly, constantly running steamers in and out of San Francisco and other California cities in February 1849. It advertised itself as the "only through line to New York," as all other boats required passengers take an overland route through Central America to meet a connecting ship in the opposite ocean. Panama was indeed where the Pacific Mail Steamship's boats made these stops, whether they were through lines or not. The ships generally left the San Francisco and Panama docks on the first and fifteenth days of each month. Rate for passage from New York to San Francisco ranged from $65 to $275, depending on the accommodations and the ship. Nothing approaching the $1,200 price the *Times* reports is mentioned. The *SS Panama* was indeed a ship in the line and was in California in January, April, and September of 1850, as well as January of 1851. One notice in the *Sacramento Transcript* from December 30, 1850 may lend credence to the mutiny story. Noting that the *SS Constitution* had arrived in San Francisco, the writer wondered as to the whereabouts of the *SS Panama*, which should have arrived two weeks

[82] Kofoed, 73; *New York Times*, May 2, 1878; New *York Sun*, May 2, 1878

prior to the *Constitution* and should have already been heading back to New York. The *Constitution*'s arrival with "no tidings" from the *Panama* suggested to the writer that "the *Panama* has met with some accident, and probably put back for repairs." The vessel finally pulled into port on January 2, though this author could find no passenger list or stated reason for the delayed arrival. Could the near mutiny recounted in the later newspaper stories have caused the delay? It is also possible that the delay, caused by something else, is what sparked unrest on board a ship that regularly made the same journey without incident.[83]

However, all the above-mentioned advertisements from 1850 show that the commander of the *SS Panama* was not a man named Hudson, but one D.G. Bailey. An ad from January, 1851 shows that the *Panama*, now having finally arrived safe at port in San Francisco, was commanded by a new Captain, named J.J. Watkins (the 1852 city directory has him as James T. Watkins), and would be connecting with the *SS Cherokee* for future journeys. The change in captains and abandonment of the "through trip" selling point may also indicate some sort of trouble on board the *Panama* during its journey.[84]

Perhaps the later newspapers did not get the captain's name wrong, but the name of the vessel on which John Morrissey and Dad Cunningham traveled. There was a Captain Hudson in charge of the steamer *Republic* in the competing Law's Line, which, by 1851, had come under Pacific Mail. Passengers and freight aboard the *Republic* were transported from New York through Panama to San Francisco via a connection with the *SS Georgia* in the same period. The *Republic* was in San Francisco in October 1850 and January 1851. Neither of the passenger lists for either of these voyages mentions a Morrissey or Cunningham on board, and the surviving descriptions of the voyages do not mention any mutinies.[85]

The first verifiable account of Morrissey's presence in California comes from a newspaper account from March 2, 1852, which of course relates the story of a barroom brawl.[86]

---

[83] *San Francisco Transcript*, September 20, 1850, December 7, 1850 and December 30, 1850; Daily *Alta California*, January 27, 1850, May 1, 1850, June 12, 1851; www.meritimehertiage.org, accessed 2/9/2020.

[84] Daily *Alta California*, January 28, 1851; *San Francisco directory, 1852-53*

[85] *Sacramento Transcript*, December 2, 1850; *San Francisco directory, 1852-53;* maritimehertiage.org, accessed 2/9/2020.

[86] *Daily Alta California*, March 2, 1852; www.maritimeheritage.org, accessed 2/9/2020.

7.

California

If John Morrissey and Dad Cunningham expected to arrive in a lively boom town bustling with possibility, they would have been sorely disappointed by the desperation that was all around them. San Francisco had endured a chaotic couple of years since Marshall's discovery of gold in the hills nearby. The influx of new residents had brought overpopulation, crime, illness, and disaster. By April of 1850, the number of newcomers residing in and around San Francisco numbered around 62,000. The arrival of outsiders reached its peak the following September, with 5,802 people disembarking at the San Francisco docks in that month alone. New newspapers, entertainment venues, and less moral businesses were flourishing to accommodate the ballooning population. Yet the city fell into devastating debt. Beginning in early 1850, the city coffers were for the first time spending more than they were taking in. With the city's credit faltering, "[claimants] against the city drew up bills for two or three times the amount of the claim, so that they might realize... the full amount of the debt in cash.... Bearing interest at the rate of thirty-six per cent, per annum." [87]

Population and fiscal problems were compounded by the elements. Beginning on November 2, 1849, flood-inducing rains continually visited the city, as much as twelve inches falling in a single day. The rainfall, sometimes replaced by hail, did not end until March 1850. Flooding turned streets into rivers and swamps, forcing many businesses to close. There were no confirmed deaths, but at least one person went missing.[88]

Ironically, the people of San Francisco probably preferred the floods to the shocking streak of devastating fires which had begun ravaging the city in December 1849. The first, called the Great Fire, destroyed fifty houses and stores, causing one million dollars in damages and prompting the city to establish a fire department. A second fire, started in a saloon in May 1850, burned down three hundred homes and killed one person, with damage estimates reaching as high as four million dollars. When the mayor subsequently refused to pay the volunteers who had labored to stop the fires from the city's struggling treasury, the city barely escaped an ensuing riot. As a massive city rebuilding project got underway in June, a third fire decimated another three hundred houses and did another three million in damage. A fourth, again started in a saloon, commenced in September,

---

[87] *San Francisco directory, 1852-53*
[88] *San Francisco directory, 1852-53*

spread quickly through the surrounding wooden tenements, destroyed 150 houses, and did a half million in further damage. When fireworks set off to celebrate the territory's acceptance as a U.S. state in October 1850 hit the building next to the city hospital, both buildings burnt to the ground. Though no one died, several patients were badly burned in the blaze. December 1850 saw another fire burn through some warehouses, consuming one million dollars in property. May 1851 brought the most destructive of all the fires, breaking out in a paint store in the center of town and leaving the city "in ruins" by the next morning. The blaze destroyed more than a thousand buildings, resulting in as much as twelve million dollars in damage, and killing "quite a number" of people. The next month saw another fire break out in a portion of the city under reconstruction, burning down another 450 buildings, causing three deaths and more than two million in damages. In the panic that struck the city after this fire, four more people died of violent causes. Yet another fire came in November 1852, though it did significantly less damage than most of the other blazes.[89]

The fires had left hundreds homeless or jobless, exacerbating the city's overpopulation difficulties. These conditions contributed to a Cholera outbreak which took as many as twelve lives a day, lasting through October and November 1850. At the time, the citizens of San Francisco regarded the multitude of fires that had repeatedly demolished San Francisco between 1850 and 1852 as all being accidental, though later historians have pointed to evidence that there may have been a single arsonist to blame. Regardless of the cause of San Francisco's dilemmas, the city into which John Morrissey stepped into at some point between late 1850 and early 1852 was one of smoldering ruins, flood damage, calamitous debt, rampant overcrowding, and pestilential disease.[90]

———

Immediately upon his arrival in California, John Morrissey made it known that he still wanted a fight with Tom Hyer, the man popularly regarded as the reigning Champion of America, though he had not fought since his victory over Yankee Sullivan two years earlier. Hyer had arrived in California before Morrissey, in hopes of striking it rich as a prospector. He refused to reenter the prize ring against anyone for less than a $10,000 stake. Proposed fights with Sullivan, New York pug Matt Gooderson, and British champion William "The Tipton Slasher" Perry had all failed to come to fruition because of his steadfast refusal to budge from this demand. As he had done in New York, Hyer plainly ignored the relative upstart

[89] *San Francisco directory, 1852-53*; Graysmith, 1-181; https://thebolditalic.com/5-times-san-francisco-was-almost-destroyed-the-bold-italic-san-francisco-697dcf1177b8,   accessed 4/29/2020
[90] *San Francisco directory, 1852-53*

Morrissey and his barroom challenges. Eventually, frustrated that his prospecting had turned up no gold and suffering from persistent illness, Hyer returned to New York.

Possibly seeing Hyer's dismal experience as an example, Morrissey and Cunningham made no attempt at prospecting in California. Noticing that the local hills and towns were teeming with criminals, desperate souls, gamblers, businessmen, sporting men, adventurers, and soldiers, the two recent arrivals realized they knew no more about gold prospecting than any of the others. But they did know a great deal about gambling, a pastime that appealed to many such men. Using the cash which their friends had fronted them, Morrissey and Cunningham established a gambling joint in San Francisco called the Gem. Their prime business was with the game of faro, which both men had dealt during their time working for John Petrie in New York.[91]

Historian David G. Schwartz describes the American version of faro as follows:

> To play, the dealer shuffled and placed the cards face up in a dealing box. He 'burned' or discarded the top card, and then began placing cards into two piles, one for the player, the other for the bank. Each draw of two cards was called a 'turn,' and each game consisted of twenty-five turns: The final card in the deck was, like the first, a dead card. Players placed their bets, either on single numbers or any one of several combinations, after the deck had been shuffled and placed in the box. Players could also 'go paroli' and parlay their winnings… if the player's card won on its first appearance, he could let his winnings ride. When only three cards remained in the deck, players could 'call the turn,' or bet on their predicted order; if they guessed right, they were paid at four to one. On 'splits' (when two cards of the same value were played), the bank took half the wager.[92]

Morrissey and Cunningham ran their faro den for eight months and, according to some sources, made a good deal of money at doing so. Morrissey was an aggressive but intelligent poker player and sometimes took part in single games that lasted days. Despite his first taste of real financial success, Morrissey's drinking and brawling ways persisted in California. A John Morrissey appears twice in the "Law Courts" section of the *Daily Alta California* newspaper in the month of March 1852 alone. The first (which might have been his first newspaper appearance ever), published on March 2, tells that an already inebriated John Morrissey entered a saloon called the Gem (his own establishment?) on Dupont Street. When the bartender refused to serve him, "tumblers were thrown, a woman kicked and a man or two knocked down." Arrested and brought

[91] *San Francisco Directory, 1852-53*
[92] Schwartz, 154

before a judge, Morrissey paid a fifty-dollar fine. Just a few days later, he pulled out a pistol "on some pretense" and "accidentally" shot a policeman in the hand. The reporter speculated that the officer would lose a finger because of the "criminal carelessness."[93]

Another disturbance nearly resulted in much more than the loss of a finger. According to some secondary sources, one of the patrons of John's gambling den, a Jim Hughes, took umbrage at a perceived injustice done to him by the house, and the proprietor was on hand to address his complaint. Violent words soon gave way to violent action. Hughes and Morrissey both pulled pistols and began firing, both missing their target. After the gun smoke dispersed, cooler heads somehow prevailed, but Hughes insisted that John meet him for a true duel as a point of honor. Morrissey agreed, if Hughes would concede the right to choose the weapons over to him. Hughes, understandably assuming his opponent was referring to the right to choose the kind of firearm to be used, consented. When the appointed time came, Hughes arrived first at the agreed upon locale, a crowd also gathering there to watch the violence play out. Then John Morrissey showed up, carrying with him the weapons for the duel: two butcher knives. Hughes, not willing to take the risk involved in calling his opponent's bluff, turned tail. John Morrissey had brought a knife to a gun fight and won.

It was during his time in California that John first met Jim Turner, a rowdy twenty-something with a penchant for violence who would become one of his closest allies in the coming years. Turner had been born in New York, but had spent a good deal of time in New Orleans working as a cooper before coming to California with the 1849 Gold Rush, where he had proven himself a vicious enough character to stand out as notorious among the many disreputable travelers flooding into the state.

If the often-unreliable Morrissey biographer Jack Kofoed is to be believed, John also amused himself in these days with the company of one Lolita Fernandez, "only sixteen years old but with the experience of twice her age and an unconquerable sensuality." They met, as Kofoed tells it, in a saloon on Broadway and John hired her to deal cards at his joint. The couple apparently continued a long sexual relationship, one that prompted jealousy from Tom Maguire, an Irish immigrant and founder of the successful Jenny Lind Theater. Kofoed gives no account of his source of this story. This author has found no mention of Lolita in any other source. Nor does she turn up in a search of California newspapers or city directories from this period, though that is admittedly not surprising. Maguire was indeed in San Francisco in this period, and his being acquainted with John Morrissey is quite plausible.[94]

[93] Bartels, 16; *Daily Alta California*, March 2, 1852 and March 16, 1852
[94] Kofoed, 76; *Daily Alta California*, May 15, 1852;
https://noehill.com/sf/landmarks/cal0192.asp, accessed 5/1/2020

Other than the above anecdotes, Morrissey's time as a faro dealer in San Francisco was apparently without incident, which might have bored a man used to adventure and brawling. Thus, when news of yet another gold strike arrived in California, John was intrigued. This time the discovery was in the Queen Charlotte's Islands off the Pacific Northwest Coast of Canada. Morrissey, Cunningham, and eighteen others purchased a schooner to take them to the islands. They hired a captain and mate for a percentage of the anticipated profits. On the day the ship set out, seeing that the men on board carried with them a total of one shotgun, forty pistols, six small cannons, and the requisite ammunition, San Francisco's customs officers understandably refused to let the boat leave the harbor. Undaunted, the band of adventurers slipped out under cover of darkness one evening.

Luckily avoiding any trouble from the law in its journey, the schooner arrived at the Queen Charlotte's Islands after eighteen days at sea. The secluded islands were inhabited primarily by the Native American Haida tribe, members of that tribe being the first to discover the gold and bring it to the mainland towns for trade. The Haida had been hostile to subsequent ships carrying American and Canadian prospectors. When this particular schooner of ambitious Americans arrived, a party of Haida came out to it in boats before the prospectors could make landfall. The Haida boarded the ship but were somehow convinced that the white men meant no harm, and all but their Chief apparently disembarked. The story goes that when the Chief refused to leave, John snuck up behind him, grabbed him, and threw him overboard. The newspaper accounts do not explain why the notoriously inhospitable Haida somehow failed to retaliate for this attack upon their leader, allowing the white men to stay and prospect for nine days on the islands. Maybe the natives knew that Morrissey and his pals would find nothing in the spot where they chose to look. After nine days without any discovery, the Americans began their return trip to California empty-handed.

The *Times* gives an account, published years later and purportedly given to them from Morrissey himself, of a perilous stopover in a port on Vancouver Island during the return trip from Canada. The day after their arrival in port, the *HMS Thetis*, captained by Augustus Leopold Kuper, arrived. Without official papers, in a foreign land, and loaded with weaponry, the Americans feared that Kuper would mistake their boat as a pirate craft, should he come aboard. Morrissey suggested that they preempt Kuper by boarding the *Thetis* first. Rowing to the gunboat's side, they boarded, and Morrissey personally explained to Kuper about their failure at Queen Charlotte's Islands and that they were innocently returning to the United States. Kuper, caught off guard by the arrival of the Americans on board and satisfied with Morrissey's explanation, received the guests graciously and hosted a dinner for them that evening. Sea-faring custom dictated that Morrissey and crew return the favor the next day, but by morning light the American schooner had already taken a quiet leave of the port. This account is verified, at least circumstantially, by the fact that the *HMS Thetis* was indeed around the area of Vancouver Island in 1852.[95]

———

The unsuccessful prospectors arrived back in San Francisco on June 20, 1852 to the further disappointing news that they had missed a prize fight that very day involving a friend of John's, Big Jack Willis of Vermont, and a well-known English pug calling himself George Thompson (his real name was Bob McLaren). Thompson had been the trainer, sparring partner, and corner man for none other than the champ himself, Tom Hyer. It was Thompson who had worked as Hyer's second for his championship fight with Yankee Sullivan. He had traveled out to California with Hyer and stayed put when Hyer retreated back across the country. Charley Duane, who had arrived in California a full year before Hyer and Thompson, idolized Hyer and thus struck up a friendship with Thompson as well. Duane had made himself even more notorious in Sacramento than he had been in New York, becoming a top aide to Democratic boss David Broderick, another transplant from New York. When Hyer returned to New York, Duane took it upon himself to look after Thompson. Duane had wanted to keep Thompson away from the attention of the Sacramento authorities that might not take kindly to yet another prizefighter arriving in town. Toward that end, he set Thompson up with a mining claim in El Dorado County until the Englishman could arrange a profitable prize fight. It didn't take long. Thompson notified Duane that he had arranged for himself a fight with Willis, and Duane rented out the Brighton racetrack in Sacramento. Charley sent out word that a $2,000 prize was on the line.

The promotion was successful. The number of spectators who turned out on the day of the match numbered about 2,500, making it the most attended fight of the Gold Rush period. Willis supporters composed most of the crowd, preferring a man from nearby Canada to a perceived invader from England via New York. Nonetheless, the betting went Thompson's way. Unfortunately, the paying public witnessed a miserable sham. A correspondent for the *Alta California* observed that the noticeably bigger Willis was "no match for his antagonist in science, coolness or courage." Neither fighter endured much punishment, resulting in "a very lame affair." After sparring his way to an easy win, the Englishman won not only the $2,000 purse, but split the $8,400 gate receipts with Duane. News later broke that the fight had been a fix. In two separate interviews, Duane gave different accounts, one acknowledging he had been a party to the fixing, and in another he claimed to have been "very angry to think that

[95] *New York Times*, May 2, 1878; http://vancouverisland.com/plan-your-trip/regions-and-towns/vancouver-island-bc-islands/thetis-island/, accessed 4/30/2020

Thompson had deceived me." In this second story, Duane insists that his anger inspired him to search for the man who could best his former friend.[96]

Having parlayed his winnings into the purchase of a bowling alley, George Thompson displayed no compunction against declaring himself the Champion of the West, despite the dubious nature of his win. Admirers bestowed him with a belt commemorating the title. Duane later insisted that it was his own indignation at the news of the Thompson fight being a fix that prompted him to convince Morrissey to enter the ring, reasoning that "he was strong and muscular and… he could win the battle." According to a later account in *The National Police Gazette*, it was boasting from Thompson himself about the talents of Tom Hyer that incensed John into his first prizefight. "Thompson announced that Hyer could whip any man in America," according to Edward Harding, one of the American prize ring's first historians, "and that statement as soon as it reached Morrissey riled him." John placed ads in several of the San Francisco newspapers, challenging Thompson to a boxing match. On July 8, the fighters signed a contract in Sacramento, each man posting a $500 deposit as forfeit if he did not show. The agreed upon date was August 20, with a $3,000 side bet placed between the participants. Morrissey, conceded the choice of ground, decided upon Mare Island, in San Pablo Bay, about twenty miles from San Francisco.[97]

Organized boxing matches were still rare enough, and his opponent well-known enough, that the promotion of John Morrissey's debut match as a prize-fighter gained attention in major newspapers as far away as Massachusetts and Maryland. Both fighters received hundreds of visitors at their respective training camps, the onlookers wishing their favorites well or sometimes wanting to judge who best to wager upon. George Thompson carried out his training at the Columbia House, built on land purchased from the nearby Mission Dolores Church by E. Carpenter & Co. His trainers were men named Ockleston and Dennison. To prepare John, Duane hired Joe Winrow, a pugilist-turned-police-officer who had been Thompson's partner in training Tom Hyer for the Yankee Sullivan fight. The location of their training is not known, but, if Duane is to be believed, Morrissey was far from an ideal student. John refused to obey Winrow's instructions and, when chided, would complain that he had no interest in training. As a result, the prizefighting novice entered the ring at Mare Island in poor condition, at least according Duane's later recollection.[98]

[96] *Daily Alta California*, June 22, 1852 and August 21, 1852; Boessnecker, 171 – 172; Graysmith, 90; Duane, 73

[97] Duane, 73; *National Police Gazette*, July 3, 1880; *Daily Alta California*, July 10, 1852; *Sacramento Daily Union*, August 23, 1852

[98] *Baltimore* Sun, August 17, 1852; *Pittsfield* Sun, July 15, 1852; *Sacramento Daily Union*, August 23, 1852; Duane, 73

The fight generated significant interest within the sporting fraternity of California and the surrounding territories. Even mainstream newspapers noted the event "has for weeks been the chief subject of conversation," some papers going so far as reporting the details of the signing of the contract and Thompson's training. With no fear of interruption from California authorities who were much less squeamish than those in the East, the fight's backers had placards placed around San Francisco, Sacramento, and neighboring areas detailing which steamers would carry fans to the site of the fight. They played up the English versus Irish ethnic angle. Most fans supported Morrissey. Both his Irish birth and the fact that he had grown up in the United States allowed his supporters to back him out of ethnic pride and patriotism, looking past the fact that he was a novice in the prize ring. John's fans argued that his ferocity would overcome his shortcomings in preparation and experience, for he was fearsome enough to "whip his weight in wild cats." Betting, though, remained rather even, indicating that sentimental favoritism didn't mean that some men were willing to bet against the Englishman's superior technique and experience.[99]

At nine o'clock in the morning on August 21, John boarded the steamship *Red Jacket*, one of four steamers set to transport fans from San Francisco to Mare Island that morning for a fee of ten dollars per passenger. A fifth steamer came from recently incorporated Sacramento. Still other fans made the journey in their own boats. By two o'clock in the afternoon, everyone had arrived. The summer sun beat down and a swarm of mosquitos descended upon the waiting crowd, which numbered about one thousand men and, to the scandal of those who would read about it later in the papers, a handful of women. The seconds shaded and fanned their fighters, while everyone waited for men to pitch the twenty-four feet diameter roped circle in the ground. Tradition required that Morrissey, as challenger, enter the ring first, and he did so to the accompaniment of boisterous cheers. John made a point of tossing his hat high when throwing it into the ring, another tradition which signified his challenge. Thompson's fluttered in shortly thereafter. "Send him back to Liverpool," cried members of the crowd. Approaching the center of the ring, Morrissey held up a bag of gold and announced its value at $2,000. He offered it as a bet on himself against any man willing to wager eighteen hundred. He had no takers, but his many supporters cheered his confidence. When John then offered the same bag against $1,500, there were still no takers.[100]

The correspondent for the *Sacramento Daily Union* noticed that Thompson and his men were relaxed professionals, while Morrissey's outrageous bravado was no more than a false cover for a novice's anxiety. Twenty-one years old, Morrissey stood five feet, eleven inches tall and

[99] *Daily Alta California*, August 21, 1832; *Sacramento Daily Union*, August 23, 1852
[100] *Daily Alta California*, August 21, 1832; *Sacramento Daily Union*, August 23, 1852; *Frank Leslie's Illustrated Newspaper*, May 12, 1860

weighed 175 pounds. The *Union* reporter noted John's "compact and firm frame" with "well knit" muscles, contradicting Duane's assertion that Morrissey was underprepared. Morrissey "looked as though it would not be his fault if he had the misfortune to lose," observed the reporter. Thompson, twenty-seven years of age, was three inches taller and five pounds lighter than his opponent. His body was "beautifully developed" with "stout limbs, brawny shoulders, and length of reach betokening that he would do fearful execution." The *Daily Alta California* gives slightly different heights and weights, having Morrissey the lighter man.[101]

Winning a coin toss, Morrissey had the decided advantage of standing with his back to the blinding sun. When the fight commenced, both fighters circled each other tentatively, both pawing with soft blows until they closed in a clinch and Thompson tackled his man to the ground. John leapt up laughing and made the scratch without delay. Again, the fighters fought defensively, though Morrissey got in a sharp blow to his opponent's mouth and drew first blood. Any cheering from the Morrissey majority stopped when Thompson threw him down a second time. Rising, John next attempted to unnerve his opponent by taunting and grinning as the men sparred each other. A veteran fighter, Thompson did not take the bait and successfully threw John again. A Morrissey supporter cried foul, but both judges refuted the claim. Infuriated, Morrissey showed much more aggression in the fourth round and landed a hard right at Thompson's left ear, "leaving a visible impress." Slipping, the Englishman hit the turf for the first time and the audience let out an approving roar. Eager to follow up on his success, John again came out brawling in the fifth, but took several hard blows in return. He closed the round by tackling his adversary to the ground, generating more uproarious applause. Morrissey put his man down again in the next round, but Thompson returned the favor in the following.[102]

By the start of the eighth, one of John's eyes was swelling badly, but he came to the scratch laughing. He "looked daggers while his adversary grinned defiance." The fighting was getting more desperate now, the punches wilder. After some viscous exchanges of blows, both men collapsed together. Both fighters took their thirty seconds rest, but it was Morrissey who came to the mark first, "game as a bantam." Thompson still displayed confidence in his expression, but his body language betrayed hints of fatigue. The fighters closed and began to exchange body blows. This time it was the Old Smoke who threw his opponent. Morrissey's fans erupted with applause once more. At the close of the next round, Thompson fell over once more after freeing himself from a Morrissey headlock.[103]

The *Union* correspondent describes the mayhem of the eleventh:

---

[101] *Daily Alta California*, August 21, 1832; *Sacramento Daily Union*, August 23, 1852
[102] *Sacramento Daily Union*, August 23, 1852; *Daily Alta California*, August 21, 1852
[103] *Sacramento Daily Union*, August 23, 1852

The utmost confusion now reigned supreme. Time was called on the men's appearance, mutual blows exchanged. They then closed, and in their struggle a cry of foul was raised against Thompson, who was said to have struck below the belt. Morrissey's judge decided it foul play and the umpire verdict demanded who is said to have said "yes," and then recalled his word. On this Morrissey broke for the colors, and ran off with them, followed by two thirds of the entire crowd. Thompson was left on the ground with his friends and other spectators, all maintaining that it was a ruse of the opposite party to pocket the bets.[104]

A correspondent for the *Daily Alta California* admitted he was not able to see if a foul had occurred and did not what had happened between the judges and umpire due to the rush of the spectators into the ring. Charley Duane remembered that the referee had ruled for Morrissey following a claim of foul, mentioning nothing of the controversy that surrounded the fight's close.[105]

The bout had lasted less than twenty minutes. After Morrissey departed, the umpire, a Mr. Rees, insisted that he had not yet decided as to whether a foul had been committed, and he steadfastly refused to declare a winner. Thompson and his men refused to pay their bets to Morrissey and his supporters, insisting upon a rematch. Morrissey's backers regarded the fight as a victory and carried him on their shoulders aboard the *Red Jacket* back to San Francisco. The boat arrived back in town at about ten o'clock that night to the sound of bands serenading the streets with horns, fifes, and drums.

On August 28, the *Los Angeles Star* indicated that a second fight was being organized, as the referee had declared the bout a draw. This rematch never came to fruition, and history records the fight as a victory by disqualification for Morrissey. Thompson later sued the stakeholder of the fight, one S.G. Whipple, for handing over the winnings of the side bet to Morrissey. Judgment went in favor of Whipple, as prizefighting was technically illegal, and any contracts drawn up in support of it consequently invalid.[106]

Writing in 1854, Edward James, early chronicler of American boxing, reported that Thompson had indeed fouled Morrissey, but did so intentionally "in order to save himself from the vengeance of an infuriated mob, should he defeat Morrissey." Edward Harding, another early fight historian, concurred that Thompson purposely fouled out, "being afraid of

---

[104] *Sacramento Daily Union*, August 23, 1852
[105] *Daily Alta California*, August 21, 1852; Duane, 73
[106] *Los Angeles Star*, August 28, 1852

being shot." This account would be the version most often retold in later tales of John Morrissey's life.[107]

Following his showdown with Morrissey, George Thompson seems to have disappeared into virtual obscurity. The California newspapers mention that in October 1852, a George Thompson suffered a gunshot wound following a quarrel with another man, the papers speculating that the wound was mortal. They make no mention if this George Thompson was the prizefighter or not, but refer to him as "leader of a gang of horse thieves and murderers." This Thompson, whoever he was, did survive the gunshot and was arrested; he later escaped police custody when his guard fell asleep. It is difficult to believe this man was the self-same who fought Morrissey just a couple of months earlier, given that the newspapers do not refer to the bandit as the well-known prize fighter at all. Additionally, newspapers describing the prizefighter George Thompson mention his profession as a political "shoulder hitter," while Charley Duane refers to him as working as a prospector in this period. Neither mentions anything about stealing horses. The only evidence this writer could find of Thompson's later life is a portrait of a middle age man, alleged to be his likeness.[108]

On the very same page of the very same newspaper that tells of horse thief George Thompson's being shot, is a separate article stating that a John Morrissey attended the Democratic County and City Nominating Convention in San Francisco as a delegate for the Sixth Ward. If this is the John Morrissey of our story, then the article in the *Daily Alta California* represents the first evidence of Morrissey parlaying his newly won fame into serious political activity and sets the stage for the success that was to follow his return to New York City.[109]

---

[107] James, *Sullivan*, 58; *National Police Gazette*, July 3, 1880; *Sacramento Daily Union*, August 23, 1852

[108] *Sacramento News*, October 15, 1852; *Daily Alta California*, November 16, 1852; *Sacramento Daily Union*, August 23, 1852; Duane, 72-73

[109] *Daily Alta California*, October 15, 1852

8.

Now Who's Champion?

By the time John Morrissey garnered his questionable win over George Thompson, he had been in the San Francisco area for approximately a year and a half. In that time, he had found some financial success as a gambling entrepreneur and brought some modicum of fame to himself with his debut as a prizefighter. Reports of his boxing debut had appeared in newspapers as far afield as his native Ireland. He set out an open challenge to face any man in California for an enormous $20,000 prize, but nothing came to fruition. As 1852 entered its final months, his restless ambition once again had him considering another cross-country trip. His motivation to return to his old stomping grounds in New York City was the very same motivation that had at least in part convinced him to stow away to California: a fight with Tom Hyer.[110]

Since his signal victory over Yankee Sullivan three years previous, Hyer had not engaged in a single true prize fight, despite the many attempts by fellow boxers to coax him into the ring. Not long after the Sullivan match, Bill Poole tried to convince the new champion to face one Matt Gooderson and the two engaged in a sparring contest at the Old Bowery Theater in New York, after which "no one could boast of the superiority of either man." However, Isaiah Rynders used his influence to put a stop to the plans for a fight to the finish, disliking the idea that two native-born Americans would be facing one another.[111]

Gooderson was one of the few American boxers whose backers had been capable of and willing to meet Hyer's outrageous prerequisite for a $10,000 side bet before he accepted any challenge. To find another potential opponent capable of coming up with the cash, Hyer himself issued a challenge to William "The Tipton Slasher" Perry, Champion of England. Famous for his marathon victories over his countrymen Tass Parker (133 rounds) and Tom Paddock (27 rounds), Perry had also held the giant American Charles Freeman to a seventy round draw lasting nearly an hour and half. Hyer offered to face Perry on his native English turf if Perry would pay $5,000 in traveling expenses. Failing this, Hyer said he would face Perry in New Foundland and this time offered to pay Perry the $5,000 in expenses. The Slasher declined both offers.[112]

[110] *Waterford News*, October 29, 1852
[111] James, *Hyer*, 22
[112] James, *Hyer*, 22

In today's boxing parlance, Hyer could be seen as "pricing himself out" of fights. Rather than appear to be afraid of dangerous opponents, one could argue, he simply demanded a side bet so high that he was sure no other prizefighter could match it. However, there is an understandable motivation for Tom to avoid the prize ring. He was the reigning champion and, as such, was feted among his fellow sporting men as the Chief, and he could depend on his notoriety to aid him in his ventures as a saloon keeper, gambling-house proprietor, and shoulder hitter. He could also pull in audiences by giving scientific sparring exhibitions with men like George Thompson. To put his status as undefeated champion on the line was to risk his only true source of livelihood. Additionally, Hyer's long term health had become a concern for those closest to him. Charley Duane records that his friend was suffering from what he perceived as rheumatism when he came to California. Before long though, Hyer was "so sick he was unable to walk," and returned to New York. The persistent illnesses which followed may have convinced the champion that any return to the ring would be his last, even if he'd never admit as much to his admirers. If he was going to gamble his future income and his life, the reward would need to be worth the risk.[113]

Since his first foray into the Americus Club in 1850, John Morrissey had been trying to garner a fight with one of the big names in pugilism, Hyer the ultimate goal. Never having much money, he never put together anything resembling the side bet the champion required. Even if he still did not have the capital to put up $10,000, he could now boast of victory (controversial though it may have been) over Hyer's friend and trainer, George Thompson. John hoped that this victory, especially considering the controversial way in which it was achieved, would push Hyer to forgo his outrageous financial requirement for want of revenge. He made plans for a return to New York City and a campaign to finally corner the Chief into a fight.

———

No details are recorded of the means of John's return East, except that it was financed by $5,000 in winnings on a bet made at a horse race in Santa Barbara, Morrissey's first recorded participation in horse racing, a past time which would play a significant role in the life to come. We can assume he again traveled by steamship with a stopover in Panama to get back to New York. It was the only way to travel from the Western end of the country to the East, except by horse. No transcontinental rail system existed yet. Certainly, John now had enough funding to travel legally, and we can assume there were no mutinies to quell. According to Jack Kofoed, John again traveled with Dad Cunningham, and the pair arrived in New York in October of 1852. Once John reached the East, he did not go direct into

---

[113] Duane, 77

New York City, but instead made a stopover for a time in Troy to visit family and friends. He made a point to call upon the home of his former employer Levi Smith, who was now the Captain of the newly launched riverboat *Francis Skiddy*. Though his visit was under the pretense of delivering a message given to him by Smith's son who had also been in California, John's true intentions involved another of Levi's children, his beautiful daughter Susie. Now about sixteen or seventeen years of age, Susannah Smith had grown into a beautiful young lady.[114]

Susan was the second youngest of six children. Her oldest sibling, William, was a few years older than John and, as of 1850, was working as a railroad conductor. Her youngest sibling, Adeline, was about eight years of age. In 1849, Susan left public school to enroll in the Troy Female Seminary boarding school, where she likely received instruction from Emma Willard, a woman of such dedication to her profession and such moral rectitude during her five decades instructing at the school that a statue to her was erected in Troy in the 1890s. Willard, the wife of a prominent Vermont physician, believed that girls and women should have the same access to higher education that their male counterparts enjoyed, and toward that end she had already set up a seminary in Waterford, New York, the first higher education institution for females in the United States. The Troy Female Seminary, the second such institution, was established in 1821, Mrs. Willard personally presiding over an all-female faculty. Upon her engagement to John in or around 1852, Susan Smith left school altogether, but the Emma Willard School, as it is now called, remains a prestigious boarding school to this day.[115]

The bare-foot street ruffian whom Susan remembered from childhood had returned a rugged man brimming with confidence, dazzling her family with tales of high seas adventure and far off California. The teenager was smitten. Likewise, he was as impressed as ever by her beauty, charm, and education. Three weeks after his return, he proposed marriage, and she accepted.

———

Having achieved one goal almost immediately after his return, John and his friends set about achieving another, getting Tom Hyer into the ring. John left Troy and arrived in New York City in the Summer of 1853. "The day I landed I challenged Hyer to a fight for $10,000," remembered Morrissey years later. John had been right in his estimation that his claim to victory over Hyer's good friend George Thompson had irked the champion. At every opportunity, Hyer publicly defended Thompson and declared Morrissey a cheater. John's backers were able to get the champion to commit to a fight, each side posting a $100 forfeit. However, when the

---

[114] Hotaling, 31; Kofoed, 89; *Manawatu Times*, February 8, 1880
[115] U.S. Federal Census, 1850; Weise, 88-91, Sage, 594

rivals and their associates came together, one or the other was unable to post the promised $10,000 and relinquished his deposit. Whether it was the champion or his challenger who was unable to come up with the cash differs by source.[116]

Convinced the Hyer fight would never come to fruition, John determined to look elsewhere for a noteworthy opponent to boost his reputation. The pickings were slim. Charley Duane and George Thompson were still in California; William Perry couldn't be convinced to leave England, even for Hyer's offer of $10,000; Bill Poole kept exclusively to lawless rough-and-tumble fights. That left one viable option, Yankee Sullivan.

In many ways, Sullivan was the perfect choice. His was the biggest name in American prizefighting, outside of that of possibly Hyer himself. Though he had not fought in four years, he could draw financial backers and a healthy crowd. Since his loss to Hyer, Sullivan had been among those trying unsuccessfully to coax the champion out of retirement. When Hyer refused to face him again and failed to meet anyone else with the championship at stake, Sullivan began to publicly call himself the champion once more, meaning a victory over him would allow Morrissey to establish a claim for himself as the true titleholder.

There were also drawbacks to fighting the aging son of Erin. Sullivan was now in his forties and noticeably smaller than John, facts that might convince fans that the fight would be a mismatch. Additionally, they were both Irish by birth. Boxing then, as today, often produces its largest crowds for ethnic, racial, or international confrontations. In antebellum America, the most public interest circled around contests between Irish and native fighters. A bout between two Irishmen would not galvanize the populace the way that the Sullivan and Hyer match had.

The impetus for the fight occurred when Morrissey and Sullivan, who had also recently returned from California, ran into each other in the Gem saloon on Broadway. Not surprisingly, the conversation turned from casual discussion to an intense argument. What is surprising is that they did not come to blows immediately but mutually agreed to meet again at another saloon on the first of September. News of the meeting spread quickly through the city's sporting circles and, a short time later, a large crowd of admirers of both men was on hand to witness the signing of contracts to fight for a side bet of $1,000 each.

That same day, Sullivan set up his camp at a place called the Hit and Miss Hotel just outside of Brooklyn, essentially acting as his own trainer. His conditioning consisted of walking and running up to thirty miles a day, lifting weights, hitting a sandbag, and sparring with pugilist friends. Entering his own camp on September 3, John trained for the match under

[116] *Chicago Daily Tribune*, August 1, 1874; *National Police Gazette*, July 3, 1880 and June 23, 1883; Gorn, 110; *New York Herald*, May 2, 1878; *New York Tribune*, March 10, 1855

the eyes of Awful Gardner and a man named Tom O'Donnell at McComb's Dam along the Harlem River in the Bronx, which was then all rural fields.[117]

Winning a coin toss, Morrissey received the right to choose the location of the fight and picked Boston Corners, an obscure location in Massachusetts, but a good place to stage a prize fight, which were still illegal in most Eastern states. Consisting of approximately fifty acres, Boston Corners had the space to accommodate a ring and large crowd. More importantly, it was just over the New York State border, out of reach of that state's law enforcement, and was secluded on the opposite side of the Taconic Mountains from Great Barrington, Massachusetts, the closest town with any substantial law enforcement. The fight's organizers were also pleased to learn that the Harlem Railroad had a stop in Boston Corners.

New York sports enthusiasts were at first put off by the unusual pairing of two Irishmen, most native-born Americans not sure who to root for. In the end, most of them settled on pulling for Old Smoke who, though Irish-born, had grown up in America. Nonetheless, nativist Tom Hyer made no bones about picking Sullivan, with whom he had reconciled years earlier. [118]

The New York police also had their own interest in the fight. In late September, warrants were issued for the arrests of both men. On September 28, Sullivan evaded capture when the arresting officer came upon the famed pugilist walking alone near Coney Island. According to the *Clipper*, the officer chickened out and left the scene, while a Washington D.C. paper reported that Sullivan had been "forcibly taken" from custody after arrest. Morrissey too evaded the officer sent to arrest him, high tailing it up to Troy, where he started a new training camp. Still, rumors continued to persist that the police had arrested both fighters all the way up until a few hours before the fight. [119]

Both principals remained free, and New York City was bristling with pugilistic fever. As if to allay the tension for the big fight to come, at least one prize fight was arranged in the meantime. On September 27, one Thomas Johnson and his adversary, a William Brady, intended to go toe-to-toe for fifty dollars a side, until police arrested them and their parties. Instead of the expected fifty-dollar winnings, the boxers paid $500 bails, ruining their chances of catching a train to the more anticipated Morrissey versus Sullivan battle.[120]

On October 10, Morrissey made the risky move of accepting an interim match with a man named Bird, "a nailer by trade.' Bird had issued a

---

[117] *New York Clipper*, May 11, 1878; *New York Sun*, May 2, 1878; Myers, "The Brawls at Boston Corners"
[118] James, *Sullivan*, 20-21; James, *Hyer*, 22
[119] *New York Clipper*, October 15, 1853; *Daily Evening Star*, September 29, 1853; *New York Times*, October 14, 1853; *Brooklyn Daily Eagle*, September 28, 1853
[120] *Brooklyn Daily Eagle*, September 28, 1853

challenge to face any man in America, and Morrissey, apparently inconsiderate of the big fight set to happen in only another three days, took him up on the offer. To the relief of both his fans and those of Sullivan, Morrissey easily demolished his opponent and walked away unscathed.[121]

At about four in the afternoon on Wednesday, October 12, the day before the scheduled fight, hundreds of excited New Yorkers crammed into Harlem Railroad cars bound for Boston Corners. "The behavior of some of them while in the cars was not such as could be described," gossiped the *Herald*; "and many acts of disorder, to use the mildest terms, were perpetrated." The four hundred passengers were incensed to learn that, because they had boarded the express, their train would not be stopping at the Boston Corners station. When the train reached Boston Corners and the conductor refused to accommodate the boxing fans, members of the crowd attacked and held down the brakeman, "while others detached the locomotive and tender from the train." Having thus disembarked, the crowd walked to the expected site of the next day's battle, where some of them, unable to find vacant lodging, camped in the open. The day of the fight saw more arrivals, bringing most published accounts of the crowd size to about 3,000. Morrissey appeared first at about two o'clock, symbolically tossing his hat into the ring to the cheers of the crowd. About five minutes later, Sullivan made his way to a prize ring for the first time in more than four years, also to applause. He had with him his seconds Andy Sheehan and Bill Wilson and his umpire, Bill Poole.[122]

The correspondent for the *Herald* noted that Morrissey's size advantage over his opponent made him appear "Herculean." He weighed 175 pounds. The writer also marveled at the extremely toned physique of the smaller man, who came in at 154 pounds. Noting the age difference between the two principals, some mused that Sullivan looked old enough to be Morrissey's father. Playing up to the nativist crowd's temporary adoption of him as their chosen favorite, Morrissey pulled out a red, white, and blue sash and tied the colors to his ring post. In answer, Sullivan wrapped a black flag around his post, which his supporters said indicated "victory or death."[123]

As the fight began, Sullivan showed no rust in getting the better of the initial action. He landed several damaging blows while Morrissey followed him, groping about but failing to hit his man. In his constant attempts to keep away from the bigger man, Sullivan accidentally fell through the ring ropes, ending the opening round. In the second, Sullivan claimed first blood from Morrissey's nose, before falling to the ground – intentionally, this time – to avoid his opponent's clumsy onrushing. Sullivan continued this strategy of hitting and purposefully falling throughout the fight,

[121] *New York Herald*, October 22, 1858
[122] *Richmond Enquirer*, October 18, 1853; *New York Herald*, October 14, 1853; *New York Clipper*, October 15, 1853; *Brooklyn Daily Eagle*, October 13, 1853
[123] *New York Herald*, October 14, 1853; Fox, 40

drawing protests from the swollen, bloodied Morrissey and his supporters. Sullivan was constantly landing four blows to one against the slower, bigger man. Early on, Morrissey's second, Awful Gardner, tried to lance the swelling of the fighter's left eye, but their efforts proved futile; it soon shut completely. Sullivan showed marks and bruises, but nothing approaching the "shockingly mangled" visage of his opponent.[124]

The fourth round proved particularly exciting as Morrissey attacked his opponent "with all the impetuosity of a wild bull." Though John landed several hard blows to the face, Sullivan returned in kind to both body and head, breaking Morrissey's nose in the process. The *Clipper* considered John to get the better of the action for the first time in the fight, with Sullivan showing signs of tiring. Both men fought viciously, and the crowd roared its approval.[125]

By the start of the sixth round, "Morrissey presented a horrible appearance, the blood streaming from his nose and mouth in profusion," but he continued to press after his opponent. John occasionally landed telling blows, but the wily Sullivan would simply keep away until he could recover his senses. In the seventh round, John landed not a single blow before Sullivan, satisfied with his own work, fell once more to the ground. Some of these rounds lasted barely one minute. Morrissey's fans finally had something to cheer for in the eleventh when he landed a punch to Sullivan's body "which made his side crack like a whip," but the smaller man continued to out-land his attacker. The worst damage Sullivan showed was a swollen left eye, the result of one of Morrissey's fingers "accidentally" going into it. As the eye began to shut, Sullivan's falls became more frequent, as Morrissey began to catch up to the forty-year-old with greater frequency.[126]

As the minutes passed, the fight became a battle of attrition, Morrissey continuing to get the worst of the punishment. When John did touch his opponent, the smaller man often staggered, but before he could land another blow, Sullivan simply fell. In a frustrated effort to keep his adversary from purposefully falling, Morrissey hit upon a strategy of cornering Sullivan and then grabbing the ropes behind Sullivan with both hands and pressing against him, holding the smaller man up with his strength and weight until he saw an opportunity to land a blow. Inevitably, Sullivan would squirm out of the hold and drop to the ground for protection, ending the round. As the fight neared the twentieth round, Sullivan showed even more concern to keep away, either to conserve energy or out of sheer exhaustion. Morrissey continued to press forward but would only manage to land a couple of blows before his opponent once more voluntarily hit the turf.

[124] *New York Herald*, October 14, 1853
[125] *New York Clipper*, October 15, 1853
[126] *New York Herald*, October 13, 1853; *New York Clipper*, October 15, 1853

Both men appeared to be tiring but Morrissey more so, as Sullivan caught a second wind. When both men toed the scratch for the start of the twenty-seventh round, Morrissey's face was ghastly, and his frustration over his opponent's tactics showed. [127]

"Now who's champion?" Sullivan taunted.

"That's to be seen," Morrissey replied, before receiving a series of punches to the body and head from Sullivan, who promptly dropped to the ground. Morrissey barely landed a blow through the next couple of rounds. The *Herald* described the sight of him as sickening, "the blood gushing in streams from his nose, mouth, and half a dozen gashes on his face." The *Clipper* marveled at how he could remain on his feet with so much blood loss. By contrast, the left side of Sullivan's face was badly swollen, but he showed little other physical damage. The smaller, older man was now landing with ease at any target he chose. Sullivan's tactics agitated Morrissey's supporters, who were losing faith in a victory for their man. [128]

The fight wore on past the thirtieth round, as one-sided as ever. John was "bearing up manfully, proving himself as game a man as ever stood up in a ring, [but] it was evident he was failing rapidly. His knees shook, and his hands were low, and his mind bewildered." Sullivan showed signs of tiring, his punches getting weaker, but he continued to out-punch his opponent. Then came the thirty-seventh round, which became such a mess that people on hand afterward argued vehemently as to what exactly had occurred. [129]

As the writer for the *Herald* tells it, Morrissey finally got ahold of his man in the thirty-seventh. He immediately threw an arm around the opponent's neck, pressed him to the ropes, and lifted him off his feet. Sullivan's men, claiming a foul, did not wait for the judges or referee Charles Allire to decide the matter, and broke into the ring. Morrissey's seconds followed suit. No one outside the fracas could see what was happening between the fighters, but their seconds were now fighting each other. Soon enough Sullivan too was in the melee, taking on Awful Gardner. When the crowd caught a glimpse of Morrissey helplessly down on his knees, some of them joined the fracas, and pandemonium ensued. Amid this mess, Allire somehow declared the fight Morrissey's, even as Old Smoke's supporters had to carry the exhausted pugilist of the ring. Outraged, Sullivan called for Morrissey's return and the fight's continuance, receiving no reply. Sullivan's seconds demanded an explanation from Allire, who offered none. The reporter later asked Allire himself, and the referee said that he declared Morrissey the winner because it was Sullivan who left the ring first, which the reporter said was a mistake. "Sullivan did

127 *New York Herald*, October 13, 1853; *San Francisco Sunday Call*, May 8, 1810
128 *New York Herald*, October 13, 1853; *New York Clipper*, October 15, 1853; *San Francisco Sunday Call*, May 8, 1910
129 *New York Herald*, October 13, 1853

not leave the ring for some minutes after Morrissey was taken away," he explained. According to a rumor reprinted in the *Times*, Sullivan, upon returning to New York, called for a rematch "in one day or sixty days."[130]

The *Clipper* tells a similar but slightly different story of the thirty-seventh. As Morrissey held him against the ropes, Sullivan executed a very clever maneuver that put his attacker on the ropes instead. From here, Sullivan dropped to his knees and then immediately jumped right back up and caught the off-guard Morrissey with a punch. Claiming a foul, Tom O'Donnell broke into the ring and shoved Sullivan, inciting the brawl between both men's seconds. As this happened, Morrissey went to Allire complaining of the alleged foul, the result of which was Allire's declaring the fight for Morrissey by disqualification. Morrissey, satisfied, left the ring with the aid of friends. Not hearing the referee's verdict, Sullivan eventually made his way back to the scratch to begin fighting again and, finding his opponent no longer present, assumed he was now the victor. When he and the crowd were told otherwise, a "general riot" ensued.[131]

The fight had lasted fifty-five minutes. The sporting press generally praised both fighters, Sullivan for showing stunning skill and athleticism despite his age and Morrissey for his perseverance and endurance. However, the result was highly controversial. That Morrissey deserved the win remained a matter of dispute for years to come. The *Herald* suggested, without saying it outright, that Allire was either corrupt or incompetent. A couple of days after the fight, the *Clipper*, declared that "if any man is honorably entitled to it, Sullivan is the man." Yet years later a writer for the same paper commented, "fault could not be reasonably found with the referee for deciding as he did." The *San Francisco Sunday Call*, in another article looking back years later, insisted "there was no doubt that Morrissey was far in the lead and deserved the victory." Nineteenth century fight historian Edward James thought Morrissey deserved the win, stating that John was present to toe the line to start the next round, and that it was clear that Sullivan would never be able to stop him. "This even Morrissey's enemies admit," James insisted. Yet another nineteenth century boxing historian insisted that it was Sullivan who did not come to the scratch, as he could not make it through the crowd of men now in the ring, forcing Allire to call the fight for Morrissey.[132]

As for the fighters themselves, while both men claimed that they deserved the victory, they apparently earned a fair amount of respect for one another in their clash. Looking back more than twenty years later, Morrissey called the match with Sullivan "the hardest fight I ever had. He was an artist, and he broke my nose, and cut me all to pieces; but I have always known that I could keep my legs and stand up until any of my

[130] *New York Herald*, October 13, 1853; *New York Times*, October 14, 1853
[131] *New York Clipper*, October 15, 1853
[132] *New York Herald*, October 13, 1853; *New York Clipper*, October 15, 1853 and May 11, 1878; *San Francisco Daily Call*, May 8, 1910; James, *Sullivan*, 21; Fox, 42

opponents were worn out." Sullivan concurred. "You might as well hit at a brick wall as hit that man on the head," he once remarked.[133]

———

Morrissey's hometown of Troy was collectively on edge awaiting news of their man's success or failure. The rest of the country might have derided boxing as morally reprehensible, but the good people of Troy were willing to set aside their judgements for one of their own, even the local clergy. On the day of the fight, the staff at the *Troy Whig* newspaper were surprised to see a "very eminent and elegant" Troy priest arrive and anxiously ask for news of the results. Upon reading the report of a correspondent, the clergyman shouted, "I would have given a quarter's salary to have seen that fight! I'm so glad that John has won!"[134]

Back in New York City, crowds awaited the return of spectators from the event at the train stations with anticipation equal to the Troy priest. When the Albany express train arrived, disembarking passengers spread various accounts of what transpired, Sullivan's fans joyously proclaiming him the victor, while Morrissey's insisted the referee had given their man the decision. Most of the praise, at least according to the *Clipper*, was for Sullivan. As news of the confusing results spread, much of the city was in "great excitement" with rumors and misinformation, the sporting houses buzzing with talk and excitement as afternoon turned into evening. Some newspapers began printing stories that Morrissey had died of his wounds. On October 15, a notice from John Morrissey (ghostwritten, no doubt) appeared in the *Times* to dispel this story:

> Having seen a statement in the *Evening Day Book* that I was dead, I beg to inform you that such is not the fact; and I hereby furnish you the best evidence, by personally handing you this communication. And I would beg leave to add, for the satisfaction of my friends, that I have received the written decision of the referee, in my favor, stating that I won the fight fairly and honorably.

Yours, JOHN MORRISSEY,

New York, Friday, October 14, 1853

An almost identical message appeared in the *Brooklyn Daily Eagle* and the *Spirit of the Times*.[135]

Despite John's insistence that everything was terrific, both fighters faced legal repercussions after the fight. Several mainstream newspapers were

---

[133] *Chicago Daily Tribune*, August 1, 1874; *New York Herald*, May 2, 1878
[134] *Cleveland Plain Dealer*, November 8, 1866, quoting *Troy Whig*
[135] *New York Clipper*, October 15, 1853; *Richmond Enquirer*, October 18, 1853; *New York Times*, October 14, 1853 and October 15, 1853; *Brooklyn Daily Eagle*, October 15, 1853; *Spirit of the Times*, October 18, 1853

indignant that authorities had allowed the fight to take place. "Those who are maimed and bruised and fleeced of their money, have already got what they deserved," editorialized the *Schenectady Cabinet*. Other papers were not so sure that more punishment was in order. With many puzzled as to why the participants were not arrested before, during, or immediately after the set-to, the *Tribune* blamed corruption within local law enforcement, noting that many policemen "associate constantly with thieves, rowdies, blacklegs and keepers of houses of ill-fame," and that these men were "all alive with excitement" over the fight. That the fight took place outside of the jurisdiction of New York law enforcement provided no consolation whatsoever to the city's mainstream papers. The *Tribune* went on to complain that Andy Sheehan, Sullivan's second, was himself a lawman.[136]

In reaction to such scorn, two weeks after the fight's completion, a Massachusetts judge finally issued warrants for both Morrissey and Sullivan, as well as sixty others who were at the fight. "By this unfeeling requisition," supposed the *Evening Post*, "a number of persons who adorn our higher circles will be accommodated with quarters in Eldridge street jail until further notice." Police arrested Sullivan on November 3, 1853 for his participation in a prize fight, sending him to the prison in Lennox, Massachusetts. Tom Hyer, showing that his longstanding rivalry with Sullivan was truly quashed, paid the Irishman's bail of between $1,500 and $2,000, a sum he was only able to raise by collecting funds from Sullivan's well-wishers among New York's sporting men and politicians.[137]

Likely looking to avoid further jail time or a fine following a trial, Sullivan skipped town and returned to California sometime in 1854. There he met a woman named Emily, who would later claim to be his wife, though both were already married to other people. Together Sullivan and Emily ventured out to Hawaii, where, the story goes, he taught boxing to King Kamehameha. At any rate, the couple was certainly back in the San Francisco area by early 1856, Sullivan earning money in his tried and true methods, as a boxer (in paid exhibitions), gambler, shoulder hitter, and ballot box stuffer. He was, wrote Ed James, "a power and a terror for miles around." Early in that year, or late in the previous, Emily gave birth to a daughter.[138]

Sullivan backed the wrong man when he stuffed ballots for one James P. Casey, an unscrupulous and violent local politico who had gotten his start in New York and had done time in Sing Sing Prison. Though Sullivan's support helped get Casey elected as city supervisor, an office for which he had not even appeared on the ballot, Casey's violent tendencies would bring about the downfall of many men associated with him. When *The San*

[136] *Schenectady Cabinet*, October 18, 1853
[137] *Evening Post*, November 8, 1853; *New York Clipper*, May 11, 1878; *New York Sun*, May 2, 1878; *Sacramento Daily Union*, August 15, 1854; *Los Angeles Star*, January 21, 1854
[138] James, *Sullivan*, 22; *Wide West*, June 8, 1856; *Daily Alta California*, February 24, 1856; *Sacramento Daily Union*, June 4, 1856

Francisco Bulletin began running articles about Casey's disreputable behavior and the questionable way by which he had come to his office, a public rivalry of slander and accusations erupted between Casey and the *Bulletin*'s founder, James King, culminating in Casey's shooting King to death in broad daylight on Montgomery Street. This crime ushered in an era of violent vigilante justice in California.[139]

Citizens of San Francisco formed a so-called Vigilance Committee in the wake of King's death. Heavily armed members laid siege to the county jail, forcibly removing Casey and overseeing his hanging. Despite this perceived justice, the Committee remained in force through the next several years, political corruptors being especially favorite targets. They counted among their numbers several high-placed members of society, all claiming to be acting righteously. They acted outside of the law, but their numbers and power were such that no official law enforcement could prevent their acts. The committee had a particularly anti-Irish bent, and men like Yankee Sullivan and Charley Duane became high-profile targets. Policemen arrested Sullivan and an associate named Billy Mulligan at Casey's funeral on May 26, 1856.

Interrogators forced Sullivan to sign a confession to political fixing and ballot stuffing under threat of violence. They held him in a former appraiser's office on Sacramento Street. The Vigilance Committee told him and the public that they did not intend to hang him as they had Casey, but instead they meant to force him out of the country. When Emily and other friends visited him, he told them of his fear of hanging. She reassured him that he would not be hanged, and then, according to her account, "he did not seem much depressed in spirits and was cheerful as usual." When she returned, he began talking of suicide, saying that as a Catholic he knew he could not go through with the act. On the morning of June 1, he awoke complaining of bad dreams, again telling others he was certain the vigilantes would hang him. At 9 AM, a man linked to the Vigilance Committee found Sullivan dead in his room. Charley Duane, who had by now publicly stated his opposition to the Committee, made his way to the scene. Seeing the corpse, "I found that the arteries in his left arm, near the elbow, had been severed and the arm was nearly cut off." Rumors immediately spread that the Committee had killed Sullivan. Sullivan's guard and the Committee insisted it had been suicide.[140]

Duane ordered an autopsy, and, according to him, the two doctors who examined Sullivan agreed that, while the wound on his arm was what killed Sullivan, the knife found in his room and delivered to them as the supposed method of suicide was so dull it could not break the skin, let alone nearly sever an arm. However, in their official findings, published in the *Sacramento Daily Union*, the doctors made no mention of this discrepancy.

---

[139] *New York Times*, June 30, 1856; *Sacramento Daily Union*, June 3, 1856; Duane, 105-111
[140] Duane, 127

Another doctor, who had been the first medically trained person to arrive on the scene not long after the body's discovery, testified in court that the dull knife had indeed been the means of death.[141]

How Sullivan died remains a mystery. Sullivan's early biographer, Ed James, insisted that a New York thug named Jessel had killed the fighter. Jessel, who had tussled with Sullivan in the past, was a guard at the prison and had connections to the Vigilance Committee, according to James. With two other guards holding Sullivan down, Jessel is supposed to have cut open the prisoner's arm with a bowie knife. James claimed this story had been personally related to him by a man who had been a prisoner in an adjoining room. As for Duane, he initially also believed the Jessel story, but was eventually convinced that America's best-known prize fighter had indeed died by his own hands. Although Duane never got along with Sullivan, he sympathized with his supposed persecution at the hands of the Committee and took it upon himself to organize the funeral. On the day before the funeral, the Committee took Duane prisoner. Back in New York, John Morrissey hosted a charity benefit for Sullivan's mother, who had followed her troublesome son to the States.[142]

Yankee Sulivan, or James Sullivan, or James Ambrose, the first widely known boxing star in America, was buried in San Francisco's Mission Dolores Cemetery. For two years, his resting place remained unmarked until a fan from Liverpool, England paid for a headstone on which read the epitaph, "Remember not, O Lord, our offenses, nor those of our parents. Neither take thou vengeance of our sins. Thou shalt bring forth my soul out of tribulation, and in thy mercy thou shalt destroy mine enemies."[143]

———

Police arrested and imprisoned Morrissey in the Massachusetts jail alongside Sullivan after their fight. A $1,200 bail secured his release. "I fought once in the States for one thousand dollars a side," Morrissey later mused, "and it cost me eighteen hundred dollars to save myself from the State prison." A year after the fight, John reported to Massachusetts with attorney Charles Bennett at his side for trial and entered a guilty plea. The judge said that, considering Morrissey's honoring his parole, he would have liked to have given the fighter no fine at all, but the law required he do so, so he ordered the defendant pay a $1,200 fine, plus court costs, or go to Lenox Prison for sixteen months. The defendant stated that he did not have such funds on hand, at which point the citizens of Berkshire County took up a collection and offered payment. John refused the donation and submitted to jail. Bennett dispatched a messenger to New York City, where the prisoner's friends collected the necessary sum and sent it back with the

[141] *Sacramento Daily Union*, June 4, 1856
[142] James, *Sullivan*, 22-24; Duane, 127-129; James, *Lives*, 71
[143] Isenberg, 78; findagrave.com, accessed 7/23/2019

same messenger by boat. Morrissey thereafter returned to New York City.[144]

Though his legal troubles must have certainly proven setbacks, John's life in the next few years would take quite a different trajectory from that of Sullivan's. He partnered with his old employer John Petrie in the running of the Gem gambling house on Broadway, close to the famous Broadway Theater, and he lived out of a room above the casino floor. A short time later, he also became a part owner of the Bella Union (also called the Belle of the Union) saloon on Leonard Street, "a resort of the worst characters." Then there were the fees he collected simply to appear at gambling and sporting locales and fraternize with the customers, who pointed him out to their friends and asked to shake his hand.[145]

———

On August 13, 1854, John Morrissey married Susannah Smith in her parents' white two-story home on River Street in Troy. It was a double wedding which included Susan's brother and his bride. They would then move into a house John had purchased for them at 55 Hudson Street in Manhattan. In those days, newspapers and correspondence recorded little of the private lives of married couples, even of celebrities, so there are scant details available of the type of relationship John and Susan had as a married couple. As with any couple together for decades, there would certainly be considerable ups and downs. Those accounts that do exist come mostly from the couple themselves, which one can assume are either biased or idealized. "I've played cards, and stood up in the ring, but I never let myself forget my domestic honor and duty. It's the first thing to take care of all the days of your life," was John Morrissey's only recorded description of his married life, made as he was approaching middle age. In her rare interviews with reporters, Susan would always describe him as attentive and sweet with her, and she lamented the public's impression that he was a brute. One old friend of the couple later remembered, "'Old Smoke' thought the world of his wife; he relied a great deal on her advice, and it was generally sound." There are no stories or evidence that John ever kept a mistress; even though such details were considered off-limits for public consumption, there were several examples of celebrity infidelities making it into the more salacious rags or into private journals in this period, including men in John Morrissey's circles of acquaintance and friendship. That no such rumor ever attached itself to John Morrissey, whose character was

[144] *Brooklyn Daily Eagle,* October 20, 1853; *Troy Weekly Times,* July 10, 1858; *New Orleans Daily Crescent,* July 17, 1854, quoting *New York Daily Tribune*
[145] *Buffalo Courier,* quoting *New York Times,* December 19, 1855

under constant attack from enemies all his life, is at least circumstantial evidence that he remained devoted to his wife.[146]

After getting married, John and Susan embarked upon a joint journey of self-improvement that began with reading lessons. "When we were married he could not read or write," Mrs. Morrissey would later remember, "and to tell the truth I was only a trifle better off... I told him we must learn to read and he said I should teach him. Well, we established lesson hours. Every night before going to bed he devoted himself to his spelling book, and in the morning one hour to writing in a copy book. The rule of study was inflexible. We made it so." The boy who had dropped out after a single year of grade school had come about as far as any illiterate could hope to go. Now, as a young man, he realized that, to take himself further toward his dreams of respectability and wealth, he would have to make up for lost time in his education.[147]

Reading would be essential in fulfilling his quickly developing political ambitions. He was beginning to make important political connections now through his fame as a prize fighter and his usefulness as a vote-getter. Literacy would provide the opportunity to provide more value than brute muscle to New York's political elite. Of course, with powerful friends come vehement enemies. In John's case, no enemies proved as dangerous as those he had by now already known for years.

---

[146] New York Genealogical and Biographical Record, 1932, accessed at www.*ancestry.com*; *Manawatu Times*, February 7, 1880; *National Police Gazette*, October 15, 1880; *Wheeling Sunday Register*, September 30, 1883

[147] New York Genealogical and Biographical Record, 1932, accessed at www.*ancestry.com*; *Manawatu Times*, February 7, 1880; *National Police Gazette*, October 15, 1880

9.

The Butcher

One early morning in 1853, shortly before John Morrissey's battle with Yankee Sullivan, Tom Hyer and Bill Poole broke into John's room above the Gem. Finding the man asleep, they proceeded to pound on him with fists and boots and, now that he was awake and badly bruised, ordered him to depart the city at once. To their astonishment, John refused to back down. "I was so determined about it that they saw that I would never leave New York till I had that belt," John boasted years later. Hyer and Poole left, but what had once been a sporting feud was now clearly escalating into serious violence.[148]

Morrissey's fight with Sullivan reawakened the sporting public's interest in a match between the controversial victor and Hyer, who had defeated Sullivan in much more convincing fashion years earlier. By 1854, Hyer was already in a noticeable physical decline at age 35, the result of alcohol-related health problems. But, as a man whose income and popularity rested solely on his reputation as a fearsome physical force, he did his best to hide his ailments and always insisted that he could not wait to meet Old Smoke in the ring. On June 20, when the two fighters and their respective supporters encountered each other at the Union Race Course on Long Island, Morrissey insisted upon fisticuffs on the spot. Hyer, knowing he was incapable of surviving a true fight, delayed, claiming he did not feel well on that day but would gladly whip the younger man at a future date. After accusations and recriminations subsided, the two parties agreed to meet for a bout at one in the afternoon on July 20, at the Old Abbey on Bloomingdale Road.

When July 20 arrived, Morrissey was not present. The Fifth Ward police, looking to prevent trouble, arrested and detained him until after the scheduled time of the fight. When news of this reached Hyer, he sent word to Morrissey's people that he still intended to fight if John, upon release, would come to the Abbey at 5 A.M. Meanwhile, the Fifth Ward Police Captain agreed to release Morrissey with the proviso that he promised not to bring a pistol to the meeting. Both fighters arrived at the Abbey in the early morning hours of July 21, with their closest friends in tow.

Though talk of the fight galvanized the sporting public as expected, the unusual hour brought few fans to the Abbey. Luckily for those who were not able to attend, they did not miss much. Knowing that his body could not withstand a boxing match, Hyer had devised a plan to avoid fisticuffs

---

[148] *Chicago Daily Tribune*, August 1, 1874

and still save face. When time came for the fight, Hyer instead pulled out two pistols and proposed they settle their differences with them. Morrissey naturally refused, and everyone left the Abbey disappointed that the most anticipated fight in years had once again dissolved. After plans for a December match also fell through, Hyer told friends he was retired from the ring, and Morrissey stopped pressing for a fight.

———

Hyer was a dangerous and viscous character, but John truly had more to fear from Tom's ally, William Poole. Like Hyer, Poole was a butcher by trade, native-born Americans having dominated that profession for generations. He was born in 1821 in Sussex County, New Jersey but brought to the city as a young child. His father ran a butcher shop in Washington Market which the son would later inherit. It was while apprenticing in the butchery trade that he first gained notoriety in the streets as a "hard customer," getting in frequent street brawls. The *Times* certainly understated the case when they described his personality as "not of the most peaceable and forbearing kind." An 1851 encounter with a couple of enemies at the Florence Hotel ended when the duo of Poole and Hyer left one man with a broken jaw and another cowering in fear. Despite – or perhaps because of – his rough edges, Poole was well-liked by his working-class customers and by many of the street toughs with whom he spent his time. He was a member of the Order of the United Americans, a "militantly anti-Catholic" group opposed to Tammany Hall's perceived pandering to the Irish. He was also a frequenter of the Whig Committees at the Broadway House, a center of nativist politics. In these pursuits, Bill would have found himself many young comrades. The huge influx of Irish immigration resulting from the potato famine had resulted in an equally abrupt backlash. Between 1852 and 1854, national membership in nativist organizations shot up by the tens of thousands.[149]

When, on July 4, 1853, a group of Ninth Ward nativist thugs attacked a meeting of the Ancient Order of Hibernians in the St. James Church of the Five Points, the culprits were said to have been "friends of Poole." The *New York Daily Tribune* considered him "a political operator and a sort of contractor for carrying primary meetings, and managing conventions…. exerting considerable influence in city politics." Such activity allowed Bill to make many important political connections, not to mention winning him a certain amount of legal and popular support from sympathetic parties within the city. By the dawn of 1855, he was said to virtually control all political activity in the city's Eighth and Ninth wards. Theodore Allen, who would later become one of the most famous sporting men of New York,

---

[149] Golway, 79

spent his early years in Poole's circle of underlings and regarded him as, "one of the best men in America."[150]

Allen was not alone; many people who otherwise had nothing to do with crime or the sporting life admired Bill's supposed fearlessness and his use of violence in the name of his nativist beliefs. It helped that he was good looking. His eyes were large and dark, and a long, straight nose (unusual in a veteran of so many fights) hung over a prominent chin. "His chest was broadly developed; he had an easy and commanding carriage, and he was expert in all his movements. The features of his face were very regular and carved; his hair was dark, and he wore a large moustache," gushed the *Times*. In the style of the day, Bill took time out of every day to curl the ends of his trademark mustache. He stood just under five feet, ten inches tall and at his best weighed near 160 pounds. To many he cut the perfect image of the streetwise sport.[151]

As a young man, Bill fell in with the unquestionably fascinating New York subculture known as the Bowery Boys. History often wrongly records the Boys (or B'hoys as they were sometimes called, referring to the way they themselves pronounced the word) as being an organized street gang. Herbert Asbury goes so far as to dub them as "probably the most celebrated gang in the history of the United States." In fact, there was never one unified Bowery Boy gang. Certainly, many street gangs were composed of young men others would recognize as Bowery Boys, but they were never a single, cohesive unit. As they usually shared the same political and social beliefs, they often traveled in packs and put up their fists for the same causes, generating the mythology of their being a single gang. Named for the street on which their kind first proliferated, they were noted for the cocksure attitude, flashy dress, and worship of an unwritten code that professed individualism, American patriotism, and settling all personal disputes with violence. They were generally Democrats, but they despised the political elite of Tammany Hall and what they believed was its cowing to the interest of immigrant voters. In other cases, Boys like Bill Poole supported the Native American or Know-Nothing Party.[152]

The first noticeable thing that marked a Bowery Boy apart from others was his appearance. He kept his hair close-cropped and greased-down. He often sported a red shirt, a symbol of his membership in one of his neighborhood's fire brigades, of which virtually every Bowery Boy, including Bill, was a proud member. On top of the shirt he wore a dark frock coat and on his legs were boots useful in fighting fires and stomping on opponents. Then there was the ubiquitous cigar which every self-respecting Bowery Boy clasped with cocksure attitude between his teeth.

[150] *New York Times*, March 9, 1855; Adams, 132; *New York Daily Tribune*, March 10, 1855; *Brooklyn Daily Eagle*, March 10, 1855; Zimmerman (e-book)
[151] *New York Times*, March 9, 1855; *National Police Gazette*, August 28, 1880 and November 20, 1880
[152] Asbury, *Gangs*, 28; Anbinder, 178-180

When not fighting fires or supporting radical anti-Tammany political causes, they usually plied at trades such as butchery, carpentry, or shipbuilding. This set them apart from a typical street gang from somewhere like the Five Points, the members of which were often from the poorest of backgrounds and worked as menial laborers if they worked at all.[153]

From his days among the Boys, Bill graduated to working for men like Isaiah Rynders as perhaps the city's most feared thug and shoulder hitter of all. He became known to the denizens of the Five Points, Washington Market, and the Fourth Ward as simply Butcher Bill or Bill the Butcher, referencing not only to his trade but his deserved reputation as "the champion brawler and eye gouger of his time." His street credibility soon attracted his own loyal following of malcontents and undesirables, many of them old Bowery Boy associates but also toughs from Washington Market and Fire Engine Company Number 34, called the Red Rover Company. These men were the terror of Christopher Street, where Poole lived in a brick row house with his wife and son. Like all the most successful shoulder hitters and sporting men, he used his influence and connections to back the purchase of a saloon, his being the Bank Exchange on the corner of Howard and Broadway. Nineteenth century sporting man and publisher Richard Fox described the Bank Exchange as the headquarters of gamblers, turfmen, politicians, and men of all stripes and callings from all over the country. A visit to Gotham was not complete until a call had been made at the 'Exchange'.... Poole's genial nature made him a great favorite."[154]

Of course, not everyone found the Butcher so admirable. "Bill Poole was the original abysmal brute," one old sport remembered of him decades later. Clearly, John Morrissey wasn't the only other sporting man who wound up on the wrong side of the man's temper. At one point, the Butcher came to blows with Yankee Sullivan. The row started as the result of an argument surrounding the results of a dog fight, Poole and Andy Sheehan at odds with Sullivan and two of his cronies. Poole and Sheehan beat their three adversaries, Bill personally "kicking, punching, chewing, strangling and tripping" Sullivan to a sound defeat. For the rest of his life, it was said, if Sullivan "even heard Bill's name mentioned he glided briskly to another and safer place." Poole had even tried to gouge out the eyes of a police officer in a courtroom before a judge and had spent a night in jail for it. Though Poole never actually took part in an organized prize fight, the fearsome reputation he gained from impromptu scraps like these (affectionately referred to as "rough and tumbles" by men who admired such violence) and from his skills with a blade in knife fights meant he was

[153] Anbinder, 178-180; Stott, 104-05; Haswell, 355
[154] Asbury, *Gangs*, 82-83; Asbury, *Sucker's Progress*, 363; Burrows, 824; Adams, 132; *New York Daily Tribune*, March 10, 1855; Stanway, 163

as respected of a fighter as any man in New York outside of possibly his good friend Tom Hyer.[155]

On the Wednesday following the collapse of the Morrissey-Hyer fight at the Abbey, John Morrissey attended a ball in Bill Poole's honor at the Chinese Assembly Rooms in New York City. He likely came looking for trouble, but he departed around ten o'clock that night, after realizing that Poole himself was not present. Making his way to the City Hotel on the corner of Broadway and Howard Streets, he was enjoying a cigar when he caught sight of Poole at the bar with Jim Hughes, who had been the stakes-holder in John's fight with Yankee Sullivan. Hughes had refused to hand the stakes over to either Morrissey or Sullivan due to the controversial nature of the fight and, seeing him there, Morrissey immediately confronted him. When Morrissey demanded the money, Hughes replied, "I'll give it up when you convince me you won the fight, and not before." Morrissey became angry, prompting Poole to tell Hughes to spend the money on rum before handing it over to the Irishman. An argument then arose as to who was responsible for the failure of the Hyer fight, with John insisting he "could lick Tom Hyer or any other man." The longstanding tensions between the two feared fighters escalated into threats and shouts until Morrissey ultimately challenged Poole to a prize fight. Poole responded that Morrissey was too big to take on under the London Prize Ring Rules, but he would gladly face Old Smoke in a knife fight. Though he paused at the proposition, John eventually agreed, but only if the battle would take place in Canada, to avoid New York authorities. Poole refused to travel. Finally, Morrissey suggested that if Poole was unwilling to face him in a gentlemanly prize fight with rules, perhaps he would like to face him in a no-holds-barred fist fight for a wager of fifty dollars. To this, Poole consented, agreeing to meet Old Smoke on the Steamboat Wharf, also known as the Amos Street Dock, along the Hudson at seven the next morning, July 26. This locale, not far from Poole's Christopher Street home, was solid Bowery Boys territory, giving the nativist a decided home turf advantage.[156]

That evening, the sporting houses of New York were again alive with rumors, betting, and arguments, everyone happy to have something to talk about after the falling out of the Morrissey and Hyer bout.

A crowd of more than three hundred people assembled on or near the wharf by six thirty the next morning, some of them having camped overnight in order ensure themselves a good vantage point of the action, some claiming spots on nearby rooftops. By virtue of the location, most were Poole supporters, and they were quick to violently discourage any

[155] *Amsterdam Evening Recorder*, July 27, 1920; *Boston Herald*, June 7, 1853; Stanway, 99
[156] *Sacramento Daily Union*, September 1, 1854; *New York Times*, July 28, 1854; Fox, 43-44

friends of Morrissey who thought to arrive early. Mountains of cordwood usually lined the pier, but men had spent the night clearing these away in anticipation of the morning's fight. Poole initially arrived at around five o'clock in the morning in a coach, accompanied by his friends Smut Ackerman, Thomas Allen, and Tommy Culkin. However, Poole got bored and, wanting to avoid the chill in the early morning air tightening up his muscles, decided to get some exercise. Allen rowed Poole, Ackerman, and Culkin across the Hudson to a resort in Hoboken for drinks. Bill rowed on the way back to warm up, returning at about six thirty. Seeing that Morrissey was still not in evidence, Poole retired to the nearby Village House to rest up. For some time, Morrissey did not appear. When seven o'clock came and went, members of the crowd speculated that the police had once more detained Old Smoke. Then a carriage pulled up and out came Morrissey, striding arm-in-arm down the dock with a lone friend, Johnny Lyng, a "notorious rough-and-tumble fighter, and an active politician in the precinct of the Sixth Ward." John stripped to the waist and threw his coat aside, appearing "as brawny a young bruiser as the most enthusiastic admirer of muscle could desire to see" in his red flannel undershirt, according to Allen. When he drew close, he asked, "Where is Poole?" and the crowd parted.[157]

The Butcher came forward, and the rivals immediately set about circling each other for a period of about thirty seconds, both men looking for an opening. Morrissey made the first move, letting loose with a left hand. Poole immediately dodged the blow and crouched down to grab John around the ankles. Throwing the bigger man "clean over his head" and down, Bill capitalized on his advantage by falling on top of him and staying there. From this position, Poole got the better of the action as both men "pounded their heads together, tearing at each other's face with their teeth and gouging for the eyes with talon-like fingers." Morrissey was clearly taking the worst of the damage, and his face was soon a soup of blood and shredded, swollen flesh. Five minutes into the fray, John finally relented with the word, "Enough." Poole then stood up and unleashed a flurry of kicks to John's arms and torso with his boots until members of the crowd pulled him off. While Poole's elated partisans boasted and cheered, most everyone else began to hastily leave the scene, knowing the authorities would likely be arriving at any moment.[158]

Eventually Poole and a coterie of friends readied for their departure, only to see either Morrissey or Johnny Lyng leveling a pistol at Bill, whose brother John flattened the gunman with a punch. A general melee then broke out among the stragglers on the dock. Morrissey's men, greatly

---

[157] *New York Times*, July 28, 1854; Asbury, *Sucker's Progress*, 366; *Lancaster Ledger*, August 9, 1854; *New York Tribune*, March 10, 1855; Boyuea, 95 – 97, quoting Thomas Allen in *Police Gazette*; Fox, 44

[158] *New York Times*, July 28, 1854; Asbury, *Sucker's Progress*, 367, quoting Thomas Allen in *Police Gazette*

outnumbered, got the worst of the action until they retreated. Lyng took the worst beating of all. While this happened, two of Morrissey's associates carried their bloodied and battered man away. However, seeing Poole's partisan's advancing, the men carrying Morrissey abandoned him and left him on the dock alone with the enemy. Someone was merciful enough put him in a wagon and drive him away "amid the jeers and hootings of the assemblage." Poole and his advocates then left the scene in a carriage "for a frolic" at Coney Island.

When John arrived at the Belle of the Union, he presented "a shocking spectacle, and scarcely could any of his friends recognize him." One of his eyes had been gouged out of place in its socket, and both were swollen completely shut. His cheek had been punctured, his nose broken again, and his lips mangled. His torso showed the bruises of Poole's kicking. A doctor reported to John's relieved friends that the wounds were not life-threatening.[159]

Morrissey awoke the next day sore, swollen, and bruised. Some later accounts supposed that he was unable to leave his bed for weeks. In fact, Morrissey was determined to give Poole no such cause for satisfaction. Despite his still horrifying visage and the pains throughout his body, he forced himself to dress and step out into the street on that first day after the fight.

In a bizarre epilogue to the story of the Poole and Morrissey scrap, Poole associate Smut Ackerman was telling others about the fight later in the day when, while demonstrating how Poole had thrown Morrissey to the ground, he fell and fatally fractured his skull.[160]

As for the victor, he was in terrific shape. The worst he had suffered was a deep gash on his cheek, where Morrissey had at some point bitten him. "We learn," read the *Times*, "that BILL POOLE and his party of Ninth Ward friends left for Coney Island, yesterday, to have a jolly time in his success in whipping the bully who has made a noise in the sporting world for the last few months." A short time later, police arrested both men on warrants of disturbing the peace. They were each released on $5,000 bond, subject to forfeit if they were again brought before the court within a year's time. Morrissey would violate this promise by September and would have to pay another $2,000 to the court.[161]

Amazingly, this glorified street fight qualified as national news, with papers as far away as Opelousas, Louisiana carrying the story. *Le Courrier de Opelousas* told the story in French. Song lyrics were even published for "Rough & Tumble, or the Amos Street Fight." As was usual when it came

[159] *New York Times*, July 28, 1854; *Evening Post*, July 27, 1854; *Sacramento Daily Union*, September 1, 1854; *Cazenovia Republican*, August 2, 1854
[160] Kofoed, 126
[161] *New York Times*, July 28, 1854; *Sacramento Daily Union*, September 1, 1854; Asbury, *Sucker's Progress*, 368; *Evening Post*, September 15, 1854; Fox 47

to a widely followed fisticuffs rivalry, newspapers were forced to walk a fine line of catering to both the lowbrow customers who wanted to read about such violence and the more squeamish tastes of their middle-class patrons. As the *New York Evening Post* candidly explained, "It engages general attention, but then it is not respectable." As indicated above, the *New York Times* covered the event in detail. As for the *Evening Post*, they kept their coverage mainly to criticism of the whole affair as a pathetic vulgarity. They did, however, take the entirely unique approach of favorably comparing the dust up to the politics surrounding the Crimean War, which was then raging in Europe and Russia. "The Czar is not a wit better than Morrissey," opined the reporter, "nor is the bloody Emperor of Austria more entitled to respect than Bill Pool [sic].... In one other respect the New York pugilists are ahead. They have less words and more blows."[162]

Bizarre analogies aside, John's friends insisted that their man had been beaten by multiple members of Poole's entourage, not just the Butcher himself, and this story has since been propagated by later published accounts (one going so far as to say that Poole wasn't even present). In a letter to the *New York Times*, Morrissey himself insisted that Poole had never hit him or thrown him once, only bit him, and that he had been "ferociously assailed by the entire mob, and I without a friend." His friends had advised him not to go that morning, he said, but he refused to appear a coward and left alone for the docks, "but little did I think that Poole had a hundred men on the ground stripped to help whip me." Morrissey then contended that he was willing to meet Poole again in a fair fight within forty-eight hours at any locale outside of Poole's home neighborhood. Most of the contemporary newspaper accounts and the few extant accounts of eyewitnesses reflect that Poole did the damage alone. "If Morrissey ever had a square deal he had it then," one nineteenth century fight man later opined.[163]

Whatever the numbers truly were, the fight had settled nothing between the principals and their associates. Tensions seemed to only increase between the two pugilists and their respective gangs. A couple of nights after the brawl on the docks, members of Morrissey's group caught up with three of Bill Poole's cronies in a saloon, among them Thomas Allen. In the ensuing melee, one policeman was killed, and Allen had both of his eyes gouged out so badly that they hung out over his cheeks until a surgeon put them back. In September, Lyng and Tom Hyer got into a tussle, during which Lyng accidentally shot a bystander. The looming elections meant that more clashes were inevitable.

------

[162] *Courrier des Opelousas,* August 19, 1854; *Brooklyn Daily Eagle,* July 29, 1854; Stanway, 177-183
[163] Fox, 47

As New York City prepared for the 1854 municipal elections, everyone expected Poole and his henchmen to be out in force in the streets, intimidating or assaulting any voters not intending to vote for Whig candidates. For the Democratic mayoral candidate Fernando Wood, Poole's intentions called for desperate measures. At the time, Wood was one of the most powerful men in Tammany Hall, the organization that dominated the Democratic Party in the city as well as the state.

"Fernando Wood and John Morrissey, taken together, reflect the perfect image of the of New York City politics," the *Philadelphia Evening Telegraph* would cynically once opine. Born into a Quaker family in 1812, Wood had lived in the city since the age of nine. His father Benjamin was a failed businessman who had desperately taken his family from Pennsylvania to Kentucky, then to Louisiana and finally to Cuba through a series of failed businesses and schemes before settling down in New York to open a tobacco shop. When that too failed, Benjamin finally abandoned his family, leaving his wife Rebecca to raise seven children on her own. Prior to his father's departure, Fernando had managed to get some smattering of private education, but with Benjamin's departure left him to gain his most important education on the city streets.[164]

Fernando Wood grew into a man obsessed with acquiring the wealth and respectability his father had always longed for but never achieved. His earliest introduction to the rudiments of business and economics came as the apprentice to a shipping merchant. During the 1830s, he used what he had gained in contacts and knowledge to open a grocer business and later a few saloons along the waterfront. Both groceries and saloons were integral centers of political activity for working class and immigrant men in nineteenth century New York City. Groceries were far from the commercial department stores of our time. They were usually small and very simple places to obtain basic foods and a cheap drink. These were the places that men spent their leisure time, usually in the company of likeminded men of similar social standing, mindset, and ethnic background. On the waterfront, those men were predominantly of Irish and German extraction.

In contrast to the image of the glad-handing, back-slapping politicians who became the stereotype of working-class New York neighborhoods, Wood employed a reserved, august manner as a tool for his rise. He set himself apart from other pols of his time and place by holding himself to a high standard of personal conduct (at least publicly) and respectable appearance. Handsome and tall, he dressed conservatively and in muted tones. He spoke softly, and friends considered him a man of good manners and even temper. Despite his chosen business, he was himself known as an abstemious drinker. Some who knew him compared him to a preacher both in dress and behavior. Nonetheless, he was a fascinating man, even if

---

[164] *Evening Telegraph*, November 19, 1866

his outward demeanor was one of quiet charm as opposed to the loud gregariousness of other men in his profession. In this way, he earned the attention and trust of his customers, who would soon become a faithful constituency.

It had been the loyalty he gained from Irish longshoremen in those waterfront days that backed his move into politics with muscle, and his association with immigrants would be a common complaint among his enemies. "Mr. Wood is greatly indebted as a politician to what are called by social philosophers the 'dangerous classes,'" noted the *Evening Post*. Even at this early stage, despite his reserved manner, he was known as an eloquent writer and moving speaker. He became chairman of the Young Men's Committee of Tammany Hall and parlayed that into winning his first term in Congress during the election of 1840. In the same period, he established himself as a successful imports merchant, which allowed him to capitalize on the Gold Rush. He invested those profits in real estate and business, the true source of a secure fortune that made him the go-to man for impresarios and politicians looking for loans and backing. An 1850 bid for Mayor as "The True Friend of the Irish" failed due to accusations of corruption from former business partners who had not shared in his success. Nonetheless, his money remained the fuel for much of Tammany Hall's activities in the antebellum period. It had all started with saloons on the New York waterfront. By 1854, he was one of the dominant figures in city and state politics and wanted another go at the mayor's office.[165]

———

Wood was intimately familiar with the dangerous political atmosphere of the New York streets on Election Day. His main concern was likely the split in the Democratic ticket. The party had become divisive, and three factions each posted candidates for every important post in the election. The Whigs by contrast had put forth a united front. That the staunchly nativist, rabidly anti-Tammany Poole and his men would be prowling around the polls threatened to turn difficulty into disaster. Wood's days drumming up votes on the waterfront in the same years that Captain Isaiah Rynders was virtually dictating the Sixth Ward vote had taught him not to underestimate the capabilities of motivated shoulder hitters. Realizing that he needed a capable thug to muster opposition to Poole, it was probably Wood who asked city councilman John A. Kennedy, another ambitious figure in the Tammany hierarchy, to find the right man. On November 7, Kennedy summoned for John Morrissey.

By the time Kennedy asked for him, months had passed since John's confrontation with Bill Poole, and he was now completely healed. In fact, he had been out carousing the night before, and he arrived at Kennedy's

[165] Golway, 57, quoting *Evening Post*; Burrows, 823

home in a disheveled state, his clothes and person showing the signs of some other tussle the previous evening. It was Mrs. Kennedy who announced the visitor's arrival to the head of the house. "There is an awful looking man at the door who wants to see you," she complained, "He is dirty and ragged, has a ferocious look, and is the most terrible fellow I ever saw." She pleaded with her husband to send the stranger away, but to her astonishment Kennedy welcomed the ruffian into his parlor. There Kennedy and Morrissey struck a deal, working out a roster of thugs to rival Poole's own.[166]

The men who assembled around John early the next morning included Orville "Awful" Gardner, his partner from his days as a river pirate and his cornerman for the Yankee Sullivan fight; Mike Murray, who had apparently buried the hatchet with John since their brawl on the docks; Johnny Lyng, noted gambler, "immense specimen of humanity," and Morrissey's companion in the Amos Dock battle; Lew Baker, a heavily tattooed, heavy-set Welsh immigrant and ex-policeman who once ran with Poole as a Bowery Boy, but now idolized Morrissey; and Baker's good friend Patrick "Paudeen" McLaughlin, an ex-con and notorious thief who specialized in kicking men when they were down and was instantly recognizable for the missing nose which had been chewed off in a brawl with none other than Murray. Diminutive compared to most of his associates, Paudeen nonetheless had as violent of a temperament as any of them. He had made recent headlines for firing a gun at Tom Hyer following an argument; he had also engaged in several noteworthy scraps with others in Poole's gang, including the Butcher himself. Dad Cunningham and Jim Turner, two close friends from John's California days, were also likely enrolled. On Election Day, these men and a team of between thirty and fifty other "desperate looking fellows," most of them Irish or Irish American, gathered in the streets around dawn, armed with pistols, knives, and clubs. They crowded inside one of the poling houses where they expected Poole and company to arrive, and they waited. The gossiping Reverend Matthew Hale Smith recalls the events of the day as given to him:

> There was no disturbance until twelve o'clock. The late [Police] Captain Carpenter was in charge. About noon a huge lumber-van drove up, drawn by four horses. It was loaded with the roughest of the rough, who shouted and yelled as the vehicle neared the curbstone. Bill Poole, at the time so notorious, led the company. They were the choice specimens of the men who then made the rulers of New York..... Bill Poole sprung to the sidewalk. Captain Carpenter stood in the door. Addressing him, Poole said, "Captain, may I go in?" "O, yes; walk in and welcome," Carpenter said, and in Poole went. He saw the situation at a glance. He measured Morrissey and his gang, turned on his heel, and, passing out, said "Good morning, Cap.; I won't give you a call today; drive

---

[166] Smith, *Bulls*, 180

on boys;" and on they went to some polling-place where they could play their desperate game without having their heads broken."

Doubtless, Morrissey and his cohorts spent the rest of the day enacting the same "desperate game" against those who entered the polling house intending to vote Whig.[167]

Fernando Wood won his election as Mayor of New York City. In the Sixth Ward, where John Morrissey and his friends had stood watch over the poling houses, he garnered 2,107 votes compared to the combined total of 724 votes for all his opponents.[168]

————

By the dawn of 1855, John Morrissey and William Poole had become heroes of the streets, and it was around them that the city's more rough-edged supporters of the Irish American and nativist causes, respectively, could rally. Morrissey was of course best known for the uncommon toughness he had shown in his set-to with Yankee Sullivan. Meanwhile, Poole's pummeling of Morrissey had in turn made him "one of the most notorious pugilists in town." The middle and upper classes of the city gasped and scowled at reports of their exploits in the city newspapers. Yet the men in the dives, saloons, groceries, brothels and gambling dens of New York City celebrated them as something like folk heroes. Supporters of Old Smoke sang his praises in the Sixth Ward, the Five Points, and Broadway, while the Ninth Ward, Washington Market, and the Bowery celebrated the Butcher. The rest of the city's more notorious sections were split in allegiance. Wherever the followers of Morrissey and Poole encountered each other, there was trouble. One account stating that brawls between the factions "were of daily, almost hourly, occurrence" may have been overzealous, but was nonetheless indicative of the gang-related tensions in New York's lower-class neighborhoods.[169]

Paudeen proved a particularly aggressive partisan on the Morrissey side. Poole's good friend Cy Shay would later testify that Paudeen practically harassed Poole day and night, insulting the Butcher in various saloons and challenging him to fights. On at least one occasion, Paudeen even went directly to Poole's home on Christopher Street and, finding Poole out, harassed a young man who worked for Poole instead. Having thrown a drink in the boy's face, Paudeen left the house before Poole returned. In virtually every drinking establishment Poole went, he would hear that Paudeen had been there first, calling him a "black muzzled bastard" and insisting he could whip the famed brawler. For his part, Poole insisted

---

[167] Asbury, *Gangs*, 84; Asbury, *Sucker's Progress*, 363-364; Kofoed, 92; *Daily National Era*, May 26, 1854, quoting *New York Times*; *Daily Alta California*, January 22, 1856; *Brooklyn Daily Eagle*, March 10, 1855; Walling, 375; Smith, 181

[168] Golway, 58

[169] *New York Times*, March 9, 1855; Asbury, *Sucker's Progress*, 368

Paudeen wasn't worth the effort of fighting, but he did visit a judge with a request to have his tormentor arrested.[170]

In January, two of Morrissey's pals, Jim Turner and Lew Baker, paid a visit to Platt's Saloon beneath Wallack's Theater on the corner of Broadway and Twelfth Street. They spotted Poole's closest friend, the retired champion Tom Hyer, sitting at the bar downing rum. Coming up on Hyer unexpected, Turner knocked Hyer's glass from his hand. When Hyer went to retaliate, both men drew their pistols on him. Despite Hyer immediately backing off, Turner pulled the trigger anyway and the ball ripped past Hyer's neck, grazing the skin but doing no serious damage. Hyer drew his own gun and fired but also missed. He then leapt at Turner, knocking his gun away before he could reload. When Baker leapt onto his back and tried to pummel him with the butt of his pistol, Hyer threw him on top of Turner. Police arrived on the scene but refused to make arrests and made a quick exit, prompting Hyer to settle matters himself by dragging Baker, who slashed at him with a knife, outside and beating him senseless. He then went back inside for Turner, only to find him gone.

The exciting tale of the near death of the Chief and his heroic conquering of his attackers spread through New York's streets, only heightening the already murderous tension between the Morrissey and Poole factions. Not long after this dust-up, Poole and Baker came face to face at John Petrie's place, the Gem, one afternoon. The pair had known each other as Bowery Boys. In fact, legend had it that Poole was the man responsible for getting Baker a post as a policeman. Then, "some election difficulty" had dissolved the friendship and Baker fell in with the Morrissey crowd. Baker was apparently "infatuated" with his new boss. According to the *Tribune*, "the hostility which Morrissey entertained toward Poole was even more ferocious in his miserable satellite." Baker later insisted that the Butcher had tried to gouge out his eyes and bite off his ear that evening at the Gem. Saved from a horrid beating by the police, Baker thereafter never left his home without a weapon and seldom without a fellow Morrissey loyalist like Jim Turner or Paudeen McLaughlin in tow. Meanwhile Poole spread the word that if he ever saw Baker or Jim Turner again, he would kill them.[171]

———

Late in the night of February 24, Bill and an entourage that included Charley Lozier (Poole's brother-in-law), Jimmy Acher, and Thomas Allen, left a saloon together and began to make their way to Poole's home on Christopher Street via Broadway. En route, they decided to make a stop in Stanwix Hall, a bar that had opened only just recently and yet already

[170] *New York Times*, March 9, 1855
[171] *New York Tribune*, March 10, 1855

attracted a frightening mix of local malcontents. "On entering the room from Broadway, the visitor may see to the right an oyster stand, and further on the bar, between which there is an open space occupied only by a washstand," described the *New York Herald*. "On the left-hand side of the room is a partition, on which is placed a number of pictures, and containing only one door, opening into a hall that runs from the street to the back yard." A politician of the era described the Stanwix atmosphere as "excessively political, without being partisan, and every man prominent in city affairs was likely to be found there. Any Stanwix hall evening was sure to show you Morrissey, Hyer, Poole, or Baker, waiting – elbow on counter – while Barkeeper Corny Campbell mixed their drinks."[172]

In a magnanimous mood, Poole offered to buy a drink for everyone in the place, except for one. That was Mark Maguire, a tough called the King of the Newsboys and a known confederate of Morrissey's. Morrissey himself was in the back room either taking his supper or playing cards, not yet aware of Poole's presence. As Maguire and Poole fell into an argument, the Stanwix proprietor, George Dean, called for a policeman to prevent a fight in his new place. Though Maguire and Poole were separated, Poole's friends continued to harass Maguire until John Morrissey walked into the main room, accompanied by his own gang.

The following account of that night is taken mostly from that of Poole's friend Allen, as told to the *Police Gazette* many years later, complimented by a few other sources, including other first-hand witness affidavits taken very shortly after the encounter. Allen's story, probably because it appeared in such a popular magazine, is the version of events most often recounted and remembered, though some it's details conflict with testimony given by others present that evening. According to Allen, the bar fight stopped immediately once Old Smoke, having overheard the fracas, entered the main room. Everyone stared at Poole and Morrissey, this being the first time that the two famed street fighters had encountered each other since Election Day. Poole and Morrissey immediately took off their coats and went toward one another. Remembered Allen:

> Some of the outsiders closed around them and tried to prevent the fight, but this only enraged Morrissey the more, and drawing a revolver, he snapped it three times at Poole's head.

> The latter was unarmed, and his calmness made Morrissey so wild that he hurled the pistol to the floor and vainly begged someone to give him another.

> George Dean had meanwhile sent for the police and his messenger had met Morrissey's friend, Lew Baker, on the way and told him what was going on.

---

[172] *New York Herald*, February 26, 1855; *National Police Gazette*, October 15, 1880; *New York Daily Tribune*, March 10, 1855; *Telegram*, August 17, 1913

Baker hurried to the scene, and, taking in the situation at a glance, made no attempt to interfere.

The police, headed by Captain Charles Turnbull himself, arrived directly after Baker, however, and arrested Morrissey.[173]

Poole and crew went to slip out a back door, with Detective Chris Hogar in pursuit. Allen turned back and delayed Hogar long enough for the Butcher to escape arrest. Meanwhile, Captain Turnbull brought no charges against Morrissey in exchange for his promise not to come back above Canal Street that night. Agreeing, Morrissey, accompanied by the ubiquitous Dad Cunningham, made his way first to Johnny Lyng's gambling house at Canal and Broadway, and then home to 55 Hudson. Poole and his friend Cy Shay, the proprietor of a Church Street saloon, then appeared at the station house demanding charges be brought against Morrissey. The police told them that Morrissey was not in custody and no warrant had been issued for his arrest. Poole and his crew then returned to Stanwix Hall, apologizing to Dean for the earlier disturbance.

At one in the morning, while Dean began closing the place down, Poole finally decided to take his leave. Making his way to the door, he was blocked by a large group of men coming through it. Among them were Dad Cunningham, Lew Baker, Jim Turner, Paudeen McLaughlin, and several other Morrissey loyalists. Paudeen, who had been the man most aggressive in his harassment of Poole in the previous months, spotted Poole right away. "There is the black muzzled son of a bitch," he shouted, gaining everyone's immediate attention. Paudeen then locked the door behind them and, telling Poole that Morrissey "can lick you on sight," spit in his face three times. He grabbed the Butcher by his collar. Someone tried to wrestle Paudeen off Poole, succeeding in distracting him enough for Poole to free himself. Poole (unarmed according to Allen's account, but carrying a pistol according to most other reliable accounts) offered to fight any member of their party one-on-one for a five-hundred-dollar bet. There were no takers. Instead, Turner drew a large revolver from a holster behind his back, leveled it at Poole in the crook of his arm, and said, "Now let's sail in," before pulling the trigger and shooting himself the arm. Turner collapsed in shock and pain onto the floor.[174]

Poole immediately put his hands in the air and cried out, "For God's sake, you aren't going to kill me, are you?" He rushed the crowd as they all began firing at him with their weapons, one bullet from Turner catching him in the leg. Seeing Paudeen headed for the door, Poole grabbed ahold of him until another shot caught him the shoulder. He fell to the floor, blocking the exit, which Paudeen had flung open in retreat. As everyone else froze in shock at the sight, Lew Baker charged forward, fell so that his knees rested on the Butcher's chest, and fired his revolver twice at Poole's

[173] *National Police Gazette*, October 15, 1880
[174] *National Police Gazette*, October 15, 1880; *New York Herald*, February 26, 1855

heart. Rising to his feet, Baker turned to look at his mortally wounded foe, and said "I have got you." Charley Lozier tried to intervene and was shot in the head and leg by Jim Turner. Lozier, somehow alive, said to a nearby friend, "Jake, Lozier is no more." Baker and Turner then fled out the door. Incredibly, Poole somehow got to his feet and started for the door but then, saying "I am shot in the leg," fell against the door and held it for about ten minutes before collapsing, at which point those present laid him out on the saloon counter.[175]

At the inquests and trials that later took place, several people gave conflicting accounts of what occurred that night, many of them partisans of either the Poole or Morrissey crowd. The Stanwix owners, John Dean and Lorenzo Deagle, would each give sworn testimony that differed from Allen's in key elements. They testified at a coroner's inquest just weeks after the actual event, and the fact that they were members of neither Poole's party nor Morrissey's tends lend them greater credibility. Deagle stated that Morrissey had arrived prior to Poole, at about 10 o'clock, drinking and playing cards with a friend in the back room of the Hall. Poole arrived with a friend, a Mr. Janeway, to eat supper and, after learning that Morrissey was in the house, told Deagle that he would leave, not intending to create a disturbance. At this, Morrissey burst in and shouted abuse at Poole, calling him a son of a bitch among other names. Following an argument, Morrissey drew his gun (according to testimony from Poole associate Cy Shay, the gun had been brought to him by an unnamed friend during the argument) but was immediately wrestled by other men in the house, including Dean, who said that Morrissey managed to fire at least twice, missing Poole each time. Dean and Deagle sent for the police during the fracas and they arrived shortly after, an officer Rue arresting Morrissey. A short time later, Dean went with Poole and Cy Shay to the station house to press charges against Morrissey, only to learn that the police had released him.[176]

Dean said that they were at the police station for a period of about forty-five minutes before Dean, Poole, and Shay returned to Stanwix Hall. Poole then apologized to both proprietors for the earlier unrest and continued to buy drinks for his party, which increased in number during the night. At a quarter till midnight the place began to close, and the owners asked Poole to leave. Deagle then went to a back room and fell asleep. According to Dean, Poole was still present at twelve-thirty when the team of Morrissey confederates entered. Paudeen, as he had done so many times before, immediately took to challenging Poole to a fight, to which the Butcher's reply was, "You're not worth it." Paudeen then spat in his face before Jim Turner broke the pair up. Incensed, Poole challenged any man in the room to a fight for $500 but received no taker. Then Turner threw

[175] *National Police Gazette*, October 15, 1880; *New York Herald*, February 26, 1855
[176] *New York Tribune*, March 12, 1855; *New York Times*, March 10, 1855; *Brooklyn Daily Eagle*, December 1, 1855

back his cape to pull the revolver from behind his back and pointed it at the Butcher, who was unarmed. After his target shouted, "Do you wish to murder me?" Turner pulled his trigger and shot himself in the arm. Falling in pain, Turner continued to fire from the floor, hitting Poole just above his right knee, causing him to drop as well. Lew Baker opened fire while rushing at Poole, missing twice, and then fell upon him and shot him in the chest, saying "I will settle you anyway." A general melee then ensued. "The firing during the affray was very indiscriminate," one city official wrote later. Shay later testified that he ran to the fallen Turner to try and take his pistol from him, but, upon hearing Paudeen shout, "Shoot Cy," he began firing his own pistol at Paudeen, Turner, and Baker, hitting Baker at least once. Paudeen shot Charley Lozier in the head and thigh for trying to pick Poole up off the floor. Amid the chaos, many onlookers made haste for cover, several hiding in a nearby closet. Paudeen, Turner, and Baker struggled to get out of the Hall and into the street. Once they were gone, Deagle heard multiple shots fired outside before the police entered. Interestingly, neither Dean, Deagle, or Shay give any indication that Thomas Allen was even present.[177]

According to Allen's account, the police arrived almost immediately after the shooting ceased, to find Poole unconscious on the counter. Sending for an ambulance, the police otherwise ignored Poole as they arrested those who remained in the Hall. "He lay on his back, covered with blood and with his clothing torn to rags, breathing in fluttering respirations…. In the wrecked saloon, filled with smoke like that which hangs over a battle-field, the dying man with a couple of his faithful friends around him, remained for some time." When the ambulance arrived, it carried Poole to his home on Christopher Street. There three doctors examined him, seeing that while one of the bullets had missed the heart, it was dangerously close and irremovable. The other had indeed hit the target and, surmised the physicians, would eventually kill the man. The victim awoke not long after arriving home and insisted to the doctors and anyone else who would listen that the shooting took place on the orders of John Morrissey.[178]

While police combed the city for Lew Baker, Jim Turner, and Morrissey's other cronies, word spread throughout the city that Bill Poole had been shot. He stubbornly clung to life for two weeks. Hourly updates as to the infamous man's condition passed from Christopher Street to the sporting dens of New York, and large crowds gathered around Poole's house. Allen later remembered that the scene "resembled a market place or camp. By day it was crowded with people who walked blocks out of their way to get a word of news about the wounded man, and at night parties of the villagers camped about a watch-fire waiting with anxious forebodings

[177] *New York Tribune*, March 12, 1855; *Brooklyn Daily Eagle*, December 1, 1855; Sutton, 143-144
[178] *New York Herald*, February 26, 1855; *National Police Gazette*, October 15, 1880

about the fatal news which they were well aware was sooner or later to come."[179]

It came on March 8 at about six in the morning. After regaining his consciousness following the initial shooting, Poole remained awake and lucid through the next two weeks, but he was aware of his impossible condition and took the time to give instructions for his burial. Hundreds of well-wishers visited him at his home. On the morning of March 8, he sat propped up in his bed talking with family members and friends. The doctor attending him that morning informed them that he could not expect to live much longer. Hearing this, Bill reached out for his friend Cy Shay, took a deep breath, and said, "I think I am a goner. If I die, I die a true American; and what grieves me most is, thinking that I've been murdered by a set of Irish – by Morrissey in particular." Shay removed Bill's hands from his shoulders and began to gently lay him back onto his pillow, only to see that William Poole was already dead.[180]

———

Accounts of the killing made the papers from as far afield as Washington D.C., Ohio, and Indiana, usually headlined as "The Poole Tragedy." The funeral was held on Sunday, March 11, "with almost regal pomp," and was later to be hailed as "probably the most extraordinary event of its kind ever seen in New York." As late as 1887, George Walling, then a police captain and later chief, considered it the most impressive funeral of his lifetime. The procession began at the deceased's home in Christopher Street, that thoroughfare having been clogged with "a perfect mass of human beings" hours beforehand. According to Allen, four people died when the rooftop of the building across the street from Poole's home caved in under the weight of people. Crowds thronged the entire course of the casket as it traveled first on the shoulders of Tom Hyer, Cy Shay, and eight others down Christopher to Hudson St. and into an open hearse decorated with the words "I die a true American." The hearse, followed by between four thousand and six thousand people, traveled down Bleecker St. and Broadway to a ferry which transported it to Brooklyn, where it proceeded through Atlantic Street, Court Street, Hamilton Avenue, and Columbia Street to Greenwood Cemetery. Included in the procession were various organizations that the Butcher had either belonged to or inspired, including the so-called Poole Guard, the Poole Association, the Order of United Americans, the Washington Association, the Bowery Association, various fire engine and militia companies from as far afield as Baltimore and Boston, along with multiple bands, players in nativist politics from throughout New York State, and hundreds of residents of the Ninth Ward. Captain Isaiah Rynders and Awful Gardner were also conspicuously

[179] *National Police Gazette*, October 23, 1880; *New York Times*, March 9, 1855
[180] *National Police Gazette*, October 23, 1880

present. A gathering of 500 butchers bowed before the hearse as it passed down Grand Street. Along the route, human beings packed the streets, windows, doorways, porches, rooftops, and climbed lamp posts and trees. The *Tribune* estimated that one hundred thousand people witnessed the funeral procession, while other accounts said the number might have reached a quarter of a million. No previous funeral held in New York, not even that of President Andrew Jackson, had drawn such numbers.[181]

Reverend J.V. Wakely delivered a eulogy that effectively canonized the deceased as a saint of nativism, and instead of invoking peace, seemed intent on riling nativists to revenge against immigrants as a matter of self-defense and defense of right. "It was the most cold blooded, diabolical, cowardly murder that ever took place in this city," declared Wakely. "'Tis singular he never struck a blow. He never fired his pistol, though he carried one to defend himself with. Are such scenes to be reenacted? Who is to be the next victim? In the name of patriotism – in the name of humanity – in the name of outraged law – in the name of trampled under foot justice – in the name of the new made widow – in the name of the lonely orphan, we answer no! The law-loving, law-abiding citizens will answer no in the most emphatic language.... If it is a crime to love our country, there are many criminals. If they are in danger of being shot for it, there are many thus in danger. If a man is liable to assassination because he first breathed American air, first trod American soil, it's time to know it, for Heaven only can tell who will be the next victim."[182]

The procession required more than 150 police officers to protect it on its journey. If Thomas Allen is to be believed, those men had their work cut out for them. According to his tale of events, following the funeral, two armed groups of mourners, the so-called Poole Guard and the Light Guard traveled together back to Manhattan and, upon reaching the corner of Broadway and Canal Streets, were attacked by a "strong party of Morrissey followers," namely the Original Hounds 36th Engine Fire Company, backed by members of the Buttenders and Short Boys gangs. The attackers had taken up position in the ruins of a house that was in the process of being torn down, using a large pile of displaced brick and wood as shelter, and they ambushed the enemy by using the same materials as missiles. Soon enough gunfire cracked above the din. Once the firemen used up their barricade, they fled the onrushing bayonets of their opponents. Poole's disciples got revenge that night by attacking the Original Hounds at their base. "When they got through with the engine house there was nothing left but four blackened and smoking walls," remembered Allen. This author

---

[181] *New York Tribune*, March 12, 1855; *New York Times*, March 12, 1855; Asbury, *Sucker's Progress*, 368-371; Gorn, "Good-Bye Boys, I Die a True American," p.390; *Daily Alta California*, April 10, 1855
[182] Stanway, 319-324

could find no New York newspaper of the period corroborating Allen's tales of riot and violence on the day of the funeral.[183]

––––––

With the slain butcher in his grave, the public's attention focused on the apprehension of his killers. The manhunt for all those involved in the Butcher's shooting was well under way before he died, and indeed had begun almost immediately after police arrived at Stanwix Hall in the early morning hours of February 25. Jim Turner, wanted not only for the attack on Poole but also for his earlier assault of Hyer, was found in bed at the home of Johnny Lyng, but the bullet he had put in his own arm apparently had him in such a fragile state as to convince the officers not to take him in just yet. He would eventually be remanded to the Tombs Prison Doctor following rumors that a conspiracy to aid his escape was under way. Then the police came for John Morrissey, finding him at the Ivy Green on Elm Street. John went along peaceably to the Jefferson Police Court, arraigned on charges of assault and battery. He posted a $1,000 bail and returned to the streets.

On February 27, the *Times* published an almost certainly ghostwritten letter from Morrissey:

> New-York, Monday, Feb. 26, 1855
>
> *To the Editor of the New-York Daily Times:*
>
> DEAR SIR: Having been made the subject of a thousand statements or rather misstatements in the public prints with regard to the late fracas in Broadway, and having been made to figure as the principal and instigator of the bloody melee, I claim as an act of justice that you admit in your columns a brief explanation of the circumstances. About 9 o'clock on Saturday evening I was at Stanwix Hall taking supper; while there Mr. POOLE and myself had a serious altercation, which however did not result in blows. To prevent a collision we were arrested. The officer having charge of me, took me as far as the corner of Broadway and Canal-street, where he released me on condition that I should immediately go home, and appear in Court at 8 o'clock on Monday morning, to answer any charge that might be brought against me. Mr. HYER [sic, referring to Morrissey's friend John Hyler, not Tom Hyer], who lives in the house where the disturbance occurred, requested me to accompany him to his rooms. I replied that I could not do so; that I was under arrest, had promised to go home, and was fearful of a renewal of the disturbance should I return there. I then *at once* went home and retired to bed. *While I was in bed*, this bloody encounter took place. The first information I had of the affair was

[183] Kofoed, 137-138, quoting *National Police Gazette*

communicated to me by an individual who called on me the next morning, and related all that happened subsequent to my arrest.

All the accounts that have hitherto appeared, hold me responsible for the blood shed and the danger incurred, whereas I was in bed at the time, asleep, and am as innocent of all blame in this matter as if I had not been in existence.

I see it stated in this evening's *Express* that one officer REED arrested me this morning at the Ivy Green. The above statement is false. I delivered myself up, according to promise, to Officer RUE, at 8 o'clock this morning, to answer any charges that might be brought against me.

JOHN MORRISSEY[184]

When Judge Stuart learned that Morrissey had been released, he ordered his re-arrest on March 12. On the evening of March 18, the jury returned its verdict against those arrested. Jim Turner and Patrick "Paudeen" McLaughlin were guilty of aiding and abetting Baker in committing murder. John Hyler, Cornelius Lynn, James Irvin, and Charles Van Pelt, all members of Baker's party that night, were guilty of being accessories before the fact. John Morrissey was guilty of both attempted murder for shooting at Poole and of accessory to murder because of his known association with the others.

Meanwhile, the man police most wanted in custody, Lew Baker, who had delivered two bullets to the Butcher's chest, eluded capture for days on end. At the time of the killing, he was about thirty years old, described as being "a large man, but not so much muscular as he is fleshy," and having "a general appearance which does not savor of a very blood-thirsty disposition." Like so many men associated with Morrissey and Poole, Baker had a checkered past. Born in Wales, he came to America as a boy and worked as a hand on a whaling ship as a young man until he deserted in Hawaii and found his way back to New York aboard a U.S. warship. Through a friendship with Poole, he found his way onto the police force, but soon had a falling out with the Butcher, who thereafter set his cronies after Baker. Baker was drummed out of the force after making a private purchase of a pistol to protect himself from Poole's boys without the required permit from the mayor's office. Without the protection that a badge brought him, Baker naturally fell in with Morrissey's crowd. He had since that time been an obsessive admirer of Morrissey's.[185]

Mayor Fernando Wood put up a five-hundred-dollar reward for any individual who provided information leading to Baker's capture and conviction. Likewise, citizens of New Jersey, Poole's home state, gathered a

---

[184] *New York Times*, February 27, 1855

[185] *Daily National Era*, May 26, 1854, quoting *New York Times*; *Brooklyn Daily Eagle*, March 10, 1955

two-thousand-dollar reward. "Scouting parties were at once organized by residence of this City and its vicinity, and numbers of dwelling-houses with the hope of tracing the culprit, but all efforts proved of no avail," reported the *Times*. A U.S. Marshal was enlisted to help track the fugitive. Tom Hyer personally scoured the streets in a hunt for his friend's killer. A description of the fugitive was published, describing him as thirty-five years of age; five feet, nine inches in height and weighing 190 pounds; bearing multiple tattoos on his arms and hands and showing several noticeable wounds from the fracas at the Hall.[186]

According to Baker's own account (later told second-hand to the *Times*) and Allen's story published in the *National Police Gazette* decades later, Baker jumped from one sporting house to another in the days and nights following the shooting, narrowly avoiding the police searches. During one such search, he hid under a pile of newspapers at Johnny Lyng's gambling house while policemen scoured the place. Shot in the side during the melee, he could barely walk and thus only relocated when necessary. He found his way to a friend's house on Broome Street and hid out there for a week while his wounds healed. He then disguised himself as a sailor and, through the arrangements of friends, got aboard the *Isabella Jewett*, a sailing ship bound for the Canary Islands off the African coast on Saturday, March 11. In his younger days, Baker had served aboard a whaler around the Hawaiian Islands and may have intended to return to that life. It was Sunday before authorities, with the assistance of Tom Hyer, learned from witnesses that their prey was already out to sea. A letter published in the *Times*, by a person claiming to know Baker, confirmed, "I think that BAKER is safe. He is now upon the High Seas." The testimony of two of Baker's friends before a judge confirmed the story. On Sunday, March 18, the steam ship *Grapeshot* left New York in pursuit of the *Isabella Jewett*.[187]

Grapeshot returned on May 15 with Baker in custody. The *Grapeshot* had caught up with the *Isabella Jewett* on April 17 off the coast of the Canary Island of Tenerife. Firing two warning shots with her guns, the *Grapeshot* crew, many of whom were familiar with Baker personally, boarded the *Jewett* and took their protesting prey forcibly into custody, while keeping the *Jewett*'s captain and crew at gunpoint. They noted that Lew still bore scars from the night of the crime. As soon as he was aboard *Grapeshot*, Baker asked his captors, "Is Poole dead? I heard he was; tell me. You would not have come after me if he was not." Upon hearing that his nemesis was indeed killed, Lew became surprisingly remorseful; telling them he wished it had been he who had been killed instead because he had no family, unlike Poole, who was a father and husband. The crew removed Lew's irons once he was safely on board and they were at sea; the captain granted him one of

[186] *New York Times*, March 12, 1855 and March 13, 1855
[187] *New York Times*, March 15, 1855 and May 16, 1855; *National Police Gazette*, October 15, 1880; *Daily Alta California,* January 22, 1856; *Brooklyn Daily Eagle*, March 10, 1855

the best cabins on the boat and free roam of the ship, albeit under the watch of a guard.[188]

Telling his version of the events of February 24 and 25 to the crew, Baker insisted that Poole had indeed been armed with a pistol and was responsible for the bullet wounds in Baker's side and head, which he claimed came from the same single shot. It was Poole who climbed on top of him, he said, and Lew only shot him out of self-defense. "I fired my pistol four times; I think I shot LOZIER; I shot POOLE in the knee... and when POOLE lay on top of me I shot him while laying on my back in the breast; he relaxed his hold and fell over on my left side." He then told them the story of his hiding out with friends and his escape aboard the *Isabella Jewett*, careful not to name names and incriminate those who harbored him.[189]

Upon the *Grapeshot's* safe arrival in port at New York, the prisoner was taken to the Tombs, where a large crowd waited outside, most of them strangers wanting to catch a glimpse of William Poole's killer and others among Baker's family, friends, and well-wishers. As guards escorted Baker down the corridor to his cell, Jim Turner called out to him from his own cell, and the two embraced, Baker in tears.

The trial of Lew Baker began on November 26. In attendance were Mayor Fernando Wood and Governor Myron Clark. None other than the New York State Attorney General, Whig politician Ogden Hoffman, served as prosecutor. Poole's great friend Tom Hyer sat in the gallery, glowering with a "determined expression" on his face. Morrissey, who was also present, was described by the *New York Times* as "a stalwart Irishman; six feet high, very broad in shoulders, with hair intensely black and coarse, eyebrows heavy and lowering, and a pair of keen eyes, black as jet. He is fashionably dressed in unquestionable broadcloth, and has a quiet manner, in ordinary intercourse." John would be present for all fifteen days of the trial, always appearing attentive and concerned from his seat beside Baker's attorneys. Shockingly, the jury was somehow unable to agree that Baker had committed murder. Two more trials followed, all inexplicably with the same result, and William Poole's killer went free. Because the gunman escaped conviction, the prosecution dropped their charges against all of those accused of aiding him in the slaying.[190]

Considering Morrissey's known rivalry with Poole, their violent confrontation earlier on the evening of Poole's murder, and the known friendship between Morrissey and every one of the men who participated in the ambush and killing of the Butcher, not to mention the dying victim's own insistence that Morrissey was behind his death, it is easy to understand

---

[188] *New York Times*, May 16, 1855
[189] *New York Times*, May 16, 1855
[190] *Daily National Era*, May 26, 1854, quoting *New York Times*; *Brooklyn Daily Eagle*, December 1, 1855

why the authorities and many others believed Morrissey to be the orchestrator of Bill Poole's murder. However, there were those who believed Morrissey's claim that he played no part in the affair and that Poole's killing was not a premeditated crime. Robert Roosevelt later told journalist Alfred Henry Lewis, "No one who knew Morrissey ever believed that he had the slightest guess at the Baker-Turner intention to kill Poole. Murder wasn't Morrissey's style, and in all chance he would have defended Poole had he been there. Morrissey was but recently married, and lived at 55 Hudson Street. Having promised the officers who arrested him that he would not go north of Canal Street again that night, he kept his word. He went home, and while in part the unthinking cause of the killing, he was in no other way connected therewith."[191]

---

[191] Lewis, 55

10.

Dead Rabbits

"WILLIAM POOLE was the ready and consistent friend of the workingman, the able and unflinching advocate and supporter of the American Principle, the faithful and fond guardian of an interesting family, who have been forever deprived of his protection and support, by the cruel, merciless and fatal onslaught of midnight murderers," read one of the resolutions of an assemblage of Ninth Ward citizens who demanded that their charter adopted on March 10, 1855 be published in the city papers.[192]

Those who knew the real Poole, even those who liked him, must have marveled at how such fine words could be published for a man who, when living, was regarded as a bloodthirsty eye-gouger, knife-fighter, and master of a team of hooligans that were the terror of Christopher Street. Yet, in the weeks and months after his demise, nativist sympathizers elevated Poole to something between a patriotic folk hero and a saintly martyr for the nativist cause. His alleged dying words, "I die a true American," became the rallying cry for Know-Nothings, Whigs, and others aligned with nativist causes. The man once known as Bill the Butcher became the hero of various plays performed before admiring crowds throughout the country, the character often spouting his famous last words whilst draped in Old Glory.[193]

Poole's murder, one of the most famous New York crimes of the nineteenth century, made John Morrissey a household name within the city and much of the rest of the country as well. The problem was that his association with the perpetrators of the Poole slaying, combined with his own well-publicized rivalry with the victim, had led many to speculate that he was the orchestrator of the slaying; and he very well might have been. If the late Poole had in death become a sanctified crusader for the good of civilization, John Morrissey became the antithesis of all of that in the public imagination, a murderous foreigner whose presence on American soil was an affront to law and order. The next several months found John repeatedly defending his reputation in the press, paying lawyers to prove his innocence in courtrooms, and enduring recriminations both true and ridiculous from all directions.

He did himself no favors by getting himself arrested on the night of December 23, 1855. That evening, he entered Lafayette Hall on Broadway and, seeing Tom Hyer there, began boasting loudly that he could "whip any

---

[192] *New York Times*, March 12, 1855
[193] Asbury, *Gangs*, 83 & 90; Burrows, 824

man in the world, Tom Hyer not excepted." Two policemen happened to be passing by and heard the commotion. After initially resisting arrest, Morrissey gave in. The next morning, he expressed his regret to the judge, insisting that he was "not himself at the time." The judge set bail at $1,000, a sum not available to Morrissey, who remained in jail until a friend came forward with the money. The next day, the *New York Times* editorialized that "The trial of Lewis Baker seems to have had no terror in the eyes of the vagabonds, who prowl nightly around the drinking saloons seeking a quarrel, and disgracing the City."[194]

This arrest aside, Morrissey was ultimately able to not only endure the Poole murder crisis but successfully turn it into an opportunity to improve upon his status in the three closely related worlds of sports, gambling, and politics. An early evidence of this eventual success exists in the presence of another name alongside his in a list published in the *Times* of those arrested for involvement in the Poole case. At the top of the list, before those of Jim Turner, Paudeen, or even Morrissey's, is that of James E. Kerrigan, "Councilman Thirteenth District." Around twenty-five years of age at the time of Poole's murder, Kerrigan was one of the fastest rising figures within the riotous political battles of the Five Points neighborhood. Like John, he was an excitable and violent fellow. However, while John was working in Troy factories, Kerrigan spent his late teens fighting in the Mexican-American War and returned a hero. Like Morrissey, he established himself as a reliable shoulder hitter in the Tammany fold, winning his councilman's seat in 1852 from which he "dominated council proceedings by the sheer force of his personality," and won reelection in 1854, the same year that Morrissey and crew had guarded polls for Fernando Wood. After Poole's murder, the *Times* accused Kerrigan of facilitating Lew Baker's escape aboard the *Isabella Jewett.* When Baker's case resulted in three hung juries, Kerrigan went free with the others.[195]

Mayor Fernando Wood's success in the 1850s had been to that point the signal victory of Tammany Hall's slow but steady accumulation of power within national politics. Begun by veterans of George Washington's Continental Army in 1788, the Society of St. Tammany or Columbian Order was one of many such clubs inspired by the Native-American Chief Tamamend of the Lenni-Lenape tribe that welcomed William Penn's arrival in the New World. Since his death, colonists had idealized Tamamend as the perfect representative of his race, and his name graced a wide range of organizations, places, and holidays. The intentions of the original membership were predominantly social, if passionately patriotic and anti-aristocratic. It was not until the closing years of the eighteenth century that

----

[194] *New York Times*, December 25, 1855
[195] *New York Times*, March 13, 1855; Anbinder, 274-275

the Society became more politicized, opposing the Federalist policies espoused by men like the late Alexander Hamilton, organizing support for the French Revolution, and promoting themselves as the champions of skilled tradesmen. Its first important organizer, Aaron Burr (Hamilton's killer), facilitated the Society's integration into the Democratic-Republican Party in 1800 to support Thomas Jefferson's presidential campaign. From then on through the early decades of the new century, Democratic presidential hopefuls continued to benefit greatly from Tammany's passionate support. However, it was not until the passage of an 1849 city charter amendment removing any property ownership requirements to vote that Tammany truly hit its stride. It was this legal change which allowed Wood to make such outstanding use of his popularity with New York City's exponentially growing (and poor) Irish immigrant community during the 1850s. "As these impoverished rural people reorganized their lives in a great and alien city, they saw Tammany as an ally – an ally who did not judge their poverty, their religion, their culture. And so the narratives of Tammany and Irish America became one," writes historian Terry Golway. Men such as Captain Isaiah Rynders, John Morrissey, and James Kerrigan had all been among the Hall's key point men in the streets at some point, organizers of the Irish into an exploitable political base.[196]

Wood's becoming Mayor was also the culmination of a trend in New York City politics that disturbed the city's upper class, both Democrats and Whigs. For years, the city's elite had been complaining about losing their previously overwhelming presence in the city's Common Council of aldermen to members of the working class. By 1850, the year after the legislature removed all property requirements to vote, large business owners comprised just fifteen percent of the city's aldermen; many of the rest were shop owners, grocers, saloon keepers, carpenters, shipwrights, and other such small business owners and craftsmen. Still, until Wood's ascent, the richest citizens could always rest easy that the mayor's office was still in their hands, as it had always been. The election of Wood, once the proprietor of a waterfront saloon, stripped the city's wealthy of their most prized political possession, confirming Tammany Hall as the premier power in New York City's Democratic Party. The New York W.A.S.P. establishment, particularly the nativists, were furious, and even some of the more conservative and elitist powers from within Wood's own Democratic Party resented his catering to the masses. Fernando Wood, by simultaneously cultivating the working-class vote and ousting the established leadership of Tammany, had placed himself at the center of city government, igniting a firestorm of controversy billowing out of the mouths of both his political opponents and his allies.[197]

---

[196] Anbinder, 144, 274-275; Golway, xvii, 1-2, and 8-9; Asbury, *Progress*, 363-364; Adler, 86 (e-book)
[197] Burrows, 823

Tammany's gathering of political might stemmed in large part from its members' effective construction of a web of patronage. For example, a city policeman's job depended on reappointment by the mayor each year. That policeman could only be brought to the mayor's consideration if his name appeared on a list of nominees presented to him by the aldermen of the ward in which he lived. Thus, any policeman looking to keep his paycheck could easily be swayed into becoming a councilman's armed enforcer, operating on the city payroll. Carpenters, craftsmen, and laborers (a great many of whom were immigrants) also found that their livelihoods were dependent on city building projects, city councilmen overseeing the disbursement of such contracts. Much like the policemen, many able-bodied men found that their families' welfare depended upon the generosity of a councilman, and they were not afraid to show their appreciation for that councilman in the streets and at the polls. Such a system also allowed a councilman to award contracts to relatives or business partners, who would in turn submit inflated bills to the city and share the profits with their political benefactor. In this way, the contracts for the rights to build the city's street railroads proved monstrously profitable for many inside the so-called "Tammany Machine."[198]

Enter the man who eventually became Fernando Wood's chief rival within New York's Democratic Party (and a man who would play an important role in the political career of John Morrisey), William M. Tweed. Born in 1823 to a family of Protestant Scottish stock. Tweed's father was an entrepreneur in multiple small Manhattan businesses, and William spent his youth studying bookkeeping, which he then applied to the family interests. Young William was known first among his public schoolmates and later among the adults of Manhattan as inordinately intelligent, physically big, and friendly. Some within Tammany Hall had already noted his talents as early as 1843, when they proposed that he run for an alderman's post, an offer he turned down in favor of continuing as his family bookkeeper. Indeed, at that time, his political sympathies may have differed from those of Tammany. During the late 1840s, he gained membership to the Order of United Americans, a nativist, anti-Catholic club offended by Tammany's pandering to the immigrant vote. In 1849, like many other tough, ambitious, working class, young men, Tweed formed a fire company with a group of friends, naming it the Americus Engine Company, Number 6 and giving it the symbol of a red tiger for a mascot. As was typical of the time and place, this company became known as much for its violent rivalries with other engine companies as it was for fighting fires. In the streets of the Seventh Ward, Tweed and his crew became known as the Big Six Company. The Big Six became so notorious for fighting other companies that the city's Chief Engineer tried to have Tweed permanently expelled in 1850, but his friendship with some aldermen turned the expulsion into a three-month suspension. That same year, the

[198] Burrows, 824-825

company elected him foreman, and he successfully arranged for the Big Six to meet with President Millard Fillmore at the White House. Though a rival fireman eventually had him ousted from membership, Tweed had already managed to earn himself a reputation as a physically strong, personally outgoing, and well-connected young politico. A fellow Tammanyite later remembered of Tweed, "there was always a merry twinkle in his eye when in the company of those he knew to be his friends; a warmth in his greeting, and a heartiness in the grasp of his hand, which were reassured to those properly introduced to him." Though the famous caricatures of him would portray him as lazy, those who knew him well were also impressed by his ceaseless energy, a locomotion of movement and business. A commanding presence, personable manner, talent for manipulation, and workaholic nature would be the tools Tweed would use to one day take command of one of the world's most important cities. Following a failed bid for an assistant alderman's post in 1850, he won an alderman's seat the next year, having this time accepted Tammany Hall's offer of support.[199]

The Common Council, of which Tweed was a member between 1852 and 1853, made graft an unwritten policy for municipal government. Before he had even joined their ranks, the members of the Council were popularly known as the Forty Thieves. Inflated civic works contracts were handed out to men who promised to split the financial windfall with aldermen on the council; valuable pieces of city-owned property like the Gansevoort Market were rented out for negligible amounts to friends; laws were passed to inhibit local businesses, only to be repealed once those business owners came forward with payoffs. In the two years of Tweed's membership, the city's expenditures increased by seventy percent. Meanwhile, men working on a meager alderman's pay were somehow retiring with ample real estate investments.[200]

In 1853, the Seventh Ward elected Bill Tweed to Congress. Despite his already fattening pockets and obvious moves up the ladder of political positions, the true source of Tweed's political strength didn't solidify until he returned from Washington D.C. in 1854, the year John Morrissey played a part in the election of Fernando Wood and Tammany Hall into the mayor's office. That year, nativist leaders repeatedly approached the personable young Tweed to come over to run on a Know Nothing ticket, promising various tantalizing rewards for the switch. The Know Nothings, as they were commonly called, were partisans of the secretive but fanatical Native American Party, hard line nativists. A few years prior to their approaching Tweed, members of the party had been questioned by police about one illegal act or another and replied simply, "I know nothing," a response that would bestow a popular name upon the party as well as other

[199] Burrows, 823; Golway, 76-78; Anbinder, 277-278; Adler, 171-176 (e-book), quoting Matthew Breen and Theodore P. Cook
[200] Ackerman, 19; Burrows, 823

likeminded organizations like the elitist Order of the Star Spangled Banner. With the stunning influx of Irish Famine refugees to American shores, Know Nothing membership swelled by tens of thousands nationwide during the years between 1852 and 1854, however 1854 would be the year of true Know Nothing dominance. In the Spring of that year, U.S. membership of the party was approximately 50,000; by October, that number had exceeded one million. The next year saw them become the second largest party in the House of Representatives (after the Democrats). It was even rumored that Mayor Wood, the self-proclaimed "True Friend of the Irish," had secretly joined the Know-Nothing ranks.[201]

It was at the height of this wave of Know Nothing ascendancy that their leadership approached Tweed with an offer of support. Each time they improved their offer to him, Tweed steadfastly refused to switch allegiances. Doing so greatly raised his profile among the Irish and German immigrants in the city, they who exerted their own ever-increasing influence in city politics. Culturally traumatized by the uncaring, distant, and accusatory ambivalence of England's government in helping them through the disastrous ruin of the potato blight, the Irish valued those who they perceived as willing to take a visible and vocal stand for them, and they heartily rewarded such displays with passionate loyalty in the streets and in the polls.

Thanks to these same immigrants and men like John Morrissey, Fernando Wood became Mayor of New York City on January 1, 1855. He barely had time to finish his oath of office before financial troubles struck the city, the culmination of several factors, including bad investments and fraud. As people struggled to find money and work, they came to blame the Mayor. The worsening winter cold exacerbated the growing tensions among the poorer sections of the city. Public demonstrations and radical political meetings were happening with disturbing frequency. Eventually the economy began to recover, but the troubles had lasted long enough to lay the groundwork for deep-rooted resentments between the working classes and those in power, who they continued to blame for the hard times.

Amid these unsettling conditions, Wood was nominated a second time for Mayor in the 1856 elections, opposed by nativist Isaac Barker. Once again both sides used gangs to help them ensure victory, Wood going so far as to dismiss most of the city's police force with orders to stay away from polling places for any other reason than to vote.

On Election Day, 1856, a large mob of Bowery Boys invaded the Five Points, staunch Democrat territory occupied by the Irish gangs. Councilman James Kerrigan led a contingent of the Molly Maguire gang into a particularly fierce confrontation with the Bowery Boys. Morrissey likely led his men in getting the vote out for Wood. The Bowery Boys

---

[201] Golway, 55, 63-66;

struck in a concentrated force at a single polling place, sending the smaller assemblage of Wood thugs running for cover. However, more Wood supporters, augmented by Molly Maguires and other citizens of the Five Points, "armed with knives, axes, brickbats, and pistols," came flooding into Paradise Square and surrounded the Bowery Boys. A small contingent of the few policemen who remained on duty responded to the scene by barricading themselves inside of a nearby home and taking shots at the various gangsters. Eventually, the violence died down and the crowds dispersed, miraculously without any deaths. Ultimately, Wood won by fewer than 10,000 votes. Naturally, Barker's supporters insisted upon fraud as the reason for their enemy's victory.

Despite getting re-elected to a second term, Wood remained a divisive figure within Tammany Hall and the Democratic Party as a whole, many still resenting his bringing immigrant interests to play in the party's politics. At the state level, many Democrats began supporting Republican-backed measures to curb Wood's power. Meanwhile, Tammany's newest power player, William Tweed emerged to challenge Wood's reformist ways at the city level. Appointed to the politically powerful and bipartisan New York County Board of Supervisors in 1857, Tweed used his new position to build a power base within the civic government, charging vendors with city contracts fifteen percent for the privilege, sharing these funds with others on the Board, and promoting friends to positions of influence.[202]

———

While Tweed gathered his strength for a coming move, other rivals made their own plays against Wood. In April of 1857, state-level Republicans (backed by those Democrats who considered Wood the greater evil) passed two laws designed to politically weaken the Mayor. The first was the Liquor Excise Law, which proposed many of the same alcohol reforms Wood himself had verbally backed but practically ignored two years prior. However, a second law established the existence of a Metropolitan Police Force controlled by a board of Metropolitan Police Commissioners appointed at the state level. The Metropolitan Police Act gave these Commissioners the authority to enforce the Liquor Excise Law, effectively circumnavigating Mayor Wood.

Provoked thusly, Wood criticized these laws to no end in the press, painting the Republicans as absentee despots looking to prevent the people of the city from governing themselves. He ordered the city police to ignore both the laws and the Metropolitan Police Commissioners. Those officers who did listen to the Commissioners, Wood fired. He then had the New York City Common Council establish the Municipal Police, a force composed of those veteran city police who remained loyal to him and

[202] Burrows, 837

refused to recognize the authority of the Metropolitan Police Commissioners and their officers. With sides chosen, Wood's Municipals outnumbered the Metropolitans by more than two to one. Then each side began to recruit new blood, the Municipals from the immigrant neighborhoods so loyal to Wood and the Metropolitans primarily from natives of Anglo-Saxon heritage, a disparity which only heightened the political anxieties already inherent in having two competing police forces.

On May 16, the Mayor had one of the new Metropolitan Commissioners forcibly thrown out of City Hall, and then he and 800 of his Municipal officers violently resisted Metropolitan officers sent to arrest Wood, resulting in multiple deaths. Only after the U.S. Army's Seventh Regiment arrived to insist the Mayor surrender himself, did Wood finally relent.

For a few weeks, the Metropolitans and Municipals would co-exist peaceably under a mutual arrangement, pending a judgement from the New York Court of Appeals. Though this agreement temporarily stopped the violence between the groups, the entire affair had been, according to George Walling (a Metropolitan Captain at the time), demoralizing for New York's citizens. "The repression of crime had been neglected, thieving had become rampant, and law-breakers had ceased to fear or respect the officers of the law." More than a half century later, Herbert Asbury put it a bit more dramatically; "an orgy of loot, murder and disorder," he called it. On July 2, the Court of Appeals ruled in favor of the State. The humiliated Fernando Wood disbanded the Municipals, and the Metropolitan Police Force had won the day. However, Wood and his supporters were far from subjugated. As Walling put it years later, "The succeeding troubles followed as a matter of course."[203]

The Metropolitans having fewer veteran officers than the Municipals, they were generally less experienced than their rivals had been, less than one hundred of their officers having more than a month on the job under their belt. The Commissioners refused to hire any of the officers who had remained loyal Wood, meaning most of the city's most accomplished and experienced police officers were out of uniform and bitter about it come July 4, 1857, which would come to be known as the day of the Dead Rabbits Riot, an event for which John Morrissey would take the blame.

While the city's new police force lacked capable officers, the ranks of the local gangs were swelling to unprecedented proportions. As of 1855, the city's gangs were some thirty thousand men strong, most residing in the Five Points, the Bowery, and the Fourth Ward. Two years later, the disarray caused by the city's two competing police forces gave the gangs an even greater foothold within their neighborhoods. The disbandment of the Municipals now meant that thousands of capable men were disgruntled, without work or income, and looking for a sense of belonging.

---

[203] Walling, 60; Asbury, *Gangs*, 101

Compounding the problem, the Metropolitans were composed almost exclusively of natives, meaning they had little experience with, and even less in common with, the immigrant neighborhoods they were now policing. They did not know the people of the immigrant communities, and the immigrants did not know them.

Unable to effectively police these neighborhoods, the Metropolitans proved no barrier to the continued gang violence which had exploded during the rivalry with the Municipals. Just two days after the Court of Appeals handed down the decision which dissolved the Municipals and confirmed the authority of the Metropolitans, on Independence Day, the powder keg which had been lit when Fernando Wood took office for his first term exploded.

Not long after midnight on the fourth, a Metropolitan policeman walking alone on his beat in the Sixth Ward heard the cry, "Kill the God Damned Black Metropolitan Police son of a bitch," just before he caught sight of a band of Five Points citizens emerging from the shadows, and first rocks, then fists began to rain down upon him. Rendered senseless and left for dead, he would indeed die of his wounds a few days later.[204]

Soon enough, the violence spread beyond the Sixth Ward and across the Bowery, the metaphorical Rubicon between Irish and nativist territories. In the early morning hours, with the sun not yet risen, a large assemblage of rowdy Five Pointers began crying the name of Fernando Wood in the streets of the Tenth Ward. They accosted multiple police officers and soon invaded the Bowery until a powerful mob of Bowery Boys sent them packing, but skirmishes continued until sunrise.

The daytime proved relatively uneventful. However, when the sun began its descent, a raging mob of Five Pointers ambushed a group of twenty-four officers with thrown rocks, bricks, and utensils. The officers formed a wall from nearby debris, but they could not break through their attackers.

Word spread quickly to the neighboring wards of a massive confrontation between Five Points rioters and a besieged party of Metropolitan Police. Hearing this, an assemblage of Bowery Boys moved into the territories of the Mulberry Boys, Mollie Maguires, Plug Uglies, and the so-called Dead Rabbits, the gang of which John Morrissey was supposed to be master. The Boys came in two hundred strong and relieved the battered, tiring police officers, who rapidly departed the scene. The Five Points gangs beat the Bowery Boys back into their own territory. Then, from behind the shelter of a construction site, the Bowery Boys mustered a counterattack using bricks and other building materials as weapons. When a fresh group of Metropolitans, in larger numbers this time, appeared at their back, the Five Pointers were sandwiched between

---

[204] Anbinder, 280

enemies and eventually broke apart, fleeing into the surrounding tenement buildings. One man fell from a roof and landed unconscious in the middle of a crowd of Bowery Boys, who proceeded to stomp him to death. The other Five Pointers now assailed their enemies, gangsters and policemen alike, with projectiles from rooftops and windows. This time it was the Metropolitans' turn to retreat, taking a dozen arrested Five Pointers with them.

The Bowery Boys, aided by their own wives and children, got busy erecting a massive barrier out of the materials found on the construction site. Soon enough, allies had armed both sides with pistols and rifles. Gunfire rang out, and people were dying. Nonetheless, hundreds of people from all over the city were now flocking to the Bowery to witness the violence and cheer for their favorites as though watching a sporting event. It was not long before a stray bullet through a window killed an innocent bystander.

The violence between the allied Five Points gangs and Bowery Boys lasted through the night and well into the afternoon of the next day, with neither side able to gain a clear advantage. City officials were at a loss. This kind of chaos confirmed that law and order was no more in New York City. Eventually, civic leaders came to a man they thought could get something done. They approached none other than Captain Isaiah Rynders, the old knife fighter and gang leader who had given Morrissey his start in the Five Points eight years earlier and who most still perceived to be the crime lord of the Five Points. At this point in his opportunistic career, Rynders was declaring himself for Tammany and the Irish, but he had walked both sides of that line, and it was thought his connection to the streets and to both factions fighting in them might give him a shot at restoring order. Rynders agreed to try, and he made his way surrounded by bodyguards toward the Bowery. Arriving there, the living legend of gang warfare waited for a lull in the shooting and made his presence known by climbing atop the barrier the Bowery Boys had built at about 7:00 p.m. on July 5 and began a public address for peace.

"I implore you to end this carnage," he said, addressing members of both parties. "You are killing each other for what purpose? To what end?"[205]

Rynders was genuinely shocked to hear catcalls coming at him from all around; from the Bowery Boys at his feet, from the windows, doorways, and rooftops which contained the men of the Five Points who had for so long been at his beck and call, from the on-looking crowd anxious for more gore. Moments later, a shot cracked from out of the crowd and boy standing next to Rynders fell dead. When the bricks, bullets, and rocks started coming for his own head, the baffled Captain made a hasty retreat toward the Metropolitans Police headquarters where, bruised, disheveled,

---

[205] English, 28

and baffled, he told the commissioners he had no idea why it was that these men who had for so long revered him would now not even bother to hear him out. Almost simultaneously, news reached headquarters that multiple fires had now broken out at the scene.

The next man to attempt to bring peace was a lone Metropolitan Police officer named Shangles who hit upon the idea of convincing all involved that the state militia had arrived and was headed there on a mission to restore order by any means necessary. At these words, the gunfire suddenly stopped, and a chorus of mumbles filled the scene. Soon enough, the men, women, and children who had survived two days of chaotic fighting were returning to their homes throughout the city. Further fighting continued through the next week, but on a much smaller scale. The total number of dead resulting from the fighting between July 4 and July 5 varies from source to source, ranging from 8 to 36.[206]

———

Though John Morrissey probably took no direct role in the so-called Dead Rabbits Riot of 1857, the press would find multiple ways in which to find him responsible. One paper believed the unrest was the indirect result of the murder of Bill Poole, of which Morrissey was still widely thought to have been the prime mover, and the government's failure to bring Morrissey and his alleged co-conspirators to justice. "[Poole's murder] is especially remarkable as having developed a state of crime and ruffianism in our city that is truly startling," it read. "The inefficiency of our present police system, the delays of justice, the frequent escapes from punishment of well known offenders, call loudly for reform; not a reform that will waste and spend itself in mere words, but for practical results."[207]

Those who saw Morrissey as the master of the Dead Rabbits gang supposed to have instigated the violence also likely blamed him for the riot. To this day, accounts of varying credibility continue to claim that Morrissey sparked the riot. Some websites will have you believe that Morrissey personally lead the Dead Rabbits onto the field of battle that day, while some others name him as the gang's founder. The first newspaper articles (loosely) associating Morrissey and Dead Rabbits would not see publication until about a year after the riots, but it is likely that rumors of their connections had been stirring a good deal beforehand.[208]

---

[206] English, 28; Nicholson, 36
[207] Lewis, 61
[208] *Buffalo Morning Express*, November 9, 1858; https://blogs.shu.edu/nyc-history/2016/12/13/morrisey-and-poole/, accessed 5/5/2020; https://allthatsinteresting.com/dead-rabbits, accessed 5/5/2020; https://irishstudies.sunygeneseoenglish.org/2018/12/02/irish-gangs-in-new-york/, accessed 5/5/2020

Morrissey's somehow instigating the Dead Rabbits to riot is likely false for several reasons. Modern historian Thomas Anbinder, in his thoroughly researched history of the Five Points, doubts that a specific Dead Rabbits gang ever actually existed, instead proposing that it might have been a catch-all derogatory term that Bowery Boys used for their Irish rivals. The Bowery Boys being sources for the stories written by reporters during and after the riot, it is easy to see how writers and their readers soon came to assume it was the official name of an actual group. According to Anbinder, the men accused of being Dead Rabbits in the riot were followers of Matthew Brennan (yet another political thug of the era, and later sheriff of New York) rather than Morrissey. Herbert Asbury, in his seminal *Gangs of New York*, proposed that the Dead Rabbits were indeed a gang. According to him, the Dead Rabbits splintered off the Roche Guard gang when someone at a contentious gang meeting angrily threw a dead rabbit in the middle of the floor, providing inspiration for a name for one of the combative factions present. As if the name was not dramatic enough on its own, the Dead Rabbits were thereafter supposed to have carried into battle with them a pike on which they impaled a rabbit. In the street lingo of the time, 'rabbit' was the term used to describe a "very rowdy, athletic fellow." They supposedly even had a junior division, the Little Dead Rabbits. Urban legends aside, there absolutely was a group calling themselves the Dead Rabbits Club in the Five Points, and they were fans of Morrissey, but the exact size of this club, the nature of its activities, and Morrissey's influence over them are difficult to separate from myth and unreliable second-hand sources.[209]

There is no known first-hand account of Morrissey being present for or actively concerned with the riot. One modern historian supposes that Morrissey played a part in Isaiah Rynders's humiliation during the riot, because he still held some grudge over Rynders's support of the Know-Nothing cause. In his book *City of Sedition*, John Strausbaugh proposes that the Dead Rabbits accosted Rynders on Morrissey's orders. In fact, Morrissey may not have even been in New York at the time, as he had just opened a drinking establishment in his hometown of Troy and would likely be interested in overseeing its first days of business. Though John did bounce between the two cities in this period, the fact that he had a new business in the making makes John's presence for the so-called Dead Rabbits Riot questionable.[210]

Even if he had no direct part in the riots, John Morrissey's interests certainly intertwined with what was happening in New York City in 1857. One need only look at the other men involved in the events of that year to understand that Morrissey would have followed the news from New York that year with great interest. James Kerrigan, the city councilman who had been named alongside him in the list of suspects in the Bill Poole murder

---

[209] *New York Times*, August 4, 1912; Anbinder, 284 – 286; Howell, 5; Asbury, *Gangs*, 21, 221
[210] Strausbaugh (e-book)

and who had worked alongside Morrissey to help get Fernando Wood re-elected a year earlier, was indeed the leader of a large number of the Five Pointers involved in the two-day gang battle. Isaiah Rynders and Fernando Wood, both of whom John Morrissey had been acquainted with for years, had also played noteworthy roles in the drama.

Speaking of Rynders, he was, for all intents and purposes, finished. Prior to July 4, 1857, any man in the Five Points would have named him the uncrowned king of the neighborhood. Tammany Hall's leadership also regarded him as a man who could deliver the vote, most notably for President Polk way back in 1844. In fact, his influence was thought to be so great that Tammany lent him out to Democrats in other states to act as a sort of consultant in proper shoulder hitting, ballot stuffing, and street warfare. Thus, it is understandable that the bosses at Tammany fully expected him to get the city's street gangs back under their control, the very kind of thing for which they kept Rynders around so long. When the time came to deliver, the old man could not pull it off. Following his humiliation on July 5, Isiah Rynders's name would disappear almost completely from city newspapers, except for colorful reminiscences of a notorious life.

With Rynders suddenly irrelevant, Tammany needed someone else to act as their go-between with the gangs of the Five Points, someone loyal to the Democratic party with sway over the immigrant wards, someone who could rally the shoulder hitters to turn out on election day but also keep the gangs relatively peaceable in the meantime, avoiding embarrassing displays like what had happened on Independence Day. There were two obvious candidates, both from the Five Points: James Kerrigan, the young city councilman who had led the Mollie Maguires to the polls in 1856, and John Morrissey, the Irish-born pugilist and shoulder hitter who had been battling nativist thugs for years. For the time being, councilman Kerrigan seemed like the brighter up-and-comer, the stronger politician, and the most likely inheritor of Rynders's once fearsome reputation. Time would tell.

As for Fernando Wood, though his public career was far from over, his reputation had also taken a beating since his re-election in 1856. As if his political losses at the state level, the lawlessness created by having two competing police departments fight it out amongst themselves, and the lethal riot that followed were not enough, the economy collapsed again in August, resulting in what would become known as the Panic of 1857. Always the demagogue, Wood had confronted this crisis by supporting the thousands who were taking to the streets calling for work and money. He urged civic leaders to support new building and welfare projects and to speed up completion of those that were already in the works. Publicly, he used class rhetoric in blaming the wealthy and businessmen for the panic and decrying their ambivalence to assist the citizens in need. These acts reinvigorated the loyalty immigrants felt for the man they saw as their champion, but eliminated what little support remained from the city's social and financial elite, many of whom saw the poor's circumstances as God's will, or the deserved fate of the lazy and sinful poor. Again, the Democratic Party fractured. Just days before the 1857 elections, a wealthy businessman and known nativist named Daniel Tiemann stepped up to run against Wood, backed by a powerful contingent of both Democrats and Republicans. Though Wood was able to rally support out of the city's immigrant communities as usual, he lost a narrow election and the mayor's office to Tiemann.[211]

In the election, Tiemann had won the backing of the majority of Tammany Hall, over which County Supervisor Bill Tweed was exerting ever greater influence. Wood's reformist stance, while more rhetoric than practice, had never sat well with Tweed's policy of sweetheart contracts, tributes from gangs and businessmen, placing his lackeys in positions of power, and treating the Seventh Ward like his personal fiefdom. Tweed had been a vocal supporter of Tiemann and, come election time, Seventh Warders came out in droves to vote for Tweed's man. Humiliated ex-mayor Wood skulked away with a few loyalists (including James Kerrigan) to form and rule his own political organization, which he dubbed Mozart Hall.

---

[211] Burrows, 850

11.

Heenan

Back in 1855, while Fernando Wood was still in his first year as New York City's Mayor, John and Susan Morrissey celebrated the birth of their first child, John Junior, in Troy on August 6. Shortly before the baby's birth, John had moved Susan out of their house on 55 Hudson in New York City and into a home he purchased in Troy. The murder of Bill Poole and all the violence surrounding that event had shown the couple that the stakes were now truly life and death, and John wanted his new bride and coming child safe. He had a gambling establishment called the Ivy Green open in Troy now, and he was making enough money to support his family in Troy while he lived out of hotels during his prolonged stays in New York City.

John was now twenty-four years old, a new father, and a full-blown alcoholic. Keeping Susan in Troy also meant that he could pursue his addiction away from his worried wife. Like a lot of immigrants of his generation, John had likely been drinking alcohol since childhood; he had certainly seen his parents drinking heavily from a very young age. By his early twenties, evidence suggests he had lost control of his own habit. Even a cursory review of newspaper articles beginning around his arrival in California circa 1852 shows repeated mentions of public drunkenness, usually accompanied by violence and legal repercussions.

Fatherhood did not change that trend. Two days before Christmas, 1855, police arrested him for public drunkenness and disorderly conduct after he got into another argument with Tom Hyer at Lafayette Hall. About a month later, he was facing charges for assault and battery against John Dean. Six months after that, he was in a well-publicized affray in New Jersey with one Harvey Young.[212]

In an article entitled "John Morrissey on a Bender," the *New York Daily Tribune* carried a particularly disturbing story about Morrissey's behavior on the morning of May 6, 1857. At 7:00 a.m., it seems John and his friend John Petrie entered the Girard House on the corner of Chambers Street and West Broadway, on the border between the Sixth and Third Wards, and proceeded to lay themselves down atop the bar, apparently intending to get some sleep after a long night of drunken carousing. Complaints from the barkeep resulted in a pathetically weak and drunken attempt at a punch from Morrissey. (*The New York Times* reported that the fight was over a bill

---

[212] *New York Herald*, October 22, 1859; *New York Herald*, July 30, 1856; *New York Tribune*, July 30, 1856; Foster, 66

for breakfast.) When another employee named William Conway tried to intervene, Morrissey drew a pistol and fired at him, the bullet missing and shattering a windowpane before passing through the hat of a bystander on the street outside. At this, Petrie, perhaps a bit more sober than his companion, convinced John to hoof it out of there and back into the street. Conway almost immediately went out the door in search of the police, taking a pistol with him for safety. Seeing him leave and guessing his destination, Morrissey turned back toward the Girard House and fired several rounds at Conway, who returned fire. Morrissey and Petrie both rushed Conway, tackling him to the ground and began beating him. Only when a group of the Girard's employees teamed up to rescue their co-worker did the two assailants resume their drunken wandering North on Broadway.[213]

They made it as far as the Fifth Ward before two policemen caught up to them. When the officers made a move at Morrissey, he drew a dagger and pointed it at one of them. "If you attempt to arrest me," he sneered, "I will rip your damned guts out with this knife." The officers relented and allowed their men to go free. However, after word reached the Fifth Ward police headquarters, the captain sent several officers to bring the perpetrators in. Surrounded by armed policemen, Morrissey and Petrie surrendered. The officers brought them to the dreaded Tombs, just a few blocks away.

Five minutes after their arrival in the jail, Morrissey and Petrie went before a judge, who set trial for 9:00 a.m. the next day. A mysterious benefactor then posted the $5,000 bail which set Morrissey free that afternoon, pending trial. The violence and the quick release brought indignation from the press, and District Attorney Oakey Hall promised the public he would send Morrissey to Sing Sing Prison. Before the trial, the story goes, Morrissey made a direct appeal to Hall himself, arguing that "in the present excited state of the community the jury will not weigh the evidence. I shall be sent to prison on my bad reputation, and not on sworn statements." At this, Hall consented to a postponement, though it seems more likely that the District Attorney, a Republican, must have needed extra incentive to accommodate a known Democratic shoulder hitter.[214]

Whatever Hall's motivations, the postponement effectively made the case disappear as far as the courts were concerned. All of the New York papers printed the details of the whole drunken affair, bringing Morrissey his worst press since Bill Poole's murder. "Law in New York is a wretched mockery," lamented the *Brooklyn Daily Eagle*. "Friendless unfortunates are hurried off to State Prison with hardly the formality of a trial while brutes like Morrissey are permitted to go at large and cut, stab, and gouge everybody they come across." More than two years later, the *Evening Post*

[213] *New York Daily Tribune*, May 7, 1857; *New York Times*, May 7, 1857
[214] *New York Daily Tribune*, May 7, 1857; Nicholson, 35-36; Gorn, 112; *New York Sun*, May 2, 1878

complained that the culprits, though indicted, had still never seen trial. "Is it because they have political influence," asked the writer, "or because they have money, or because their services are useful in smashing ballot-boxes and carrying elections?" The answer was likely a combination of all the above.[215]

In 1857 alone, John would be arrested three separate times for attempted murder. His reputation was at its lowest point. The "respectable" people of New York saw him as a violent immigrant and a drunken thug, which, at this point in his life, seems to have been an accurate impression. However, to his confederates inside the saloons and gambling dens of the Sixth Ward, Morrissey was something of an anti-hero, increasingly a figure of urban legends and tall tales. To them, his arrests for drunkenness and violence were to be commended. It should be noted that heavy drinking was not unusual among Irish immigrants in the Five Points; in fact, alcoholism was rampant. In Morrissey's circle, there would have been no one to criticize John's behavior or to help him curb his drinking. It is entirely possible that even he had no conception that his drinking had become a problem, as many in American sporting culture viewed a man's masculinity as proportionate to his ability to drink alcohol in large quantities. Virtually all his noteworthy friends appear in the papers for similar behavior and with similar frequency. His wife, who might have had a thing or two to say about his arrests if nothing else, was rearing their child up in Troy and thus unable to keep a watchful eye on her husband's activities in New York City. Meanwhile, after each arrest, Morrissey somehow made bail, suggesting that well-to-do or politically influential friends were enabling his bad behavior.[216]

———

In August 1857, just over a month after the Dead Rabbits Riot, John Morrissey sat ringside at the most anticipated boxing match since his own fight with Yankee Sullivan roughly four years prior. The participants were not among pugilism's finest, both being saloon owners from Philadelphia with limited experience as professional fighters. However, prize fights were so rare and the animosity so great between these two rivals that the event generated tremendous interest among the sporting men and also members of the upper classes. Newspapers refused to print the names of the more respected individuals who came to Buffalo, New York to see the fight, but were eager to report that both Morrissey and his longtime nemesis Tom Hyer were both conspicuously present. After almost three hours of mostly even battle, a man named Dominick Bradley emerged the bloodied, exhausted winner over one S.S. Rankin.

[215] *Brooklyn Daily Eagle*, June 16, 1857; *Evening Post*, February 21, 1860
[216] Nicholson, 35-36

In some corners, certainly in his hometown of Philadelphia, Bradley won acclaim as the new champion pugilist of America. Most still saw Morrissey as the rightful title holder by virtue of his win (however disputed) over Yankee Sullivan, though Bradley's supporters pointed out that John hadn't been in the ring for nearly four years.

Still others insisted that Tom Hyer remained champion, because he had beaten Sullivan first and had yet to meet defeat in the ring. Both the supporters of Bradley and those of Morrissey saw this as a preposterous assertion, as Hyer, who continued to suffer from debilitating health concerns, had also failed to meet any opponent in the ring in over eight years.

At about the same time as Bradley's victory, another emerging fighter was brought to John Morrissey's attention, a man whose name was all too familiar. In their youths, John Carmel Heenan had fought alongside Morrissey as members of the Down Town Gang in Troy. Heenan was four years Morrissey's junior, but even when they were teens, he towered over all other boys, Morrissey included. The pair had never liked each other, but as the roughest, toughest young men in town, and as compatriots in the same gang, they shared at least a begrudging respect.

Heenan was born on May 2, 1835 in the Naval Arsenal of Troy, where his father Timothy had been employed, and his native birth was enough to make some fight fans prefer him over Morrissey already. As had been the case with Morrissey, the adventure of a journey West had lured Heenan to California during the Gold Rush. Heenan was only sixteen or seventeen years of age when he made the trip. In California, his large frame won him work as a laborer for the Pacific Mail Steamship Company in Benicia, the site where the company's steamers came for repairs. Swinging a thirty-two-pound hammer, moving steel, and working as a fireman for Pacific Mail swelled his six-foot two-inch body with nearly two-hundred pounds of muscle, unusual statistics for a man of his era.

Heenan was by most accounts a soft-spoken, peaceable man, if dim-witted. One old friend thought him to be "as impressionable as a twelve-year-old." However, men of considerable size and strength often find themselves challenged by others, and he refused to back away from any man. This led to several "rough and tumble" encounters. During one such fight, where he was dealing out a beating to a New Yorker named Sam Banta, three others tried to intervene on Banta's behalf and received similar treatment from the big youngster. In yet another violent encounter, Heenan was surprised by a gang of armed hoodlums hired to kill him by a wealthy local man he had offended. Heenan rendered three of his attackers senseless before the rest took off running.[217]

---

[217] *New York Herald*, October 22, 1859; Lloyd, 38; Foster, 65.

Heenan met slick-talking Jim Cusick while in Benicia. Cusick was himself a former prize-fighter and liked to boast of his time sparring England's famous champion, Tom Sayers. Ever the opportunist, he recognized Heenan's physical gifts as a fantastic way to make money and told him so. Cusick and Heenan became friends and business partners, Cusick always on the lookout for ways to exploit Heenan's size and strength to both of their advantages. Following a failed attempt at mining, they relocated to San Francisco, where locals regarded the hulking youngster as the Benicia Boy.

Like so many working-class, well-muscled young men in San Francisco, he found quick work as a shoulder-hitter for the local Irish politicians. This is likely how he became known to former boxing champion Yankee Sullivan. Impressed by Heenan's size and reputation, Sullivan took the youngster in as a sort of protégé and sparring partner. They gave several friendly boxing exhibitions together in San Francisco theaters, earning Heenan "high commendation as a pugilist." Eventually the sporting public of that city began to clamor for a real prize fight between the legend and the upstart, but Sullivan balked at the idea. Careful not to give the impression of cowardice, he insisted he avoided fighting because he wanted to remain friends with Heenan. However, Sullivan hinted at one day returning to New York with Cusick and Heenan to organize a fight between his promising discovery and John Morrissey. Of course, Sullivan met an untimely end in the custody of the local vigilance committee before this could happen. After Cusick learned that his name was also on the committee's naughty list, the Benicia Boy and his manager thereafter set a course back East.[218]

In New York City, Heenan had become a political thug in the employ of Tammany Hall, for which some political benefactor rewarded him with a cushy job in the New York Custom House, always a center for government patronage jobs. Meanwhile, friends and benefactors kept insisting that the young man try his hand at true prize fighting. The peaceful natured Heenan remained reluctant. He knew how to handle himself, but his taste for bloodshed was limited. Even so, Cusick was not about to let his friend's serene nature get in the way of serious money. He convinced the hesitant Benicia Boy to give it a go.[219]

It was likely Cusick and others in Heenan's circle who made trips to the *New York Clipper* issuing challenges against Morrissey in Heenan's name throughout the Summer of 1858.

Cusick had proven an adept promoter and manager. The gifted fighter Aaron Jones, Professor of boxing at Oxford University, took Yankee Sullivan's place in training the young man in the rudiments of boxing at Cusick's side, and Heenan was matched with another highly-touted young

---

[218] *New York Herald*, October 22, 1859; Foster, 66.
[219] Lloyd, 38

fighter, Joe Coburn, for a brief exhibition on December 10, 1857 at the National Hall in New York City. Despite Coburn's being a bit more experienced and having bested some good competition, Heenan possessed an obvious size advantage and a natural athleticism that easily dominated the abbreviated competition. Eventually, Coburn accepted a position in Heenan's camp to assist Jones and Cusick with the upstart's training. Morrissey had attended the Heenan-Coburn exhibition, and even though Heenan had yet to participate in a to-the-finish prizefight, the clamor for Morrissey to get in the ring with this hulking young bruiser became incessant in sporting circles, particularly among nativists. Heenan's blood might have been just as Irish as Morrissey's, but he had been born on American soil, and that was enough for the Bowery Boys and Know Nothings to embrace him as their latest hope of wresting the championship from the hands of the man they believed had killed their hero, Bill the Butcher. Bill's old friend Tom Hyer himself, finally giving up any illusions of a return to the ring, loudly sang the praises of the Benicia Boy.[220]

Though Morrissey continually responded to the challenges with insults against Heenan in print, in truth he was reluctant to fight. He was a husband and a father now, and his wife was steadfastly against his return to the ring. He hadn't been in a prize fight in nearly five years, and he was now more interested in drinking, politics, and his gambling businesses than in the decidedly strenuous activity of boxing. To flee the constant demand for a fight with the bigger, younger man, John headed North to Troy.

––––––

Hiding out in his hometown did little to save John's reputation within the fighting fraternity of New York City, even among those who were once his supporters. On the evening of March 20, 1858, Morrissey's closest New York Associates, John Petrie and Dad Cunningham were drinking at a dance hall on Howard Street, along with Patrick "Paudeen" McLaughlin and another man named Patterson. Cunningham bought a round, and the conversation turned to Morrissey. "It's no use talking about him," said Paudeen, "he is a big cowardly loafer." Paudeen had once been a Morrissey partisan in the conflict with Bill Poole, but Morrissey's retreat to Troy had obviously changed his opinion. Cunningham immediately got to his feet and grabbed Paudeen by the collar, ordering him not to say another word about his best friend. Most present in the hall happened to agree with Paudeen and interfered on his behalf by sending Cunningham scrambling for safety behind the bar. When Paudeen and others in the crowd began mocking him, Cunningham came out onto the floor again, but with his pistol held nervously in front of him. Following another argument with Paudeen, Cunningham again fled behind the bar. This time, it seemed that cooler heads would prevail when Paudeen returned to his seat at the bar

[220] Lloyd, 38; Foster, 66

and agreed to leave if Cunningham would share a drink with him. Cunningham refused, and the two began to scuffle once more. Cunningham threatened that if Paudeen did not let go, Cunningham would shoot him. He counted to three and then kept his word, sending the wounded Paudeen to the floor with a bullet in his chest. Threatening the fallen man's friends to keep away lest he shoot them too, Cunningham made a panicked exit. Patrick "Paudeen" McLaughlin, twenty-six years old, later died of his wound in the hospital. Despite protests from Cunningham's friends that the murder was a case of justifiable homicide, police arrested Cunningham, and a judge ordered him held without bail. A jury later found him not guilty by reason of self-defense. The killing made headlines as far away as England.[221]

There is a small article which appeared in several papers in early May 1858 indicating that Morrissey also ended up in a brawl during his time in Troy. "A fight occurred in Troy, N.Y., Monday morning between John Morrissey, the well-known pugilist, and a countryman named Bennett. Morrissey was badly bruised and had to be carried from the ground by his friends," the article reports. Insisting on repairing the damage this did to his reputation, John challenged Bennett to a real boxing match, but Bennett refused. Publicly, Morrissey claimed that Bennett's refusal had satisfied his honor as a fighting man. However, being carried away from a loss might have privately had some effect on John's feelings about the proposed fight with Heenan.[222]

The retreat to Troy had proven futile, anyway. Heenan's supporters followed their quarry North, insulting and baiting Morrissey in person, as well as in the papers. Even Morrissey's own friends pestered him about silencing the young upstart and his loud-mouth manager. "I was worried and set upon in and out of print," Morrissey later remembered. Morrissey could take no more when a group of Heenan men "whipped my old father and abused my family."[223]

Enraged, John went to his wife, who had been pleading with him all along to stay away from the ring. "I can't live this way," he confessed. "I shall have to fight that man."[224]

Susan was not happy at the news; "my soul revolted at the thought of a prize battle," she later recalled. However, after the thugs had attacked old Tim Morrissey, she understood that she had no chance of dissuading John now. She gave her consent, and her husband thereafter began the most disciplined training regimen of his life, splitting his time between Levi Smith's farm and the Abbey in Lansingburgh, New York, not far from his wife and son in Troy. He gave up drinking and carousing for serious

---

[221] *New York Times*, March 22 and 26, 1858; *London Evening Standard*, April 6, 1858

[222] *New York Tribune*, May 5, 1858; *Daily Dispatch*, May 7, 1858; *Richmond Dispatch*, May 7, 1858; *Buffalo Morning Express*, May 7, 1858; *New York Herald*, October 22, 1858

[223] *Chicago Daily Tribune*, August 1, 1874

[224] *Chicago Daily Tribune*, August 1, 1874

preparations, perhaps convinced of the necessity by the defeat at the hands of Bennett. Meanwhile, representatives of each fighter drew up a contract, John Petrie acting as Morrissey's agent and one James Hughes serving the same role for Heenan.[225]

The fight was initially set to take place on December 30, 1857 in the Stryker's Bay section of Manhattan along the North River. However, by the day of the fight, city authorities had already gotten wind of the plans, and the Deputy Superintendent mobilized the policemen of the Nineteenth and Twenty-second Wards, who converged upon the scene and arrested all involved, including Morrissey and Heenan.[226]

In the long-term, the breakup of the fight proved beneficial, because it generated a great deal more public anticipation for the day when Old Smoke and the Benicia Boy would finally collide in the ring. Petrie and Hughes simply rescheduled the bout for October 20, 1858 for $2,500 a side at an as yet undecided locale in Canada, to avoid American authorities. This time, the public demand for the fight would be much more intense.

The particulars of when, how much, and generally where now settled, the focus of the combatants was now preparation. In the five years since he had faced Yankee Sullivan, John Morrissey's weight had risen to a fleshy but still muscular 208 pounds. His training began at five o'clock each morning. On waking, he first bathed and then laid for a rub-down before dressing. After downing some sherry mixed with raw eggs, he would warm himself up by lifting dumb bells, and then start off on a five or six-mile walk. Then it would be off to the farm's workshop, which had been converted into makeshift training quarters. There he worked pulleys attached to thirty-five-pound weights for about an hour and a half, before switching over to pounding a sandbag which was suspended on a rope from the workshop roof, and lifting a series of dumb-bells for about a half hour. After this, he returned to his room and undressed for another massage. Putting on clean attire, the famished fighter allowed himself a breakfast of unseasoned, broiled meat (chicken or mutton) with tea and toast at about eight o'clock each morning, followed by a half hour's period to talk with friends and digest his food. Then he was off for another long walk until about eleven in the morning, when he would return to the workshop for another half hour of working with the bag, weights, and a jump rope. His noon meal consisted of steak and bread, rinsed down with a glass of sherry, and the requisite rest period of a half hour. A third walking jaunt lasted until about half past four in the afternoon, followed by a third trip to the workshop, this time to spar with one of his attendants, a Mr. Lawrence. Having earned another massage, he returned to his room, and then attended supper for broiled chicken and unsweetened tea. The evening saw Morrissey either taking another walk, or occasionally rowing a boat for

---

[225] *Manawatu Times*, February 7, 1880; *Chicago Daily Tribune*, August 1, 1874; Fox, 52
[226] *Evening Post*, December 31, 1857; *New York Times*, December 31, 1857

miles before closing his arduous day with a one-hundred-yard sprint race against his friends. After a final massage, Morrissey made sure to be in bed by nine o' clock each evening.

As the day of the fight drew nearer, the noticeably trimmer and more muscular Morrissey cut his total daily walking distance from a maximum of forty miles per day to a maximum of twenty-four miles. "He is in splendid fettle," observed one of the many writers attending Morrissey's camp, "his broad shoulders, tapering waist, massive arms and upper works being supported by the strongest-looking pair of pins we ever saw. He has no superfluous flesh at all on any part of him." The other professional athletes who visited John's camp were amazed at his transformation and the speed with which he won each evening's foot race.[227]

"Mr. James, you can form no idea of the glorious feeling that a man experiences when he gets himself into perfect condition," John later told early sportswriter Ed James, remembering the shape he was in before taking on Heenan. "Everything in the world looks different to him from what it does when his system is clogged up with bile, and he is carrying a quantity of flesh that is only a burden to him. It is almost impossible to get a man when in such condition into a bad humor. He feels like a young colt, and wants to kick up his heels and have a good time with everybody and everything he meets."[228]

Mobs of onlookers, from locals to New York sports, surrounded the champion's training grounds to catch a glimpse of the country's most famous athlete in action. When cornered by members of the crowd, Morrissey did his best to hide his annoyance at the dozens of preposterous questions put to him. One fellow went so far as to interrupt a focused and sweating Morrissey's training camp to suggest he switch to a diet of raw meat.[229]

Morrissey may have been frustrated by the crowds, but even more onlookers swarmed his opponent's camp. Heenan's team had selected Rock Cottage Hotel as the site for their man's training. The Hotel was only a half hour away from New York City by cart or carriage, and tremendous crowds arrived from the City each day to find that the young fighter was focused on building both stamina and muscle. On at least one occasion, Heenan raced a horse in a sprint between two houses. Granted "what was considered a fair start," he emerged the victor. As reported by the *Albany Knick*, the Benicia Boy got out of bed at four o'clock each morning for a twenty to twenty-five-mile walk, followed by two to three hours of punching a bag. He was in bed by eight o'clock each evening. As of early

---

[227] Kofoed, 160-162, quoting *New York Herald*
[228] James, *Practical*, 49
[229] *New York Times*, September 1, 1858

August, he weighed 193 pounds, fifteen pounds lighter than when his training had begun.[230]

Anticipation for the fight obsessed the press and public, arguably even more so than had been the case for the already legendary contest between Hyer and Sullivan the prior decade. That was certainly the case in Troy, hometown to both competitors. The *Troy Evening Times* reported that "the mania created in anticipation of this fight exceeds any before ever known." Troy was not alone in its excitement; fight fever infected New York City as well. Careful to maintain any sense of dignity, but unable to resist the boost in sales that the fight promised, newspapers like the *New York Daily Tribune* feigned disgust as it delivered every detail of the fighters' preparations and of course of the fight itself. "No event for years has created so much excitement in the city, and, indeed, throughout the country," the *Tribune* reported, balancing complaint with excitement; "a fact most disgraceful to any civilized country, but as a fact compelling us to recognize and record it."[231]

Both fighters also gave multiple boxing exhibitions to whet the public's appetite for their eventual showdown and to finance their continued training. Morrissey participated in exhibitions in Buffalo, Boston, and New York, one of them garnering him an extra $2,500 payday equivalent to the one contracted for the actual fight with Heenan.[232]

The promotion for the fight, played out largely in the newspapers, painted Morrissey as the villain. Most literate folks in the urban areas of the country were middle to upper class people of Anglo-Saxon heritage, who were more apt to appreciate the native-born John Heenan over his rival, who was painted by most reportage as being the personification of all the things natives found so abhorrent in immigrants, the Irish in particular. Of course, he did match several of the stereotypes applied to Irish in this period of American history: criminal, alcoholic, and hot-tempered. John's barroom exploits and the murder of Bill Poole had made him one of the most notorious men in the country. To some, just the fact that he was an Irish prize-fighter were enough to despise him, whoever the opponent might be. Morrissey recognized the anti-Irish prejudice behind those calling for his defeat. "Every effort was made to bring the whole sentiment of the United States up against me," he later recalled. "You can't tell how many years and how much pain I have had to bear for that perfectly unjust odium of seeking to challenge an American as an Irishman." Meanwhile, the press propped up Heenan as a respectable working-class boy who made good on the American dream, taking advantage of the chance of a lifetime.[233]

---

[230] *Troy Weekly Times*, August 14, 1858; *Sunbury Gazette*, October 30, 1858

[231] Kofoed, 163 – 163; Gorn, 121, quoting *Troy Evening Times*, *New York Daily Tribune*, October 22, 1858

[232] Gorn, 116

[233] *Chicago Daily Tribune*, August 1, 1874

The Troy Weekly Times, hometown newspaper for both pugilists, had the following to say about each fighter:

> You hear men give their opinions just as they are friendly to the expected contestants. Morrissey might win the fight easily if he was in the same train and condition in which the Benicia Boy is. The latter is about twenty-three years of age, stout built, and has muscle like iron; Morrissey is much older. If the Benicia Boy has any science at all he should beat Morrissey, who, of late years, has been careless of himself as Tom Hyer. Late hours, night gambling and irregular living are sufficient to put a better man than Morrissey out of train for a prize fight forever. Morrissey can take a great deal of punishment, and if the Benicia Boy can do the same, the contest will be of some interest to the scientific world, as well as the b'hoys, for then it will show how far a man can with impunity destroy his constitution, and, when necessary, bring it back to its old condition in a given time."[234]

———

Organizers for the fight designated Buffalo, New York as the gathering place for both participants and their fans, from which they would then depart for Long Point, Ontario, a peninsula on the opposite side of Lake Erie. As the fighter's trains began to make their way across New York State, lawmen intent on arresting both principals made some efforts to pursue, forcing both parties to put their trip on hold and disappear into Pennsylvania for some time. When they were satisfied that they had dodged the law, the fighters arrived in Buffalo, Morrissey and crew taking up temporary residence at Cold Spring Hotel, while Heenan and his party split their stay between the Eighteen Mile House and the home of a friend. Large numbers of "roughs and sports, and fancy men of every variety" began descending upon Buffalo on August 14.[235]

On October 18, about four hundred fight fans, including Morrissey himself, attended a sort of appetizer for the fight to come when the gifted American lightweight champion Young Barney Aaron took on Brooklyn native Patrick "Scotty" Brannagan, who took Aaron's title in a surprising upset. Heenan did not attend this event; for reasons then known only to his closest friends but soon to be revealed to the public at large, he stayed conspicuously out of sight for a week prior the fight. As midnight struck on October 19, the fighters got on separate steamboats in Lake Erie and made their way to Long Point.[236]

[234] *Troy Weekly Times*, August 14, 1858
[235] Kofoed, 163; *New York Daily Tribune*, October 22, 1858
[236] *Frank Leslie's Illustrated Newspaper*, October 30, 1858

Only the most complimentary observer could have described Long Point as a small hamlet at best. There were no docks, and the steamers could not get close enough to shore, so all passengers had to board smaller boats and row near to shore. However, they soon found themselves confronted with an impassible sandbar and had to wade on foot the rest of the way to shore. Those with extra pocket change were willing to pay others for a piggy-back ride to stay dry. Once he reached dry land, one writer felt as though he had arrived in some ancient wasteland, Long Point looking "as if abandoned by civilized humanity long ago, and left in the charge of a barbarous race, who have allowed it to run back into a normal condition of wildness." It was precisely for this remote nature that the site was chosen, for it provided open land for a crowd, there was no local police force, and it was entirely out of the jurisdiction of any United States authority. There was only one building intended for public accommodations, and Morrissey's party, arriving first, took up the entire place. October 20 dawned with clear weather, the temperature comfortable, and the breeze from the lake refreshing. Organizers immediately set about constructing a ring in the sand of the beach. Though some of their handlers were concerned about the unusual ground, neither fighter objected to fighting in the sand, and thus men set about efficiently constructing a ring.[237]

When Heenan and his team arrived and were not able to find any private accommodations, it became immediately clear just why Heenan had sequestered himself away for the prior week. Disembarking from his boat, two of Heenan's handlers had to practically carry him for the half-mile to the spot of the ring's construction. A sore which had previously been on the fighter's ankle had reappeared and gradually become infected. His leg "from near the knee to the ankle was one mass of sore," recorded the *New York Times*. "Being most of the time bed-ridden, his skin had become yellow, his flesh flabby, and a heavy dumbness around the eyes betokened that he was in no condition to last long," observed writer Edward James. Though he had gotten his weight down to well under 190 at the close of his training, the illness demanded inactivity, and he now weighed about 215 pounds. With no protection from prying eyes, his disabled condition would be known to the gathering crowd of fight fans and, most importantly, to Morrissey and his team. Where there had previously been excitement that John Morrissey would finally get his comeupance, there was now silence among those at ringside. Betting as to who would win was almost non-existent, as no one dared place a dime on the limping, sickly man resting in a stupor on a stool in the sand.[238]

---

[237] *New York Herald*, October 22, 1858, quoting *Troy Times*; *New York World*, September 27, 1867

[238] *New York Times*, October 23, 1858; Kofoed, 164, quoting Edward James; *New York Herald*, October 22, 1858

As for John Morrissey's condition, he "was fine as a star," reported James, "a perfect beauty, the embodiment of health, strength, and endurance, and probably the best trained man that ever entered the American prize-ring." Though his party had packed the nearby house, the fighter himself chose to spend most of the time before the fight outdoors with friends, who strolled with him back and forth along the shore for hours. As more fans and reporters waded their way onto the beach, they repeatedly asked Old Smoke about his condition and how he felt. He replied with the only comparison that made sense to an avid gambler, "like a race horse." When word reached Morrissey of his opponent's condition, his confidence flooded over, and he ordered that a telegraph be sent as soon as possible to friends who had remained behind in New York, telling them to "bet all the money they could rake and scrape... he had a sure thing."[239]

Fans came from as far afield as New Orleans, though most hailed from Buffalo, Troy, Albany, and New York City. The writer for the *New York Daily Tribune* was very disturbed by the character of the crowd, which included Lew Baker and Dad Cunningham, notorious for their killings of Bill Poole and Paudeen McLaughlin respectively. Tom Hyer was also present. "Probably no human eye will ever look upon so much rowdyism, villainy, scoundrelism, and boiled-down viciousness, concentrated upon so small a space, as was, compressed into the few feet of seeing room about the ring..." he reported. "Scoundrels of every imaginable genus, every species of every genus, and every variety of every species, were there assembled; the characteristic rascalities of each were developed and displayed in all their devilish perfection." The *New York Times* agreed emphatically. "Indeed, did his Satanic Majesty desire to raise a special body-guard for state occasions he could not have sent his recruiting sergeant to more admirable grounds," mused their correspondent. Considering the quality of men present, some of whom came from rival factions back in New York, it was not surprising that multiple melees broke out among the crowd before the real fight got under way.[240]

The fighters had contracted to enter the ring between noon and 2:00 p.m., agreeing that if either fighter failed to appear in that time frame, he would forfeit the fight and his pay. When neither fighter appeared for the first hour of the afternoon, the air echoed with chants of "Bring your men!" Rumors soon circulated that Heenan would not fight, that he believed Morrissey's partisans, heavily armed as they were, would not allow him a fair fight. Englishman Aaron Jones, Heenan's trainer, had been aghast at the sight of knives and guns at ringside, the possession of which was banned in English prizefighting, as a matter of gentlemanly honor. Word began to spread that Jones did not intend to let his man out amid such

---

[239] Kofoed, 164, quoting Edward James; *New York Herald*, October 22, 1858
[240] *Evening Star*, October 21, 1858; *New York Daily Tribune*, October 22, 1858; Nicholson, *Notorious*, p. 42, quoting *New York Times; New York Herald*, October 22, 1858

weaponry. "It's not the way they do such things at 'ome," the disgusted Briton complained. At this, the Morrissey crowd predictably accused the Benicia Boy of cowardice, denied any accusations that they would interfere with what happened in the ring, and offered to shoot Heenan there and then if he did not come and fight their man. The murderous tension subsided when Heenan's other trainer, American Johnny Mackay, stepped forward and confirmed that his charge did intend to fight and had never thought to do otherwise.[241]

At 1:19 p.m., Heenan threw his hat into the ring and made his way through the ropes, accompanied by Jones and Mackay. Someone cried, "Give him a cheer, boys," and an uninspired spattering of voices briefly shouted their support for the Benicia Boy. Dressed in a heavy overcoat and blue woolen leggings, he immediately sat down on a stool placed in his corner, sullen and quiet. When Morrissey threw his hat in and stepped into the ring, a much louder cry accompanied him. His own seconds, William "Dublin Tricks" Hastings and Australian Jem Kelly followed him into the ring. After his entrance, Morrissey, garbed in his own overcoat, immediately strode to the other corner and greeted Heenan with a pleasant handshake. Heenan made it to his feet and returned the cordial greeting to his old Troy gang leader. Heenan's expected size advantage was even more pronounced once they stood together. He was at least two and half inches taller and heavier by almost thirty pounds (though much of that difference had turned to useless flab). Morrissey then returned to his corner and took a seat on a stool provided him.[242]

The principals having made their appearances, the next concern became security. Considering the dastardly appearance of the some in the crowd, both camps agreed that each would get to select twenty-five trusted men to serve as security around the ring. After lengthy discussion which frustrated the crowd, the men were chosen, brought forward to encircle the ring, and armed with clubs. After this, the fighters stripped, and the parties reviewed the rules. Both men agreed to file down the spikes on the bottoms of their shoes, Morrissey finding Heenan's too long while Heenan thought Morrissey's too sharp.

Morrissey then called out to the crowd, "I'll bet $1,000 to $700 that I win this fight," but there were no takers. He turned to Heenan and offered a side bet, but Heenan declined, citing a lack of funds on hand to meet the amount required. The two camps spent a great deal of time deciding upon a referee, always customarily chosen on site. Both camps steadfastly disagreed, and the crowd became noisy and anxious, prompting two men,

[241] *New York Daily Tribune*, October 22, 1858; *New York Herald*, October 22, 1858; *New York Times*, October 23, 1858; *Sunbury Gazette*, October 30, 1858

[242] *New York Daily Tribune*, October 22, 1858; *Sunbury* Gazette, October 30, 1858; http://www.cyberboxingzone.com/boxing/morrisey.htm accessed 5/30/2020

both unknown to either of the principals, to simultaneously serve as referees, where there was traditionally only one.[243]

After a final handshake, the fight began at 3:30 p.m. Both fighters initially circled each other, posing, jockeying for position, and feinting for a few minutes. Perhaps wanting to end things before the sore on his leg became a serious liability, Heenan made the first significant play at an attack, which failed embarrassingly. "Not this time, my boy," teased Morrissey. Still, Heenan began to get the upper hand, blocking a series of wild swings from his opponent and countering with straight, skillful blows which landed to the face. He drew first blood from Morrissey's nose with a hard left. Remembering the moment years later, Morrissey told a reporter, "he could strike the most powerful blow of any man I ever saw." Clearly bothered by the punch, Morrissey staggered back to the ropes, where Heenan capitalized on his advantage with a series of ferocious shots that had many thinking Old Smoke was already finished, "as helpless as a child." The *New York Daily Tribune* writer counted twenty-five landed blows to Morrissey's face without an answer. Adrenaline surging, Heenan prepared his feared left hand for the finishing blow, but Morrissey, his fighting instincts still intact, sensed the danger, and he ducked. The punch flew over his head and smashed into the wooden ring post behind him. His third and fourth knuckles now broken, Heenan winced, and his punches stopped. Morrissey, recovering his senses and recognizing this was his opportunity to catch a much-needed rest, forced himself off the ropes and forward, holding Heenan around the arms and chest to buy some time. Not to be denied, the bigger man ignored the pain in his left and tossed Morrissey down to the sand, ending the first round.[244]

All ringside could see that Morrissey, his handlers, and his previously vocal supporters were shocked. They had come to the ring expecting to fight a big, cumbersome amateur crippled by pain and sickness in his leg. Instead, it was their man who took a sudden and humiliating, almost ruinous beating at the hands of the upstart. Aaron Jones, Heenan's second, considered the beating of the first round to be "the severest he ever witnessed in the ring." Between rounds, a clamor arose ringside from those suddenly wishing to bet on the Benicia Boy.[245]

Both men rose for the second round "panting like locomotives." Morrissey attempted a rally by focusing on his opponent's clearly soft mid-section. Still, Heenan landed sharp, damaging shots to Morrissey's face and threw him once again to the ground, eliciting a roar of excitement from the astonished crowd. "Morrissey, where are you?" cried a flabbergasted fan at ringside.[246]

[243] *New York Daily Tribune*, October 22, 1858; Nicholson, 43
[244] *New York Daily Tribune*, October 22, 1858; *Chicago Daily Tribune*, August 1, 1874; Lloyd, 36
[245] *New York Times*, October 23, 1858
[246] *New York Herald*, October 22, 1858, quoting *Troy Times*; *New York Daily Tribune*, October 22, 1858

In the third round, the fighters employed the same strategies they had in the second, but now both fighters were clearly fatigued, and this time it was Morrissey who threw Heenan down, giving his own supporters their first opportunity to cheer. Excited by this sign of hope, Morrissey became more aggressive in the fourth round, and Heenan seemed to be wilting under the fast pace of the fight. Both men got in terrific shots, but the best was a devastating uppercut from Morrissey. At the round's close, they both wrestled and fell into the sand, Morrissey landing on top of his opponent.[247]

Morrissey became so aggressive in the fifth, likely hoping to bring an end to the contest, that he began walking into well-timed, straight punches from Heenan, a pair of which dropped him hard to the ground. By now, Old Smoke's face presented a frightening visage. A torrent of blood streamed over his face. Heenan's face was in much better condition, but it was clear that he was in pain and tiring. Though both men were hurt in the sixth, Morrissey got the better of the action and threw Heenan to the sand, falling upon him once more for good measure. The "dreadfully disfigured," Morrissey again tossed his tiring opponent to end the seventh. Heenan could not hold his hands up any longer, but bravely toed the line for the eighth. Morrissey charged at his man, who managed to muster only a few weak punches before collapsing from sheer exhaustion without Morrissey having to land a blow.[248]

Somehow still able to come up for the ninth, Heenan tried desperately to land something that would keep his opponent at bay. He threw wild, ill-timed punches that not only missed, but had him clumsily careening around the ring from the force of his own blows. Morrissey was also tired and not able to take full advantage of these moments, but clearly got the better of the action and put the Benicia Boy down with a blow to the neck. Despite clearly struggling to fend off exhaustion, Morrissey, "a tottering tower of blood," continued to land the harder shots in the tenth and threw Heenan once more. [249]

Heenan struggled to make it to the scratch on his feet for the eleventh, but somehow did so. Unable to defend himself, he went down from the first significant blow from his opponent, which landed on his throat. Heenan toppled forward, landing face first in the sand. Jones threw his sponge into the ring signaling surrender, and the fight was over.

Morrissey's partisans rushed the ring, surrounding their exhausted hero, who was too weak to speak. He did force a smile, however, which one reporter found "a most ghastly thing to see." One of his eyes was nearly closed; blood ran out of his badly swollen mouth, but not as much as hemorrhaged from his flattened nose. Heenan's visage was much more pleasant to behold, but his handlers took a half hour to rouse him from his

---

[247] *New York Daily Tribune*, October 22, 1858
[248] *Memphis Daily Appeal*, October 27, 1858
[249] Hotaling, 36

sleep. By that time the winner was inside, cleaned up, bandaged, and rested. At news that Heenan was awake, fans brought Morrissey out of the house on their shoulders and put both men in a horse-drawn carriage together, holding a bizarre, impromptu parade on the barren peninsula in their honor.[250]

—

At 2:30 a.m. the next morning, the citizens who lived along the banks of Lake Erie in Buffalo were awaked by the startling sound of fireworks. Looking out of their doors and windows, they saw that the ruckus was coming from a riverboat on its way to shore. The boat carried the battered but victorious John Morrissey and his elated followers. Despite the hour, some people made their way down to the docks to excitedly welcome and congratulate the champion, while the rest returned grumpily to their beds.

In New York City, the press struggled for days to keep up with the public's demands for any details about the fight. On the day of the fight itself, thousands of people surrounded each of the city's major newspapers, awaiting the results. No fight, not even that between Yankee Sullivan and Tom Hyer, had elicited so much public fascination. Newpapers in England carried round-by-round accounts of the action. The subsequent articles describing a bloody, grueling affair, fought without any serious fouls or controversy, with multiple turns in momentum and bravery to be admired on both sides confirmed for boxing's fans that the fighters deserved the accolades and attention given them. The fight having temporarily assuaged the animosity between the participants, Morrissey openly complimented Heenan to newspaper reporters and admitted that the battle had been much harder than he had expected.[251]

For most in the middle class and those convinced that boxing was a sign of degenerating morals and increasing foreign influence in America, the news only convinced them of the disgusting barbarity of it all. (The *Buffalo Republic* had even printed that Heenan had died during the fight, a rumor subsequently carried by other national papers.) Regardless of how one felt about the participants and their sport, both the victor and the loser were now household names throughout the United States.

Though eager to return home to Troy and New York City, Morrissey first gave an exhibition at the St. James Hall in Buffalo the following Saturday evening. Fewer than two hundred people, patrolled by a hefty contingent of watchful police officers, paid fifty cents each to watch six matchups, the final one to be between Morrissey and Australian Kelly. Though John's stated motivation for the event was to show that he was not

[250] *Sunbury Gazette,* October 30, 1858; *New York Daily Tribune,* October 22, 1858
[251] *Penny Press,* October 26, 1858; *New York Times,* October 23, 1858; *Era,* November 14, 1858

so badly hurt from the fight that he could not give an athletic demonstration, a reporter present noted that his face was "decidedly ugly from a badly bunged eye." When the star of the show came upon the stage, someone hailed him as the Champion of America, to which Morrissey replied that, yes, he had won the title, but he no longer intended to defend it, "so that anybody that wants it may take it for I shall fight no more." He then set about sparring Kelly, who did well to hold his own with the bruised champion.[252]

That night, the champion boarded a train for his hometown of Troy, many of his supporters who had witnessed the fight coming along. "No city ever rejoiced more at the departure of an invading army that does this at the receding roll of every train which carries off a detachment of 'Dead Rabbits,'" reported a *New York Times* correspondent from Buffalo. The scene aboard Morrissey's train was particularly chaotic. To the chagrin of the conductor and employees, many had boarded without paying fare, the staff being too frightened of the type of men boarding to ask them for their tickets. One brave soul had tried to collect a fare, only to withdraw the demand when the passenger produced a pistol and held it to the conductor's head. Several people on board were robbed and, on one occasion, as the train passed through the Utica station, a man was yanked from the platform, stripped of his belongings at gunpoint, and thrown out of a train window back onto the platform below.[253]

After reuniting with his wife and son in Troy, John then set off eagerly for New York City, where there was rumored to be a massive celebration awaiting his victorious return.

[252] *Middlebury Register*, November 3, 1858, quoting *Buffalo Advertiser*
[253] *New York Times*, October 23, 1858

12.

Purposes More Laudable and Advantageous

"Morrissey says this is his last fight, and it is to be hoped he will keep his word," editorialized the *Memphis Daily Appeal* a few days following John Morrissey's hard-fought victory over bigger, younger, but obviously ill hometown rival John Heenan.[254]

Heenan, of course, insisted that the fight had been unfair. It had been his first prize fight, he explained, and he had come in sick and in pain, and had lost six precious days of training to his illness. He had broken his hand in the early goings. These excuses, along with a promise that he was improving himself for a second attempt at glory, appeared regularly in the New York newspapers. Though Morrissey had publicly announced his intention to retire from the prize ring, Heenan insisted that his rival was privately insulting him during visits to Philadelphia and Albany, saying he could beat Heenan anytime, regardless of his condition. Citing this as his reason, Heenan insisted upon a rematch, "a challenge which, if he has the spirit of a man, he cannot decline after his recent vauntings." The Benicia Boy also proclaimed his readiness "to fight any man in Europe or America for any sum up to ten thousand dollars." Even Heenan's trainer, Aaron Jones, having returned disgusted to his native England, now challenged Morrissey to a match, offering to pay for the American's fare across the Atlantic Ocean.[255]

Morrissey remained insistent that he would not return to the ring against any man and, for a good while, refused to publish any response to Heenan, whose challenges (or those of his handlers) became more extreme, eventually threatening John with bodily harm if he should decline to sign for another organized fight. Only after Heenan's published threats appeared did the following letter to the editor, signed with Morrissey's name, appear in the *New York Tribune*:

> Sir: Previous to my recent engagement with Mr. Heenan, I publicly announced that it would be my last fight. At its conclusion I proclaimed the same determination. Circumstances, seeming to me imperative, forced me into that contest. I considered myself obliged to make the match and fight it, determined by it to

---

[254] *New York Times*, October 23, 1858; *Memphis Daily Appeal*, October 27, 1858
[255] *Daily Dispatch*, December 11, 1858; *New York Times*, October 23, 1858; *Louisville Daily Courier*, October 27, 1858, quoting *New York Express*

vindicate my honor and manhood, and to relieve myself from the persecution and assaults of my foes. I consider the first of these objects accomplished. No one has or can complain of the manner in which myself or my friends have conducted the fight. I had hopes that my second objective would also have been secured. I have no desire for further contest with any man. My duties to my family and myself require me to devote my time and efforts to purposes more laudable and advantageous. I hope to be permitted to do so without further interference from my late antagonist or his friends. I am aware of his published challenge and threat. It seems to be the determination to force me into another match, or assail me openly with violence. I now repeat that I shall never enter the prize-ring again, and those who knew me will not misapprehend the motives of the resolution. It arises from no fear of any man, but from a desire to more fittingly discharge my duties to my family and society. Nor shall I be driven from this purpose by any threats of unlawful violence. I shall trust to the laws and the just influence of public sentiment to preserve me in the common privileges of an American citizen. If assaulted, I have no fear of my ability to defend myself, unless overcome, as I have been heretofore, by cowardly combinations. I shall exercise the right of defending myself, and trust to the countenance of all fair men to sustain me in my peaceable determination. Before the fight with Mr. Heenan, I declared publicly on the ground that if he vanquished me, I would take him by the hand and acknowledge my defeat without cherishing any animosity. My treatment of him and his friends after it was all over is well understood. It certainly was not illiberal or unkind. It is not for me to proclaim or boast of it, but I am entitled to say that it ought to protect me from all abuse from him or them.

JOHN MORRISSEY[256]

John had returned to New York City to find the entire Sixth Ward alight with bonfires in his honor. A banner hung across Mulberry Street which read "D.R.C. – Morrissey Victorious," with images of dead rabbits in each of the sign's corners. D.R.C. stood for Dead Rabbits Club. People cheered and mobbed him in the streets. "Pugilism maintains its ascendancy," observed the *Spirit of the Times* a few weeks later, "and, probably, no man in the city excites more general interest and attention than John Morrissey, as he walks along Broadway, in his seal-skin coat.[257]

On Saturday, November 13, 1858, various personalities within the sporting community held a benefit to honor the Champion at Hoym's

---

[256] Kofoed, 171-173, quoting Morrissey in *New York Tribune*
[257] *Daily Milwaukee News*, October 27, 1858 quoting *New York Post*; *Wheeling Daily Intelligencer*, October 26, 1858, quoting *New York Post*; *Era*, December 12, 1858, quoting *Spirit of the Times*, November 20, 1858

Theater in the Bowery. Aaron Jones had held a similar event for Heenan a few days earlier at the same locale, ending with Heenan publicly challenging his conqueror to a rematch. At the November 13 event, Morrissey was to give an exhibition, and other advertised participants included notables Aaron Jones and Young Barney Aaron, among others. A reporter for the *New York Times*, an account of the scene:

> Some of our readers may associate with prize-fighting, or exhibitions of the science thereof, ideas of sawdust and dirt, and suppose that nobody with good clothes is ever present at such occasions. We must beg leave to correct so erroneous an impression. The performance last night was upon the stage of a very neat and roomy theatre, - with footlights and a *very* brass band, - in front of a splendid scene in which mountains and cataracts and clouds vied with each other to ravish the heart of the beholder, and a painted footpath led to a painted bower upon the painted side of a painted mountain. The attendance was very numerous and somewhat miscellaneous, but, on the whole, quite as respectable as any average political assembly, and a good deal more *distingue* than any primary meeting of any party... in any Ward in our City. The parquet, which would seat about 200 persons, was in the main occupied by gentlemen of Irish birth, who had come from the markets and mechanical labors of the day, for an evening of rational and relaxing recreation. The dress circle was densely filled with just such persons as you may see daily in Broadway, or any other crowded street, with a liberal sprinkling of Federal and State government officers, members of the Common Council, magistrates aad [sic] others who bear the honors, as well as perform the duties which pertain to the services of the Commonwealth. The private boxes were mainly monopolized by the magnates of Wall-street, - the Bulls and Bears of the Stock Exchange, who seek in these serene and soothing amusements relief from the harsh and exhausting conflicts of their daily pursuits.... The theatre was packed from the floor to the ceiling. Every available standing place was occupied, and hundreds went away who could not obtain admission.[258]

One reporter estimated that the 200-seat venue accommodated 2,000 people that night, collecting a gate of at least $1,500. Spectators even took up half of the stage area, and quickly found that having close seats did not translate into greater entertainment when the brawling performers kept careening into them.[259]

The bouts began at eight o'clock that evening. To the disappointment of many Aaron Jones failed to appear, but the show went on as fighters

---

[258] *New York Times*, November 13, 1858
[259] *Era*, December 12, 1858

named Jim Ball and Young Sweeny were the first to take the stage, followed by famed lightweight Young Barney Aaron and a man from Brooklyn named Kerrigan. Third came one Morris Leonard and another Brooklynite, this one named Scotty. Australian Kelly and Con Fitzgerald followed them. The violence was suspended for boisterous music from the orchestra pit, which heralded the appearance of dancer and comedian Johnny Aaron, who many felt provided the best entertainment of the evening. Finally, Morrissey came to the stage and stood before the crowd in his sparring gloves, arms folded for several minutes to admire the applauding crowd before him. The *Times* described him as "a well-built man – not large and powerful as has been represented, but muscular, active, with a bulletty head, short hair, sprouting beard and a not unpleasant face." An Editor of the *Clipper* stated that he would at last hand the Champion his stake money from the Heenan fight, which rumor had it was $5,000. He then handed an envelope holding the cash to John, who promptly tossed it into the thrilled crowd. The Editor then brought forth an open jewel case and told John that "a small circle of Mr. Morrissey's personal friends," had gone in together to purchase a token to honor the fighter, especially considering his recent decision to never fight again, a promise they hoped he would keep. Inside the case was an emerald breast pin surrounded by diamonds. Taking this gift and stepping to the stage, John addressed the crowd.[260]

"I thank you very much for this large attendance," he said. "I said, before my fight with Mr. Heenan, that it should be the last prize-fight I would ever engage in, win or lose – and I shall keep my word. If I ever had any animosity against Mr. Heenan, it ended with the fight. I have nothing against him or any of his friends. I would much rather be on good terms with the whole of them." After uproarious applause, he proceeded to spar lightly with a Mr. Orrignon, a portly fellow nonetheless described as a "well-known teacher of gymnastics." The reporter for *The Spirit of the Times* was impressed by Morrissey's skills and reflexes. "His guard is not very good, but he is quick on the legs and understands how to use both hands with effect." Having satisfied the crowd that he could have dispatched his obese sparring partner at any moment he chose, the champion departed to further cheers.[261]

Less than two weeks later, John gave a similar exhibition in Philadelphia at Franklin Hall before a crowd of about one hundred onlookers of similar varied background as the New York show. He again sparred with the "hugely obese" Orrignon. Then, on March 24, 1859, he returned to Hoym's Theater for another friendly match against the smaller Australian Kelly.[262]

---

[260] *New York Times*, November 13, 1858; *Era*, December 12, 1858, quoting *Spirit of the Times*, November 20, 1858

[261] *New York Times*, November 13, 1858; *Era*, December 12, 1858, quoting *Spirit of the Times*, November 20, 1858

[262] *New York Times*, November 25, 1858; *New York Times*, March 25, 1859

As if to convince the sporting crowd that they no longer held grudges against one another, Morrissey and Heenan took part in yet another exhibition at Hoym's on April 4, 1859, this one a charity event. Other famed fighters, including Barney Aaron and Joe Coburn, gave exhibitions, but it was the appearance of Morrissey and Heenan which filled the house "almost to suffocation." The two rivals gave a lively account of themselves but displayed no malice in their sparring. No other details survive of this encounter, other than that Susan Morrissey made an appearance at ringside, the only time she did so in her husband's career in the ring.[263]

Despite their profession to have settled their differences, Old Smoke and the Benicia Boy never developed any true friendship in their lifetimes. By that autumn, it appeared the two were once again on a collision course. On October 11, the *New York Times* published a letter from John Heenan claiming that Morrissey had been telling others he would meet Heenan in a prizefight for $10,000 a side. Heenan accepted the offer, saying that he intended to fight English champion Tom Sayers soon, but that he would be willing to face Morrissey in a rematch before or after that event, at Morrissey's choosing. The same day saw the *Times* publishing a reply from Morrissey insisting, "I will avail myself of the privilege he has tendered me, and agree to fight him after his battle for the championship of England, whether he win or lose it, for $10,000 a side, within four to eight months after the date of his fight in England, just as he may choose." He went on to defend his reasoning for a return to the ring by pointing out that Heenan had been threatening his friends, and he felt it a matter of personal honor to defend them. He also wished Heenan victory in the proposed match with Sayers. To show his intentions were serious, Morrissey left a fifty-dollar deposit on this offer with the Editor of the *Spirit of the Times*.[264]

The day following the publication of these letters, the two fighters wound up coincidentally running into one another near the recently opened Central Park. Morrissey went straight to his challenger. "So, here you are, God damn you," he growled; "come into the Park and I'll fight you now for two hundred dollars." He then reached out and smacked his hand across Heenan's shoulder. Heenan reached into his pockets and pulled them inside out to show them empty.

"Mr. Morrissey, I have not got two hundred dollars about me, and therefore I cannot fight you," he said. At this, Morrissey again cursed and offered to fight the Benicia Boy for free. He struck Heenan on the shoulder again.

By now a large crowd was growing around the adversaries. Careful to stay calm, Heenan refused to fight for free, insisting upon facing Morrissey in a true, organized prize fight. Morrissey, incensed at Heenan's unruffled demeanor, looked as though he was about to attack the other man right

[263] *Brooklyn Evening Star*, April 5, 1859
[264] *New York Times*, October 12, 1859

there, prompting some of the crowd to intervene and draw the fighters apart from one another.[265]

A few days later, the Deputy Sheriff of Buffalo arrived in New York City to arrest Morrissey, Heenan, and thirteen other men, warrants having been issued by a Buffalo Grand Jury for the complicity in a prize fight between Boston's Ed Price and New York's Australian Kelly, which had taken place in Buffalo on October 6, 1858. Morrissey submitted to arrest at his home and was transported to Buffalo for trial. He was in Buffalo for one day before he acquired the services of an attorney who facilitated his return to New York City. On February 2, 1860, he returned to Buffalo and pleaded guilty to the charges against him. The next day, he paid $300 in fines before returning once again to New York City.

Ultimately, nothing seems to have come of the arrangements for a second meeting between Morrissey and Heenan, and the former did keep to his word about retiring from the ring, also turning down a challenge from English wrestler Sam Hurst. "He is a shrewd, strong-headed fellow in more senses than one," observed one reporter of Morrissey after the Heenan fight, "and has far more brains than most of the crowd around him." He did indeed have new interests which he regarded as more important now that he had made a name for himself. Just how "laudable and advantageous" these new interests were would certainly be a matter for debate.[266]

_____

"A prize-fighter can graduate with no other avocation equal to his start," Morrissey later reflected. "I have always played cards more or less." Not only had he been playing cards, he had dealt them at least since first gaining employment with his friend and mentor John Petrie when still a recent arrival to New York City. He had used a loan to open his first gambling joint, called the Gem with partner Dad Cunningham upon arriving in San Francisco sometime around 1852 and, upon his return to New York, opened a saloon, also called the Gem and likely with gambling as an attraction, on Broadway. Shortly thereafter, he bought a stake in the Bella Union Hall on Leonard Street, a sign of his steadily increasing financial gains through the 1850s. He sold both businesses opening a new gambling parlor and saloon in Troy called the Ivy Green.[267]

With the Heenan fight out of the way and the appearance fees he had won as a result, Morrissey was free to focus on his expanding business interests by 1859. He partnered with fellow New York gambling personality Matt Danser in opening a new parlor at the corner of Broadway

[265] *New York Herald*, October 13, 1859

[266] *New York Times*, October 23, 1858; James, *Lives*, 52

[267] *Chicago Daily Tribune*, August 1, 1874; Asbury, *Sucker's Progress*, 372

and Great Jones Street. In no time, the place was turning a tremendous profit and John's pockets were full of cash.

The financial windfall generated by this new venture is part of the extreme highs and lows represented in the Morrissey family's fortunes through 1859 and 1860. On one hand, John had just conquered one of his oldest rivals, who happened to be a bigger, younger man. He was now famous around the country for something more than his alleged role in the death of Bill Poole, even if fighting for money was still cause for disgust among much of the public at large. The hard work and discipline of his time training for the Heenan fight had brought him to possibly the best physical shape of his life. Always muscular, he was now trim and, circumstantial evidence suggests, drinking significantly less. The frequency of newspaper reports about his carousing, public drunkenness, and barroom brawls taper off significantly after the Heenan battle and disappear almost completely from 1861 forward, suggesting either that Morrissey was drinking less or that his increasingly powerful political connections were suppressing the stories. Matthew Hale Smith, who was acquainted with Morrissey, attributed his new discipline to his expanding gambling interests. "To do this he knew he must dress well, behave well, be sober, and not gamble," wrote Smith. "These resolutions he carried out." Perhaps most satisfactory to the doting father was that he was now able to provide his family with financial stability for the first time.[268]

However, a morbid pall seemed to spread over the Morrissey family, making its first appearance just as the year 1859 was getting under way. There is a lone account published in Grand Rapids, Wisconsin paper on January 15 indicating that Susan Morrissey had failed at two suicide attempts. The reporter does not specify her reasons for the attempts, but recorded her preferred method as laudanum, the popular opiate used as medicine throughout the nineteenth century. Apparently, the hasty intervention of a doctor saved the woman's life on both occasions. This single article is the only source this author could find indicating any hint of clinical depression in Susan Morrissey, let alone suicide attempts. The reporter does not name the source of his information.[269]

A few days after Susan's reported attempts to kill herself, on January 19, 1859, Captain Levi Smith, the man who had years earlier given a Troy hoodlum work aboard his riverboat and later consented to that same young man marrying his cherished daughter Susannah, passed away while in New York City. He was 53 years old. After the funeral, grieving John, Susan, and John Jr. moved in with Captain Smith's widow in Troy, to look after her. For most of the year, though, Morrissey was in New York City looking after his business and political interests. After one of his returns to Troy, Susan became pregnant a second time. However, tragedy struck once more

[268] Smith, 182
[269] *Wood County Reporter*, January 15, 1859

in November, when the baby boy died on his fourth day of life. John Sr. would make no public comment about this child for the rest of his life, perhaps a sign of the unspeakable sorrow the death brought to his heart. The Morrisseys would have no more children.

Perhaps the most heart-breaking of this string of personal losses for John came shortly after the opening of the new decade, on March 14, 1860. At about six a.m. that Wednesday morning, two men walking alongside the Poestenkill Creek near Second Street in Troy sighted a human body floating in the water. Drawing the body to shore, they found it to be a female and very shortly later authorities recognized it as that of Julia Morrissey, John's mother. By the time of her death, Julia had accumulated a notorious reputation throughout Troy as a vagrant drunk. "During nearly a year past the unfortunate woman had been an inmate of the Troy county house, which she left only a day or two ago," reported the *New York Times*, adding that she "has since been quite intoxicated." A coroner's inquest that afternoon declared that Julia must have gotten drunk and accidentally fallen into the creek on the prior evening and drowned. News of her demise made newspapers around the country. These stories incorrectly reported her name as Joanna, a mistake which thereafter has appeared in every published biography of her son. Julia Morrissey had been just 54 years old at the time of her death.[270]

Outside of a token statement he made, John's emotional state upon receiving the sad news of his mother's death cannot be known. He had just boarded a Royal Mail steamship called *Africa* in Jersey City with three friends bound for England amid a chorus of cheers from admirers. Someone came aboard to express their condolences, which was the first he had heard of her passing. In response, he simply stated that he "had the consolation of knowing that the last sad rites would be properly attended to." Just as had been the case with his dead infant child, John would make no further public comments regarding his mother's fate or its effect upon him.[271]

———

The *Africa* was to take Morrissey and some American friends of his to England in advance of the much talked-about boxing match between John Heenan and Tom Sayers, the Champion of England. The fight generated more anticipation than any previous on either side of the Atlantic, the first to be billed as the "Championship of the World," where the individuals popularly recognized as the champions of their respective nations were to meet in a prize ring. Many in the press and in the sporting world insisted

---

[270] *New York Times*, March 19, 1860; *Daily Empire*, March 22, 1860; *New York Times*, March 15, 1860; findagrave.com, accessed 12/9/2016
[271] *New York Times*, March 19, 1860; *Daily Empire*, March 22, 1860; *New York Times*, March 15, 1860; *Sporting Life*, March 28, 1860

that Heenan would have won his fight with Morrissey had it not been for his handicaps. He had certainly shown the better "science" in the early goings. Since Morrissey had declined a rematch with Heenan, and no one else in America stepped forward with the money he and his handlers requested for a battle, many in America were now willing to recognize the Benicia Boy, who had yet to win a fight, as the Champion of America, at least for the purposes of this high stakes international bout. Morrissey himself had observed that the American public's anticipation for Heenan-Sayers was "beyond description." Perhaps missing some of the attention he had gained in the prize ring, he intended to be among the many Americans setting sail for England's shores, and would constantly put himself before the reporters and sporting men conversing about the fight, stealing whatever limelight he could from the two fistic stars about to do battle. Perhaps more out of this need for attention than any serious intent to fight, Morrissey continually insinuated to reporters on both sides of the Atlantic that he would face Heenan again after the Sayers bout. When friends asked him who he thought would win, Morrissey insisted Sayers would emerge the victor, and he placed multiple bets to back this opinion before departing New York. Some said his pick reflected continued resentment for his old Troy rival; others wondered if Old Smoke knew something they didn't. "Morrissey seemed uncommonly confident," remarked a friend. "He had, he asserted, ten thousand dollars which said that Heenan was beaten."[272]

In the months after his fight with Morrissey, John Heenan had met and fallen in love with Adah Menken, a Broadway actress of dubious talents but bountiful body who had among her admirers Frank Queen and Edwin James of the *New York Clipper*, men who also spent a great deal of time in Heenan's entourage. Pretentious and narcissistic, Menken was known for manipulating men for the purposes of gaining fame and money. She had already been married twice and, when the smitten and famously gullible Heenan proposed to her not long after their first meeting, the fighter's friends shook their head in disapproval. The marriage occurred with similar rapidity. Together, the pair became the most notorious couple in the growing culture of New York celebrity, scandalous rumors constantly circling about them (The most inflammatory of these was the discovery that Menken had never divorced her second husband). The self-appointed watchdogs over public morality routinely decried Heenan as a savage man-child and Menken as a money-grubbing slut. For both, all the outrage only heightened their notoriety and the attending financial prospects.

In sporting circles, Heenan's marital bliss, combined with rumors that he was now drinking heavily and had fallen out of physical condition, made even his supporters shake in their confidence as to how he might perform against the Englishman. When reporters discovered that Menken's previous marriage had never ended, some wondered how this revelation might affect her latest husband's concentration. Ada Menken was not on

[272] *Daily Empire*, March 22, 1860; *Sporting Life*, March 28, 1860; Lloyd, *Prize Fight*, 94

board when her new husband and the ever-present Jim Cusick arrived in England aboard the *Asia* on January 16, 1860, months before news of Menken's prior marriage had arrived. She stayed behind in New York to suffer the public dishonor alone.

The Benicia Boy initially set up camp along the Trent River, but authorities arrested him shortly thereafter, causing a sensation among the public, many of whom mobbed the police station. After posting a bond of one hundred pounds, Heenan snuck out of the back door to avoid the crowd and headed for London, where he languished while his handlers searched for a new training ground.

After news of Heenan's setbacks reached Morrissey, he offered his services to Tom Sayers as an advisor on Heenan's style and weaknesses. His trip to England would now not only be as a betting fan of fisticuffs and a man intent on regaining a modicum of public attention, but a matter of getting yet another victory over his old rival, even if by proxy. The *Africa* hit England's shore at Liverpool at four o'clock in the morning on Monday, March 24th, after a twelve-day journey. Morrissey disembarked with his good friend Dad Cunningham as well as John Lawrence and Morris Barron, two cronies from his days in Troy, and another friend named William Lindsay.

John had not expected to be well-known in England, yet he and his party soon found themselves surrounded by as many as a thousand people, some cheering his name while others were trying to shake his hand and offer words of welcome. When things got a little too stressful for the Americans, they ducked into a nearby hotel, only to find that the crowd was continuing to gather outside. One of John's companions slipped out to buy them all train tickets to London, and the friends made their way out of Liverpool via the London and North Western Railway that evening only to find a similar crowd cheering Morrissey upon their arrival.[273]

At around eight o'clock that evening, the Sayers camp heartily welcomed the Morrissey party into their headquarters, ex-boxer Owen Swift's hotel on Tichborne Street. The English champion was not present, having ventured off for training in Newmarket, but Morrissey and his friends spent the evening at the hotel, eating and conversing with two of Sayers's backers, John Gideon and Farmer Bennett. Someone broached the subject of Morrissey himself engaging in a prize fight during his stay, but the American insisted he was only present as a spectator to support Sayers.[274]

After this, John set off on his own to tour London's sporting houses. "I did not miss one," John wrote home, "but served them all alike; and I must say I was never more cordially received nor better treated in my life." He was pleased to find that the patrons all recognized him "yet not one of

---

[273] *New York Herald*, April 18, 1860
[274] *New York Daily Herald*, April 14, 1860; *Sporting Life*, March 28, 1860; Lloyd, 116; James, *Lives*, 51

them had any reason to believe that I was in the country, much less coming to see them that night." He was also satisfied to hear some criticize Heenan for not visiting them as Morrissey had. Having gotten to know the sporting crowd of London and fed his ego on its adulation, John made his way back to Swift's hotel for the night around eleven in the evening.[275]

The next morning, John, dressing himself in a fur-lined overcoat to protect himself from the English winter, paid a visit to the editor of the *Sporting Life* newspaper with William Lindsay. After Lindsay presented the editors with a letter of introduction, Morrissey proceeded to charm the reporters, who found him a "fine, handsome, unobtrusive fellow, well built, and with a mug that indicates a generous and thoroughly game disposition." He told them that he felt healthy except for a sore throat which was improving.[276]

Tom Sayers greeted Morrissey outside Swift's hotel as Old Smoke returned after his outing. After finally making each other's acquaintance, Morrissey, Sayers, and their respective parties all became immediate friends, with Sayers charmed by the American fighter's "frank and manly address," and Morrissey impressed by the "athletic, powerfully built *physique*" of Sayers. Morrissey presented his English counterpart with the gift of a trophy dating back to his own fight with George Thompson in his California days. The solid gold trophy was of a horse and included the inscription, "Made and presented to John Morrissey, Champion of California, by James H. Moore, Sacramento City, Cal." The Englishman graciously accepted the gift. The pair of prize-fighters sat up until ten in the evening talking until Sayers's trainer insisted that he get some rest. John would end up staying on as a sort of mascot and consultant for Sayers; the fact that Morrissey had beaten Heenan before, whatever the circumstances of the win, proved a considerable boost to camp morale.[277]

Newspaper writers made note of the newly grown, thick, bristling beard on Morrissey's chin, which a *New York Times* writer had noticed beginning to sprout a year earlier. In years to come, the beard would be something of a Morrissey trademark. In England, some whispered that Morrissey had grown the beard to cover scars from his own encounter with Heenan.[278]

As of Morrissey's arrival, Heenan was in jail again, the police having picked him up at his new training camp near Bath. Rumors circulated that Sayers was behind the arrest this time, allegedly because he feared the hulking American. Sayers refuted this with a letter to the editor of the *Spirit of the Times*. Likewise, Morrissey wrote a letter to the same paper offering to pay bail for his former adversary. "I know he don't like me," he wrote, "and there is no reason why I should like him; but I want him to have a fair

---

[275] *New York Herald*, April 18, 1860
[276] *Sporting Life*, March 28, 1860
[277] *New York Herald*, April 14 and 18, 1860; *Sporting Life*, March 28, 1860; Lloyd, 116; James, *Lives*, 51
[278] *New York Times*, November 13, 1858

chance, and will go as far as you or any other American will, to see that he gets it." Heenan apparently received bail, from whom is not clear, but he thereafter switched camps yet again, this time to a village outside of Bedford.[279]

Morrissey was fascinated by Sayers's training regimen, or lack thereof. "He is the best man of his size I ever saw," he wrote to the *Spirit of the Times*, "and his confidence is perfect. His system of training is different from that of any man you ever heard of – no sparring, no fighting of bags, no nonsense of any sort, and he does at any and all time, pretty much what he feels like doing at the moment." Intending to lose a little weight on his trip, Morrissey agreed to work with Sayers in whatever training he did accomplish. When he wasn't attending the Sayers camp, Morrissey continued his rounds among the sporting taverns of the region: The Horseshoe, Cambrian, Black Horse, and the George and Dragon. He met some of the noted champions of the British prize ring, including Ben Caunt and William Perry. He also paid a visit to Frank L. Downing, the Editor of *Bell's Life*, that country's premier sporting rag. The Heenan and Sayers camps had selected Downing as the stakes holder for the fight. A reporter on his staff noticed "a look about [Morrissey] that convinces one at once that he would prove a tough customer to any one [sic]." The same writer echoed the question as to whether John intended to find a fight for himself in England, to which the American replied that he had simply made the trip to visit and to see the fight. The patrons and press listened intently to Old Smoke's criticisms of his former rival and insistence that the Englishman was guaranteed to win, to the point that "his biased opinions and expressions had affected the confidence of even Heenan's friends." He told a reporter at the Horseshoe Tavern that "Heenan was not much of a man." He also continued to take wagers on the fight, always betting on Sayers. Some fight fans, both American and English, found his favoritism of the Englishman and personal attacks on his fellow American distasteful, but their criticism seemed to matter little to Morrissey.[280]

The ballyhoo and excitement over the meeting between Heenan and Sayers made it the most anticipated prizefight on either side of the Atlantic to that point in modern history. Every major periodical from both nations, sporting or otherwise, carried at least some news or opinion piece concerning the event. Hopes and predictions from reporters as to who would win unsurprisingly split along national lines. Queen Victoria, along with Princes Albert and Alfred, even attended a comedic play put on at the Olympic Theater about Heenan, entitled *B.B.*, as in Benicia Boy, and rumor had it that Her Majesty had insisted that any news of the fight be brought to her immediately so that she might know the outcome before anyone else.

---

[279] *New York Times*, April 26, 1860
[280] Kofoed, 188, quoting *Life in London*; Kofoed, 191, quoting the *London Sporting Telegraph*; Lloyd, *Prize Fight*, p. 120; James, *Lives*, 31; *Frank Leslie's Illustrated Newspaper*, April 28, 1860; *New York Herald*, April 18, 1860

The "Great International Fight" was set for Farnborough in Hampshire on the afternoon of April 17, 1860. In London, train tickets went on sale for fifteen pounds each to a ravenous crowd around three o'clock that morning. The intention of the high-priced tickets, according to the *New York Times*, was to keep attendance exclusive to the higher rungs of the sporting crowd. Morrissey found his trip to the station delayed by an astounding amount of traffic on London Bridge for such an early hour. Arriving at the station, he witnessed an even more fantastic sight. Encircling the train station and bunching up at the gates was "an immense crowd, all desirous of entering... There were dukes, lords, earls, and even ministers; there were the first members of the press, merchants, lawyers." Among these were also politicians, judges, doctors, authors (William Makepeace Thackeray was present), dramatists, college professors, architects, engineers, soldiers, sailors, boxers, craftsmen, "every class of society." A few hours later, the people of Farnborough barely had time to rub the sleep from their eyes before this massive, mottled mob of men descended upon their small town and made its way to a large field to pitch a boxing ring, John Morrissey among them.[281]

All this time, John Heenan and Tom Sayers had never met face to face. Their intermediaries had made all arrangements for the fight. Sayers was smallish for a heavyweight boxer, even by nineteenth century standards. Standing just over five feet, eight inches tall and never weighing more than 152 pounds in a fight; Heenan dwarfed him. Born in Brighton, England in 1826, Sayers had battled Heenan's former trainer Aaron Jones twice, to a draw on the first occasion and beating him handily on the second. He was known as a defensive-minded fighter whose skills and athleticism allowed him to best bigger men, including William "The Tipton Slasher" Perry (who outweighed him by as much as fifty pounds) on the day he won England's heavyweight laurels. By the time of his match with Heenan, Sayers had made four successful defenses of his new title.

————

The fighters entered the ring at approximately 7:30 a.m. As combat got underway, it seemed that Heenan got the better of the action by taking advantage of his size, though Sayers did use his skills to land some good blows and evade any punches that would prove too dangerous. A continuous ebb and flow of control in the action marked the earlier rounds. In the sixth round, a blow from Heenan shattered a bone in the Englishman's arm. Unfortunately for the American, he was not able to enjoy the obvious advantage for long. A multitude of swift, straight, and stiff blows from Sayers swelled Heenan's eyes nearly shut, turning his target into a floating haze before him. Amazingly, two hours of this kind of action passed, both fighters showing signs of fatigue and serious injury but

[281] *New York Times*, April 30, 1860; Lloyd, 120-121, 125; Gorn, 153

using to relent. Sayers was going down much more often than Heenan ...d was clearly on the worst side of the action, but he remained dangerous ...nd determined.

As bedlam ensued inside the ring, back in the town of Farnborough, the local constabulary had been unprepared and undermanned to handle such a large congregation of people, legal or not. The constable sent word to the surrounding towns that Farnborough was under siege, and that he would appreciate any assistance from his neighbors. Policemen from throughout the region responded and began marching their way to the horde of humanity in the field under the local constable's leadership. When they arrived, no one moved aside to let them through. Despite the constable's harshest orders, not a budge. The constable decided his men must make it to the ring, by force if necessary. This caused the people in the back of the crowd, closest to the police, to press into the crowd under the force of the police incursion behind them. In turn, the people close to the ring surged forward against the stakes and ropes, pushed by those behind them.

While all this was happening, the fighters continued their struggle. Sayers, his broken arm swollen and flopping about, was barely able to stand from the exhaustion, pain, and punishment he had endured. Heenan, both eyes swollen shut, simply stumbled about the ring flailing at shadows and sounds. Eventually, Heenan's hands found his foe's throat and grabbed ahold. He pushed Sayers to the ropes and began to strangle him, illegal by any boxing rules. However, the referee had lost sight of the fighters, having been consumed by the crowd of fans which had by now spilled into the ring. Blind, Heenan had no clue what was going on with the crowd and continued to choke his foe, whose face was turning purple as he struggled to remain conscious. "That's murder!" someone cried. Then someone purportedly cut the ropes, and chaos ensued. Many reporters lost sight of the fighters as the entire space of the ring was flooded with battling boxing fans and policemen. Other people went scrambling toward the trains to avoid arrest. The referee, yelling over the tumult, declared the fight at an end.[282]

Somehow, a team of Heenan's supporters were able to force the police back. Though there were no more ropes, and partisans of both sides rioted around them, the fighters themselves agreed to continue without the referee. Sayers had since gotten loose from Heenan's grasp, and the American was now flailing blindly around the ring, hitting and knocking down anyone nearby, including Sayers's seconds. An exhausted Sayers, having been battered about within the violent crowd, collapsed against Heenan, and both fell into the dirt. At that point, the referee forced himself through the crowd and again declared the fight at an end. Having seen enough, most fans at last began to disperse toward the trains.

---

[282] Lloyd, 150

Even as the crowd made its way on board the trains, easing the stress on local law enforcement, arguments began as to who had won. The referee, in stopping the contest twice, had failed to indicate a victor. Heenan's partisans insisted that, since he had the upper hand before someone cut the ropes, the American should be the winner. Sayers's supporters pointed out that choking was illegal, and that the referee should have disqualified Heenan, giving their man the win. Though both fighters and their countrymen would continue to insist that the win was theirs, history records the bout as an inconclusive draw. There was also debate as to exactly who had dared cut the ropes, possibly saving the life of the British champion but ruining the fight.

———

Morrissey, Dad Cunningham, and their friends caught the *Canada* back to the States a few days after the fight, arriving in Boston on May 4. Though many in that city cheered John's arrival and followed him around looking for stories of the fight, others criticized his backing of an Englishman against an American. There were even published accusations that "evil-minded" Morrissey had been the man who cut the ropes toward the fight's end, allegedly to save Sayers or, at least, prevent a Heenan victory. Heenan's fans in Boston were not happy to see him, some of them hanging an effigy of him in the streets with a sign which read, "Morrissey the traitor." Still battling a bad cough which had plagued him on and off since before he left the States, John declined to respond to the accusations verbally, but delivered a written statement published in many of the country's prominent newspapers:

> There appears to be some ill feeling toward me for the part I took in the late fight. For the opinions of the fighting fraternity I care little, but I do wish to have myself placed in the proper light to the public…. In betting my money on Sayers and going to see the fight I did no more than many other citizens and why I am singled out as a target against which public opinion should be directed I do not know… I did not cut the ropes and watched the fight without making a demonstration. The ropes were not cut whatever.
>
> The stakes were merely pulled out of the ground and the ropes thrown down. I defy any man who was there to say that I opened my lips to say anything from the beginning of the fight to the end of the fight. I spoke to no one during its progress, but stood quietly by and saw the whole affair without making any demonstration whatever.[283]

———

[283] *Albany Evening Journal*, April 30, 1860; *New York Times*, April 30, 1860; *Evening Journal*, May 4, 1860; *New York Times*, May 7, 1860; *New York Herald*, May 7, 1860

The *Clipper*, known for its strong backing of Heenan, was historically very critical of Morrissey, but on the matter of cutting the ropes they defended him. Their correspondent for the fight confirmed "that he was in close proximity to Morrissey at the fight, that he observed him closely, and that he did not cut the ropes, or assist in breaking up the ring." Few first-hand accounts provided any clue as to who did cut the ropes, or if they were indeed pulled out of the ground as Morrissey claimed. Nonetheless, the *Canada* left under cover of darkness at nine in the evening on May 4 to keep John and his friends safe from "rough treatment" by Heenan's fans. A "large police force" escorted him safely aboard.[284]

Even before Heenan's return to the States, rumors circulated of a second match with Morrissey. The newspapers could not resist publishing any such information that came their way. "We understand that John Morrissey, the pugilist, is going into training at the 'Abbey,' with a view of fighting Heenan in August," reported the *Troy Budget* on June 12, a tale with no validity at all. When Heenan's boat, *The Vanderbilt*, arrived in mid-July, the rumor mill only increased in production. A challenge, allegedly penned by Morrissey, then arrived on the desk of the editor of the *New York Times*, declaring, "I will fight [Heenan] in four months from signing articles, for from $10 to $10,000 a side; and as it seems paradoxical to me and my friends to see a man dubbed 'Champion of the World,' who has never won a fight in the ring, I will now give him the chance he wants, although I only stipulated to fight him again as a winner." Heenan was quick to publish a reply, "I at once accept all the terms he offers, and choose for stakes the highest sum he names."[285]

On July 17, the real John Morrissey penned a letter declaring the widely read challenge a hoax and a forgery, stating clearly "I am not the author of this challenge, nor have I authorized any person or persons to issue such a challenge in my name. Moreover, I am not training for any fight, but am here for my health, and have business of more importance on hand than preparing for such a contest."[286]

———

John penned and sent the above letter had from the enormous Congress Hotel in Saratoga Springs, New York. Native Americans had valued this area and its many natural salter-water springs for various health-related purposes before and during the colonial period. The story goes that the natives introduced nearby colonists to the springs, and tales of their invigorating and healing properties later drew Revolutionary War officers stationed at nearby Fort Saratoga. Thus, General George Washington,

[284] Kofoed, 202, quoting *New York Clipper; Evening Post*, May 4, 1860
[285] *New York Times*, July 16, 1860, quoting *Troy Budget; New York Times*, July 18, 1860; Kofoed, 203, quoting Heenan in *New York Herald*
[286] Kofoed, *Brandy*, 204, quoting Morrissey in *New York Herald*

touring the region as the war was winding down, first encountered what were then known as the "salt springs" in 1783. It was Washington who, enamored of the place and its potential as a real estate investment, first referred to the area as "the Saratoga Springs" in a letter to Governor George Clinton. The future President was foiled in his prescient plans for the area when Clinton informed him that the natives had too strong of a claim on the springs, and so Washington could not purchase the land. Four years later, though, tourism was on the rise at the springs thanks to a feature in *Columbia Magazine*, and the first commercial building, a tavern (naturally) opened on a bluff overlooking some of the springs. Lumberman Gideon Putnam began designing the outline of an imagined town there in 1800 and built what would become the Grand Union Hotel there two years later before dying in a construction accident while building a second hotel, becoming the first person installed in the cemetery he had designed. The Union Hotel and the hotels that sprang up its wake (the Congress Hotel, the Gideon Putnam, and – most luxurious of all - the United States Hotel) pioneered a new trend in American leisure: the resort. These were more than simple room and board providing accommodations on a journey. More extravagant and luxurious than anything on American soil at the time and situated near natural springs said to provide health and relaxation, the hotels themselves became a destination to which people could travel from afar, not simply a meager stop over. Those who could afford it came here to heal wounds and ailments; still other wealthy came just for the pleasure of it as part of the first generation of a new type of American, the recreational tourist.[287]

For tourists, relaxation can threaten to turn into boredom, and thus, over the next few decades, Saratoga Springs and the surrounding areas became known for opportunities to drink alcohol, eat fine food, dance in astonishingly vast ballrooms, play billiards, admire fine art, fish the nearby Lake Saratoga, stroll through the gorgeous Congress Park, or, should the whim arise, pray. These were the activities available to men like John Quincy Adams, Andrew Jackson, Martin Van Buren, and Joseph Bonaparte (brother to Napoleon) when they visited Saratoga during the 1820s. Horses, long a subject of fascination for the aristocratic on both sides of the Atlantic, came to Saratoga too. The tourists brought their favorite horses with them, and they enjoyed racing them down the resort's thoroughfares for wagers, sometimes drawing large crowds of onlookers who openly ignored the laws locals had passed forbidding such activity. With the betting begun in this manner, gambling had come to Saratoga in a big way by the early 1840s, when the village's first gambling houses opened. Shooting galleries, taverns, and high-class bordellos were not far behind.[288]

Visiting for what was apparently the first time that July in 1860, Morrissey noticed the money pouring in from the upper crust of New York

[287] Hotaling, 1-8
[288] Hotaling, 14-27

society, the very people with whom he had long sought to associate himself, people like the Astors and Vanderbilts. Morrissey himself lost $10,000 playing faro there that August. Here was a serene locale where the mineral waters, luxury accommodations, and beautiful scenery provided an escape from the poisons, tenements, and filth of the City, the Five Points in particular. However, outside of the scenery and amateur amusements, there appeared to be nothing substantial there to entertain this enclave of social and financial elites. The men especially seemed starved for excitement. Morrissey made note of this and began making connections among the Saratoga Springs wheelers and dealers. By September, he opened a "faro bank" there, but his ambitions were much bigger than a simple gambling den. He had a plan which he hoped would turn this sleepy town into a personal mint.[289]

John eventually returned to his wife and son in Troy, and to attending to his increasingly profitable business interests in New York City. On July 24, 1860, a census taker visited the Morrisey home, still the official property of Adeline Smith, the late Captain's widow. The census man listed the household members as Adeline, aged 47; John Morrissey, aged 29; Susan Morrissey, aged 24; John, Jr., aged 5; Addie Smith, aged 15; and David Smith, aged 26. He listed John's profession as "Prize Fighter & Gambler" and valued his personal assets at $10,000. Taking his interest in New York City gambling ventures into account, it is very likely that Morrissey was a far wealthier man than this. However, he intended to become still richer in the coming years. Just as his single-minded ambition once drove him to become a champion boxer, so now it pushed him toward a new dream centered on the tranquil spas of Saratoga Springs.[290]

[289] *New York Herald*, September 6, 1860
[290] 1860 United States Federal Census

13.

Boss Tweed and the Draft Riots

On February 26, 1860, the Sunday school superintendent at the Five Points House of Industry was distracted from his teachings by the arrival of a man he had never seen before. The House of Industry was home to a rather radical charity group intending to reform the locals, particularly the Catholics, through Protestant teachings and lessons in temperance. They also adopted many children, sometimes forcefully, from those deemed unfit for parenting. "One Sunday morning I saw a tall, remarkable-looking man enter the room and take a seat among us," recalled the school's superintendent later. He was so struck by the stranger's apparent interest in the teachings that he asked the stranger if he might like to speak to the students, an offer the stranger accepted. The man gave an impromptu talk "which at once fascinated every little hearer and hushed the room into silence." When the stranger finished, the children called out for more, but the speaker said he must take his leave. As the man made his way to the door, the superintendent asked him for his name. "It is Abraham Lincoln," replied the visitor, "from Illinois."[291]

The tall, lanky tourist had arrived in New York City the day before with little fanfare. This was his first visit to the great metropolis. He had made a name for himself in national politics and was certainly recognizable throughout the Midwestern states now. However, in New York City he found that he was mostly anonymous, catching the eye of locals only for his conspicuous height. Though he was in town for a speech at the Cooper Union Hall scheduled for February 27, Lincoln had arrived a couple of days early and intended to make his rounds through the city streets to get to know the people, their concerns, and their ways of living. He spent most of February 26 traveling through the city unattended, visiting Broadway and the Five Points, among other locales.

On February 27, Lincoln made his appearance at Cooper Hall, delivering a speech he had painstakingly researched, written, and edited for weeks. In it, the Republican presidential hopeful referred to his rival Steven Douglas's assertion that the founding fathers created the United States of America with the intention of continuing and supporting slavery. He proceeded to tear apart Douglas's claim by explaining in meticulous detail that twenty-one of the thirty-nine signers of the U.S. Constitution believed it important that the federal government control slavery for the purposes of preventing its expansion.

---

[291] McClure, 246

Though Lincoln's first speech and appearance in New York did much to expand his popularity in the city, the Republican Party faced an uphill battle there. The city had deep financial and business ties to the slave-holding South, and Lincoln's proposed quarantine of slavery found opposition from many in both the upper and lower classes of the city. The rich did not want their business interests threatened by a challenge to slavery or a split, already political and threatening to become violent, between the North and South. Working class whites already found themselves in competition with free blacks for employment, and they were resentful because of it. Restrictions on slavery, in their view, only promised to exacerbate the problem. Immigrants, who made up a great deal of the working class and were always reverently loyal to Democrat Fernando Wood, had managed to get their man elected Mayor for a third term. Benjamin Wood, the Mayor's brother, picked up on this tension and fanned the flames of discontent by promising that, should the Republicans get into the White House, "we shall find negroes among us thicker than blackberries swarming everywhere." Lincoln, of course, wound up winning both the Republican primary and the general election. That December, two thousand New York merchants drafted a resolution to support the South's right to secede, should they decide to do so, and that, "if ever a conflict arises between races, the people of the city of New York will stand by their brethren, the white race."[292]

John Morrissey, being a Democrat with ties to Fernando Wood, likely agreed on very little with Republican Lincoln, but did make his first known trip to Washington D.C. for the new President's inauguration on March 4, 1861. A reporter waiting outside Willard's Hotel where Lincoln was staying was amused to spot Morrissey passing in and out of the hotel wearing a stovepipe hat not unlike Honest Abe's.[293]

Back in New York, Mayor Wood, always a fan of keeping government as local as possible, had long been vocal against the Republican Party and federal involvement in the slavery issue. Following a second visit to the city by newly inaugurated President Lincoln, Wood met with the city's Common Council, proposing that, should the South in fact secede, New York City would also split with the Union.

———

On April 21, 1861, Southern forces opened fire on the federal garrison at Fort Sumter, South Carolina, and the Civil War had begun. News of this took days to reach New York City, but the effect it had on public opinion was radical. Despite the strong sympathies many in New York City held with the South, the nation's biggest metropolis was not immune to war fever. Seemingly at once, New York City's sentiments turned pro-Union.

---

[292] Burrows, 865
[293] Hotaling, 37

Thousands answered the new President's call for volunteers, the Irish immigrants among the most enthusiastic.

One interesting case was that of James Kerrigan, the Five Pointer who had been suspected of collusion with John Morrissey in the Poole murder, who, like Morrissey, had fought to protect the vote for Fernando Wood, and had been a leader of the Five Points gangs in their 1857 battle with the Bowery Boys referred to as the Dead Rabbits Riot, a calamity for which many still blamed Morrissey. Kerrigan was now a prominent figure within Mozart Hall, the Democratic organization created by Wood as an alternative to Tammany Hall, from whose leadership Wood had been ousted after his defeat at the polls in 1857. Following Isaiah Rynders's embarrassment during the Dead Rabbits Riot, Kerrigan had stood as the most prominent gang leader in the Sixth Ward, with Morrissey as the only possible competition for the premier place.

Before the attack at Fort Sumter, Kerrigan had been a vehement anti-abolitionist opposed to all things Republican, going so far as to publish a notice in the *New York Herald* calling for the formation of a volunteer militia to support the city's rights against federal intrusion "in the event of a revolution." Following the events of April 21, Kerrigan's sympathies immediately switched to the Union, though he remained a steadfast Democrat and critic of the new President. A congressman at the time that war broke out, Kerrigan abandoned his political responsibilities to be among the first wave of Lincoln's requested volunteers. Using his position and connections, he found himself a colonel in charge of the Twenty-fifth Regiment of New York Infantry, assigned to protecting Washington D.C. from Confederate invasion.[294]

Kerrigan's elevation to Congress and his subsequent departure with the Union Army left John Morrissey as the uncontested master of the Irish Five Points gangs, the coveted intermediary between the city's Democratic politicians and the working men and women of the neighborhood. Following his inspirational stopover in Saratoga Springs, he had returned to tend to his gambling enterprises in New York City, though his residence of record remained Troy. He did not volunteer for military service. At the time of the fighting at Fort Sumter, he was recovering from a life-threatening bout with diphtheria. In early April, newspapers mistakenly reported his death. He did survive and recover, but still avoided military service. His life through 1861 and 1862 would remain unusually quiet as he separated himself further from the streets and began cultivating his business interests and political connections.[295]

One of those connections, Fernando Wood, left his third mayoral term in 1862, succeeded by Republican George Opdyke. Unlike Kerrigan and Wood, Morrissey remained aligned with Tammany Hall. In 1860, no

---

[294] Anbinder, 297 - 299
[295] *Northern New York Journal*, April 9, 1861; *Evening Post*, April 9, 1861

Tammany man was on the rise quicker than Bill Tweed, whose emergence as the city's most powerful pol would be complete by the end of the war.

———

The Civil War lasted longer than most anyone in the North had expected, including the President and the series of commanding generals he went through during its course. Families in New York City, particularly those of the working class, lost their husbands, sons, brothers, fathers, and their enthusiasm for war, all at an alarming rate.

Soon enough, the Union was once again desperate for good fighting men. Battle, disease, and desertion were all taking a toll. The Enrollment Act introduced in March 1863 instituted the first draft in American history. Most New Yorkers resented this measure. Worse yet, the Act allowed for someone to avoid conscription if they paid $300, an unattainable sum for most of the city's working class. With the President's Emancipation Proclamation in January, the war had been increasingly identified as being fought for the freedom of enslaved blacks in the South, a cause for which the urban working-class whites cared little, or to which they were completely opposed. Making matters worse, inflation was pushing up the cost of goods and housing much faster than the average income, creating unprecedented fortunes for the few but ruinous poverty for the majority. In the minds of many of the city's immigrants and other poor, they would now be forced to leave their desperate families without a breadwinner to fight a war that would free men who surely intended to settle in the North and take their jobs.[296]

That July, Union forces emerged victorious at the Battle of Gettysburg in Pennsylvania, but at tremendous cost, making the Army even more desperate for conscripted troops. Saturday, July 11 saw the draft come to New York City. At each draft office, an official spun a wheel to determine who would be drafted, and the papers published the results the next morning. Those chosen were to report on Monday. Instead, an entire mob of men and women from the poorer wards of Manhattan reported to the streets at about six o'clock that morning. The crowd grew ever larger, collecting more numbers in each neighborhood as it proceeded north. By the time they reached the draft office up town on Forty-Sixth Street, the procession was so long that it took as much as twenty-five minutes to pass a single point, according to one witness. Soon enough, other mobs were forming outside of other draft offices around town. John Kennedy, Superintendent of Police – and the man who had years earlier recruited John Morrissey to "protect" the polls on behalf of Fernando Wood – put his men into action.[297]

---

[296] Ackerman, 12 – 13; Stiles, 380
[297] Asbury, *Gangs*, 116

The officers who arrived at the draft office on Third Street found themselves in immediate trouble. For much of the morning, the crowds had only been peacefully protesting. However, a volunteer fire engine company whose leader had been drafted arrived at the Third Street office intent on smashing the draft wheel and the office records. The police mounted a resistance until a gunshot erupted, sending the crowd into a frenzy, the fire company at the fore of the attack. Facing overwhelming odds, the policemen retreated inside. The firemen and rioters gave chase and burst inside, again overwhelming the police, who this time fled the building for Second Avenue. They put the draft office to flame, the firemen blocking attempts by other brigades to save the building. Soon enough, an entire city block had burnt to its foundations.

Superintendent Kennedy, meanwhile, set off for the bigger mass at Forty-Sixth Street dressed in plainclothes. Arriving, he found that they too had begun setting fire to that draft office. Someone in the mob recognized him, and a group violently accosted him. He fled, but another mob caught sight of him and ran him down. Pummeling him savagely, they left him for dead. A concerned citizen saw to his safe transfer back to the police station, where he received medical attention. Despite his dire condition, the Superintendent continued to bark out orders, assigning more men to reinforce those now under siege at both locations.

Governor Horatio Seymour was vacationing on the New Jersey shore when two military men delivered a telegram carrying news of the riots. Seymour had been one of the most visible opponents of the war and had personally warned President Lincoln against instituting a draft, trying to explain that New York's citizens would not stand for it. His warning clearly not heeded, he now set course for home, but was not overly concerned; New York had seen and survived its share of riots. The telegrams failed to communicate the magnitude of just how bad the riots had gotten. Seymour took an indirect means of travel to get to the city, even spending a restful night in New Jersey before finishing his trip back.

As the unconcerned Governor took his time crossing New Jersey on July 13, the increasingly violent rioters pushed back wave after wave of policemen, many of the officers taking severe beatings. When fifty members of the Veteran Reserve Corps arrived on the scene, a hail of bricks and stones killed one of the soldiers almost immediately. The Corps fired blanks at the crowd. The intention had been to frighten them into submission, but the effect was the exact opposite, serving only to enrage the rioters further. They fired a second volley into the crowd; this time they used actual ammunition and killed multiple men and women. The mob temporarily shuddered backward but then recovered and came rampaging forward, overcoming the soldiers and tearing their guns away from them. The Corps went into retreat, leaving behind dead or injured brethren who were promptly and quite literally torn to pieces by the mob.

Through the afternoon, heavily armed crowds numbering in the thousands laid siege to and destroyed both the State Armory and the Eighteenth police precinct. At the State Armory, scores of people on both sides of the law died in the fighting. Even more died after someone set the building on fire. Rioters died choking on the smoke, trapped in the fire, or leaping to the sidewalk. By the time the fire died, and the Armory lay in ashes, "more than fifty baskets and barrels of human bones were carted from the ruins and buried in Potter's Field." All over the city, rioters chased African Americans through the streets, murdering three before nightfall. As the sun set, multiple city blocks which had been sturdy and peaceful at sunrise, were now smoldering cinders. The State Armory was no more. Rioters surrounded the *New York Times* and *New York Tribune* buildings. Others destroyed or looted shops and businesses. Corpses of rioters, policemen, and innocent bystanders lay in the streets all over Manhattan. Poor families were homeless. The upper classes were sneaking away by the thousands and by any means available, most by train. Those African Americans who could afford it also understandably fled the city in droves. Meanwhile, none the wiser, Governor Seymour slept peacefully in a New Jersey bed.

The Governor was astonished by the chaos and destruction before him when he finally arrived in New York City via a ferry from Jersey City on July 14. A cacophony of warlike sounds echoed around him. Smoke and flames filled the skies. Seymour shook hands with county supervisor William Tweed, who had braved the chaos to meet him on the pier and brief the Governor on what was happening. Tweed had been in the streets for most of the prior day and night trying to prevent all Manhattan from burning down, in some cases successfully convincing angry crowds to leave the abandoned homes of the wealthy unmolested. Mayor Opdyke had abandoned City Hall, holing up in the St. Nicholas Hotel. The police were disorganized, leaderless, fatigued, and injured. Rioters had destroyed telegraph wires, crippling any hope the Governor had of requesting outside military aid. All kinds of horrific and paranoid rumors filled his ears from citizens and assistants. He soon learned that citizens of individual communities had taken up arms to defend their families and homes against the advancing rioters, threatening to provoke a miniature Civil War. Confronted with all of this, Governor Seymour made his way as quickly as possible to the St. Nicholas Hotel, which lay virtually in the center of Manhattan, under guard from Tweed and a few others. There the Governor spent an hour in indecisive panic.

Finally, Seymour settled upon a strategy. He left the hotel and risked his own safety by walking twelve blocks on foot to City Hall, Mayor Opdyke, District Attorney A. Oakey Hall, county supervisor William Tweed, and other political officials behind him. As he did so, policemen, militiamen, and citizens began to also follow. A mob had surrounded City Hall all night. The police and militiamen provided protection for the Governor as he made his way up the front steps and turned to face the crowd. Seymour appeared calm and confident, but Opdyke was frightened to the point of visibly trembling. In a brief but compassionate speech, Seymour told the crowd that he would ask the federal government to suspend the draft and promised that it would not be enforced until a court ruling was passed down as to the validity of the Enrollment Act. "I will take care that justice is done you," he assured them, "and that your families shall be fully protected." He then ordered the nearby militiamen to lay down their arms. In a short time, the pacified crowd at City Hall had dispersed, returning to their homes or joining other rioters at other key points in the city.[298]

As news of the Governor's speech spread through the city, many of the "respectable" citizens who remained were disgusted. To them, the politician had betrayed the rule of law to satisfy looters, murderers, and arsonists. The Governor and most of his party subsequently returned to the safety of St. Nicholas Hotel, but one man remained in the streets, determined to do what he could. This was William Tweed, recently made the chairman of Tammany Hall that January but already referred to as the Boss by Tammany's inner circle. His presence in the streets for the past day and night was important to the city and to Tammany in particular; many in the crowd were immigrants who provided the constituency which kept Tammany in control of city politics. He himself came from the Seventh Ward, also home to many of the rioters. To them, Bill Tweed could be trusted. He understood their struggle and their anger. Face to face with rioters, insisting that he sympathized with their cause, he and his men urged calm and patience, which at times successfully prevented more death and destruction. Still, mayhem continued to reign over Manhattan clear through to Thursday, when the combined efforts of Union troops from the Gettysburg battlefield, Army officers, police officers, volunteer citizens, and city employees personally led by Tweed himself made a forceful, unified surge through the city, sending the spent and disorganized rioters back to their homes.

It had been the worst riot America had ever seen. Entire city blocks were simply gone. The air still smelled of smoke. The wealthy of Gramercy Park returned to vandalized and looted houses. Homeless poor people found shelter wherever they could, usually in the open streets. Somewhere around one hundred people from all sections of New York's society were dead, their bodies in piles along the city's waterfront, including at least eleven lynched black men and two black children. Army canon fire had killed a mother and her daughter. Rioters later captured the officer responsible for giving the order to fire the canons. They dragged him through the streets and tortured him for hours until he died. Now U.S. Army soldiers marched in patrols throughout New York City, a reminder of what was effectively martial law.[299]

---

[298] Ackerman, 16
[299] Hotaling, 41; Ackerman, 23; Stiles, 381; Golway, 96-98

Though much of the city's institutions and neighborhoods were in shambles, if anyone had emerged a hero of the New York City Draft Riots, it was William Marcy Tweed. In the aftermath, the city and its politics seemed at an impasse. Mayor Opdyke was at odds with Senator Seymour over the draft. Seymour was not able to get a suspension of the Enrollment Act out of President Lincoln, failing in his promise to the rioters. Republicans, nativists, and merchants demanded the arrest and punishment of those same rioters, amounting to thousands of people. Tammany Hall and their immigrant constituents warned of more violence if the draft continued or if the authorities made any incursions into immigrant wards to try and make arrests.

To avoid violence, satisfy the grievances of the poor, and still get the Army the men it needed, Boss Tweed and fellow county supervisor Orison Blunt drafted a plan for compromise which would allow the draft to continue, but provided ways in which some of the men of the lower classes could avoid conscription without having to come up with the impossible $300 requirement. The plan exempted firemen, policemen, and militiamen, while other working-class men who had families would be reviewed on a case-by-case basis. A bi-partisan County Substitute and Relief Committee would judge each case, with Opdyke, Blunt, and Tweed among the membership. Tweed and Blunt would meanwhile supply the Army with new recruits, offering the recruits sign-on bonuses of three hundred dollars each, paid out of the New York City treasury. A special two-million-dollar fund created from bonds sold on Wall Street would alleviate the resultant strain on the treasury.

The only problem was that the New York Board of County Supervisors to which Tweed and Blunt belonged had no control over the rules of the federal Enlistment Act or how the government instituted it in New York City. That Fall, Tweed and Blunt took a trip to Washington D.C., where they met with Secretary of War Edwin Stanton and U.S. Army Provost Marshal General James Fry, successfully selling the deal. They returned the heroes of the New York poor, lauded in newspapers and congratulated by the people in the streets as tensions subsided.

Most importantly, this move strengthened Tweed's hold over the city's huge immigrant population. Since he and some of his cronies were on the board reviewing who would go or not go into the Army, it helped to be on his good side if they drew your name. This meant that avoiding conscription might not mean simply having extenuating circumstances to make your case convincing, but it could also mean doing favors for Tweed or otherwise proving your loyalty to Tammany. Likewise, someone who earned his ire or disrespect could expect little mercy should their name come up before the board. Immigrants and others in the working classes felt reassured that he was a trustworthy politician genuinely on their side, and they were elated when Tammany inevitably elected him their Grand Sachem (the organization's highest position) in August.

Cleverly, Tweed also took measures to please those who still cried for justice against the rioters. Two of Tweed's most loyal political cronies, District Attorney A. Oakey Hall and Judge John Hoffman held very public trials that put dozens of alleged rioters in prison. He was careful to put pro-Union rhetoric in his newspaper interviews and public speeches. He was the master behind massive, patriotic recruitment drives for Army volunteers, making sure the public was aware of the large numbers of recruits he had brought to the Union cause (though Army officials routinely complained about the quality of men that New York sent their way). By the war's end, William Tweed was effectively the unchallenged master of all New York City.

———

John Morrissey seems to have taken no direct part in the Civil War Draft Riots of 1863. According to biographer Jack Kofoed, he came down to the riotous metropolis from Troy on the third day and holed himself up in an office on Twenty-Fourth Street, which he had boarded up for protection. There he lunched with one Colonel Edward Jardine, an Army officer whom John had met in Saratoga, and who was determined to assist the city with putting down the riots by any means necessary. Later that afternoon, Jardine would be one of the leaders of a band of two hundred current and former soldiers armed with two howitzers who marched against the large group of rioters on First Avenue. Jardine's would be badly wounded in the fighting and left for dead by those of his surviving men still able to flee. He watched helplessly as rioters proceeded to beat two other wounded men nearby to death. One of the rioters recognized Jardine as a friend of Morrissey's and convinced the murderous mob to leave him be. Some good citizens brought him to a surgeon. Though he later recovered from his wounds, his injuries meant the end of his military career. This story is the only specific mention of John Morrissey related to the Civil War Draft Riots, but their impact upon his life and role in New York City would be important.[300]

No sooner had the riots in New York ended than similar unrest, though on a much smaller scale, broke out in Troy, again in reaction to the draft order. Rioters attacked the *Troy Times* building and accosted several black citizens. When a mob arrived at one of John's taverns, the Troy House, insisting that the black waiters be handed over, the proprietor, only just returned from witnessing the chaos in New York, presented himself instead. Morrissey told the crowd that his black employees had already fled

[300] Kofoed, 222; Asbury, *Gangs*, 150-151

for their lives, but that he "was at their service if they desired." For this, Morrissey received a blow from a brickbat, but seemed to not be badly hurt. The mob moved on, and the violence in Troy eventually subsided without nearly as much property damage and bloodshed as had been the case in the metropolis to its south.[301]

In August, newspapers listed "John Morrissey, pugilist" among those selected for the draft. The papers listed his address as 678 Broadway, but John received the news while attending to his broadening business interests in Saratoga. He notified a banker in his employ to find a replacement and offer $5,000 to the willing man. A George F. Eberley accepted the offer, allowing John to continue with his plans for Saratoga Springs undistracted by patriotism.[302]

———

Morrissey's growing number of gambling halls in New York City survived the Draft Riots unmolested, probably because most of them existed on the southern end of Manhattan, where many of the rioters lived. Most of the violence had happened in the Northern wards, the location for public buildings, private shops, and the homes of the wealthy. Morrissey had by this point been working hard to separate himself as much as possible from direct involvement in street-level activities like gangsterism, shoulder hitting, fighting, rioting, and drinking. Police arrested him in December after he beat up Yankee Sullivan's old friend Andy Sheehan (Sheehan was the alleged aggressor in this affray), but such encounters were no longer the norm. Names of men like John Petrie and Dad Cunningham, who had once been his inseparable companions, would cease to appear alongside his own in print, evidence that Morrissey was now seeking out a different class of companion. Though the nature of his gambling business required that he not lose touch completely with the man in the street, Morrissey now had ambitions of being accepted as a respectable gentleman worthy of the company of the wealthiest and most powerful men in the city or even the country. It was a tall order for a semi-literate man still regarded by the middle class as despicable for his criminal record and violent past.

The riots and the consequential rise of Tweed to uncontested power within Tammany provided an opportunity for Morrissey to make another step in the direction of true power as well. The old guard of New York politics with which Morrissey had associated himself in his twenties, men like Sixth Ward power broker Isaiah Rynders and ex-Mayor Fernando Wood were now either irrelevant to or absent from local politics. As he would always be able do in his life, Morrissey recognized that a change was

---

[301] *Albany Evening Journal*, July 16, 1863
[302] *Fort Edward Ledger*, August 21, 1863; *Mexico Independent*, August 27, 1863; *New York Herald*, August 21, 1863; *Daily Telegraph*, August 29, 1863; *Manhattan Nationalist*, September 13, 1863; *Birmingham Daily Post*, September 19, 1863; *New York World*, August 21, 1863

in order if he was to continue to flourish. Aligning himself firmly inside of what would later be known as the Tweed Ring provided him an opportunity to have a real say in Tammany politics, a role more relevant than causing havoc on the streets each Election Day.

Likewise, John knew he had to have something to bring to the table if Tweed was to make him part of his inner circle. His reputation on the street and his position as the unofficial boss of a legion of two-fisted cronies certainly represented part of that something. An 1862 article in the *New York Herald* describes a Democratic Council meeting at Mozart Hall, Fernando Wood's headquarters, intended to designate a Comptroller which broke into violence. Morrissey was present, "the center [sic] of a circle of admirers, who seemed to attach oracular import to every word which fell from his lips, and listened with eager interest to his opinions on the important subject of the Comptrollership." Such loyalty could pay dividends for pols like Tweed. [303]

John also knew that the best way to impress the Tammany leaders would be through election rigging, a topic in which they might trust he would have some expertise, thus making them more willing to pay attention. Years later, Tweed would testify in court as to Morrissey's prowess for organizing voter fraud, specifically that he had introduced a "repeating" strategy to the Tweed Ring which he had picked up during a trip to Philadelphia. By this means, Morrissey and his co-conspirators transported voters from one voting house to another on Election Day, voting under their real name once and false names on multiple other occasions. "As an organizer of repeaters," Tweed would later compliment Morrissey, "he had no superior." Having gotten his toe in the door as a shoulder-hitting youth, John Morrissey now intended to pull that door open and take a big step inside the corridors of power. [304]

---

[303] *New York Herald*, November 20, 1862
[304] Asbury, *Sucker's Progress*, 386

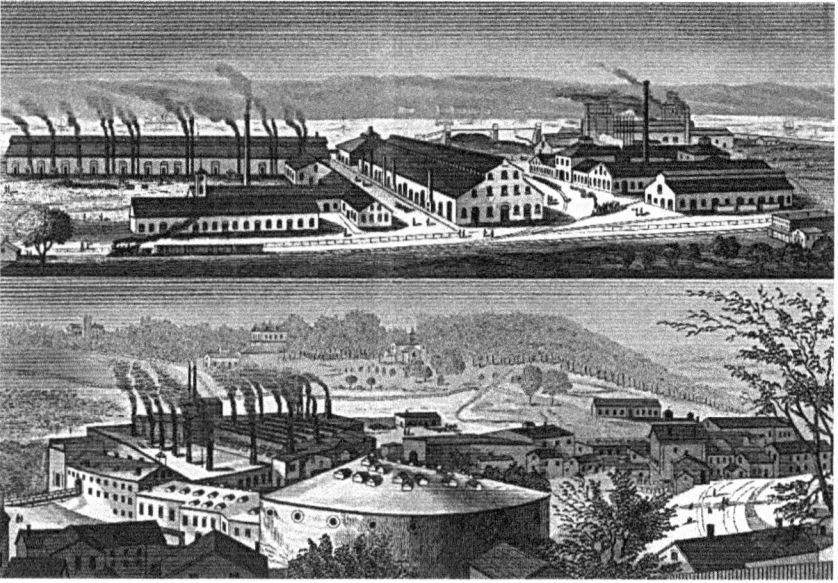

Troy's Burden Iron Works, where John Morrissey labored as a teen, 1876.

Yankee Sullivan, America's first boxing star, 1846.

A wealthy family goes slumming in the notorious Five Points with a police escort.
Frank Leslie's Illustrated Newspaper, 1885.

A typically crowded Five Points boarding house in a tenement cellar, 1872.

JOHN MORRISSEY,
Born February 5th 1831.
HEIGHT 6 FEET, WEIGHT 170 LBS

Beat Thompson, Aug. 31. 1852, 11 Rounds 16 min.
$ 2000 a side. _ California.
Beat Yankee Sullivan, Oct. 12. 1853, 37 Rounds 55 min.
$ 1000 a side. _ Boston Corners N.Y.

Beat John C. Heenan. __ "The Benicia Boy" Oct. 20.
1858, 11 Rounds, 22 min. $ 2500 a side.
Long Point Canada.

John Morrissey, pugilist, circa 1852.

Streetfighter William "Bill the Butcher" Poole, in whose murder Morrissey was implicated.

Newspapers blamed John Morrissey for the "Dead Rabbits Riot," *Frank Leslie's Illustrated Newspaper*, 1857.

JOHN C. HEENAN, THE CHAMPION OF AMERICA.
(THE BENICIA BOY.)
Born at West Troy New York, May 2 1835. Height 6 feet 1½ inches. Fighting weight from 192 to 195 lbs.

John "Benicia Boy" Heenan, of Troy, New York, who had known Morrissey for years before their famous ring battle, circa 1860.

John Morrissey (left) vs. John Heenan (right), Long Point, Canada, 1858.

John Heenan (left) vs. Tom Sayers (right),
the first fight for the Heavyweight Championship of the World, Fainborough,
England, 1860. Morrissey is standing facing the artist wearing the hat in Sayers's
corner.

Commodore Cornelius Vanderbilt, once the wealthiest man in America, and Morrissey's mentor on Wall Street.

Rioters burn the Colored Orphan Asylum during the New York Draft Riots, 1863.

John Morrissey, politician and gambler, 1865

Illustrator Thomas Nast accents the differences between two politicians: wealthy, educated Horace Greeley (left) and man of the streets John Morrissey (right). Notice "The Ring" snake emblem to the right of Morrissey, the first time the term appeared in print in reference to a Tammany Hall politician. *Harper's Weekly*, 1866.

James Fisk, Jr., the man arguably most responsible for Black Friday.
Harper's Weekly, 1869.

Morrissey's infamous Club House in Saratoga Springs, New York as it appeared in the early 20th century.

Susannah Morrissey, considered one of the great beauties of her time.

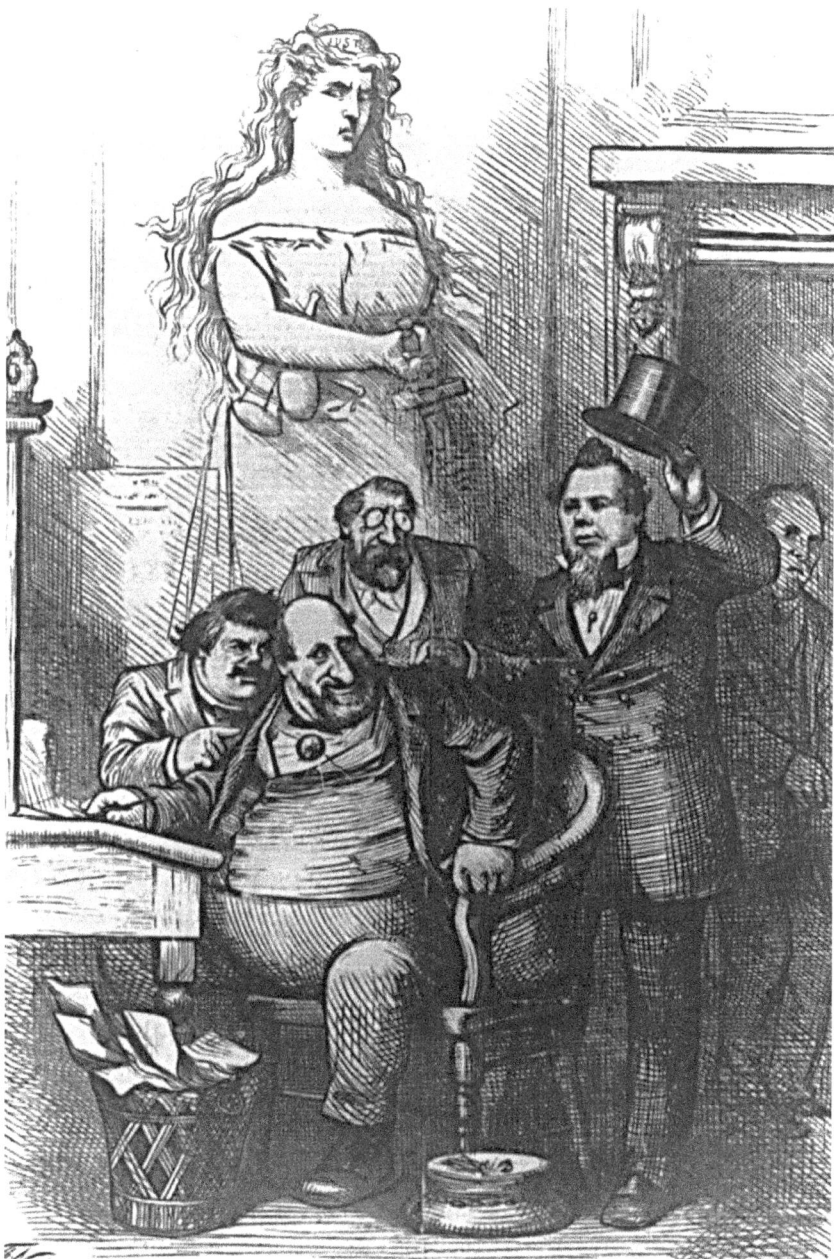

Sheriff Matthew Brennan (standing, right, raising his hat) arrests Boss William Tweed (sitting), along with Peter Sweeny (whispering in Tweed's ear) and A. Oakey Hall (standing behind Tweed). Lady Justice looks on, prepared to draw her sword, illustrated by Thomas Nast, *Harper's Weekly*, 1871.

"Hercules Morrissey." Morrissey became a favorite target of Thomas Nast's cartoons. Here he stands atop a defeated Boss Tweed (with a money bag for a head) while the Tweed-backed *Sun* and *World* newspapers look on. *Harper's Weekly*, 1873.

Honest John Kelly, Morrissey's rival for control of Tammany Hall and New York City.

Presidential candidate Samuel Tilden relied on Morrissey for Irish American votes.

"A Jewel Among Swine." Another Nast cartoon questions how low Morrissey sank in trying to get Tilden elected. *Harper's Weekly*, 1877

14.

Saratoga

While he was establishing himself on the perimeter of the Tweed Ring, John also furthered his status as a top figure in New York City gambling. He had parlayed his reputation into becoming master of the illegal "policy" game in Manhattan, a kind of lottery popular in poor urban communities where, for a fee, men and women would pick a three-digit number and hope that it was pulled in the daily drawing, for which they would receive a large portion of the pot. If run correctly and without controversy, policy was always a tremendously profitable enterprise for its boss. Morrissey used the firm of Charles H. Murray and Company as a proxy to handle the details of this illegal enterprise, but he was the major shareholder in the company.

Not long before the outbreak of the war, he purchased yet another gambling parlor at 818 Broadway, which was meant exclusively for the upper crust of New York's gamblers. One such sucker lost as much as $35,000 to the house in a single evening. A writer in 1868, while Morrissey was still owner, described it as "a favorite resort for many persons of good standing in society, and for 'the fancy' of New York…. The landlord is married, and very careful that everything is carried on in an orderly manner. Women are not admitted into the gaming rooms, or even into the parlors of the house. An elegant supper is served up, every evening, to frequenters and visitors." Likewise, another account insisted that "His table, attendants, cooking and company are exceeded by nothing on this side of the Atlantic." In the eight years that John Morrissey would run this establishment, it yielded him an estimated total profit of over $700,000.[305]

By 1861, John had ended his business partnership with noted gambler Matt Danser and gone into business alone, buying the already established gambling hall at 8 Barclay Street from Charles Ransom, yet another well-known gambler with whom Morrissey would enter into several business agreements in the years to come. The 8 Barclay Street purchase would prove the best business deal so far in Morrissey's life. Under his ownership, the hall flourished. He spared no expense in providing the lushest accommodations possible, hired private detectives to work security, and his notoriety as a prizefighter brought in sporting men and gamblers from

---

[305] Asbury, *Sucker's Progress*, 373 - 375, quoting anonymous, *Asmodeus in New York*; Smith, *Bulls*, 182

every level of society. In the five years that he owned this establishment, it would generate one million dollars in profits.[306]

By 1864, John allegedly had a financial stake in no less than sixteen gambling dens inside of New York City, just as his ambitions for Saratoga Springs had also solidified from dream into reality. In 1861, he had made his first business foray there by opening a gambling hall on Matilda Street, said to be a favorite of Army officers, as well as the gigolos who accompanied the well-to-do ladies frequenting the resort. Gambling was still technically illegal in Saratoga, but his experience running similar businesses down in New York City made him adept at ensuring that the proper authorities, as well as the people of Saratoga themselves, were happy to see his operation go smoothly. He bribed those who needed bribing, made generous (and very public) donations to local churches and charities, paid for the construction of a school, paid the necessary fees for young men to avoid conscription, stopped a woman's house from being foreclosed upon, and bought municipal bonds, all covered adequately by the press, and all ensuring gratitude among important folks of Saratoga, who could now be trusted to protect him against the moralists, middle class, and "old rich" who protested his presence.[307]

By 1864, many already regarded John as the resort's prime master of gambling. A New Orleans newspaper, under the title "Dark Side of Life at Saratoga," complained that "the vice of gambling has assumed a fearful magnitude at Saratoga.... Young men of respectability, officers of the army, men who at home are reported staid and untainted, are alike drawn into the gambling vortex, and in time are reduced the pecuniary and moral ruin." According to the writer, this vortex sucked the money of Saratoga's victims into the pockets of John Morrissey. Morrissey called this new establishment his Club House, but he was likely already making plans for another, even more decadent and resplendent Club House to be constructed soon, one that would become the crown jewel of his gambling empire in the years to come.[308]

––––––

During one of his increasingly frequent visits to Saratoga, John had managed to meet and make the acquaintance of "Commodore" Cornelius Vanderbilt, who was nothing less than the richest man in America. There is a story that Vanderbilt once won sixty thousand dollars in a single evening playing faro in one of Morrissey's gambling halls, certainly an event that would have brought the pair into contact with one another. Like Morrissey, Vanderbilt came from humble beginnings. He was born on Staten Island in

[306] Asbury, *Sucker's Progress*, 373; *National Republican*, August 1, 1864; *New York Herald*, May 2, 1878

[307] Hotaling, 64; *New York Sun*, May 2, 1878; *Daily Albany Argus*, August 9. 1871

[308] *Daily True Delta*, August 13, 1864

1794 and quit school at age eleven to work for his father, the owner of a ferry that operated in New York Harbor. With a one-hundred-dollar loan from his father, Cornelius purchased his own ferry and went into business for himself at just sixteen years of age. A boy with tremendous drive and ambition, he was uncommonly serious about his job, which caused other ferry captains to jokingly call the boy "Commodore," a nickname which remained with him long after his death.

Adept at business and the law, the young Cornelius eventually became the business manager for a steamboat company. In time, he would open his own line, making it one of the largest and most successful in or around New York City, as well as expanding into real estate. By the close of the 1830s, he was a wealthy man. Beginning with the Gold Rush of 1849, he capitalized on the craze by expanding his steamship business into the ocean and transporting people and goods from one side of the North American continent to the other.

Tall and strong, Vanderbilt had a run-in with Morrissey's old rival Yankee Sullivan back in 1844. Sullivan was calling himself the Champion of America then, his fight with Tom Hyer still five years off. He was also working as shoulder hitter for the Tammany Democrats. Vanderbilt, the fast-rising entrepreneur, had put together a nighttime parade in honor of Whig Party Presidential candidate Henry Clay, whom Sullivan's backers vehemently opposed. As Vanderbilt led the parade down Chatham Street on horseback, Sullivan and other Tammany hooligans charged out of a nearby watering hole intent on violence. Sullivan grabbed the reins of Vanderbilt's horse, intending to rip him off the steed. Instead, to the shock of the prizefighter and his cronies, Vanderbilt got himself down and proceeded to whip the feared pugilist where he stood, leaving him in a "nearly senseless condition" before proceeding on with the march.[309]

By 1859, Vanderbilt could see that the steam engine and continent-spanning railroads were to be the future of transportation, and he knew he had to plant his flag in that frontier if he expected to survive against his competitors. He began quietly buying stocks in the aging and struggling New York and Harlem Railroad at eight dollars a share, intending to slowly combine the company's tracks with other local railroads to expand their reach – and his – to even further distances without alerting rivals as to his plans. As a member of the Board of Directors for the Harlem line, Vanderbilt was able to position several of his other cronies in key positions and they in turn made him President of the company in May 1863. When word got out that the Commodore was buying stock in the Harlem line, most on Wall Street laughed incredulously. Undeterred in the least, Vanderbilt assured Morrissey and others that, "if properly managed, it will be as good property as there was in the state." As yet another means of finding real wealth and power for himself, Morrissey had been investing

---

[309] Renehan, 146; Bartles, 29, quoting Wheaton Joshua Lane in *Commodore Vanderbilt*

portions of his income from his gambling ventures in the New York Stock Exchange as early as 1861, but the New York and Harlem was his first major play at true stock market success.[310]

Inspired by the tremendous financial fortune made by mutual friend John J. Tobin in following Vanderbilt's past advice, Morrissey eagerly listened to the Commodore, buying shares in the New York and Harlem line. "Morrissey himself is one of the Commodore's favorites," noted Wall Street watcher James Knowles Medbery a few years later, and his friendship with the master investor inspired Morrissey's own natural competitiveness to gamble big in the stock market. Suddenly, Vanderbilt's fellow investors on Wall Street began noticing the presence of men with "strongly Celtic faces, sixth-warders by the cut of their jib," hanging about the city's financial centers.[311]

More than several of those Irish faces belonged to city officials who, aware of the fact that Harlem needed approval from them to lengthen their rail down Broadway (which would give the company access deeper into Manhattan and proximity to the city docks), hatched a plot against the Commodore and his company. Using this insider information, some of the city fathers had taken it upon themselves to purchase stocks in Harlem in 1863. As Vanderbilt biographer T.J. Stiles describes it:

> Their plan was simple: to sell Harlem short, *revoke* the Broadway franchise, then buy in at a profit after the price tumbled. They would use their official powers to destroy the share value of one of the city's largest companies and most important transit lines. The result would devastate the railroad's shaky credit as the price of its securities collapsed.

The plot backfired on June 25, 1863 when the ingenious Commodore caught the conspirators in a trap which not only saved the company, but further enriched him and ruined them. The financial genius set about cornering the market, picking up every share available from the brokers representing the aldermen and councilmen. "When the short-sellers went into the market to buy shares in order to deliver them to Vanderbilt's brokers, they would find none – and still less money," explains Styles. With one brilliant move thereafter called the Harlem Corner, Vanderbilt had become the undisputed master of the company with the fastest rising stock in the city.[312]

As a result of the Commodore's retaliation, John found himself at a loss of $70,000, though he had not gone in with the conspirators against Vanderbilt. The Commodore would have viewed this as collateral damage necessary to maintain his reputation and interests. Having only $50,000 at his disposal, John brought all of this to Vanderbilt's brokers and signed a

---

[310] Medbery, 163; Bartles, 29; Stiles, 371-375
[311] Medbery, 163; Bartles, 24 – 34
[312] Stiles, *Tycoon*, 375 - 376

note saying he was good for the remaining $20,000. He then presented himself personally to the Commodore, finding him at his horse stables. Vanderbilt expressed concern. "John, they tell me you lost heavily in Harlem. How much did you lose?"

Morrissey made no attempt to cover for himself. "About $80,000," he replied, "all I have in the world. I am now going to Saratoga, and merely want to say I have not come here to cry or make a poor face; I only wish when you have something good, that you will allow me to come in."

Vanderbilt loaned Morrissey $20,000, refusing to take a note in exchange. "If your word is not good," insisted the Commodore, "your note is certainly of no account."[313]

Vanderbilt himself was planning a trip to Saratoga. He was proud of his stable of horses there but, after arriving, was astonished when a faster horse passed his trotter on the street. The driver of that other horse was none other than John Morrissey, who was there investing the $20,000 loan from Vanderbilt into expanding his business interests in the resort. Intrigued by the magnificent horse, the Commodore later visited Morrissey at his stable and offered to buy the impressive animal. "No," Morrissey replied, "but I will give him to you!" The next day, Vanderbilt arrived at his stables to find the same horse there with a tag on it which read, "with the compliments of John Morrissey." "Had I sold the horse to Mr. Vanderbilt for a round sum," Morrissey later confided to an interviewer, "he would at once have concluded that I had no gratitude, and merely desired his acquaintance for selfish purposes."[314]

By January 1864, Morrissey's share in Harlem Railroad stocks had profited him a reported $250,000. However, 1864 brought a second threat to Vanderbilt's and Morrissey's Harlem interests, this time from within the company. Daniel Drew had been a rival of Vanderbilt's from their days running competing steamship companies. However, by the late 1850s, they had put their differences aside to combine their business skills in railroad investments, the Harlem line included. Drew was a director of Harlem when he perceived what he felt was an opportunity to pull off a coup and manipulate Harlem's stocks in a manner similar to that used by the city politicians the prior year. His plot proved as miserable of a failure as that of his predecessors, the Commodore again orchestrating a masterful plan to corner the market on the stocks.

As Morrissey later told it, in order to punish Drew and his failed co-conspirators, Vanderbilt subsequently intended to drive up the cost of the shares in Harlem to $1,000 each, to "break every man who was 'short of it,'" but Morrissey convinced him that to do so would profit nothing, and the Commodore decided to move on. In the end, Drew wound up paying

[313] *Wheeling Daily Intelligencer*, January 5, 1867
[314] Medbery, *Men*, 163-164; *Raftman's Journal*, October 17, 1866; *Wheeling Daily Intelligencer*, January 5, 1867

Vanderbilt one million dollars, and the railroad's board stripped him of his position. Meanwhile, the shares that the genius Vanderbilt had initially bought at eight dollars a share had peaked at $285 a share. Vanderbilt did not actually own all the stocks in the company, but he controlled nearly all of them. Most of the stocks he did not own had been bought up by his flunkies and friends, men he could trust to use their shares as he instructed, men like John Morrissey, who, thanks to Vanderbilt's advice, was on the right side of the struggle this time and benefitted greatly. His friends later told the papers that, within eighteen months, Morrissey's accounts enjoyed another $400,000 surge thanks to the Commodore's friendly advice.[315]

In return for Vanderbilt's generosity of information, Morrissey readily supplied his own. His establishments in Saratoga acted as a hub for stock information for the wealthy and powerful who frequented the resort. "He may be seen daily at the telegraph office in Congress Hall," wrote a correspondent from Saratoga, "during the hours when the New-York stock board is in session in electric communication with his broker on the subject [of railroad stocks] that is thought chiefly to interest him." At times, word reached Morrissey in one of his gambling halls of a rival's plot against Vanderbilt's interests, and John dutifully passed this information along to the Commodore.[316]

As he fended off attempts by rivals to subvert his plans for the Harlem line, Vanderbilt manipulated himself into unofficial control of the competing Hudson River Railroad and had negotiated a mutually successful agreement with the larger New York Central company. The genius investor's plans for dominion over the New York railroad system fell into place just as he planned.

Making friends with the Commodore was no small feat. Journalist Junius Henri Browne, a contemporary of Morrissey's, wrote of Vanderbilt, "Many fear, but few love him; nor has his course been such as to endear him to any very large number of people." Known to be deeply serious, highly competitive, and a bitter holder of grudges, Vanderbilt's closest relationships were either familial or fiscal in nature. However, he did enjoy socializing with an insular group of wealthy associates who shared his enthusiasm for competition, men with names like Belmont and Jerome. His obsession with winning at all costs made him partial to sports and those who won at sports. Thus, Morrissey's reputation as an undefeated champion prize-fighter was likely the first thing that endeared the notorious Irishman to the accomplished businessman.[317]

Morrissey's friendship and influence over the Commodore instigated the rumor that Morrissey was behind the fall of John Tobin from the

---

[315] *Sonoma County Journal*, January 8, 1864; *Wheeling Daily Intelligencer*, January 5, 1867; *New York Sun*, May 2, 1878; Stiles, *Tycoon*, 394-397

[316] *New York World*, July 12, 1865

[317] Browne, 333

Presidency of the Hudson River Railroad's board. As the story went, Tobin was unable to immediately come up with the $25,000 he had lost after an unlucky night at Morrissey's gaming tables. Morrissey, in recognition of a friendship with Tobin, gave him a week to come up with the funds. After a week passed, Tobin failed to present himself, forcing Morrissey to go looking for him. Once tracked down, Tobin said he would not pay. Indignant, Morrissey spread word of Tobin's refusal to pay money he owed around the financial centers of the city, and the story reached the ears of the Commodore, who had just recently become the main stockholder in the Hudson River Railroad. Less than a week later, or so the story goes, Tobin handed in his resignation to the railroad's board.[318]

―――――

Their friendship and business relationship now well established, the Commodore introduced Morrissey to a class of extremely prosperous businessmen and politicians, some of whom would join them in railroad investments and other future business ventures, including attorneys William Travers and Leonard Jerome, political heavyweights August Belmont, John Hunter, Erastus Corning, and James Marvin, and an ambitious young investor named Jay Gould.[319]

Most, if not all these men were frequenters of the luxury hotels at Saratoga Springs and also fans of horse breeding and trotting (Jay Gould would have been the lone holdout, having no taste for the vulgarities of sporting culture.). Morrissey himself had been betting on horse racing and buying horses at least since the late 1850s, some of his larger losses appearing in newspapers around the country. The frequent sight of Morrissey racing his own harnessed horses with his new, well-placed friends in amateur trots down Harlem Lane likely unnerved the blue bloods of the neighborhood. As a relative of Jerome's later recalled, "Well-bred folks disapproved but could not resist watching as the suave intruder with the broken nose matched his horses in Harlem Lane against those of Vanderbilt, Jerome, and Belmont."[320]

In Saratoga, horse trotting (or harnessed racing) had been a popular entertainment for a time; the famed "Old Gray Mare" Lady Suffolk had caused a sensation when she first raced at the brand new trotting course there in August, 1847. However, horse trotting's allure had faded nationwide during the 1850s "because of the imposters and swindlers connected to it." Actual thoroughbred (non-harnessed) horse racing, as an organized sport, was virtually non-existent at Saratoga and indeed the entire North. John Morrissey had been looking for an opportunity to somehow

[318] *Burlington Daily Times*, July 11, 1865
[319] Bartles, 24 - 34
[320] Bartles, 33, quoting Anita Leslie

make a fortune at the resort, and his friends' interest in horses provided him a means of doing just that.[321]

For years now, he had dreamed of doing something special with Saratoga, and of ingratiating himself with the 'fancy' of the town. Now a more specific inspiration had come to him. As the man himself later told it, "[I saw] that the racing stock of the South was nearly extinct, owing to the horses having been killed in the cavalry. Said I: 'Them people will return to Saratoga as in former years, and bring their horses, when they can revive and reimport them. I will anticipate the time and buy a track.'"[322]

In May 1863, John placed advertisements in all the major New York papers, as well as the popular sporting rag *The Spirit of the Times*, and the local *Daily Saratogian*. Thoroughbred races featuring the best horses from both the United States and Canada were to be held at the largely forgotten Saratoga Trotting Course that August. He put up $2,700 of his own money to lease the grounds, which were about one mile from the town. Though the stables featured a gorgeous view of the valley below, the track itself was not well-suited to a thoroughbred race, nor was it an ideal spot for a large spectator event. Designed for harness racing back in 1847, the track was too narrow and too short, and the turns dangerously tight. Buildings, trees, and plants obscured much of the view of the track from the bleachers. However, it was the best option Morrissey had for putting on the event anywhere near Saratoga.

Anticipation for the first major thoroughbred races in the North spread to the press. Interestingly, the *New York Times* reported that "to the great credit of Mr. John Morrissey, the proprietor, gambling will not be permitted inside the Course." That the king of New York gambling would forbid its practice at a race which he himself had organized was of course a blatant falsehood, and the writer of the article probably knew it. But all parties also recognized that it was important to give off the image of respectability to attract some elements from New York City.[323]

For all his gambling interests, John was not a bookmaker. He left that to others. However, he did act as a stakeholder for the larger bets on the races in Saratoga, charging a five to fifteen percent rate to do so. The man who handled most of the actual betting at Saratoga was Dr. Robert Underwood, an Irish Jew who came up from Lexington, Kentucky. His official occupations were veterinarian and horse breeder. Today, historians regard Dr. Underwood as the father of modern American bookmaking. While in Saratoga, Underwood, "a little fellow, with a pleasant, red face, and queer, cracked voice," ran his operation discreetly but profitably out of the

---

[321] Hotaling, 26-27, Kofoed, 228
[322] *Chicago Daily Tribune*, August 1, 1874
[323] *New York Times*, July 29, 1863; Bartels, 38

basement of the United States Hotel, which was conveniently near the first gambling house Morrissey had purchased there.[324]

Come August 3, the opening day of the scheduled four days of races (less than a month after the New York City Draft Riots), an estimated 3,000 people paid one dollar each to attend, ensuring that the promoter would make back his investment. Many were New Yorkers and members of the "turf crowd," a horse-obsessed subculture not unlike the "sporting men" who obsessed over prizefighting. As it had previously been an exclusive resort catering to only the wealthiest Americans, most attendees had never set eyes on Saratoga before. On first arriving by train, these newcomers marveled at Saratoga's main thoroughfare, Broadway, which was far different from its claustrophobic and sin-ridden namesake in Manhattan Saratoga's Broadway was "a canyon flanked by magnificent elms and gargantuan hotels and jammed with men in expensive black broadcloth and women in the latest fashions." Other than Morrissey himself, the most noticed men present were William H. Vanderbilt and Cornelius J. Vanderbilt (sons of the Commodore), as well as John Clay (son of onetime presidential candidate Henry Clay) and wealthy investor Leonard Jerome.[325]

The official listing declared the opening race as being for one mile (one lap around the course, which in fact was 297 yards short of a mile) for three-year-olds, the prize for the winner being $1,000. Initially eight horses were slated to complete and post a $200 entry fee. However, six of the teams backed out and paid the $50 forfeit fee because they considered the level of competition too great. The two remaining competitors were the colt Captain Moore and a filly, Lizzy W., each considered an excellent match the other. This inaugural heat began at 11:30 a.m. and Captain Moore took the early lead, only to eventually lose steam, allowing Lizzy W. to pass. On the backstretch, Captain Moore rallied to pull up even with and eventually win narrowly over Lizzy W. However, the filly got revenge on the following two heats, winning their matchup overall.[326]

Morrissey had one of his own colts, named John B. Davidson, in the second race. He had bought the horse from John Clay for $3,000. John B. Davidson would be running for two miles against Thunder, an undefeated horse who had been one of the main attractions for the event. The fact that Morrissey had hired Gilbert "Gilpatrick" Patrick, one of the nation's most accomplished riders, to jockey John B. Davidson managed to make the promoter's horse the favorite in the betting over the unbeaten opponent. Two fillies, Sympathy (older sister of Lizzy W.) and Echo, would also compete, but thoroughbred insiders thought the true match to be between the colts.[327]

---

[324] Schwartz, *Roll*, 326; *Daily Albany Argus*, August 26, 1869
[325] *New York Times*, July 29, 1863; Bartels, 38; Mooney, 136; Hotaling, 42-44
[326] Bartels, 24 and 38-41
[327] Bartels, 41-42

Thunder took the lead at the outset and widened it through much of the rest of the race. However, his inexperienced jockey had pushed him too hard, and Thunder tired dreadfully on the backstretch, allowing both John B. Davidson and Sympathy to catch up. In the final strides, all three horses were neck and neck, but it was Sympathy who scored the upset by crossing the finish line first, with John B. Davidson taking second and Thunder third. Echo pulled in last.

Three more days of racing between some of the best-known horses in the nation followed. Most of the races were competitive and entertaining. The only blemish had come on the final day when the handlers of Thunder, a heavy betting favorite, had to pull him from a race after suspicion arose that someone had fed the horse a poisoned apple the prior evening. Still, the event was a massive success by any sporting standards of the day. National newspapers covered it. Between all four days, a total of 15,000 spectators paid for the one-dollar tickets, garnering its organizer a significant profit.[328]

Morrissey's financial success at putting on the first major thoroughbred races in the North at Saratoga Springs convinced him and his friends that the resort was ready for more – and so were their balance sheets. Thus, just days later, the first official meeting of the newly chartered Saratoga Racing Association took place. Morrissey's less than savory reputation with the public meant that more respectable names had to be the nominal leaders of the group, at least on paper. During the two-hour meeting, they elected attorney William Travers as President, with Leonard Jerome, the so-called "King of Wall Street" (and grandfather to Winston Churchill) as Vice President. Jockey John Purdy became "second vice president." Others on the executive committee included Vanderbilt, his son-in-law George Osgood, stable owner John Hunter, New York Central Railroad boss Erastus Corning, hotelier and congressman James Marvin, riverboat owner John Davidson (in whose honor the horse had been named), and Saratoga's own John White. Years later, Morrissey would estimate that the united wealth of the members of the Saratoga Racing Association amounted to more than one hundred million dollars.[329]

Because he had so successfully pulled off the prior event, and in consideration for his experience as a gambling hall operator, the executive committee made Morrissey the unofficial manager of the Association and its projects. "Much credit is due to the lessee for the energy he displayed in the outset, in originating the plan of the operations," read an article in the *Spirit of the Times*; "but his only connection with the club, and the only one he desires, will be in an executive capacity." In this role, he would be the man truly running things at Saratoga Springs from behind the scenes.[330]

---

[328] Bartels, 47-48
[329] Bartles, 48; Hotaling, 48-49; *Chicago Daily Tribune*, August 1, 1874
[330] Hotaling, 50

Given the title of secretary but acting as a sort of consultant and assistant in managing the establishment and running of the new course was Charles Wheatley, the experienced secretary and manager of a track in Lexington, Kentucky, where thoroughbred racing had already been popular for decades. His advice, support, and management skills would be invaluable to making sure things progressed properly and efficiently. The Association paid Wheatley $1,200 annually.[331]

Aside from memberships and positions, the committee also settled upon the establishment of a new track, better suited for thoroughbred races and large crowds, to be located across from the original on Union Avenue. Toward this end, Morrissey personally handled the collection of $20,600 from among the Association members to purchase the necessary 125 acres of land and construct the course and its accommodations. Vanderbilt contributed $3,000 of the funding. For his work on the purchase, for his management of the track, and for his own financial contribution, Morrissey would receive one-third share of the track's income, making him the largest stakeholder. The Association also purchased the original trotting course for just over $7,000.[332]

Things proceeded smoothly and quickly on the project, and within just a couple of months workers had already laid out, leveled, and fenced the track, with the grandstand completed. Morrissey and the other Association members were so confident of the completion and success of the new course that in December they published advertisements for four more days of races to take place the following August.

With operations going so well in Saratoga, John bided his time before the next year's event by looking in on and expanding his interests in New York City. His luxury gambling hall at 8 Barclay Street was to this point the crown jewel of his growing gambling empire, but he soon turned his property on West Twenty-Fourth Street into an even more palatial venue. With a $50,000 investment from fellow sporting men Price McGrath and John Chamberlin, he opened what the *New York Sun* later described as, "the most successful game ever established in the city." As one visitor marveled:

> The halls are fitted with superb furniture and appointments. On the frescoed and gilded walls are grouped copies of gems of modern and ancient art. Couches, divans and lounges are scattered about, heaped with cushions of purple, green, gold and crimson. Upon the marble tables are vases of alabaster or Bohemian glass of every hue, and quaint jars of porcelain. The lamps are veiled until their lights softly float in the air. The keepers of the faro banks deal cards from ornamental silver boxes.[333]

---

[331] Bartles, 34 & 48
[332] Bartels, 48-49; Riess, 19
[333] *New York Sun*, May 2, 1878

A reporter in 1871, taking a tour of the gambling dens on or near Broadway, called the West Twenty-Fourth Street house, "probably the most successful institution of its kind in the city," warning that it's tables were a "swindle for strangers, but fair for those who know the game." Within two years of the house's 1864 opening, John and his partners divided $800,000 in profits.[334]

———

Considering his interests, properties, and accounts, John Morrissey was worth an estimated total of $500,000 in 1864, at age thirty-three. His annual income for that year was $50,000. This was nowhere near the wealth enjoyed by his millionaire friends in Saratoga and Wall Street. However, it was a tremendous sum for a man who had come to New York fifteen years earlier owning little more than the clothes on his back. Morrissey was proud of his rise and not ashamed to flaunt his newfound prosperity. He constructed a four-story home in Troy for his father. He began to cultivate different images for himself, dependent upon locale and the character of his associates in that locale. Matthew Hale Smith, a New Yorker contemporary of Morrissey's, and no fan of his, noticed that the ex-prizefighter dressed differently between Saratoga and New York City, to give off different impressions. At the resort, Morrissey wore bright suits and gaudy jewelry, giving off a showiness that embarrassed those more accustomed to wealth. In New York City, he dressed much more conservatively but not without style, wanting to give off the airs of a responsible businessman, yet still clearly wanting attention. Wrote Hale:

> Now, John Morrissey at Saratoga, in his white flannel suit, huge diamond rings, and pin containing brilliants of the first water, and of immense size; tall of stature, a powerful-looking fellow, walking quietly about the streets, or lounging at the hotels, but seldom speaking, is not a bad-looking man. Seen in New York in his clerical black suit, a little too flashy to be a minister, yet among bankers, merchants, or at the Stock Board he would pass very well as one of the solid men of the city.

Even Hale, who always saw Morrissey as a cancer on the morals of his fellow New Yorkers, had to admit that Morrissey cultivated an impressive (if to Hale's mind deceptive) image.[335]

———

In February 1864 John became desperately ill from a bacterial skin infection called erysipelas. Within forty-eight hours of infection, those

[334] Riess, 24; Kofoed, 174; *New York Tribune*, December 16, 1871
[335] Riess, 20; Smith, 180-181; *New York Herald*, July 6, 1865; *National Republican*, August 1, 1864; *Times-Picayune*, June 9, 1865

stricken with the illness can start to experience high fevers, chills, fatigue, headaches, and vomiting. The skin can develop swellings, lesions, rashes, and even necrosis. Erysipelas was seriously life-threatening in the nineteenth century, and reports spread that John Morrissey's days were numbered. However, after a few weeks of terrible sickness, he began to recover and announced his eagerness to return to business.[336]

John was not the only notable ex-prizefighter in a battle for his life that year. Tom Hyer had lived a life of debauchery that made the young John Morrissey seem like a teetotaler by comparison. Although married with children, he was an admitted frequenter of prostitutes, and bragged about consuming as much as a dozen alcoholic drinks a day. As a result of such excesses, he had transformed over the past decade from a man admired as Young America, a virtually flawless physical specimen, into a forty-five-year-old invalid "leaning on crutches, almost doubled up, as helpless as a child, haggard, ill-clad, and never free from pain." His old friend Robert Roosevelt was shocked to find the once "straight as a spear" former athlete "crippling about, broken, bent, an old man." Having avoided the prize ring since his 1849 battle with the late Yankee Sullivan, Hyer had tried his hand as a saloon owner and manager, but with far less success than Morrissey. By 1964, he was destitute and clearly headed toward death. Friends held at least two benefits that year to get him enough money on which to live. It is not likely Morrissey, with whom Hyer had carried out a prolonged rivalry, attended either of these. John Poole, brother of Tom's late friend Bill the Butcher, organized the last one, which took place on June 21 at the Stuyvesant Institute. It would be Hyer's last public appearance. As the crowd cheered him repeatedly, Tom raised his cane in acknowledgement but did not speak. Four days later, he died in his bed. A coroner proclaimed cardiac dropsy his cause of death, but also noted that "the liver was very much diseased."[337]

It does not appear that John Morrissey attended his old rival's funeral. However, he was the first to propose that a fund for Hyer's widow and mother. John started the collection with a $250 contribution but was unable to collect much more from his associates, the total sum given to the two grieving ladies coming to somewhere around $500.[338]

―――――

That same month, Morrissey traveled to Paterson, New Jersey to attend the Jersey Derby, where a much-anticipated race between three-year-old colts Kentucky and Norfolk, half-brothers by the legendary sire Lexington, was to take place. There he fell victim to a scheme by jockey, gambler, and

---

[336] healthline.com, accessed 7/31/2019; *Alexandria Gazette*, February 16, 1864; *Daily True Delta*, March 5, 1964

[337] James, *Hyer*, 26; *New York Times*, June 27, 1864; Lewis, 51, 59-60; Gammie, 294

[338] James, *Hyer*, 26

con man James Eoff. For days leading up to the race, Eoff had been making a tour of gambling halls and saloons, convincing local sports that he was the owner of Norfolk, the favorite in the race. Claiming dissatisfaction with the betting and prize, Eoff insinuated that Norfolk would not start the race. This generated wild speculation and rumors within the sporting community in the days and hours leading up to the race. Eoff then presented himself to Morrissey and, failing to mention that he had been the source of the rumors, offered to bet $6,000 against Morrissey's $2,000 that Norfolk would win the race, along with a separate bet that Norfolk would start the race, with Morrissey betting that he wouldn't. Morrissey, feeling he had the inside track based on the rumors from those supposedly "in the know," took the bets.

Seeing Norfolk ready to start the race and witnessing a mad rush to bet on the favorite, Morrissey suddenly understood the scam to which he had just fallen prey and the street-level ruffian in him exploded to the surface. Incensed, John made sure all nearby were aware of his opinions about Eoff. "The roars of the enraged 'tiger' when he found himself enmeshed… shook the very earth at Paterson," reported the *Spirit of the Times*. Meanwhile, Norfolk came out "like a bullet from the jump" and never gave up the lead, winning the race. By scamming Morrissey and others, Eoff walked away from the Jersey Derby with an estimated $20,000.[339]

Despite his fury at the ruse, Morrissey appears to have regained his composure well enough to keep himself from destroying Eoff physically. However, the Passaic County Agricultural Association, the organizers of the Jersey Derby, did call the jockey to appear before them to account for himself. After he gave a surprisingly candid confession, the Association banned Eoff from the Paterson track for life. Because one of Eoff's co-conspirators in the scheme had been one of Norfolk's handlers, the Association also suspended the horse indefinitely.

As John organized the 1864 races at Saratoga, he left Norfolk off the list of horses to compete, doubtless a bit of revenge. Noting this, Eoff composed a letter to the *Spirit of the Times*, adding insult to the injury, "Mr. Morrissey probably knows that he has been beaten out of his money and I guess that is all he knows, only that he has had me and Norfolk, the best race-horse he ever saw, without any cause, only feeling." The con man's words might have been bold, but he knew enough to not show his face around Morrissey after publishing them. Eoff disappeared from the thoroughbred racing scene and returned to working as a jockey in harness races.[340]

The August 1864 races at Saratoga, opening with the first annual Travers Stakes, were a tremendous success. *The New York Times* marveled at the new accommodations erected in the previous year. "Neither pains nor

---

[339] Bartles, 55-58
[340] Bartles, 63

expense have been spared to render it perfect in all its departments," raved the writer. "The spacious grandstand is a model of elegance, with its covered balconies, broad stairways, retiring and refreshment rooms, ladies' boudoirs and every needful convenience." Notably present was a large contingent of women, who enjoyed the "champagne on draft" distributed in the stands, not to mention the ice cream, soda water, and lemonade from the concessions. That Vanderbilt and the rest of the rich and powerful members of the Saratoga Racing Association were there, along with plenty of other high-placed sporting men, businessmen, and politicians, established Saratoga as the fashionable place to be each year, come racing season. The President's son Robert Lincoln was there, as were aristocratic sports enthusiast William B. Astor, immensely wealthy wholesaler and real estate investor Alexander Stewart, the Commodore's sons William and Cornelius, the Commodore's railroad investment rival Daniel Drew, and a host of people with last names like Roosevelt, Rockefeller, and Delano. Morrissey's partners in the Saratoga Racing Association now knew they could trust him to efficiently manage their interests in Saratoga and make them - and himself - a heap of money year upon year.[341]

―――――

Susan Morrissey often joined her husband in Saratoga. In time, they would become permanent residents. Reveling in their newfound wealth, they were together at the center of the well-to-do sporting society there. John would hold court over his casino, dressed in a "tall beaver hat, a swallow-tailed coat, striped trousers, patent leather boots, and white kid gloves with a $5,000 diamond on his shirt and smaller diamonds in his cuff links." For all John's attention-grabbing attire, those who knew him in this period of his life described him as sober and quiet, changed from the drunken braggart of just a few years earlier. A Boston reporter visiting one of Morrissey's gambling halls during the 1865 racing season observed that, "Mr. Morrissey is looked upon here by many persons as a sort of Napoleon who, by suppressing, for his own advantage, the minor and meaner descriptions of 'sporting men,' is himself a benefactor of society." Susan was described as a "a beautiful woman with great sparkling black eyes, and queenly form, and a dashing manner," by one writer, and a "handsome woman, who attends the balls, but has no social passion" by another. She was so elegantly dressed that she was part of the allure for tourists, who, upon arrival in one of Morrissey's establishments there, would often ask where they could find Mrs. Morrissey, for no other reason than to simply marvel at her attire and jewelry.[342]

[341] *New York Times*, August 4, 1864; Hotaling, 5-53, 67
[342] Bartles, 64; Hotaling, 65; *Chicago Daily Tribune*, August 1, 1874; *New York Semi-Weekly Express*, August 11, 1865, quoting *Boston Poet*

When not engaged in ostentatious public displays of wealth and fashion, the couple continued their long-standing tradition of spending their time at home engaged in self-improvement. Susan (or "Baby," as John affectionately called her) had been teaching her husband how to read and write since they were first married, roughly a decade earlier. These kinds of rudimentary skills long since accomplished, they both began to study other subjects which would improve their minds and conversation. Susan studied during the day, while her husband was out in the world seeing to his businesses and finances. When John returned home in the evenings, she would then instruct him in what she had learned. Topics ranged from current events in Europe, famous speeches, and history, to the writings of men such as De Quincey and Carlyle. When she would begin a new subject, John often found it difficult to concentrate, complaining, "Now, this is no good for me, Susie." In time, though, he would warm up to the topic and his interest in learning would outpace hers "with indomitable perseverance," she would later remember.[343]

One evening, Susan was engaged in the difficult task of getting John to understand fractions. Her frustrated pupil eventually threw his work on the ground, exclaiming, "I don't care about all these fractions – they're only part of a thing anyway! What's the use of all this study, Susie?"

Mrs. Morrissey was not shocked. She knew math was particularly difficult for him, and she was by now used to his tantrums. "John," she calmly replied, "if you don't beat those fractions, you will never go to Congress."

For a moment, John was confused. He had never mentioned such ambitions to his wife. In fact, to that point, he had never harbored any desire of the kind. Then he realized that the ambition was hers, a secret reason for her insistence on improving her husband's mind all these years. "Oh," he said with a smirk, "that's your way out for me, is it?"

"It is indeed, my boy," she replied, returning his grin.

His trademark toughness dissolved away by his wife, John calmly picked the book up and sat back down. He knew there was no point in arguing. "All right, my dear," he conceded; "we'll go to Congress."[344]

---

[343] *Manawatu Times*, February 7, 1880; *New York Herald*, May 5, 1878
[344] *Manawatu Times*, February 7, 1880

15.

Have Ye Asked Morrissey Yet?

President Abraham Lincoln liked to tell jokes and anecdotes. During the Civil War, the President had been frustrated by his generals' lack of decisiveness. One of them had a particularly annoying habit of cabling the War Department before taking any sort of action. This general's delays were resulting in a waste of money, men, and time. When Secretary of War Stanton came to the President with yet another telegraph from this general, the President made an interesting comparison.

"This general reminds me of a story I once heard about a Tammany man," Lincoln said to Stanton. "He happened to meet a friend, also a member of Tammany, on the street, and in the course of the talk the friend, who was beaming with smiles and good nature, told the other Tammanyite that he was going to be married.

"The first Tammany man looked more serious than men usually do upon hearing of the impending happiness of a friend. In fact, his face seemed to take on a look of anxiety and worry.

"'Ain't you glad to know that I'm to get married?' demanded the second Tammanyite, somewhat in a huff.

"'Of course, I am,' was the reply; 'but,' putting his mouth close to the ear of the other, 'have ye asked Morrissey yet?'

"Now, this general of whom we are speaking, wouldn't dare order out the guard without asking Morrissey," concluded the President.[345]

Lincoln's anecdote is indicative not only of the general's indecisiveness, but also of John Morrissey's growing reputation during the early 1860s as one of the true powers of Tammany in New York. Working closely with Boss Bill Tweed, he had also developed friendships and business relationships with August Belmont, John Hunter, and Erastus Corning, wealthy Democrats powerful enough to operate outside of the confines of Tammany and Tweed's influence. For men like these, Morrissey's familiarity with the people in the streets of Manhattan made him invaluable. Through many techniques they likely preferred not to know about, John made sure that the people of New York voted for Tammany candidates and that the proper dollars got into the proper hands to grease the gears of political necessity. In return, Tweed rewarded him in 1865 with a seat at his side on a committee to ensure the election of Judge John Hoffman as Mayor of New York City.

---

[345] McClure, 443-444

High-ranking Republicans like Lincoln regarded this kind of backroom conspiracy as everything that was wrong with American politics. Thus, the President's story was as much an insult to John Morrissey and men like him as it was an indictment of the insecure general and his incessant telegrams. However, Lincoln's joke was not far off the mark in its accuracy. As a reporter later noted, Tammany men berated Old Smoke with a chorus of "Johnny, what had we better do about this?" "Johnny, what had we be better do about that?" and "Johnny, can you suggest any way of raising money to accomplish so and so?"[346]

There is a story that the President and the ex-prizefighter met during one of Lincoln's rare visits to New York City. Back in 1861, en route to his inauguration, Honest Abe made a stopover in the metropolis he had visited just a few months earlier as a candidate. That initial visit was mainly for a campaign speech at the Cooper Union Hall. This time, the President Elect and future First Lady made their visit a mostly social one. Mr. Lincoln breakfasted with local merchants and visited with Mayor Wood and others at City Hall, while Mrs. Lincoln took in the sights at Barnum's American Museum. That evening, they were both present at a special Republican gala in their honor at the luxurious Astor House on the corner of Broadway and Vesey. According to Morrissey biographer Jack Kofoed, Both John and Susan Morrissey were present at this event. John was apparently the only Tammany man to attend this gathering of his rival Republicans, supposedly doing so out of some newfound idol worship ("He's a man, Susie, the kind o' man I wish I was," he is supposed to have told her). Kofoed tells that the President Elect of the United States and the coming king of New York gambling shook hands and exchanged pleasantries before Lincoln moved on, but that "though he opposed the President in principle, [Morrissey] was one of his most enthusiastic personal supporters."[347]

While the Lincolns were certainly present at the Astor on February 20, 1861, this author could find no primary sources indicating attendance by the Morrisseys at this event, and Kofoed gives no indication of how he learned of this story. Kofoed's use of imagined conversations, meetings, and events in other parts of his book suggest that this tale may also have been entirely fictional. Most Tammany men and Irish immigrants despised Lincoln, and this author found no credible account of John Morrissey ever speaking sympathetically of Lincoln, except to place a $2,000 bet back in 1860 that he would indeed become President, and a $100,000 bet that he would be re-elected in 1864. Even with that money at stake, Morrissey insisted on voting for Lincoln's Democratic opponents, Stephen Douglas and George McClellan. He did, however, attend Lincoln's inauguration in Washington D.C., where a reporter spotted him coming and going from the

[346] *New York Times*, October 22, 1870
[347] Burrows, 866-867; Kofoed, 209-210

President's hotel; that is at least circumstantial evidence that he had some interest in the President.[348]

_____

If Kofoed's story and his description of John Morrissey's feelings about Abraham Lincoln are true, then the news of actor John Wilkes Booth's assassination of the President on April 14, 1865 would have surely disturbed him. Overall, though, it would have been a lone spot of bad news in a period of constant prosperity for John. The success of the 1863 and 1864 races at Saratoga had prompted funding for still more renovations for the racecourse from the Saratoga Racing Association, with Morrissey and secretary Wheatley responsible for the completion of the project prior to the 1865 season. By now, the public regarded the racecourse as essentially Morrissey's, and its success bolstered his reputation as *the* name in thoroughbred racing in New York State, if not the entire North. His gambling interests in New York were proving tremendously profitable and his investment in the Harlem line perhaps even more so.

In late 1865, the success of the Saratoga course inspired John's attorney friend Leonard Jerome, the so-called King of Wall Street and the vice president of the Saratoga Racing Association, to open a course inside of metropolitan New York. Toward this end, he established the American Jockey Club, its membership consisting of some of the same men who belonged to or were involved with the Saratoga Racing Association (Belmont, Travers, and Wheatley), as well as Bill Tweed. In all, these men put up an astounding $750,000 intended mainly for the establishment of the new track. Jerome put up $25,000 of his own money. Jerome Park, immediately a contender for the best racetrack in the country, opened on September 25, 1866. Morrissey was not a member of this association, but several of his associates clearly were, and he was among the 25,000 people (including the guest of honor, General Ulysses S. Grant) who turned out to see the inaugural races.

If Morrissey was worried that having a superior track closer to home might dissuade New Yorkers from traveling north to Saratoga and his own course, he need not have done so. Jerome Park proved the proverb that a rising tide raises all ships by further cementing thoroughbred racing's status as one of the most popular past times of post-war America. The fact that Jerome's races took place a month after the ones at Saratoga meant that fans would not have to choose between visiting one course or the other. After all, Grant had also attended the Saratoga races that same year.

Morrissey had been correct in his prediction years earlier that, at the close of the war, Americans from the Confederate states would come

[348] *Jeffersonian*, September 6, 1860, quoting *Troy Times; Rutland Weekly Herald*, October 6, 1864; *Cleveland Daily Leader*, October 12, 1864; *New York Tribune*, September 1, 1860; Hotaling, 37

North to attend the races. The carnage of war had indeed claimed their own best horses, and it would take time to breed or import new quality stock. Saratoga Springs was now one of the few places where thoroughbred racing could be enjoyed in the North, and many among the crowds during racing season at Saratoga in the 1860s and 1870s hailed from Kentucky, Virginia, and the Carolinas. Jerome Park's representing competition in New York or not, John Morrissey was still the undisputed lord of Saratoga's sporting culture. "In all matters pertaining to the races he is the oracle consulted by every one, and on games is equally well posted," noted one reporter after a visit to Saratoga. *Harper's Weekly* declared the 1865 races at Saratoga "the most splendid ever witnessed on this continent." If mastery of gaming and gambling was a race itself, he was certainly enjoying a big lead.[349]

Soon enough, Morrissey entered an entirely different kind of race. John's politician friend James Hayes mentioned to him that he would support him should he run for Congress, a commitment that brought Susan's prior suggestion back to mind. Morrissey pretended that the idea had never occurred to him. "Hold on! I don't know as I want to go to Congress," he replied. Hayes pointed out that British boxer John Gully had once been a member of Parliament. Morrissey feigned reluctant consent. "Well, all right, I'll do it."[350]

By the autumn of 1866, the press began reporting on rumors that he was a shoo-in for a congressional nomination on the Tammany ticket for New York's Fifth District (consisting of the seventh, tenth, thirteenth, and fourteenth wards) against Republican candidate Eneas Elliott. Union Brigadier General Nelson Taylor, the Democratic incumbent, posted no threat to Morrissey in terms of popularity. Politically, the Fifth was an important district and represented a great opportunity for advancement for its congressman, which had previously been the position of none other than Fernando Wood himself (Wood was now a candidate to represent the Ninth District). Organizers waited until just a few days before the election to confirm Morrissey's candidacy, ostensibly to avoid much time for the rival party to mount a campaign of character assassination against the ex-prizefighter and noted gambler who had been the alleged boss of the Dead Rabbits gang and had been mixed up in the murder of Bill Poole.[351]

Considering his new political ambition, John made a risky move in September 1865. During the middle part of the decade, the Fenian Brotherhood was in America looking for funding for a proposed Fenian Rising, an outright rebellion against the English crown. The Fenians, as

[349] Hotaling, 66, quoting *Harper's Weekly*; *Evening Telegraph*, July 25, 1866
[350] *Evening World*, February 6, 1891
[351] *Herkimer Democrat*, November 7, 1866

they were commonly called, were a not-so-secret society who had been funding, arming, and taking part in smaller scale violent uprisings for decades. They were controversial to say the least, but certainly loved by a large section of the Irish Americans who represented most of John's constituency. Besides, he was an Irishman himself, raised on his father's tales of England's abuses of his countrymen. When the Fenians came to Griswold Hall in Troy, he was there to give a speech. "I am an Irishman," he said to them, garnering applause for that statement alone, "and I want to do something for the land I was born in, and that is what I came here for to-night. Knowing your private objects, I know that money will be needed for them... Put me down for one thousand dollars." He then sat down as the crowd cheered his name. Several New York City papers carried the news, which could not have endeared him to a certain section of the City's population. However, the *Irish American* gave the meeting and the speech the most coverage, and their readership was certain to appreciate Morrissey's words and contribution more than the W.A.S.P. New Yorkers reading the *Times, Herald,* or *Tribune.* When the Fenians next came to Cooper Hall in the metropolis itself, rumors circulated that Morrissey had promised them $100,000. Similar rumors would follow Morrissey through the next couple of years.[352]

To this point, Morrissey had valued behind-the-scenes power, despite his very public career as a prizefighter, his ostentatious dress, and his fame throughout the country. The Saratoga Racing Association had kept his name out of its official officers roll, even as he had been the strongest force in the new track's success. He had operated for years in the anonymous streets doing unscrupulous work for politicians like Fernando Wood and Bill Tweed. Only occasionally would his name pop up on the list of individuals present at a political convention, or of members of the Tammany General Committee. Having a spotlight thrust upon his political activities certainly would not have been a prospect to which John would have warmed easily.

Nonetheless, he considered his own reputation as a thug and a gambler and then considered his son. John Junior was now twelve years old and living very much in his father's shadow. Despite growing up with financial means his father could only have dreamed of at the same age, the boy still had the elder Morrissey's wild streak. He had trouble staying focused in school and was known as an incorrigible troublemaker. John Senior wanted to leave more than a bad reputation and a talent for violence to his boy. "My general reputation amongst Americans, I felt, required me to do something to start my boy, for whose character I live at present in a great degree," Morrissey explained to a reporter years later, "and I chased up the seat in Congress." Of course, he could not ignore Susan's ambitions to see

[352] *Irish American*, September 16, 1865 and October 9, 1865; *New York World*, September 28, 1865; *New York Herald*, May 23, 1867

her husband take a seat in Washington, but he made sure to omit to the press that his wife was the original inspiration behind his campaign.[353]

Various local Democratic organizations confirmed John as a nominee at an evening meeting in the Fifth District on October 27. After Gilbert Wood presented the nomination with a brief speech promising that those present "shall use our utmost endeavors to elevate you to the position, and shall, as the representatives of the Democracy of the district, do all that is required on the day of the election," the man himself came forward to address the assembly.

> GENTLEMEN: It is gratifying for me to receive these manifestations of the confidence of the different organizations that are represented here to-night. Although much has been said which ought not to have been uttered. I stand here as one of the humble exponents of the principles of the Democratic Party. That it is necessary for men in high position to fill our offices of honor I do not believe. Other men who have the heart and have the disposition to place themselves before the great tribunal of a public vote have the right, and I am one of those men. With all due respect for my opponents, I do not think that my Democrat friends will regret the action they have taken. They will always find me a trusty friend.[354]

Many within the district and outside of it were outraged by Tammany's choice. Morrissey's residence was still officially in Troy, and he now spent as much time in Saratoga as he did in New York City. He had never been a resident of the Fifth District at all, pointed out a speaker at a bi-partisan, anti-Morrissey meeting on October 29. Newspapers spilled more ink ridiculing and criticizing him than at any point previous in a life filled with controversy and violence. "In all the crime and wickedness of New York," decried the *Newark Daily Advertiser*, "in all that is demoralized and vile, John Morrissey is the acknowledged chief." Morrissey's opponents also brought up his foreign birth, his shady history, and his lack of military service in a scramble to avoid what they saw as Tammany foisting a corrupt and cowardly outsider upon the public. The *Northern New York Daily Journal* went so far as stating that Morrissey had bought his way into the nomination by paying a $75,000 purchasing price to the Democratic Committee. Of course, most of these printed accusations mattered little to the illiterate masses of Morrissey's district. When one public speaker railed against Morrissey, asking what he had ever done for the working man, there arose a response from an anonymous member of the audience, "Be jabers, he licked John C. Heenan and Yankee Sullivan!" When the rest of the

---

[353] *Chicago Daily Tribune*, August 1, 1874; *New York Herald*, December 31, 1865
[354] *New York Times*, October 28, 1866

crowd erupted in laughs and cheers, the frustrated speaker grumpily departed his stage.[355]

If John's nomination disgusted the rest of the nation, many in the city of Troy, New York were proud of the hometown kid's expected elevation. "There are whole classes in this community who swear by John Morrissey," the *Troy Whig* reported, "and would prefer his election to that of any or all other men in the State." The paper went on to praise his ability to rise from the humblest of beginnings to a place of influence and power almost exclusively by his own character and action.[356]

Some of John's friends suggested that he give up his gambling interests in order to ease the concerns of the reformers and moralists so offended by his candidacy, but he saw little chance of those individuals coming around to vote for him either way, and he knew that his income as the gambling king of New York City was far more lucrative than a congressman's salary. He insisted that, if the people were to vote him into a seat in Washington, they would have to take him as he was.[357]

Those within the Democratic Party who were distressed by Morrissey's candidacy supported and voted for the incumbent, General Taylor, a Harvard graduate who had been a hero of both the Mexican and Civil wars and now had his own law practice in the city. Though born in Connecticut, he was now a resident of the Fifth District. Most people knew Republican candidate Eneas Elliott stood no hope against Morrissey or Nelson in a district historically dominated by Democrats. There was the minor threat that Morrissey and Taylor would split the much larger Democratic vote, allowing Elliott a chance, but insiders felt that enough Democrats would turn out to overwhelm the Republicans, split or not.

Morrissey spent $10,000 of his own money on his campaign. Always self-conscious of his raspy voice, he despised public speeches, and although he recognized the need to speak before large crowds, he usually kept them brief but powerful. When called upon to speak before audiences in his first campaign, he would simply stand and say, "This is your fight – not mine. I win my fights." He much preferred to do his campaigning on a face-to-face basis. He and James Hayes would canvas the district on foot, Morrissey approaching a prospective voter with the words "Say, do you know who I am? I'm John Morrissey." The other party, astonished to meet the famed fighter, would inevitably promise his support when solicited. Women turned out conspicuously at John's rallies, and he proved especially effective with the wives of local merchants in person as well, particularly if the husband was away from the establishment. Mustering all his considerable masculine charm, the handsome hero of New York's working classes would

[355] *Wheeling Intelligencer*, October *31, 1866*, quoting *Newark Daily Advertiser*, *Northern New York Daily Journal*, November 6, 1866; *Evening World*, February 6, 1891
[356] *Cleveland Plain Dealer*, November 8, 1866, quoting *Troy Whig*
[357] *Wheeling Daily Intelligencer*, January 5, 1867

introduce himself and offer his hand, convincing the lady to influence her husband's vote. "John always caught the women!" Hayes later recalled.[358]

James Hayes would become perhaps Morrissey's most loyal supporter in his coming political life. Born in 1829, he had first entered politics as a volunteer fireman, like so many street-level characters of the day. Somehow landing first on the Common Council and then the Board of Supervisors, he finagled himself into becoming a protégé of Boss Tweed himself, his bank account benefitting greatly from that favoritism. Hayes had amassed half a million dollars in real estate at the Boss's side in a matter of a few years but lost it just as quickly during the Panic of 1873. As one contemporary said of him, "Mr. Hayes is an uncompromising Democrat, and one not easily turned aside from the object he has in his view, and it has been the untiring energy he has ever manifested in the behalf of his friends that has rendered him as popular as he is." Hayes would continue to spend that untiring energy on John Morrissey's behalf for years to come, even when disagreements between Tweed and Morrissey tested his loyalties.[359]

On November 5, the day before the election, some unnamed enemy of John's handed over to the *New York Tribune* his complete arrest record from Troy, certified by New York District Attorney A. Oakey Hall, beginning with "The People against John Morrissey – December term, 1848. Indicted for assault with intent to kill," and ending with a charge of beating and stabbing three men on May 6, 1857. In total, the list included four charges of assault with intent to kill, three charges of burglary, and one charge of disturbing the peace.[360]

The *Tribune* allowed the accused to publish a letter in his own defense. It read:

ANSON HOUSE, SPRING-ST., NEW YORK, NOV. 3, 1866.

To the Editor of the Herald,

SIR: My attention has been called to an editorial article in The Herald of this day, in which it is stated that I have been indicted for "burglary and other offenses."

It is a duty not only to myself but to the people of the Vth Congressional District, for whose support I am a candidate, that I should state the facts. When I was a boy, but 16 years of age, I and a few friends were engaged in an altercation with a party of young men, and in that altercation there was a door of a house kicked open. It was charged that I was one of those who kicked open the door and struck one of the opposing party. An affidavit was made by one of the men engaged in the quarrel that I had broken open

[358] *Evening World*, February 6, 1891
[359] Gover, 74; *Irish American*, March 22, 1897
[360] *New York Tribune*, November 5, 1866

the door and struck him. I was indicted for burglary and assault and battery. The indictment for burglary was never tried. The District-Attorney regarded the charges as too frivolous to be prosecuted, and summarily dismissed it. I was tried for the assault and battery and found guilty.

Before entering upon my canvass for the position to which I aspire, I referred to my past life, which, until within the last eight years, was one of adventure, in consequence of the poverty of my parents and the few advantages I had in my early youth. I commenced to labor for my own livelihood and to assist in the support of my father and mother at the early age of ten years. At that time most boys are under the influence of domestic discipline, and have the advantages of regular educational training. Is it, therefore, strange that I should have committed errors in my early life? There are few boys that have not been guilty of a trifling assault and battery. If I had had influential parents and friends I would have been permitted, probably, to have escaped with a reprimand; but having no one to say one kind word for me – a poor, rough boy, working in a foundry – I suffered the slight penalty due to my boyish folly.

During my whole life no man can say that I have ever wronged him, defrauded him of a dollar, or even broken my given word. I have had during the last eight years business relations and connections with many of the best men of this city, and not one of them will say I am other than a man of my word and of strict integrity; I have endeavored by my conduct to atone for the mistakes of my youth. Although successful in accumulating a competence, I have never forgotten that I was once poor. I have never turned a poor man from my door, or deserted a friend in his need. There has been much criticism in the newspapers in reference to my being a candidate for Congress. It is natural that I should meet with great opposition. A man who has passed through such varied and strange scenes of life as I have must expect to make bitter enemies and warm friends, and jealousies and hostilities are inseparable from political contests. But, Mr. Editor, I will state to you my motives in being a candidate for Congress.

I have one boy, who is now 12 years of age, who will have the benefit of the best education this country can afford, and will have better opportunities than I had, at his age, to start upon an honorable career. I feel it a duty that I owe to him, my only child, to make my record as clear and honorable as possible, that my manhood may atone for the follies and errors of my youth, and leave behind me memories of which my son in after years may be proud, and that will cast no shadow upon his path through life.

I respectfully solicit, as an act of justice, that this reply should be published in your paper. JOHN MORRISSEY[361]

Much of the press reacted to John's letter with skepticism, making note that he was a prizefighter (considered a brutish, dishonorable profession) as an adult, not a boy, and that he was still New York City's leading proprietor of gambling, a vice regarded by many as a scourge on public morals. One paper editorialized, "when a man is simply *notorious* for some of the worst vices that corrupt the community, it is expecting too much that the public shall cast the mantle of forgetfulness over his past career when he seeks honorable and respectable public station." They also questioned if his reasons were more selfish than simply leaving a better legacy for his namesake.[362]

The last obstacle in the way of his election came from the Republican Party, members of which made it known that, should he be elected, they would prevent him from entering the House, as they did not believe he had been naturalized. Having been born in Ireland and brought to this country as a small child, Morrissey was not sure that he was an American citizen. He certainly had no papers confirming it. Morrissey subsequently asked Edwin M. Haggerty, the Clerk of the Board of Councilmen, how to go about getting naturalized. Haggerty and Morrissey then went to a judge, who explained that it was necessary for a witness to attest that he had known Morrissey in the United States for at least eighteen years. As it turned out, Haggerty had known of Morrissey just that length of time, though they had not been acquainted with one another that long.

"You were pointed out to me on a towboat near Washington Market as a fighter from Troy," explained Haggerty. "You wore a pair of dirty overalls with one suspender, and I remember you as a hulking big 'Mick' with a curly head." Haggerty gave his signature that this was the case, Morrissey took his oath, and walked away with his naturalization papers, putting a stop to Republican plans to block him.[363]

Come Election Day, the Democrats of the Fifth Congressional District turned out to cast 9,159 votes for John Morrissey and 6,451 for General Taylor. Republican Eneas Elliot received 2,292 votes.[364]

Newspaper writers from as far away as Illinois and Missouri decried the result, the *Chicago Republican* going so far as to suggest that Morrissey's fellow Congressmen ignore the election results and refuse to allow him into the Capitol when he arrived. Still more papers published accusations that Morrissey had bought his way into putting the M.C. (Member of Congress) behind his name.[365]

---

[361] *New York Tribune*, November 5, 1866
[362] *Evening Telegraph*, November 12, 1866
[363] *New York Sun*, May 2, 1878
[364] *Holt County Sentinel*, December 14, 1866
[365] *Troy Weekly Times*, November 24, 1866

The *Daily Alta California* and other papers published lyrics in a mock Irish folk song style accredited to a fictional Army private Miles O'Reilly humorously addressing Morrissey's rise from boxer and faro dealer to national politician, insinuating that, in terms of corruption, he would be in over his head with Washington D.C. politicians. The true poet was Charles Halpine, an Irish immigrant, Union Army officer, journalist, and editor who had created O'Reilly as a caricature of immigrant Civil War soldiers, and as a pen name for publishing humorous or bawdy poetry. The closing verses went:

> John Morrissey, my Jo, John,
>
> These politicians deal
>
> From a faro-box false-bottomed,
>
> Wi' springs o' patent "steal;"
>
> Will yer scruples never melt, John,
>
> When to Congress now ye go?
>
> Can ye deal the same square game ye dealt,
>
> John Morrissey, my Jo!

> John Morrissey, my Jo, John,
>
> It ne'er was kenned your plan,
>
> To kick a fallen foe, John,
>
> Or spurn a helpless man;
>
> But ye'll find a different ride, John,
>
> When to Congress now you go –
>
> For they kick the South, having gagged its mouth,
>
> John Morrissey, my Jo![366]

A letter from a female reader to the editor of the *Urbana Union* came to John's defense by pointing out a similar contrast between he and his future colleagues in Washington. "John Morrissey has hitherto associated with brave men; he now seeks nominal affiliation with cowards," the writer commented; "he has fought his own battles, and the foe went down before his own strong hand; but the fellows whose association he now covets were craven in the hour of conflict, and forced better men to brave the blows which their coward soles dared not encounter." The same letter proposed that Morrissey's "innate magnanimity of character, inspire the belief that he will, by the contrast of his noble nature, sink the Radical Congress lower in

---

[366] *Maryland Free Press*, March 7, 1867; *Daily Alta California*, March 17, 1867

public estimation than plummet ever sounded!" Addressing the "Puritans" who cringed at a prizefighter's elevation to Congress, she asked, "Do they forget that a gladiator – one who had fought with wild beasts in the amphitheater at Ephesus – was yet deemed worthy to be a minister of Christ, and the chief Apostle of the Gentiles?"[367]

Others who came to Morrissey's defense pointed out that "He is liberal to the poor, giving thousands of dollars yearly to objects of charity, he pays a hundred cents on the dollar for all he owes; he moves in the best society of New York; he is a clear-headed business man, with broad, liberal, national views." One writer made a comparison between Old Smoke and Honest Abe, describing them both as self-made men who rose from poor beginnings to national office. Similarly, others liked that he was not an aristocrat, those supporters feeling that he understood the woes of the common people of New York.[368]

The notoriety of his congressional run brought rare news regarding one of John's sisters from Chicago. "Much excitement was caused here by the discovery of a family named Morris starving to death. The wife says she is the sister of John Morrissey, member of Congress elect." The husband, John Morris, an ex-convict, had been arrested for beating his wife Mary, Morrissey's sister. Mary, blind following an untreated eye infection, was now supported by her twelve-year-old son, John, Jr. who had saved her from his father's fists.[369]

———

At about this time, when John Morrissey was thirty-five, a reporter made one of the most illustrative accounts of his looks and manner ever put on record by a contemporary, which would be reprinted years later in the *New York Herald*:

> Morrissey's personnel is that of a man of great muscular strength, indomitable perseverance and untiring energy. He stands about five feet nine inches in height, is very broad across the chest and shoulders; has a large head, covered with bushy black hair; a broad, full face, usually illumined with a smile; speaks moderately, but with determination; has a deep, sonorous voice, and impresses the stranger at once with an idea that he is going to be fairly dealt with as long as John Morrissey has anything to say in the matter. His eye is dark, sharp and stares you straight in the face while you are talking, looking neither to the right or left. His admirers say of him "his head covers as big a brain is there is on top of the planet, and his heart is as big as a bullock's." His countenance bears marks of

[367] *Urbana Union*, November 28, 1868

[368] *Memphis Public Ledger*, December 12, 1866

[369] *Daily Journal*, November 22, 1866, quoting *Chicago Herald; New York Times*, November 25, 1866; *Chicago Daily Tribune*, June 20, 1878

the many encounters he has had, and in which he has received punishment such as few men could have survived. His nose is somewhat indented, and there is an ugly mark on the side of his face. In manner he is polite and agreeable, courteous to everybody; has a great memory of faces and friendly shake of the hand for all. He is no wonder to his friends who know him intimately, but into the presence of the stranger who has already regarded him as unpolished rough and an unworthy member of society, he comes as a gentleman and an agreeable surprise.[370]

Rumors of Morrissey's participation in an unusual conspiracy threatened the forthright image he was now cultivating. Dean Richmond had died on August 27, 1866, just months before Morrissey's nomination. Richmond, as one of the nation's most powerful railroad magnates and the longtime chairman of the New York State Democratic Committee, making him the master of New York State politics. His death left that position vacant, and there had been wide speculation as to who would fill that void, with Commodore Vanderbilt among those eyed for the position. With the announcement of John Morrissey's candidacy for Congress, many came to conclude that he was to be Richmond's heir apparent. Democrat Morrissey, so the conspiracy theorists supposed, was part of a triumvirate that included Republican Secretary of State William Seward and Republican newspaper publisher Thurlow Weed, this trio allegedly intending to monopolize political power within the state, regardless of party politics. "The startling antecedents of Mr. Morrissey, the historical record of Mr. Seward, and the legislative experience of Mr. Weed make a very strong combination," proposed the *New York Herald*. According to this theory, Morrissey would do the bidding of Seward and Weed on the congressional front, while Seward exercised his influence over President Johnson, and Thurlow Weed manipulated public opinion through the press and his business interests. It should be noted that one of Weed's properties was the *Evening Journal*, a competitor of the accusing *Herald*.[371]

Before his own election, Morrissey's first assignment as part of this supposed political "firm" or "Corporation ring" was to see to the nomination of Judge John T. Hoffman for Governor of New York at the Democratic Convention. Hoffman, at the time the Grand Sachem of Tammany, was a patently corrupt pol, the type of man political reformers despised. Morrissey had allegedly been the central figure in Hoffman's election to Mayor, and so Seward and Weed apparently felt he was the best man for the job of getting the same man into the governor's mansion. Morrissey's efforts, "by which all other candidates were made to throw up

---

[370] *New York Herald*, May 2, 1878
[371] *New York Herald*, September 16, 1866

the sponge," proved successful, which was presumably the cause for his being rewarded with a last-minute candidacy for Congress.[372]

In late October, shortly after Morrissey's nomination for Congress, the *Herald* published a story accusing Hoffman, Seward, and Weed of seeking to betray him. The paper did not specify the so-called ring's reasons for wanting to do so, but the writer insinuated that the trio had some difficulty in separating themselves from Morrissey and the stigma that came with him. "They have the wrong customer to deal with," observed the *Herald* writer, asserting that in the gubernatorial race, "it would be an advantage to the State if we could swamp off both [candidates] for such a man as John Morrissey…. He has many praiseworthy, honorable traits about him, and is at least a man of decision of character and firmness of purpose." In the end, Hoffman lost the gubernatorial race to Republican Reuben Fenton.[373]

———

Strangely enough, after nearly a decade away from boxing, and amid all his political and financial dealings, John Morrissey unexpectedly entered the ring once more during the late 1860s. A fighter named Ned O'Baldwin out of Linsmore, Ireland arrived in the United States sometime in 1857 or 1858 looking for a match with the reigning world champion, Jem Mace, and had caused quite a sensation in sporting circles. O'Baldwin, whose height was reportedly anywhere from six feet, two inches to six feet, seven and a half inches, was renowned as the Irish Giant, and thought to be among the hardest hitters in the sport's history. The masterful boxer Professor Mike Donovan considered O'Baldwin the best fighter he had ever seen.[374]

Morrissey, who still retained a strong interest in the sporting world, was curious about the newcomer from his native land and paid a visit to the House of Commons on Houston Street in New York, where the Irish Giant was said to be holding court of late. On his first visit, O'Baldwin's handlers told Morrissey Ned was out, so John returned the next day to find the boxer present. Morrissey, who had always prided himself on being able to handle any man's punch, could not resist someone's suggestion that he go a few rounds against the sensational young slugger. The House's proprietor, a Bob Smith, produced gloves for the two to spar with. Morrissey, despite being almost a decade older than his opponent, showed surprising aggression and energy against the bigger, younger man, and he got the better of the in-fighting. However, when O'Baldwin was able to extend his left and get full momentum behind it, he dropped Morrissey to the floor twice. Morrissey admitted defeat and offered to assist O'Baldwin in his pursuit of the championship stateside. Despite Morrissey offering

[372] *New York Times*, October 22, 1870; *New York Herald*, September 16, 1866; *New York Herald*, October 18, 1866
[373] *New York Herald*, October 18, 1866
[374] Fleisher, 50; Redmond, 32; *Idaho Semi-Weekly*, October 12, 1875

$10,000 to Mace to fight O'Baldwin, the Irish Giant never got his shot before a business partner murdered him in 1875.[375]

———

The Morrisseys moved to Washington D.C. in early 1867 so that John could join the 40th Congress in March. Before ever casting his first vote, Morrissey entered the House of Representatives as one of its most famous members. "Of all the members of the new Congress," reported the *New York Times*, "Mr. Morrissey, of this City, appears to attract most interest in Washington. We are told that when he made his appearance to be sworn in on Monday, the anxiety of the House and the galleries to get a glimpse of him was intense…. Members crowded round his seat to congratulate him, and the brilliant array of ladies who on this occasion were settled all over the House, gave evidence of something more than curiosity concerning him." Many men asked those who knew John to bring him by so that they might be introduced to the new local celebrity, but Morrissey seems to have quickly tired of all the attention. "I am here at my desk," he told those seeking to take him to meet one representative after another; "if anyone wishes to see me let him come here." Clearly, the House had no intention of following the suggestion of the *Chicago Republican* that it bar Morrissey from entering the premises.[376]

Upon Morrissey's arrival in Washington, famed journalist Benjamin Perley Poore, who had a side job as the compiler of the *Congressional Directory*, approached him. It was Poore's duty to include a brief sketch of the new congressman's life thus far and he asked Morrissey how he would like to have his occupation listed in the book. Morrissey referred to his job as a youth in Troy in the iron works; thus, Poore listed John's occupation in the *Congressional Directory* as "iron-molder."[377]

There is another anecdote told about Morrissey's initial days in Washington, printed nearly two decades later, that deserves mention only because it is so preposterous as to be amusing in its unlikelihood:

> At a reception in Washington [Morrissey] was introduced to a venerable attaché of one of the foreign legations, and just as they were shaking hands some unprincipled person shouted "Time!" The word at once brought Mr. Morrissey back to the days of his battles in the ring, and he completely forgot his surroundings. He backed away from the old gentleman, put up his fists and danced around him, and then made a sudden rush upon him and knocked him to the floor. After waiting 15 seconds for him to come to time, while the other gentlemen in the room stood paralyzed with

[375] Fox 59-60; Fleisher, 50; Gorn, 173
[376] *New York Times*, March 6, 1867; *Bismark Tribune*, September 10, 1873
[377] *New York Times*, May 6, 1878

astonishment, Mr. Morrissey screamed "Judgement!" rushed into a corner, fell into a chair, and called for somebody to sponge him. He was deeply chagrined upon realizing that he had forgotten himself, and for a long time after the occurrence there was an aversion to being introduced to him apparent in Washington society.[378]

In truth, Morrissey was more than aware of the criticism and expectations of him because of his morally dubious background, and he went to great pains to disprove them by his behavior in Congress right away. "Knowing that he is such a prominent target," observed a correspondent for the *Daily Albany Argus* in March 1867, "he conducts himself with the utmost indifference to surroundings, although never being entirely at his ease." His new position may have bored John out of his mind, but he was not about to give his critics the satisfaction of reverting back to his Old Smoke ways in the House of Representatives.[379]

For all the hoopla over his nomination, election, and arrival, Morrissey's record through his first term as a Congressman would be disappointingly nondescript. In the face of so much controversy over his candidacy, Morrissey's determination to win the seat might have become less about improving his son's opportunities in life or helping the people of the Fifth District than it was simply a matter of proving his critics wrong. Years later, the *Herald* supposed that he had "wanted the place simply as a lesson to his enemies, who boasted that he could not in any event be elected." Once he got to Washington, Morrissey showed little interest in the job, other than the political clout it gave him to aid his own ambitions and those of his friends.[380]

There is a story of John's earliest days in Congress that is illustrative of his ambitions – or lack thereof – in his new position. One day, Speaker Schuyler Colfax noticed John Morrissey's large frame passing nervously back and forth in front of Colfax's office door. Colfax had been discussing the formation of congressional committees with a few other men at the time. When these men left, Morrissey cautiously entered the Speaker's office, careful to make sure that no one else was within earshot.

"Mr. Speaker, I have a fine box of Havana cigars I am going to send you," the new Congressman began. "Will you accept them?"

"Oh, yes, certainly," was the reply. "Anything in that line is acceptable."

"All right," Morrissey responded, which was then followed by a prolonged, awkward silence before John blurted out, "Mr. Speaker, I have a favor to ask – I want you to put me on a certain Committee," to which Colfax asked Morrisey which committee.

[378] *New York Times*, September 14, 1885
[379] *Daily Albany Argus*, March 9, 1867
[380] *New York Herald*, May 2, 1878

"I want you to put me on that committee where I have damned little work to do," Morrissey requested. Doubtless amused, Colfax consented, and John found himself assigned to a minor position on the Committee on Revolutionary Pensions.[381]

The *New York Times* provides another of the best accounts of Morrissey's behavior and reputation during his rare appearances at his desk in an article entitled "Useless Member":

> He wastes no time in reading or writing when he is in the House. He is always listening to the proceedings – though what he thinks of them must be left entirely to conjecture. He has never favored the world with his opinions on public affairs. Still, one only has to look at him to feel quite sure that the country is safe in his hands. His constituents, then, may well feel aggrieved at his inattention to their affairs. He has been away from his post nearly four months, and on the principle of 'no work, no pay,' he ought to return about $1,700 to his constituents. To the House and the people he can make no adequate compensation.[382]

Morrissey began to avoid New York City as well, for every time he returned to the city, every acquaintance would accost him with the question, "Why are you out of your seat?" Occasionally, he had legitimate family and health reasons to be away. In the Summer of 1867, Tim Morrissey fell ill, and John went to Troy to look after him. The next Spring, he traveled to the spas at Hot Springs, Arkansas for his own health, "to be treated for the asthma, with which he has long been afflicted." Once breathing became easier, he returned to Washington, but remained conspicuously absent from his seat.[383]

If his responsibilities as a congressman did not keep his attention, power plays on Wall Street continued to obsess him. 1867 saw Morrissey both win and lose enormous sums of money playing the stock market. In January, he was reported to have lost $400,000 in a failed corner of the Cumberland Coal Company, an astounding sum partially recouped that summer when he won $200,000 playing the stock market inside of a single week (said to be possibly the largest single week haul in American history to that point).[384]

———

The overall challenge meeting the fortieth Congress at its start was healing the wounds of the Civil War. Many of the Southern states were not yet fully allowed back into participation in the national government. "The

---

[381] *Watertown Times*, March 30, 1870; *Brockport Republic*, April 21, 1870

[382] *New York Times*, May 4, 1870

[383] *Memphis Daily Appeal*, April 19, 1871; *Public Ledger*, March 7, 1868; *Daily Albany Argus*, July 26, 1867; *Commercial Advertiser*, July 26, 1867

[384] *Albany Evening Journal*, January 30, 1867; *Daily Albany Argus*, January 31, 1867; *Daily Albany Argus*, July 26, 1867; *Commercial Advertiser*, July 26, 1867

first public act of Mr. Morrissey after being sworn in was to enter his protest, in company with his fellow Democrats, against the exclusion of the Southern representatives from their seats in Congress, and the protest received emphasis from the fact that he joined in it," reported the *Times*. The Federal Government and the former Confederate states were politically at odds over a series of Reconstruction Acts which essentially imposed military rule over the former Confederate States and established various political requirements that each rebel state meet before being admitted back into Union and being allowed representation and participation in national politics, one of which was the ratification of the Fourteenth Amendment to the U.S. Constitution.

Simply put, the Fourteenth Amendment limits the control states have over voting in national elections. Most controversially, it specified that all men born or naturalized in the United States are citizens and therefore have the right to vote. To the South, this meant that, to rejoin the Union, their states must recognize that African Americans were in fact U.S. citizens and could vote. In addition, the Amendment required that the states afford all citizens equal protection and rights, again an open challenge to the South's ability to discriminate between people of different heritage.

John Morrissey's very public joining of the protest of the obstruction of the Southern Democrats from Congress seems to have stopped at protest. While many of his forty-five Democrat allies, including Fernando Wood, voted nay to the Amendment, Morrissey was among the thirteen Democrats who abstained from voting. There can be little doubt, however, that he was not a fan of the amendment. At one point during the discussion, the habitually mute Morrissey is said to have impatiently blurted out, "If any gentleman on the other side wants his constitution amended, just let him step into the Rotunda with me." The Amendment passed the House by a wide margin of ninety-four votes in July of 1869.[385]

Building on the promises of the Fourteenth Amendment, the Fifteenth Amendment, also placed before the fortieth Congress, specifically said that states could not prevent a citizen from voting based on their race, skin color, or having previously been a slave. The political fight over this one was long and hard at every level of its ratification. In the Congressional vote on January 30, 1869, John Morrissey again abstained. The Amendment passed Congress by an even wider margin of 108 votes.[386]

Morrissey was also conspicuously absent from voting on the other huge political issue of the day, the impeachment of President Andrew Johnson for various acts which his opposition considered beyond the powers of his office. One of the major political battles of the Reconstruction period, this ended when Congress did impeach Johnson on March 2, 1868.

---

[385] www.govtrack.us, accessed 11/1/2016; www.nysun.com/calendar/old-smoke/13666/, accessed 12/7/2016
[386] www.govtrack.us, accessed 11/1/2016

Despite his abstaining from the voting, there can be little doubt that Morrissey would have been on Democrat Johnson's side in the impeachment dispute. In fact, allegations that he had used bribes to protect the President turned into a minor scandal later in the year. George Wilkes, the less than scrupulous publisher of the *National Police Gazette* and *Spirit of the Times* and staunch Republican, informed Ben "Beast" Butler, Republican lawyer, Union General, and leader of the movement to impeach Johnson, that he had a confidential source close to lobbyist Sam Ward who insisted that Ward, a man Butler already greatly despised, had personally handed $12,000 to a freshman Senator out of Kansas named Edmund Ross to vote against impeachment. That cash, said Wilkes, had come from John Morrissey.

In true Wilkes fashion, the rumors got even more scandalous from there. The middle "man" between Morrissey and Ward was said to be an individual currently going under the name Charley Morgan. Morgan was in fact a cross-dressing woman who allegedly enjoyed sexual relationships with both Sam Ward and Susan Morrissey. Intrigued, Butler called Ward before a House committee investigating the impeachment and grilled him on various coincidences relating Ward to the impeachment proceedings. Thanks to his connection to the case being purely circumstantial, as well as Ward's discretion and Butler's refusal to believe some of the more salacious details of Wilkes' story, Morrissey's name was left out of any of the public proceedings related to this investigation.

Whether or not Morrissey was indeed behind the $12,000 allegedly paid to Senator Ross cannot be known now. Wilkes had a deserved reputation as a sensationalist publisher and a blackmailer; the information in his papers was notoriously unreliable. However, there is circumstantial evidence to suggest Morrissey's involvement in the bribe would be possible. Sam Ward, who would slowly build his reputation as the King of the Lobby in the coming years, did insinuate in correspondence to his family that Morrissey was one of his primary clients, and journalist Benjamin Perley Poore later remembered that Ward had been one of Morrissey's advisors during the latter's first congressional run. According to a *New York Times* article published after Ward's death, the lobbyist had worked on Morrissey's behalf in Washington in support of a bill which would impose a national tax on gambling lotteries, effectively legalizing them. Beyond the legalization the bill promised, Morrissey, who had the funds to pay the tax, saw this as a means to discourage the smaller lottery operators who chipped away at his businesses. Ward, allegedly funded by Morrissey, wined and dined a congressman and convinced him to change his position on the bill, though it never did come to fruition. "Charley Morgan" was a real woman, albeit with an assumed name, who apparently did have some sort of relationship with Ward, but there appears to be nothing connecting Morgan to Morrissey or his wife. At any rate, it does not seem that Morgan would have been necessary as a go-between for Morrissey and Ward. If the men were looking to handle the money exchange discreetly and thus not meet in person, using a bisexual, cross-dressing mistress hardly seems the most inconspicuous choice.[387]

Morrissey does seem to have also had at least a working relationship with Johnson. It is clear from their correspondence that they met in person on multiple occasions to discuss matters of policy and appointments. *The New York Sun* went so far as to say that Morrissey's "personal magnetism was so great, that he is credited with having had more influence with Johnson's Administration than many out-and-out Johnson men." [388]

On July 26, 1868, Morrissey wrote a letter to the President from the Metropolitan Hotel in the District of Columbia that might have seemed of mediocre important at the time, but in hindsight is quite intriguing:

> I have called to see you in relation to the appointments of which I spoke to you at our last interview. I recommended the nomination of Simeon M. Johnson of New York as Com. Of Internal Revenue and of General Chester A. Arthur of New York as Surveyer [sic] of the Port of New York.
>
> I told you that if these two names should be sent into the Senate together, they would both be confirmed. I am assured of this, and I trust you will now send the names in. You know all about Mr. Johnson. In regard to Genl Arthur, I enclose letters from two members of your Cabinet, who are both his friends, from which you will be satisfied that he is eminently a proper person to be appointed Surveyer [sic], and that he has always been a friend of yours.
>
> The appointment of General Arthur, is for many reasons especially and exceedingly important to me personally, in the contest which I expect to have in New York, and I beg that your Excellency in carrying out the wish you have kindly expressed to gratify me, by some such appointment *will make this one.* The present incumbent of that office certainly has no claims upon you for his retention, and his removal would gratify all parties in New York.
>
> I have taken the liberty of writing this note, as the little time left for the consideration of this matter makes the obtaining of a personal interview uncertain.
>
> John Morrissey[389]

Chester A. Arthur was a little over a year older than John Morrissey, the son of an Irish immigrant Baptist preacher. Though born in Vermont, he had grown up in North Troy. Raised in better economic circumstances than Morrissey, Arthur attended Union College in Schenectady, New York

---

[387] *Indiana Herald*, August 5, 1885; *New York Times*, May 20, 1884
[388] *New York Sun*, May 2, 1878
[389] Bergeron, 434

and the State and National Law School in Ballston Spa (not far from Saratoga Springs), New York in the years John was working in Alexander Hamilton's brothels and aboard Captain Smith's riverboat. He had been a schoolteacher, school principal, and New York City attorney before getting involved in politics, his opposition to slavery eventually leading him to join the new Republican Party during the 1850s. He joined the New York militia in 1858, and through his political connections steadily collected promotions until becoming Quartermaster General of the New York Militia in 1862, conducting his duties impressively and displaying a talent for organization and leadership. After the war, he fell in with the New York Republican political machine and became a favorite of Republican boss Roscoe Conkling, earning a reputation for being dependable and hard-working for the party. The Surveyor of the Port of New York position was a political appointment on which a man could grow very wealthy. How exactly Arthur came to Democrat John Morrissey's attention and what his appointment to the lucrative spoils position meant to Morrissey's "contest" in New York is not known. A Democrat himself, Johnson unsurprisingly did not give Arthur the appointment, which must not have sat well with his petitioner. Even so, John Morrissey's working to promote a future President of the United States into the favor of the sitting President is nonetheless indicative of the level of politics to which the once impoverished immigrant had risen.[390]

In July 1868, John returned to New York City to act as a delegate at the Democratic National Convention held at the brand-new Tammany Hall in Union Square. Three stories of red brick with marble inlays, the Hall featured a large concert room capable of seating 5,000 people, as well as multiple lobbies, smoking salons, and a library. A larger concert hall was already under construction. The ornate architecture and luxurious accommodations, all overseen by Boss Tweed, had cost a staggering grand total of $300,000, a sum to which John Morrissey likely contributed.[391]

Morrissey worked hard at the convention to make sure that his fellow New York delegates supported the incumbent President. He personally corresponded with the President in the days preceding the convention, urging Johnson to "Be deaf to false counsels and when you have done your duty the civilization of the age will solve the balance of the problem." In the end, Morrissey and Samuel S. Cox, another congressman, were the only New York delegates to support Johnson over Governor Horatio Seymour for the Democratic ticket. "He is a peculiar man," a mutual acquaintance wrote to Johnson of Morrissey shortly after the convention's close, "is wholly relied upon by all parties, for his integrity and sagacity."[392]

Many others were equally impressed with Morrissey's qualities of restraint and party loyalty as a congressman. Considering the outrage that

[390] Pafford, 10-50 (e-book)
[391] *New York Sun*, May 2, 1878; Ackerman, 49
[392] Bergeron, 296 – 434; *New York Times*, January 20, 1878

had accompanied his initial nomination and election, the simple fact that he had not resorted to flat-out fisticuffs on the floor of the House was probably enough to surprise some. "His courteous demeanor and unassuming ways won him many friends from both parties," one reporter later remembered. Despite his lack of activity in the House, John Morrissey garnered nomination for a second term in Congress with the 1868 elections looming.[393]

The 1868 elections in New York would become the subject of more investigation and scandal than any prior election year. Among the Tammany-backed candidates for that year were Horatio Seymour for President (the current Governor), John Hoffman for Governor (the current Mayor of New York City), New York Supreme Court incumbent George Barnard, A. Oakey Hall for Mayor of New York City (the current District Attorney), and Morrissey for Congress, all of whom were closely connected with Senator William "Boss" Tweed, who was up for re-election as County Supervisor himself.

In addition to the long-practiced voter intimidation and the "repeater voting" introduced to Tammany by John Morrissey, new techniques for wholesale naturalization of fresh immigrants and post-election manipulation of ballot numbers were also used to influence the success of Democratic candidates for every position. Immigration statistics had been on a steep incline since the 1850s and did not abate after the end of the Civil War. Investigations by a congressional committee, a U.S. marshal, and the local press would all expose Tammany's unscrupulous practice of taking advantage of the new arrivals when the citizens of New York went to the polls in 1868. Various local judges churned out approved naturalization papers with factory-like efficiency, none more prolifically than State Supreme Court Judge (and 1868 candidate) Barnard. Many of the names on these papers did not meet the requirements of citizenship, either because of age, residence, or because they were entirely fictional. The congressional investigators later discovered that New York judges processed 41,112 new citizenships in the weeks leading up to Election Day. Many of these new Americans were also willing participants in repeat voting, given assumed names and transferred to different polls around New York City by Tammany men.[394]

U.S. Marshal Robert Murray, having discovered the conspiracy of selling citizenships, had dispatched men all over the city on Election Day. In retaliation, Tammany-backed Sheriff Jimmy O'Brien immediately deputized two thousand men and sent them into the streets as enforcers of the Tammany agenda. Meanwhile, Mayor Hoffman offered a $1,000 reward for

[393] *New York Sun* May 2, 1878
[394] Ackerman, 39-41

each arrest these men made of anyone "intimidating, obstructing or defrauding any voter in the exercising of his right as an elector." Hoffman's presence on the Tammany ticket meant that his offer was a code calling for the obstruction of any Republican, U.S. Marshal, or anyone else who got in the way of Tammany's corruption of the vote. Obeying the Mayor's call, O'Brien's men arrested at least three poll inspectors and threatened to arrest others who watched the polls too closely; they also acted as armed guards for the parties of repeat voters bouncing between polling places across town.[395]

Marshal Murray did manage to make dozens of arrests of alleged repeat voters and fake citizens, but almost as quickly as he could bring them in, they were back on the streets, Tammany-funded lawyers and judges having been placed on call for just such assistance. Judge Barnard himself signed the release papers of twenty-seven such men on a single order.[396]

The congressional investigation would also discover a circular put out on Election Day by the Democratic State Committee with the signature of Samuel Tilden, a high-ranking and wealthy power within the party who was close friends with, and the primary advisor to, Governor Seymour. The letter, distributed in the hundreds throughout the state to various important Democratic politicians, asked the reader to "at once communicate with some reliable person in three or four principal towns and in each city of your county, and request him… to telegraph to William M. Tweed, Tammany Hall, at the minute of closing the polls… such person's estimate of the vote. *There is of course an important object to be obtained.*" Tilden would later claim to have no knowledge of the letter. A. Oakey Hall, District Attorney and Tammany candidate for New York City Mayor, had been the leaflet's true author. The message's implication was that Tammany wanted these early numbers from Republican-friendly rural areas in order to have time to manipulate City ballot results to get the statewide majorities required for their candidates.

Brought before the congressional committee later, Boss Tweed made no attempt to cover his position at the center of Tammany's web of political influence ("I have that reputation, and I think it is pretty well deserved."). He also made no attempt to cover up Hall's role as the letter's author. The reason for it, he explained, was to get a good idea of the legitimate numbers, in case the Republicans decided to manipulate the results. Essentially, he was accusing the Republicans of intending to use the various strategies which Tweed himself had in fact overseen for the Democrats.

After the polls closed, Tammany operatives used various methods to delay counting, stuff ballots, lose Republican votes, cause confusion, and otherwise manipulate the final numbers. The congressional investigators later estimated that 50,000 of the 156,054 votes cast in New York City had

---

[395] Ackerman, 55
[396] Ackerman, 56

been illegal or fraudulent. In fact, that total number of votes cast exceeded the number of eligible voters in the city by more than 8 percent. In the end, Presidential candidate Horatio Seymour defeated Ulysses Grant at the New York polls by a suspiciously round number of exactly 10,000 votes. John Hoffman took the Governor's office, and Tweed and Barnard were re-elected to their posts, all by wide margins. A. Oakey Hall replaced Hoffman as Mayor, and John Morrissey received his second term as congressman by a wide margin of over 13,000 votes over his opponent, railroad entrepreneur George Francis Train. "The machinery of local government is in working order," Hall bragged; "every office is filled with capable men."[397]

John Morrissey's name was not at the center of the congressional investigation into New York State voter fraud the next year. Doubtless, as a Tammany man with at least some connection to every man involved in the corruption, Morrissey was at least complicit if not directly active in the various schemes the Democrats had going that election season. Certainly, historians can blame him for the use of repeat voting, which he had introduced to Tammany years before. However, either because he was not directly involved or because of friends at each level of the political stratum, Morrissey emerged from this election as a two-time congressman with his reputation relatively unmarred.

––––––

As had been the case with his first term, Morrissey was largely an absentee congressman through much of his second term. One reporter found Morrissey's long absences appropriate, sarcastically suggesting that "he could not more fittingly represent the class of Democrats who elected him than by remaining at home and attending to his faro business, as he is said to do." Morrissey would later complain that he had lost a half million dollars in opportunities related to his gambling businesses because of his time in Washington. He remained determinedly ambitious for furthering his career as the overlord of New York gambling, another likely explanation for much of his absence from his government position in Washington. An 1867 raid on his place at 808 Broadway by an anti-gambling society barely amounted to a nuisance. $25,000 placed in the right hands saw the charges dropped. That same year, the people of Saratoga watched with curiosity as workers in Morrissey's employ filled in a vacant, swampy mire on Congress Street with dirt. Once the workers completed that job, they placed wooden planks over the dirt and began erecting the frame of a curiously large brick

[397] Ackerman, 56-58; *New York Herald*, May 2, 1878; *New York Times*, May 2, 1878; *Danville Express*, May 9, 1878; Wingate, "Municipal Government," *North American Review*, January 1875

building on top of them. Visiting the construction site, John envisioned in his mind's eye the completion of the crown jewel of his gambling empire.[398]

Everyone else's eyes were dazzled by Susan, who enjoyed flaunting her husband's wealth as much as he did. Even the early women's rights paper *Revolution* objectified the woman as a "large fine looking woman" before describing the material adornments for which she was famous. Whether in Saratoga or the District of Columbia, Mrs. Morrissey's beauty and diamond-laden fashion continued to astonish those who met her, and she enjoyed the attention. She was most conspicuous when attending the opera in Washington, making sure everyone noticed her $75,000 Lemaire of Paris opera glasses, encrusted with diamonds and sapphires, a gift from her husband to celebrate winning his congressional seat. Sometimes she would come to sessions of Congress to see her husband at his work and appear in the gallery "dressed in a complete suit of crimson, and blazing with diamonds" valued at $25,000. Both the New York and D.C. papers marveled at "the charms of the strong man's better half" and proclaimed her among the great beauties of their cities. When the couple appeared at the inaugural ball for President Ulysses S. Grant on March 4, 1869, Susan once more outshined her husband in her black velvet dress, point lace and diamonds.[399]

Despite the refinery of her dress, Mrs. Morrissey hailed from a working-class background like her husband, and her rougher edges amused some of those who knew her. One friend noted her obsessive reading of boxing news, and that, despite being "amiable and charitable," she was not opposed to putting up her fists against those who sorely offended her, rendering a female neighbor senseless on at least one occasion. Similarly, a newspaper correspondent recorded that, when a young man presumed to speak to Mrs. Morrissey too familiarly in a public street, "an arm of steel sprang from a sealskin muff, and a blow that might have felled an ox laid the young fellow sprawling against a stoop."[400]

As a new decade approached, John Morrissey was ten years removed from his ring career. He was a father, investor, and a congressman. He had powerful allies and friends, and he was married to one of the most famously beautiful women in America. Some said he was now himself a millionaire. Little did he know that the coming year would threaten many of those relationships, as well as his financial and political futures.[401]

[398] *Raftsman's Journal*, May 11, 1870; *Memphis Daily Appeal*, April 19, 1871; Asbury, *Sucker's Progress*, pp. 375-376, 383
[399] *Charleston Daily News*, October 11, 1867; www.nysun.com/calendar/old-smoke/13666/ accessed 12/7/2016; *New Orleans Crescent*, March 16, 1869; *New York World*, July 31, 1866; *Daily Albany Argus*, March 25, 1868, quoting the *Revolution*
[400] *Morning News*, March 1, 1889; *Helena Independent*, March 3, 1889; *Albany Evening Journal*, November 15, 1876
[401] *Evening Telegraph*, July 25, 1866; *New York World*, July 12, 1865

16.

Black Friday

John Morrissey was by most accounts a very wealthy man at the dawn of 1869, wealthy enough to forget about $50,000 in cash he left in a hotel room. While spending the night in Albany's Delavan House, the congressman thought it a good idea to place the large sum of cash under his pillow, presumably to protect it from theft while he slept. However, upon rising the next morning, he hurried out the door of the hotel in such a rush that he did not remember the money under his pillow until a half hour had passed aboard the train out of town. Disembarking at the next station, he impatiently waited for the next train back to Albany, then rushed into the Delavan's lobby and inquired about the money hours after he had departed. To his relief, the desk clerk handed over a wad of cash to Mr. Morrissey, who counted it and found it all there to the dollar. Told a chambermaid had brought the money down to the desk, Morrissey asked to meet her. The elderly chambermaid presented herself, and the grateful John Morrissey peeled off a $500 bill from the roll of cash and presented it to the astonished lady.[402]

As part of his expanding business interests, Morrissey allegedly enjoyed behind-the-scenes ownership of one of the first professional baseball teams in America, Troy's Haymakers, and it was supposedly he who caused one of the sport's most noteworthy early controversies. In 1869, when the Haymakers walked out of a tie game with the undefeated Cincinnati Red Stockings after a violent disagreement over an umpire's call, it was rumored that Morrissey had ordered the team to do so, knowing he had wagered $60,000 on the game. The Red Stockings were taking control of the game, and a tie game would mean all bets were off. Apparently, walking out on a game did not mean a forfeit in those days.[403]

As great as Morrissey's wealth and political influence might have been at this stage in his life, there were still those close to him who had the power to tear it all down. One of those was the acknowledged master of New York politics, William Tweed. Morrissey and Tweed do not appear to have ever been exceedingly close friends. As important figures in the New York Democratic Party in general and in Tammany specifically, they were allies for a time. They certainly had plenty of things in common. Both were physically big men for their era. Both had laid the foundation of their future political strength at the street level with the working men and lower

---

[402] *Daily Albany Argus*, March 14, 1871
[403] *Jackson Standard*, September 2, 1869; *Daily Dispatch*, August 22, 1869; Ginsburg, 7-10; Laing, 30

classes of Manhattan, where they both learned the tactics of political fixing that would serve them in later years. Their political bases (the Sixth Ward for Morrissey and the Seventh for Tweed) were just a few blocks apart from each other. Both had quickly grown wealthy in the years immediately following the Civil War (Tweed would once boast of being worth twenty million dollars) and were looked down upon as "shabby rich" by the men supposed to be their social betters. They were both sporting men who liked to gamble, dabble in the stock market, and flaunt their wealth. They knew, socialized with, and worked with many of the same people.[404]

However, beyond the circumstances of time, place, and politics, Morrissey and Tweed were very different men in several ways. The perception of Morrissey was of a quiet, brooding man when sober, and of a man belligerent to the point of violence when drunk. His best political tools were his black-browed scowl, his reputation as a fighter, his plain-spokenness, and raw physical intimidation. Tweed, by contrast, was boisterous and gregarious, greeting his friends and enemies alike with a big smile, a hearty handshake, and a disarming joke. Day-to-day management bored Morrissey: he had no patience for the nuances and details of the capitol or a board room. Tweed, on the other hand, was a born administrator. His background was in bookkeeping, and for years he deftly managed the complex web of politics, corruption, and finance that composed the day-to-day operation of New York City. Certainly, Morrissey's past work on behalf of Fernando Wood, who had once stood in the way of Tweed's ascendancy in Tammany, did not help their relationship.

In terms of political influence, Tweed had long been Morrissey's superior. Being the older of the two and a native New Yorker, he had entered the city's political circles earlier, and had since gone about methodically centralizing first Tammany and eventually the entire city government around himself over a period of two decades. At the time that Morrissey was beginning to pull himself out of the mire of the Five Points, Tweed was already a power in Tammany. Morrissey had brought himself into the Tammany inner circle in part through his value to Tweed as a hero of the Sixth Ward, not to mention by bringing "repeater" voting strategies to Tweed's attention. As the 1860s neared an end, Tweed was at the very height of his powers, even if his name was not yet infamous to the city newspapers or the national public at large. However, it was becoming increasingly clear that Morrissey's status within Tammany was rising; his own amassing fortune, congressional seat, and powerful connections within both finance and politics made him a real power in New York's Democratic Party and a potential threat to the Boss.

The first signs of serious strain between Morrissey and Tweed appeared as far back as 1868, when Tweed opposed John's nomination for a second term in Congress. According to the *New York Herald*, Tweed had approved

---

[404] Wingate, "Municipal Government," *North American Review*, January 1875

Morrissey's initial nomination "in consequence of fear of his strength and popularity than for any other object." Tweed apparently hoped that giving Morrissey the seat in Congress would satisfy his ambitions, turning him from a potential threat to a mollified lackey. By 1868, though, Morrissey's association with men like President Johnson, Cornelius Vanderbilt, and August Belmont, all of whom were too big for a local political boss like Tweed to control, gave Morrissey too much independence, as far as Tweed was concerned. Thus, as the elections drew near, Tweed and his cronies began criticizing Morrissey to others in Tammany as a "drag chain" on the Democratic Party, his reputation as a drunkard, gambler, and criminal potentially stigmatizing the other candidates on the 1868 ticket. They went so far as to blame John Hoffman's defeat in the 1866 gubernatorial race on his association with Morrissey. They argued that Hoffman's return as a candidate meant that Tammany should not allow Morrissey to run as well, in order to prevent a repeated result. Hoffman, as Morrissey once described him, was "like wax in the hands of Tweed and [Tweed Ring member Peter] Sweeny," and so was preferable to Tweed's mind than the more independent Morrissey as an elected official. However, the Tweed Ring's whispers could not overcome John's popularity in the largely Irish Fifth District, who wanted Morrissey again. Seeing this and hearing rumors that Morrissey was threatening to defect to a rival organization, the Tammany leadership reluctantly threw its support behind Old Smoke for re-election.[405]

During the same election, Morrissey had favored Joseph Shannon, the President of the Board of Aldermen, for Sheriff. Initially, the rest of Tammany had approved and, according to Morrissey, promised the position to Shannon. However, when Jimmy O'Brien came along, Tweed and his cronies forgot this promise and instead named O'Brien to the post, a move which only served to infuriate Morrissey further.

———

That same year, the Wall Street struggle which became known as the Erie Railway War also likely widened the gap between Old Smoke and the Boss. Jay Gould, a rising figure on Wall Street, had joined a group of investors led by John Eldridge of Boston, who sought to remove Cornelius Vanderbilt's longtime rival and sometime friend Daniel Drew from the board of the Erie Railway and take full control of the line. Gould approached Vanderbilt in person in 1867. Vanderbilt reluctantly joined this conspiracy to finally do away with Drew, though he plainly expressed his distrust of the upstart Gould to the man's face. The Commodore's reservations would prove correct.

---

[405] *New York Herald*, May 2, 1878; *New York Sun*, May 2, 1878

The reasons and details of the Eldridge and Gould plan are intricate and not consequential here. Suffice it to say that, learning of the plot against him too late to do anything else about it, Drew pleaded with Vanderbilt to reconsider his alliance with Eldridge and Gould, which the Commodore did. Naturally, Eldridge and Gould were upset by the Commodore's change in position, but they now had little option but to agree to a deal. Eldridge, Gould, and Vanderbilt associate Frank Work would assume positions on the Erie board, along with the relative neophyte stockbroker James Fisk, Jr. Drew lost his seat, but after another board member quickly resigned, Vanderbilt and the rest allowed him to fill the vacancy as part of the deal.

In the next year, Drew began a series of manipulations and betrayals with the Erie stock that left Work and other Vanderbilt allies (possibly even the Commodore himself) at a financial loss and feeling cheated. Work filed a complaint with the New York State Supreme Court, asking for an order to prevent further Erie stock trades by Drew and recompense for the losses Work and others incurred. The case came before none other than George Barnard, Boss Tweed's man in Albany. Barnard did stop Drew's trading and eventually ordered his temporary removal from the board. Vanderbilt then went about cornering Erie's stock, motivated almost entirely out of a desire for revenge against Drew, rather than any plans for the company.

Seeing Vanderbilt's move, the members of the Erie board, Eldrige, Gould, and Fisk among them, interpreted this as a threat against their own control of the company and aligned themselves with Drew, the very man they had originally intended to oust. "In essence, they would drown Vanderbilt in new shares, created under cover of the law that permitted the conversion of bonds into stock" explains Commodore biographer T.J. Stiles. In the meantime, the conspirators found another Judge to remove Work from the board and suspend all his lawsuits, resulting in Drew's ability to once again trade Erie. Drew and his new allies then executed a series of financial moves that culminated with Drew secretly selling huge amounts of Erie shares short to Vanderbilt through various intermediaries. Determined to finish his corner and unaware that these sellers were fronts for Drew, the stubborn Commodore just kept buying, even as Erie's value obviously began to turn.[406]

Judge Barnard, having kept a close eye on this activity, issued citations against the entire Erie board, forcing the conspirators to flee to New Jersey, taking their cash, bonds, and stocks with them. By now, the public had realized what was happening, as had Vanderbilt, whose financial losses were in the millions. Possibly because of the Commodore's known friendship with John Morrissey, word soon spread that the Commodore was hiring thugs to track down and exact revenge upon his enemies in their hotel. These henchmen never materialized.

---

[406] Stiles, 456

As the press and public surrounded the conspirators in their New Jersey hotel, Work, Vanderbilt, and their enemies continued their fights in the state courts. Bribes were flagrantly dispersed, with Albany legislators with $300 annual salaries pocketing cash in the thousands as the price for a single vote. Possibly due to their mutual association with Morrissey, Boss Tweed (who included State Senator among his many titles) initially threw his political influence behind Vanderbilt, as evidenced by Tammany judge Barnard's support of Work. Soon enough though, Tweed's influence and money switched allegiances to Eldridge, Gould, and Fisk. His reasons for doing so are not clear. Perhaps he sensed that he had initially backed the wrong horse and wanted to realign with those he perceived to be the eventual winners. Perhaps also he saw this as an opportunity to weaken John Morrissey's political strength, which had always been backed by his good friend Vanderbilt.[407]

The lives of fugitives holed up in a hotel, combined with other pressures of the fight with Vanderbilt, took their toll on Drew and Eldridge, who soon enough were willing to negotiate with the Commodore. Likewise, Vanderbilt's financial losses had been great enough to also put him in a mood for peace talks. A deal ended things with Vanderbilt selling 50,000 of his shares back to the Erie board for $3,500,000, only a portion of the money he had lost. The board then paid the Commodore another one million dollars for the option to buy his remaining 50,000 shares at a lesser sum within sixty days, which they eventually did. Frank Work and others also worked out deals to sell their watered-down shares back to the board.[408]

In the end, the Erie Railroad War proved to be the most humiliating and financially disastrous affair of Commodore Vanderbilt's great railroad investing career. Jay Gould and James Fisk, Jr., seen as the victors in the dispute, were now extremely wealthy men who had earned serious reputations for themselves on Wall Street, along with the Commodore's begrudging respect. Senator Tweed's backing in Albany had apparently been a big help to the Erie board, as Gould subsequently rewarded the Tammany boss with his own seat on the board. This would be the beginning of a long working relationship between Gould, Fisk, and Tweed, with the financiers becoming integral parts of Tweed's Ring.

Hot tempered and loyal to a fault, John Morrissey would not have taken well to Bill Tweed betraying Vanderbilt. By the close of 1868, Morrissey had come to recognize Tweed as an enemy. "Night and day," a writer for the *Herald* later remembered, "in public and in private, whenever an opportunity arose, he denounced Tweed in the most bitter terms." John openly offered a bet of $50,000 that Tweed would be in prison within three years. What had started as a cold war of whispers and secret alliances

---

[407] Ackerman, 52
[408] Stiles, 464-465

between two of Tammany's most powerful figures was quickly becoming a very public row.[409]

That Tweed next set his political sights on another of Morrissey's Saratoga circle, August Belmont, could only have made things worse. For years, Belmont had been the chairman of the Democratic National Committee. His wealth, connections, and status within the party placed him well outside of Tweed's expanding control, something the Boss sought to remedy with a plan to oust him from the chair and take that coveted position himself in 1869. Through his various subordinates, Tweed initiated a publicity campaign to paint Belmont as an aloof aristocrat disloyal to both the Democratic Party and the country as a whole because of his connection with high finance in Europe. The move proved self-defeating. Unbeknownst to Tweed, Belmont had been considering resignation from the chair, but the challenge from Tweed convinced him to stay and stubbornly fight for the position as a matter of pride. Morrissey and Belmont's other friends within the party rallied to his cause, and Tweed eventually backed off.

———

As Morrissey and Tweed drifted irrevocably apart, Tweed drew closer to his friends on the Erie Railway board, Jay Gould and particularly Jim Fisk. He would participate with these two in yet another Wall Street conspiracy, one that would this time have dire consequences for the national economy at large and prove particularly detrimental for John Morrissey. Gould and Fisk initially intended to drive down the cost of American exports overseas, thereby resulting in a boom for the railroads they owned, as farmers became desperate to get their in-demand crops to the coasts and the docks. Approaching President Grant, the pair convinced him to limit the sale of government gold, another part of their plan. Gould had been buying and stockpiling gold for months.

Meanwhile, Cornelius Vanderbilt had separately been moving toward his ultimate ambition of connecting his New York railroads (Harlem, Hudson River, and New York Central) with those of Chicago, a plan he hoped to bring to fruition by the close of 1869. As he had done with all three New York lines, he brought John Morrissey in on the deal, advising him to buy up stock in Chicago's Lake Shore Railroad. Gould was making similar moves with the Erie Railway, leasing lines around the country to connect with his own, thereby making the Erie more attractive and efficient for growers, manufacturers, and sellers looking to transport their products. Just as the Commodore had been taking a financial interest in Lake Shore, Gould and Fisk began secretly making plays to take control of the Lake Shore board and connect it with Erie. Soon enough, Gould revealed

[409] *New York Herald*, May 2, 1878; *Chicago Daily Tribune*, August 1, 1874

himself and got the upper hand in this struggle. In retaliation, Vanderbilt began selling off stocks in Lake Shore and New York Central. The value of the stock still owned by Gould and his fellow conspirators plummeted. At the same time, as other New York investors jumped on the opportunity of buying up the Commodore's stocks, the men of Wall Street became suddenly cash-strapped and credit became tight.

All this had happened simultaneously with Gould and Fisk attempting to corner the nation's gold market through their manipulation of the President. Gould, in retaliation for the Commodore's strike at Lake Shore's value, began to bid up the price of gold. All these schemes and manipulations, combined with the lack of credit and cash available to Wall Street investors, threatened to wreak havoc on the national economy. Worried about suspicions circling the White House's involvement in all of this, President Grant ordered the Treasury to release millions of dollars in gold into the market, hoping to offset Gould's manipulations. The move proved a disastrous over-correction.

On Friday, September 24, 1869, gold prices collapsed, sending the national economy into its worst crisis in over a decade. In a single day, more than a dozen brokerages folded. Credit faltered nationwide, sending down the value of stocks in most of the country's major businesses. The day would become almost immediately known as Black Friday.

At Vanderbilt's urging, John Morrissey had bought big into the New York Central Railroad and the Hudson River Railroads, inspired by the Commodore's intentions to combine them into a single line. The Commodore's flooding the market with his own Central stocks weakened the value of Morrissey's shares. The collapse of Black Friday only made this trend worse. Through September 24, Vanderbilt worked hard to maintain his control of, and protect the value of both lines, which he regarded as a single investment. While he had some success at both, he could not prevent the share values from taking a downturn. The *New York Times* later estimated Morrissey's losses in New York Central at $600,000.[410]

Amid the wild rise and drop of gold prices, the brokerage firm John used had lost money to Fisk as part of the gold corner and was now on the verge of collapse, threatening Morrissey's already dwindled finances further. "Mr. Morrissey had nothing directly to do with Fisk or his gold *corner*," reported the *Times* a few days later, "but he had to do with a highly-respectable firm of young brokers who were nearly ruined on the occasion." Differing sources place the losses that Morrissey's friends experienced as part of the Gould and Fisk gold manipulations between $50,000 and $82,000, a sum that Old Smoke fully intended to recover from Fisk himself.[411]

[410] Stiles, 493; *New York Times*, May 2, 1878
[411] *New York Times*, October 5, 1869; Medbery, 164

A former waiter and dry goods salesman, Fisk had risen from near poverty and complete obscurity to outrageous wealth and infamy as one of the true robber barons of Wall Street in just a couple of years. Flamboyant in dress, personality, and spending, he delighted in the high life and in his friendships with men like Gould and Tweed. He openly kept a mistress, furnishing her with her own riches and apartment. Fisk's Grand Opera House, constructed the previous year on the corner of 8th Avenue and 23rd Street, was his pride and joy. Here and elsewhere, he wined and dined and openly bribed the politicians and lawmakers who aided him in his piracy. For many, Jim Fisk was a living embodiment, a walking caricature, of a Wall Street robber baron, a reputation that did not work to his benefit once Black Friday hit.

Following the stock market collapse, the press and public all pointed their fingers at Fisk. Neither he nor Gould nor Vanderbilt had intended to crash the market with their maneuverings. They all lost money on Black Friday, but their reserves were strong enough to allow them to ride out the crash with minimal difficulty. The same had not been the case for others who had invested in the stock market, many of whom lost their fortunes, their businesses, or their credit, and these people now made the extravagant Fisk the focal point of their ire.

Fearful of the public's rage, Fisk had been holing himself up in his Grand Opera House office for days when John Morrissey made moves to collect on his losses. As Wall Street chronicler James Knowles Medbery recounted the tale a year later, Morrissey personally forced his way inside of Fisk's office at the Opera House to confront the robber baron in person on the day of the collapse. He demanded that Fisk return the $50,000 to him and his stockbroker friends, to which Fisk replied he would see them in court. The former Five Points gangster scoffed at the idea of settling a personal dispute in the courts. "Bah! we are not going to the law. I've evidence enough, and you may as well pay without more bother."

The threat was obvious. Shifting in his chair and too fearful to raise his voice above a choked whisper, Fisk told Morrissey to see his lawyer. Morrissey made no move to leave. He again demanded a check. At this, Fisk sprang out of his chair to ring a bell chord which would bring the authorities. Morrissey got to the bell first and, standing between Fisk and the chord, demanded payment once again. A few minutes later he was back out on the street, a signed check in his hand.[412]

The next day, a rumor spread throughout New York that a vengeful John Morrissey had shot and killed Fisk on the street, and later yet another circulated that Fisk had shot Morrissey, but the newspapers were quick to investigate and disprove these stories. A *New York Times* article printed a few days after the event says that nothing so dramatic as Medbery's story, and certainly not murder, was necessary for Fisk to reimburse Morrissey

---

412 Medbery, *Men*, 163-165

and his friends. Old Smoke's reputation had preceded him well enough that Fisk saw no reason for a physical meeting to produce the check, which the *Times* listed as being between $80,000 and $82,000. "The summary process used was not of a corporeal nature," insisted the reporter, "but simply an intimation, in very emphatic terms, through a mutual acquaintance, of what would follow in a week, or in six weeks, or whenever he dares show himself outside hi [sic] intrenched [sic] office if the money was not forthcoming at once, to the uttermost penny. The money came." Clearly supporting Morrissey's case in the matter, and, like many papers, condemning Fisk for his part in the gold corner and Black Friday, the *Times* went on to say that "Mr. Morrissey is known for his prompt and quiet way of doing business in Wall-street, and is never ruffled by losses great or small when fairly and squarely incurred. But there are some 'hard cases,' it seems, he will not stand, and Fisk, Jr. is one of them."[413]

Accounts of the period differ as to exactly how much John lost through his investments during the events of Black Friday. At the very least, it seems the event had sapped all his ready cash, and he very likely began accruing the considerable debts that would later come to light. Technically, he still had his congressman's pay, as well as much more money coming out of his various business interests, not the least of which was his gambling empire. He was by no means ruined, but if any of his other businesses would happen to take a turn, he would no longer have the cash reserves to repair the damage and reverse his fortunes. He saw no other option other than to borrow heavily until he could replenish his finances.

The financial stresses began to take their toll on Morrissey's carefully constructed image of respectability. In the closing weeks of 1869, he wound up in a tussle at the Capital, a saloon owned by Jem Mace, the British boxing champion. Seated at a table with several other men, John wound up in an argument with George "Coolie Keys" Hill, a "desperate character" whose arrest record would ultimately include everything from woman beating to forgery in his lifetime. An aspiring gambling kingpin himself, Keys had been a nuisance to Morrissey for years, and was now running the gambling enterprises in Mace's place. When the confrontation at the Capital broke out, Hill spit in Morrissey's face, bringing out the drunken rage of Old Smoke for the first time in years. John stood and drew a derringer, leveling at Hill, who then pulled his own revolver. Luckily, Mace was presiding over the evening, and seeing that blood was about to spill on his floor, leapt into action. Grabbing Morrissey up, he dragged the enraged fellow pugilist into another room and left him there behind a locked door until he sobered up and left peacefully. Both Mace and Morrissey subsequently tried to prevent the story from getting out, but the *Times* inevitably got ahold of the tale and printed it.[414]

[413] McAlpine, 435; *New York Times*, October 5, 1869; *Chicago Tribune*, January 24, 1870
[414] *New York Times*, December 31, 1871; *New Orleans Republican*, April 11, 1875

After his first election to Congress, Morrissey told a Cincinnati interviewer that he intended divest himself from his gambling businesses; it was a lie. He certainly paid less attention to his gaming empire, but it remained his main source of income. In the last month of the decade, Morrissey became embroiled in a legal case concerning his illegal policy (or lottery) business in Manhattan which compounded his losses from Black Friday. Investigations by the District Attorney's office and the Internal Revenue Service had brought the business into the newspapers and the courts after one of the policy game's operators, a W. Van Vorst, was arrested for failing to pay the proper taxes derived from his income in the illegal operation. Morrissey had been the behind-the-scenes master of the policy game for years, and it had been easy money, requiring little management and providing big returns. Back in 1863, Benjamin Wood (brother of Fernando and former a former congressman himself) and his partners had weaseled in on Morrissey's business, Wood promising to pay Morrissey $5,000 a month, which Morrissey alleged had never been paid. In time, it would be learned that both men had interests in a network of policy games which stretched well outside of New York State, even as far as Virginia and West Virginia. Since the lottery was now in the open, John felt it appropriate to fight the matter of an illegal business in a legal court battle.[415]

In some ways, the move makes sense. Participating in a lottery game was a misdemeanor punishable by a fine. However, the lucrative receipts from the lottery in Manhattan trumped any such penalties. The *New York Times* noted that, in past cases of illegal lotteries, judges referred the case for investigation to a grand jury, which usually resulted in no convictions and no substantial change. However, the unusual case brought before the courts by plaintiff John Morrissey would prompt a whirlwind of contradictory orders from two New York Supreme Court judges.

On Tuesday, December 6, Judge Albert Cardozo gave a shocking order that Morrissey and his partners in the policy game hand over their business, including "property, assets, credits and effects," to Wood, who was supposed to sell off these assets and extricate himself from the business. Morrissey, being the one who had issued the complaint in the first place, was doubtless shocked and enraged at this. Then, come December 19, Judge Barnard issued a new ruling, acting as though the original had never existed. Barnard's father-in-law, a tobacconist named John Anderson, was also among those implicated in Morrissey's policy game as well, giving him a significant conflict of interest. Nonetheless, Barnard got himself involved and made Morrissey the receiver of the business and its assets. Naturally,

[415] ; *Wheeling Daily Intelligencer*, January 5, 1867; *New York Times*, December 15, 1869 and January 27, 1870; *New York Herald*, January 27, 1870

Cardozo responded with yet another order that the business be handed over to Wood on December 21. Both Cardozo and Barnard were subservient to Tammany Hall. Their bickering through competing orders represented a growing rift within the organization itself. "Order, counter order, disorder," mused the *Times*. The *Herald* found less humor in the situation. "This is a most bare-faced prostitution of the intent of the law and a disgraceful evidence to the people who elect the judges of our courts of the degeneracy into which the holders of this high office have fallen," decried one of their writers, going on to insinuate that a vigilance committee should cleanse New York of its judges, "from the highest in the State down to the lowest." As far as can be gathered from the papers of the day, Cardozo's December 21 order, confirmed in another hearing the following January, was the last in the matter and the policy game, illegal though it might have remained, was legally put completely into Benjamin Wood's hands, the decision representing a complete reversal of Morrissey's original intent in bringing the suit and robbing him of one of his most rewarding incomes, although some sources report that Morrissey continued to be secretly involved in policy at least through the next few years.[416]

---

[416] *New York Times*, December 15, 19, and 22, 1869; *New York Herald*, December 20, 1869 and January 27, 1870; Wingate, "Municipal Government," *North American Review*, January 1875; *New York Sun*, May 2, 1878

17.

The Young Democracy

In the Spring of 1870, word reached John Morrissey that Boss Tweed had ordered his death. As outraged as John was at this news, he could not have been surprised; the prior year's events had been pointing at an irrevocable split not just between Tweed and Morrissey, but between two warring factions within the entire Tammany organization.

Tweed's failure to wrest the New York Democratic Party Chairman's seat from August Belmont in 1869 did not prevent him from working to expand his power within New York City. Since the days of Fernando Wood's struggles with the state legislature, the state government in Albany had been consolidating its influence over the city's politics to the point that demand for "Home Rule" had become a universal lament of the people and politicians of New York City, Democrat or otherwise. Senator Tweed issued a new charter for the city, which he publicly passed off as a push for Home Rule. In truth, Tweed's brilliant and secretive right-hand man Peter Sweeny had drafted it, and it promised to consolidate the entire city government around the Boss. It also threatened to relegate the rest of Tammany Hall to perpetual subservience.

Under the charter, power over city construction and finances would be split between four offices, that of the Mayor (currently Tweed's close ally A. Oakey Hall), the Comptroller (another Tweed Ring crony, Richard "Slippery Dick" Connolly), the Commissioner of Parks (soon to be Sweeny), and the Commissioner of Public Works (Tweed himself). The charter gave Mayor Hall the power to appoint all these positions but his own elected office, a power previously held collectively by the city aldermen. Once in place, the office holders would keep their positions for terms of six to eight years, depending on the office, meaning they would hold these titles even if a mayor disloyal to Tammany entered office after Hall. Only a unanimous decision from the six judges of the Common Pleas could impeach one of them from office. If Mayor Hall should somehow be removed from office before a replacement could be elected, his powers of appointment would pass to the comptroller, Connolly.

Despite the obvious movement of power away from Albany and despite the consolidation of that power within the Democratic Party and Tammany Hall in particular, the main objection to Tweed's charter came from inside Tammany. That Tweed had left them out of the offices of power – and the corresponding opportunities for graft and patronage – offended many high-placed figures within the organization. At the forefront of those protesting the charter was John Morrissey, who used the exclusivity of the charter as a reason to rile up discontent within Tammany. In this way, he found an important ally in the already disgruntled Sheriff Jimmy O'Brien.[417]

Born in Ireland, O'Brien had come to the United States only a few years previous at age twenty. Like Morrissey, he had little time for school as a youth; unlike Morrissey, he had never taught himself to read. Like Tweed, his first significant connections with local politics had come as the foreman of a fire company, a frequent route into ward politics in nineteenth century New York. Early on, he had not been a favorite of the Tweed Ring. Judge Barnard had sentenced him to time in Blackwell's Island prison for participating in an election riot and, after his release, Peter Sweeny had tried unsuccessfully to prevent his election to alderman. However, the charismatic, ambitious young man proved effective enough at the job to turn the Ring's opinion of him, the result of which was their approval of his installment as sheriff. For a time, the gregarious and ambitious sheriff considered himself something of a protégé of Tweed's, whom he regarded as a personal hero. John Morrissey had a different opinion of Tweed of course, and thus Morrissey and O'Brien had initially been at odds with one another.

In his position as sheriff, O'Brien had been at the center of the Tammany-backed voter fraud of the 1868 New York elections, the leader of thousands of deputies sent into the street to protect repeat voters from interference from political opponents and U.S. marshals. He was right to think that Hall and Tweed owed their lucrative positions, at least in some part, to his activities. A dispute had already arisen between O'Brien and Connolly, the Sheriff claiming that the comptroller had failed to pay him properly. When a friend of his went to prison for murder, eventually to be hanged, O'Brien blamed the conviction on Tweed and Sweeny, furthering his grudge against the Ring. Only in his twenties, O'Brien was still young and impatient for respect and money. When the Tweed charter left him out of its exclusive dispensation of power, O'Brien was finally ready for an open fight with Tweed. Morrissey and O'Brien suddenly found common ground. After a New Years' Day, 1870 meeting at Morrissey's Twenty-Fourth Street office, Morrissey, O'Brien, and many other figures in the Tammany fold united in their opposition to the Tweed Ring. They came to call themselves the Young Democracy.

Almost from the start, the Young Democracy found a highly respected benefactor in Samuel J. Tilden, a wealthy and influential Democrat in national politics. A Yale graduate who hobnobbed with the most powerful politicians and patricians in the country, Tilden despised the kind of local swindling represented by Tweed and his cronies. He and his kind looked down upon the "new rich" that had risen out of the Civil War, men like Tweed, whom they regarded as uncultured, corrupt, and undeserving of social status. Likewise, Tweed and his men liked to call Tilden's kind of

417 Wingate, "Municipal Government," *North American Review,* January 1875

Democrats "swallowtails," mocking the formal jackets that they wore at exclusive social clubs like the Manhattan Club, which had turned up its nose at Tweed's request for membership. Though many of the Young Democrats hailed from poor families, lacked formal education, and were themselves corrupt, reformer Tilden regarded them as the lesser of two evils and put his significant support behind them. Soon enough, every one of the city's alderman had also joined the Young Democracy cause.[418]

Tilden's support brought added visibility to the Young Democracy movement, and soon enough newspapers such as the *New York Sun* and *New York World*, both traditionally pro-Tweed, were editorializing in favor of the rebellion within Tammany. The *World* went so far as to declare "war to the knife, and the knife to the hilt" on the Tweed Ring. Meanwhile, O'Brien, still bristling under the insults of the Ring, was running around the city spewing insults against Tweed and Sweeny. He was asking every Tammany man he knew that wasn't directly connected to the Ring to swear allegiance to the Young Democracy on a Bible he kept in his pocket; it was hardly a subtle means of recruitment. Initially, Morrissey had intended to make the group's maneuverings secret, hoping to surprise the Ring by planting Young Democracy delegates at the 1870 Democratic Convention. However, with the publicity generated by men like Tilden and the hotheaded O'Brien, there was no more sense in being subtle. Tweed knew.[419]

Realizing that a divided Tammany Hall would not be advantageous to his plans to control the city at large, Boss Tweed met with the insurgents shortly after their existence came to his attention. For weeks the two sides tried to negotiate a settlement, to no avail. According to one account of the conflict, "To save himself, Tweed opened a half-way understanding with the Young Democracy chiefs, by which he was to join them and abandon Sweeny. Tweed even offered – though vainly - $200,000 outright if he would swerve the Young Democracy to his interest." This strategy failing, Tweed next invited five State Senators who had joined the rebellion to his mansion. Mayor Hall was also there. The seven men reached an agreement, swearing to it over the Bible. Tweed left thinking he had settled the matter, but he had failed to invite either Morrissey or O'Brien, and the Senators had made their deal without the knowledge or consent of the rest of the Young Democracy. The rest of the rebels refused to acknowledge the agreement and demanded more. Both sides prepared for internecine war, the battleground to be Albany and the fights to be over Tweed's charter and the 1870 elections.[420]

"I have known these men for years," Morrissey explained to famed newspaper publisher and reformer Horace Greeley at Delmonico's restaurant, referring to the Tweed Ring, "but I was never indebted to them for a single favor. I fought and won my election in spite of them. They will

---

[418] Ackerman, 37-46; *New York Sun* May 2, 1878
[419] Wingate, "Municipal Government," *North American Review*, January 1875
[420] Myers, *Tammany*, 269; Ackerman, 73-74

never forget or forgive any man who is in this fight against them, no matter what he does... I want you to open the eyes of these republican Senators," John told Greeley. "You can control them." Greeley said that he would do what he could. A former congressman himself, Greeley was arguably the most famous man in New York and maybe the country. A respected journalist, publisher, politician, and man of letters, he had risen from poverty to wealth a self-made man, helped to found the Republican Party, created the *New York Daily Tribune*, and was an eccentric but highly influential reformer. "He finds his chief happiness in work, as other men do in recreation," admired a fellow journalist.

Greeley likely disapproved of Morrissey's background as a boxer, just as he had been a critic of Morrissey's initial elevation to Congress. Greeley had once complained in his newspaper that pugilism's "natural gravity of baseness... stinks. It is in the grog-shops and the brothels and the low gaming halls." However, a mutual friend, General Edwin Merritt, later remembered that Greeley told him that Morrissey "had a reputation as an honest man and that he believed he would not sell his vote." For Morrissey's part, he thought Greeley "a good friend to the poor." Whatever his reservations about Morrissey's background, Greeley despised Tweed practically more than anyone else. He blamed his own losing run for congress back in 1866, (the same year John Morrissey had won his seat) on lack of support from the Boss. Greeley had been among the first people to criticize Tweed publicly ("fat, oily, and dripping with public wealth," he had called him), before most of New York knew who he was. Apparently agreeing with Sam Tilden that the Young Democracy was the lesser of two evils when compared with the Tweed Ring, the staunch moralist became one of the rebellioin's most ardent supporters, both through the press and through his connections in Albany.

A single reporter was on hand for this meeting between the radical reformer and one of the most notorious men in New York. His transcript of what went on at Delmonico's instantly filled the New York papers with rumors and speculation. Astonished over the alliance between a highly educated moralist, a founder of the Republican Party and a street-smart, ex-boxer Democrat, the *Times* marveled, "The age of wonders is not ended."[421]

The Young Democrats were not the only people offended by Tweed's charter. The politicians in Albany widely condemned and the Ring abandoned it, a fact which Morrissey and his allies hailed as a victory. Soon enough, the Young Democracy ranks were swelling with Tammany men looking to back the winner. Emboldened by their success, the Young Democrats next introduced a series of bills to the Legislature which, taken altogether, formed their own charter. These had been composed by Tilden, Greeley, and a few other figures from within the Young Democracy fold.

---

[421] *Brooklyn Daily Eagle*, April 4, 1870; *New York Herald*, May 2, 1878; *New York Times*, April 4, 1870; *Irish American*, October 19, 1867; Isenberg, 71; Browne, 216; Merritt, 22; Adler, 203 (e-book)

However, they were soon humbled when a bi-partisan vote struck down the key bill, putting the two factions at an apparent stalemate.

Disturbed at the news that all but his most loyal friends on the Tammany General Committee were abandoning him for the rebels, Tweed again attempted to mollify his opponents. He offered Sherriff O'Brien $200,000 to support a bill composed by Tweed's men, even going so far as to give the Young Democracy the opportunity to make changes to their satisfaction. O'Brien refused, sending Tweed back to the drawing board. Tweed next took the advice of Judge Cardozo (who sympathized with Morrissey and company) and called a meeting of the entire Tammany General Committee, which included several adherents to the Young Democracy, on March 28 at 7:30 p.m. However, he had no intention of adhering to Cardozo's suggestion of reaching a compromise at this meeting. Instead, he devised a ploy to lull the insurgents into a false sense of strength and then destroy them.

Before the scheduled meeting, Tweed stepped down voluntarily from his position as Deputy Street Commissioner, allowing a rumor to spread that O'Brien had orchestrated his removal from the post. More rumors followed, intimating that Tweed feared that O'Brien was going to remove him from the Tammany Hall General Committee at the meeting, and he was in tears with worry. Excited by this news, Morrissey, O'Brien, and the other Young Democrats who sat on the committee gathered their forces at Irving Hall across Union Square from Tammany Hall. They numbered 174 men to the eleven expected to represent the Tweed Ring. Surging with confidence, they then made their way through a downpour of rain toward Tammany Hall.

"They've killed me dead, they think," Tweed confided to a supporter that evening, "perhaps they have, but I'm Tweed now and I'll be bound if I don't show that I mean to kick the lid off the coffin pretty lively." He then sent word to Police Commissioner Henry Smith that his opponents had threatened bodily harm to the Tammany leadership, and he expected a riot to ensue at the Hall that night. Smith then mobilized eight hundred police officers to the Hall with orders to surround it and the nearby buildings on all sides and prevent the entry of anyone that did not have Tweed's approval. No sooner had the Young Democrats arrived at Tammany's doors than thousands of rain-soaked onlookers gathered in Union Square, their curiosity drawn by the police presence. Some of the crowd supported them, others shouted praise for Tweed. Intimidated by Tweed's flexing of his political muscles, the rebels backed off, retiring demoralized either to Irving Hall or to their homes. Soon enough, Morrissey and O'Brien would find that men who had pledged themselves as allies were no longer enthused for their cause and were avoiding meetings. Their numbers were dwindling.

"It astonished me," Tweed lied to a reporter who visited his home after the meeting. He insisted that he had had nothing to do with the police blockade, insinuating that the police had arrived without his prompting to stop intended violence on the part of his enemies. As the Young Democrats struggled to recover their prior momentum following the unexpected events of March 28, Tweed cleverly pressed his advantage in Albany. His cronies introduced a new charter, revised but not all that different from the original, and pushed through with urgency. Taking no chances this time, the Boss initiated a flurry of bribes and promises, including at least $200,000 divided among five Republicans (Morrissey would later claim that the figure was one million dollars). Such dealings managed to switch important Young Democrats back into the Tweed Ring's fold and garner their votes for the passage of the charter. Once they caught on, the remaining Young Democrats also flooded the capital with cash. Tilden and Greeley vehemently opposed the charter in the State Senate, but it was to no avail. Distracted by their embarrassment at Tammany, the Young Democrats had been too slow to respond to Tweed's killing stroke. The charter passed the Senate by a vote of 30 to 2.[422]

Back in New York City, Tweed managed to spin public opinion to believe that the Young Democracy had intended to start a riot on March 28 and that the passage of his charter was a victory for Home Rule because it took control of their city out of the hands of Albany politicians. The trade off, of course, was that it put control of the city exclusively into the hands of a very few men, each hand selected by Tweed himself, but few among the public objected at that moment; the Boss was cheered as a hero by hundreds in an extravagant celebration on the corner of East Broadway and Canal Street, an area that would afterward be known as Tweed Square for decades.

The short-lived Young Democracy was essentially no more, much of its roster having quietly skulked away from Morrissey and O'Brien, back into the mainstream Tammany ranks. Looking to steer his political fortune clear of the defeat, Horace Greeley abandoned the fight. The final "Waterloo defeat" occurred on April 18, the day that Tammany came together to elect its officers. Ballots for officers were clearly divided between the two warring parties. Of the 265 votes cast, 242 supported Tweed and his cronies, and Tweed himself once more obtained the organization's highest post, Grand Sachem. A. Oakey Hall, Peter Sweeny, Richard Connolly, and their friends made it on the roster of sachems and officers. Morrissey, Samuel Tilden, John Fox, Augustus Schell, and all others associated with the Young Democracy failed to gain a single seat on the council.

"Now is the triumph of Tweed complete!" declared the *Times* on the 19th. "In the innermost recesses of Tammany the two factions met last night in mortal conflict – and the representatives of the Young Democracy were left upon the ground, helpless and humiliated." That day, Tammany issued a statement to the New York papers concerning the humiliation of

---

[422] Ackerman, 74-80; *New York Times*, September 18, 1877

the insurgents. It specifically named Morrissey as being under investigation by the council for his "effort to break down the organization of the Democratic Party in this City." The statement went on to accuse Morrissey of surreptitiously working in the interest of the Republican Party during his time in Washington. It was signed, WM. W. TWEED.[423]

Morrissey did not deny working with Republicans at times, and was proud of the fact, insisting that he was wealthy and respected enough to not have to resort to partisan politics. "While I am a staunch Democrat," he explained to a reporter in a story published exactly one year after the Tammany statement, "I am so unquestionably sound that I could afford to vote in opposition of my party whenever I thought that more partisanship diverted it from paths of duty and right and patriotism."[424]

Having confirmed his strength, Tweed was not of a mind to be lenient on the leaders of the rebellion. "The sword of the 'Boss' first fell on the broad shoulders of Morrissey," the *New York Herald* commented years later. Tammany essentially excommunicated him. With his second term in Congress set to end in the Spring of 1871, expulsion from Tammany gave him little hope of securing a third term, which might have seemed just as well to Morrissey considering his desire to focus once more on his gambling interests.[425]

It was around this period that word reached John of an alleged conspiracy by the Tweed Ring to kill him. The supposed assassin was George "Coolie Keys" Hill, with whom Morrissey had once quarreled in the Jem Mace's saloon, the Capital. According to the story which reached Morrissey's ears, Keys was to gather about him other thugs, who were to act not only as aids in the killing if necessary, but also as witnesses for him once the job was done, testifying that he killed Morrissey in self-defense. At this news, Morrissey confronted Keys in person and told him what he knew. Whether the rumor was true or not, Keys never made a subsequent move against the congressman.[426]

[423] *New York Times*, April 19, 1870 and September 18, 1877
[424] *Memphis Daily Appeal*, April 19, 1871
[425] *New York Herald*, May 2, 1878
[426] *Pilot*, December 27, 1879; *New York Herald*, April 26, 1871

18.

Exile

Considering his political humiliation and the rumored assassination plot, it is not surprising that John Morrissey chose to spend much of the remainder of 1870, and most of the next year too, in places other than New York City. He was clearly not welcome at Tammany, and he had plenty of interests to look after elsewhere. His sudden and unannounced return to his desk in Congress on May 4, 1870 after four consecutive months of absence caused a shock to his fellow representatives. Just a couple of weeks earlier, Boss Tweed had stood before the New York State Assembly in Albany trying to get John vacated from his seat in Congress on the grounds that he had been away from the House so long that he might as well be dead. Ironically, it was partly the fight against Tweed which had kept him in New York for so long that, upon his return to Washington, "people stared at him as if he had descended – or ascended – from another world." He had a little less than a year remaining in his term, but, not surprisingly, the legislative life was not able to keep his attention through that summer.[427]

He was back in Saratoga in June, supervising the opening of his new Club House. Perhaps the troubles incurred on Black Friday, in the courts, and at Tammany Hall explain why his dream project, which had begun construction back in 1867, took so long to complete. Perhaps, too, it took so long because it was just that magnificent. For people of his time and the generations that immediately followed, John Morrissey's true legacy would be his Saratoga Club House on Congress Street. Widely regarded as America's premier gambling resort for decades to come, "the Baden Baden of America," the large, red brick edifice featured a tastefully decorated salon, "Gorgeously furnished toilet rooms, Faro parlors, and drawing rooms carpeted with soft carpets and decorated with rich carvings and bronzes." Just outside of the new Club House's door was a brand-new racecourse, its accommodations improved over the course built in 1863. This one would inherited its predecessor's reputation as the premier horse racing site in the North for years to come. A visitor from the *Boston Journal* shortly after its opening described the house as follows:

> John Morrissey's new house… is far the most gorgeous house for play on the continent. The main floor is divided into three rooms, two of which are devoted to play and one for dining. The fitting

---

[427] *New York Herald*, April 23, 1870; *New York Times*, May 4, 1870

up of the rooms is simply magnificent. The floors are covered with scarlet and white velvety tapestry. The furniture, sideboards, cornices, mantels and mirror frames are French cheval, inlaid with gold. The curtains are silk and damask. The monogram "J.M." flames out on all sides. Over the massive mirrors are carved tigers' heads, with mouths wide open to devour, an emblem of the tiger persons will fight within the walls. The chandeliers are gold gilt, and the brackets are burnished in the same style. On the saloon floor there are one hundred and twenty-five lights, and two hundred and seventy in all the house. Private staircases lead to rooms aloft, and these rooms, on the two-stories above the parlors, are gorgeously fitted up for guests. The lower floor is for the kitchen, wine cellar, laundry and for domestic uses.[428]

A visitor in 1871 was impressed by the "English and French cooks" and "attentive waiters," and an overall opulence "on a scale of such lavish elegance as would cause profound wonderment in the minds of ordinary mortals." This writer was equally impressed by Morrissey himself, whom he described as "a plain, honest looking fellow, with immense largeness of heart, as well as of size…. [He] produced a favorable impression upon his visitors that evening, not only by the excellence of his liquors, but by the off-hand suavity of his manners."[429]

An expansion, with even more resplendent features, including a library, was completed in 1871. Two separate buildings for more gaming and a third one to house the approximately fifty employees were part of this project. Morrissey agreed to pay a church $1,000 a year to rent the adjacent land and keep it vacant to allow sunlight on the house and give the appearance of a larger estate.

John Morrissey slept very little. People who visited the Club House noted that he was usually the last person in bed and that, no matter how early they got up, they would find him already dressed and leisurely strolling the grounds or standing on the veranda in serene thought. Expecting the violent sinner of old, they were astonished at the proprietor's self-discipline and manners. The man was normally quiet, and when he did speak, took care to avoid colorful language. The once notorious alcoholic never drank in front of his customers, nor did he personally gamble.

To ensure that the customers' spending at the roulette and poker tables would not be hampered by the watchful eyes of wives, and to avoid the potential scandal of having ladies present at all, Morrissey gave the order that no women were to be allowed in the gambling parlor, though they were allowed in any of the other public rooms of the house. 25,000 women visited the mansion in 1870 alone, a number which prompted indignation

---

[428] *Manchester Journal,* September 11, 1873; *Democratic Advocate,* June 30, 1870
[429] Asbury, *Sucker's Progress,* 383; Schwartz, 826; *Chicago Daily Tribune,* August 1, 1874.; *Watertown Re-union,* June 29, 1871

from Saratoga's most conservative citizens. Eventually, John closed women out altogether to avoid further controversy. The same rule applied for Saratoga residents, the proprietor not wanting to further raise the ire of local reformers by corrupting Saratoga's men.[430]

A visitor from the *Chicago Tribune* noted that actors, sporting men, Wall Street brokers, journalists, politicians, and speculators made up the main section of the Club House's gambling customers. "I have seen Senators of the United States inhabitants of his place, invited there as his guests," the writer gossiped, noting that Morrissey put on a different front for his more dignified guests. "He is always a master of the situation, somewhat modified and softened in his manners, but his rights he demands with as much ferocity and directness as in his former days." Among the many noteworthy figures who would visit the famed mansion during Morrissey's tenure as its manager would be President Grant, Samuel Clemens, John Rockefeller, and of course Cornelius Vanderbilt.[431]

All told, the Club House and its expansions had cost an estimated $200,000 to complete, and the new race track another $125,000, right around the time that Morrissey was struck by the bad fortunes of Black Friday and the lottery case. By April of 1871, one newspaper estimated that John now had just $90,000 to his name, which, if accurate, would have still made him very well off for the period, but a far cry from the millionaire he was supposed to have been just a couple of years previous. In desperate need of ready cash after all the expenses of the Club House, he was forced to immediately sell half of its ownership to a man named Reed Spencer that Summer for a sum of between $80,000 and $100,000. It was also rumored that August Belmont and William Travers were brought in as silent partners as well. He did stay on as co-owner and manager, however, and he remained the visible face of the business. The Club House would go on to gross over $250,000 in a year's time, doing much to help put its proprietor back on his financial feet. The next year, someone offered John half a million dollars to buy out his remaining interest in the enterprise. By then, he felt financially secure enough to turn them down.[432]

The Club House was not open long before the Young Men's Christian Association of Saratoga began making noise about shutting it down. They raided the place and took an inventory, demanding that all the contents be handed over. Morrissey consented that he would willingly close if that was the wish of the people of Saratoga. However, he pointed out that closing the Club House meant that he would also have to cease operation of the new racetrack. The organization owned property adjacent to the racetrack,

[430] *Chicago Daily Tribune*, August 1, 1874; *Watertown Re-union*, June 29, 1871; *Ithaca Journal*, July 11, 1871; *Daily Albany Argus*, June 20, 1871

[431] *Chicago Daily Tribune*, August 1, 1874

[432] Hotaling, 85; *Watertown Re-union*, June 29, 1871; *Chicago Daily Tribune*, August 1, 1874; Schwartz, 326; *Alexandria Gazette*, April 15, 1871; *Bossier Banner*, July 15, 1871

the value of which had increased exponentially by its proximity to the course. John subsequently had no more troubles from the Y.M.C.A.

———

John Morrissey was never a devoutly religious man. His parents hailed from a part of Ireland that had a Protestant Church, and Susan was raised Methodist (she would later convert to Catholicism), but there are no stories of his attending any church with any regularity, either as a child or adult. He did, however, enjoy a long-lasting friendship with a Catholic clergyman in Saratoga, one Father McMenomy. The priest would pay visits to John quite often, taking care to avoid religious topics so that the noted sinner would not cast him out. Eventually, after two or three years, McMenomy could no longer hold his tongue and broached the subject of faith. "Mr. Morrissey, we have now been acquainted for several years," he began cautiously. "You have uniformly treated me with attention and kindness, always responding to the charitable requests I have made; but somehow I have failed in the discharge of a more important duty. I have always wanted to converse with you about religion. – Are you willing to hear me?"

Expecting this topic to come up eventually and knowing that the priest considered this a crucial moment in their friendship, John gave him his undivided attention. "Certainly," he replied.

"I am confident that a man of your intelligence, absorbed as you have been and are in worldly things, must have reflected upon what concerns your future existence." John's reply in the affirmative encouraged the priest. McMenomy was also happy to hear John confirm that he was in fact a "believer." "Then," the priest continued, "if you are willing to state it, I should like to know just what you do believe."

The famed gambling kingpin paused for a moment in thought and then replied simply, "I believe in doing as we agree." Though he was never a devoted Catholic, Morrissey always favored Catholicism over Protestantism, both in words and political deeds; his wife had become a devout Catholic. John did not attend church as regularly as Susan, but Father McMenomy came to view him as "almost his son."[433]

Through July and August of 1870, John oversaw the annual thoroughbred races held at the new course. Each year thus far since the inception of his races, the attendance numbers had increased, and pleasant weather made sure that 1870 would be no exception. One reporter could not help but notice that the grandstand was "completely filled in every part with elegantly attired ladies, who manifested the warmest interest in the different races." The presence of well-to-do women at the Saratoga races had become something of a novelty each year, speaking to the reputation of

---

[433] *Ogdensburg Journal,* November 12, 1877; *New York Herald,* May 5, 1878

the events as being peaceful and elegant when compared to most other sporting events, which any respectable woman was expected to avoid.[434]

The Saratoga course's reputation for security and serenity was something Morrissey prized, in part because it meant wealthy families felt safe to spend money there, and in part because it furthered his ambitions to be seen as an upright member of society. When, on the first day of the 1870 races, John recognized four men in an approaching carriage as notorious criminals from New York City, including Swaggers gang member John Casey, he made a quick move to prevent their entry into the course. Having bought a ticket, Casey ignored him and went to enter anyway.

"Think it over first coolly," Morrissey warned him; "you might think better of it." Again, Casey paid little heed, forcing Morrissey to grab him around the collar.

"This is a public track, and I'm going in anyhow," Casey insisted, reaching for his pistol.

"I'll make you think it is a church before I am through with you," Morrissey replied, "and if you dare draw that pistol on me, I'll make you eat it." The arrival of police officers prevented the necessity of Morrissey having to resort to his Old Smoke instincts. Casey was hauled off to the local jail, and one assumes his cohorts set a course for home.[435]

———

As of March 4, 1871, Morrissey was officially free from his obligations as a congressman, not that those obligations had ever weighed too heavily on his mind. The *New Orleans Republican* commented, "We are persuaded that his resignation is as satisfactory to the representative body he leaves as it can be to him…. Mr. Morrissey did not shine in the legislative hall, for, although the place has been enlivened with an occasional knockdown, there never has been a regular set-to, such as he has been accustomed to, and as for the continuous wagging of tongues going on there, he, as a man of action, must have regarded that with contempt." The paper expected that John would return to his gambling halls, at which the writer speculated he would be much more successful. In truth, Morrissey was packing his bags for the *Republican*'s hometown.[436]

In April, John boarded the steamer *Great Republic*, headed to New Orleans to attend a horse race there. Susan presumably stayed behind with John, Jr. in D.C. The boat kept a black bear named Bruin as a kind of mascot. One evening during the trip, the bear broke out of his container and found his way into the servants' quarters. He terrified a female employee named Becky by climbing into her bed, waking her. Leaping

[434] *New York Times*, August 14, 1870
[435] *Ogdensburg Journal*, July 25, 1870
[436] *New Orleans Republican*, June 2, 1870

startled to her feet, the woman fled from her room and ran screaming through the halls, the bear following. Not realizing that Bruin had escaped, most of the passengers awoken by her cries thought that the boat was sinking. Morrissey, having gone to bed only a short time earlier, stepped out of his room to see the bear following Becky and quickly snatched up the rope that was tied around Bruin's neck. He pulled the animal away, Bruin ripping up the carpet in an effort to extend his freedom just a little longer. As John put the bear back in his cage, others attended to Becky, who had collapsed.

Several Southern papers carried the anecdote about the bear, but another reporter was more interested in interviewing Morrissey about his political mindset, which the ex-congressman granted upon arriving in the Big Easy. He seemed mostly happy to be free of his congressional seat. Expressing satisfaction but also disinterest, he closed his period in Congress with the words, "I have done a share of good service."

Nonetheless, he still sounded like a professional politician in expressing sympathy for the post-war South to the correspondent, whose story would appear in a Memphis paper. "Your section has been desolated; your people lost all that we won. While you were impoverished, we have been enriched; while you have gone backwards, we have rushed forward," expounded the man from New York. He criticized President Grant's request that Congress grant him the ability to suspend *habeas corpus*. "Give him that power, and he need ask no more." He believed that Grant was promoting "absurd stories about Ku-Klux outrages" to convince the House to allow him to declare martial law and steal the next Presidential election. Morrissey seemed convinced that, if not given this tool to punish those who vote against him, the President would be willing to fight another war and "sacrifice a million men" to maintain the White House at the end of his term. Morrissey and Grant had been on decent terms personally; Grant was a patron of his Saratoga club house, they traveled together on occasion, and Morrissey had been a guest at Grant's inauguration ball. However, Democrat Morrissey and Republican Grant were clearly not on the same page politically.[437]

The reporter was surprised by Morrissey's assertion that there could be a second Civil War, but admitted that Morrissey seemed to have a firm understanding of Grant's character and did not seem prone to exaggeration. "John Morrissey is not a scholar; I don't think he ever read a book, save that of human nature, over which he has bent more studiously than the profoundest thinker over the pages of Locke or Newton. His habits of life have made him an adept in reading the character of individuals. He knows Grant thoroughly, and Morrissey's opinions are worth more, in a matter of this sort, than those of philosophers or statesmen." The reporter went on to note that, though Morrissey was an Irishman by birth, "he is utterly

[437] *Memphis Daily Appeal*, April 19, 1871; *Daily Albany Argus*, September 7, 1869

devoid of blarney." After enjoying the races and buying a famous thoroughbred named Defender for several thousand dollars, John departed New Orleans by steamer on April 22 looking forward to uninterrupted management of his New York City gambling empire for the first time in years.[438]

The transition from the Big Easy to the Big Apple did not go well. Lack of political protection from Tammany meant that his gambling interests in the City were in jeopardy. Tammany now favored John's biggest rival for supremacy in New York gambling, Johnny Chamberlain, formerly of Pittsfield, Massachusetts. Chamberlain and Morrissey had partnered in the gambling house on Twenty-Fourth Street, but by 1869, when Chamberlain opened Monmouth Park, complete with a racecourse and a Club House not unlike those at Saratoga, they were clearly professional rivals. Much to Morrissey's consternation, this resort proved more financially successful than his own Club House and track in Saratoga at times, benefitting greatly from its proximity to the City. Monmouth Park had been in part funded by two of John's other enemies, Tweed and Fisk, who encouraged their wealthy associates to bring their business to Chamberlain's houses. Meanwhile, the Tweed Ring let it be known to the authorities that it was open season on the businesses owned by John Morrissey, as far as Tammany was concerned.

At one o'clock in the morning on May 9, twelve policemen raided the lucrative gaming hall John and his partners operated at 818 Broadway. John was not present, but the police picked up two of his partners and all the patrons inside. They seized gaming tables and devices, along with a small amount of cash. "The house is one of the most elegant and frequented in the City," reported the *New York Times*, "and it's seizure, late as was the hour at which it was made, created great consternation among the gamblers as the news spread among them with marvelous rapidity." Morrissey had been staying at the Hoffman House, an elegant, male-only hotel also on Broadway. Hearing of the raid later that day, John presented himself to the court at the Tombs Prison, where he stayed in a cell until a friend arrived with $1,000 bail. Because the house's iron doors had slowed the entry of the authorities, the men inside had had time to disassemble or destroy most of the evidence and put themselves in positions where none of them were caught participating in gambling; thus, the next morning, a judge was forced to release them all. Morrissey's business manager later tried to convince a reporter than John had no financial interest in the business whatsoever.[439]

[438] *Memphis Daily Appeal*, April 19, 1871; *Daily Ledger*, April 22, 1871; *Nashville Union and American*, April 23, 1871
[439] *New York Sun*, May 2, 1878; *New York Times*, May 9 and 10, 1871; legendsofamerica.com, accessed 11/19/2016; *Public Ledger*, May 20, 1871

It was likely after this event that Morrissey had a secret vault installed in one of the walls of the cellar at 818 Broadway, meant for hiding gambling paraphernalia. In 1880, when the business was under another owner, police raided the place again, and the authorities would frustratedly admit that they found neither gamblers nor gambling equipment. Only after a construction crew discovered the vault in 1900 would the mystery be solved.

Raids were part of the overhead of running gambling businesses, and it is not likely that this one would have presented any immediate threat to Morrissey legally or financially, especially considering his continued interests in both Troy and Saratoga. In most cases, the owner of a gambling hall would just wait a brief period for the authorities and reformers to find other distractions, and re-open for business. Nonetheless, Morrissey's establishments had previously boasted a reputation as being safe from raids, allowing customers peace of mind. That each of the customers arrested wound up having their names printed in the papers would have wounded that house's reputation for discretion. It was also confirmation that Tammany no longer protected him or his businesses.

Saratoga and Troy were now safer and more lucrative places for John and his family, and he made moves to improve his reputation and image with the respectable citizens of both towns. His first strategy toward this end was through philanthropy, particularly on a local level. "Morrissey divides the profits of his sinning with the good people of the village [Saratoga] with a generous hand," noted one writer. His personal secretary, a Mr. Scribner later attested to his boss being regularly visited by members of various religious organizations, or at other times by struggling local businessmen, and that Morrissey would often tell Scribner, "Give these people a check for $500 or $1000." Scribner even remembered two high ranking politicians, one a governor and the other a mayor, each borrowing at least $5,000 dollars from Morrissey. To Scribner, John "might as well have taken his money and thrown it in the gutter," but Morrissey saw these kinds of donations and loans as a means to an end. He made sure the press covered his donations to the churches and civic organizations (if not to the politicians) of the various cities and towns in which he operated.[440]

Coming to Saratoga inspired in Morrissey a strong desire to assimilate into the aristocratic class that vacationed there. "He was very ambitious to learn, to know, to do" the *Herald* once reported about Morrissey; "he desired to know what highly bred people thought, because he could only guess what that class of people were thinking about." He began appearing in public with a swallowtail jacket (the stereotypical jacket of the upper-class men of the day) stretched over his muscular frame, leather boots on the feet that had once not been able to afford any shoes, and white gloves on his infamous brawler's hands. He also fancied beaver-pelt coats and top hats for outdoors attire and travel in a custom-ordered, gold-embroidered

[440] English, T., 42; *New York Herald*, May 2, 1878

carriage rumored to have cost $2,000. He certainly now had the money, but his new ostentation did nothing to improve the opinions of New York State's old rich elite, who would always consider him an oafish immigrant criminal and his wife pretentious and gaudy.[441]

If Saratoga's elite refused to take him seriously, John hoped that the respectable folk in his hometown of Troy would at least be more accommodating, but he received no such satisfaction. While they were establishing themselves in Saratoga, John and Susan made plans to purchase a new home in Troy's most blue-blooded neighborhood. Scandalized by even the possibility of having an ex-prizefighter in their midst, their prospective neighbors colluded in their snobbery to buy the property out from under the couple and leave it vacant. Out of sheer spite, Morrissey instead bought a large plot of land that ran behind the neighborhood and oversaw the construction there of a soap factory. When it was eventually completed, the building "produced more vile odors than it did soap." His need for revenge satisfied after a few weeks, Morrissey sold the factory at a profit to the very people who had conspired to keep him out of their neighborhood, and they eagerly shut it down.[442]

———

By July 1871, John and his family had spent a little over a year avoiding New York City, returning only on rare occasions. They had been forced out by John's failure to oust the Tweed Ring from power and his subsequent expulsion from Tammany. However, as 1871 progressed, rumors started making their way to Saratoga and elsewhere that Tweed's days at the helm of America's greatest metropolis were numbered and that there would soon be a power vacuum at Tammany Hall, a tantalizing prospect for the exiled Morrissey.

In the summer of 1870, the political magazine *Harper's Weekly* published a cartoon by its artist Thomas Nast entitled "Senator Tweed in a New Role," depicting the Boss as Shakespeare's Queen Gertrude from *Hamlet*. The bearded Queen cradled Tweed's infamous charter in his arms like a newborn babe, while Hamlet lectured him with lines from the bard himself, "'While rank corruption mining all within, Infects unseen. Confess yourself to heaven. Repent what's past; avoid what is to come." Nast had criticized Tammany corruption in cartoons before. In fact, a mean-looking, cigar-smoking John Morrissey had been the first subject in a Nast cartoon to be associated with Nast's emblem of the Ring (a snake devouring its own tail), which hung on the wall beside the illustrated Morrissey during John's 1866 congressional run. Four years later, the Queen Gertrude cartoon was the first to place Tweed front and center. It was far from the last.[443]

[441] Nicholson, 89

[442] English, T. 42; Asbury, *Sucker's Progress*, 385; *New York Herald*, May 2, 1878

[443] Ackerman, 98-99; Adler, 203 (e-book)

Thomas Nast was a passionately Republican, vehemently anti-immigrant, and obsessively anti-Catholic man in his thirties during the early 1870s, even though he himself was a German immigrant raised a Catholic. He had come to New York City as a child and grew up idolizing William Tweed, the heroic (in his eyes) leader of the local Big Six fire brigade when Nast was a boy. As a teenager, he got his first art job as an illustrator for *Frank Leslie's Illustrated Newspaper,* one of the most widely read papers in the country. Somewhere along the way, he had become a passionate Republican, envisioning himself as a courageous crusader against Democrats, Tweed, immigrants, and the Catholic Pope. *Harper's Weekly*, owned by the famously nativist Harper brothers, picked him up in 1859. Nast's most outrageous cartoon for *Harper's*, entitled "The American River Ganges," appeared in September, of 1871. It showed Catholic bishops as a horde of crocodiles emerging onto a riverbank looking to devour New York children trapped on the beach by Tweed, Hall, Sweeny, and other Tammany men, who were sticking around as spectators to the carnage. Only a lone young man (Nast's vision of himself) stood heroically between the helpless children and the man-eaters. Behind it at loomed a large edifice intentionally made to look like a melding of Tammany Hall and the Vatican, as Nast believed that the Pope in Rome was the true master of Tammany.[444]

Not long after *Harper's* published the cartoon, the *New York Times* soon joined in the fight against the Tweed Ring, a risky move when the Ring was at the very apex of its influence and Tweed himself was revered by many throughout the City as a hero for his championing of "Home Rule." On September 20, the *Times'* editor, Louis Jennings fired the first salvo of what would become the most storied journalistic crusade against civic corruption in America's history. This first attack was pure editorial, focused more on criticism than exposure of any hard facts. Jennings marveled at Tweed's mastery of "the art of growing rich" in the span of just a few years. He had gone from being a local bookkeeper and volunteer fireman in a poor urban community to the third largest landowner in New York State. "How is it done?" was Jennings' rhetorical inquiry. "We wish Mr. Tweed, or Mr. Sweeny, or some of their friends would tell us. The general public say there is foul play somewhere. They are under the impression that monstrous abuses of their funds, corrupt bargains with railroad sharpers, outrageous plots to swindle the general community, account for the vast fortunes heaped up by men who spring up like mushrooms." More editorials followed in quick succession, increasingly accusatory in their tone but offering little evidence. The paper called for comptroller Richard Connolly to release the city's financial statements for journalistic and public scrutiny, a request Slippery Dick refused.[445]

To many, the attacks on Tweed and Tammany seemed to be purely politically motivated, particularly after President Grant consented to a

[444] Adler, 101-118 (e-book)
[445] Ackerman, 100; Adler, 155-156 (e-book)

Republican petition that he send thousands of U.S. troops to New York City to police to the polls on Election Day and A. Oakey Hall and John Hoffman were both re-elected to the mayor's and governor's offices respectively. Before the eyes of the public, Tammany seemed vindicated, and Tweed seemed to be a victim of his political opponents. Still, neither Nast nor Jennings let up.

Neither did John Morrissey's old Young Democracy ally, Jimmy O'Brien. O'Brien, still smarting from the humiliation of his rebellion's defeat and still disgusted with comptroller Connelly for not paying him the $350,000 he felt he was owed, set in motion the events that would finally undo the Tweed Ring. He had a good friend in William Copeland, who happened to be a clerk in the comptroller's office. For most of 1870, Copeland had been discreetly stealing away with and hand copying the ledgers and account books in that office. He prepared three separate copies of these and, in the last weeks of the year, brought them to O'Brien, who hid each copy away in a separate place. O'Brien's next move was to again submit a bill to the city for the $350,000 in fees, this time threatening to release incriminating information about the Ring if payment was not forthcoming. The Ring again refused to pay up. For the time being, O'Brien held onto the documents, considering his options.

While O'Brien plotted, the *Times* began to finally uncover evidence of corruption: 1,300 people collecting city paychecks without actually reporting to a job, and circumstantial links between the county auditor's purchase of the Broadway Hotel and a simultaneous Tweed-backed bill to widen the street in front of the hotel, which granted the new hotelier a $150,000 compensation check from the city, among other similar tales of fraud. Still, this was not enough to turn the tide of public opinion against Tweed or warrant serious inquiry from the government into a broader Tweed Ring conspiracy.[446]

Previously, Tweed and his cronies paid only bemused attention to what *Harper's* and the *Times* had been saying about them. Now, by coming up with actual numbers, the *Times* had managed to rile the metaphorical Tammany tiger. Both the magazine and the newspaper came under Tammany attack through attempted takeovers, intimidation of their business partners, and public smear campaigns. In response, the publications courageously doubled down on their criticism of the Tweed Ring.[447]

Then came the Orange Day Riot of July 12, 1871, in which dozens of people, as many as 130 (more than the Civil War Draft Riots), were killed. Orange Day was an Irish Protestant holiday celebrated with a parade in New York City on July 12 which the Irish Catholics of Manhattan found offensive. Wanting to avoid some of the inter-Irish violence which had

[446] Ackerman, 131
[447] Adler, 157-161

disrupted parades in prior years and show support for their Catholic constituents, Tweed, Hall, and Connolly agreed to prevent this year's parade, and Hall gave the order to the police to stop any such gathering that may arise. Then Governor John Hoffman, seizing an opportunity to publicly separate himself from the corrupt image of Tammany for his prospective run at the Presidency, issued a contradictory order, supporting the parade and ordering a police and military escort. The war of words between Hall and Hoffman fought in the city papers wound up making things worse. On July 12, a bloody, armed confrontation left the bodies of men, women, and even children lying motionless or screaming on the street in the wake of the parade, which continued marching to its conclusion at Cooper Union Hall. All sides blamed Tammany, either for allowing the parade, failing to control the Catholics, or for heightening the already dangerous tensions between Protestants and Catholics with their contradictory orders and publicized bickering.[448]

The *Times* was relentless in its coverage of the riot, of the funerals for the dead, and of Tammany's irresponsible squabbling, which they blamed for inciting the chaos. Still, these criticisms would always seem to be politically motivated until the paper published cold, hard evidence of intentional fraud. Then Jimmy O'Brien walked into editor Louis Jennings's office on July 18 with an envelope. "Here's the proof to back up all the *Times* has charged…. They're copied right out of the city ledgers," the ex-sheriff said, placing the envelope on the editor's desk. O'Brien then turned and left, leaving the speechless newspaperman to marvel at what had fallen in his lap.[449]

Jennings and his most trusted writers spent a full day pouring through the contents of the envelope, three years' worth of hand-copied ledgers from inside of comptroller Connelly's office. They then developed a strategy for releasing the information to the public, portion by portion, to galvanize the attention of readers and draw out the humiliation of the Ring. The first article, detailing $941,453.86 in city funds paid over a nine-month period (most of it within just thirty days) to just four contractors for carpentry, plumbing, plastering, and furniture (including $7,500 for thermometers and a whopping $170,729.60 for chairs) approved by Connelly and Mayor Hall, was printed on Thursday, July 20, 1871. On Saturday, the *Times* released details of $5,663,646.83 in additional expenditures to contractors for various services (including $125,830 for cabinetwork in the courthouse). The article also outlined that, though the bills were paid to different contractors, all the money ended up in a single account of Ingersoll & Company. The company, they reported, was owned by one James Ingersoll, a Tweed family friend, whom the times declared "a well-known agent of the Ring." In total, the *Times* estimated that the city had paid Ingersoll $9,789,482.16. Ingersoll, the *Times* later revealed, had

---

[448] Ackerman, 154-158
[449] Ackerman, 161

been the bag man for the Ring, accepting the payouts from the city treasury and then distributing them back to his Ring masters, for a healthy fee. Further sums of $62,488.18 and $64,090.49 were paid to R.J. Hennessey and T.C. Cashman respectively. The *Times* found no evidence that either of these men existed at all. For days and weeks to follow, similar reports were detailed line by line on the front page of the *New York Times*, each day's new information often reaching more than a million dollars in city payouts for services or items that did not seem to even approach the necessary expenditure (for example, $800,000 for safes). Accompanying each dry list of hard numbers would be an editorial from Jennings imploring readers to hold Connelly, Hall, and their accomplices accountable. To close out July, the paper distributed a pamphlet entitled *How New York is Governed* throughout the city, reviewing details previously published on its front page and revealing more information as well.[450]

After several days of accusations from the *Times*, Mayor Hall, who was still, along with Connelly, the main focus of the paper's ire at this point, simply said that the information had been obtained from a "dishonest servant" of the city, a paltry defense which the paper amounted to an admission of guilt. Soon enough, Tweed's and Sweeny's names began appearing alongside those of Connelly and Hall as the orchestrators of the outrageous frauds. The accusations continued unabated through August. At one point, Connelly paid an unannounced visit to the office of George Jones, owner of the *Times*, and offered him five million dollars "in five minutes," if the paper would stop its attacks. The Ring had been paying off reporters and papers for years; an estimated eighty New York City newspapers took payments from members of the Ring at some point, either for advertising, for support, or to drop a story (while the *Transcript* and the *Leader* were out-and-out Ring mouthpieces). When Connelly tried the same strategy with Jones, however, Jones refused him. An attempt to bribe Nast at *Harper's Weekly* had the same result.[451]

Amid the sensation of the *Times* articles, public opinion was swiftly turning. Other newspapers were still cautious about criticizing the Ring; they were afraid to lose the millions of dollars in payoffs the Ring had been making to them for years; In some cases, Ring members were part owners or even editors of the papers; then there was the fact that Tweed himself owned the printing company which supplied some of them with contracts. Still, there were now citizens associations publicly denouncing Tammany. The Ring was now the constant subject of Nast's increasingly popular cartoons in *Harper's Weekly*. The city's most successful businessmen, returning concerned from their summer holidays at places like Saratoga, picked up the *Times* to receive confirmation that their taxes had paid the lion's share of the fraudulent expenditures, and that the city's credit was

---

[450] Ackerman, 165-170, 179; *New York Times*, July 20 and 23, and August 2, 1871; Mandelbaum, 79; Adler, 353-354

[451] *New York Times*, July 23, 1871; Ackerman, 172-173; Adler, 132-133 (e-book)

faltering, a fact which threatened disaster for their own credit and fortunes. City politicians who were not in on the fraud now understood why their city debt had gone from about thirty-six million dollars in January 1869 to ninety-seven million dollars a little more than two years later. The proverbial rats leaping from a sinking ship, some of the contractors mentioned in the *Times* exposes were offering to come clean about their own deals with the Ring in order to spin the information in their favor and paint themselves as whistle-blowers in the scandal, rather than participants.[452]

The men at the center of the scandal, Tweed, Sweeny, Hall, and Connelly failed to come up with an agreed upon strategy for confronting the accusations. Hall repeatedly blamed the *Times* for using less than gentlemanly means to come up with their information, accusing George Jones of blackmail. Yet, by admitting that the books came from the comptroller's office, Hall essentially admitted that the figures published were true. Simultaneously, Connelly had attempted bribery and failed, proving that Jones's motivations went beyond money. Observing that these efforts from their colleagues had only further incriminated them, Tweed and Sweeny (or Tweedledee and Sweedledumb, as Thomas Nast had once caricatured the pair) left the city on vacations and remained publicly silent on the matter.

On September 4, a gathering of the city's social and financial elite, men with names like Astor and Roosevelt, met at the Cooper Union Hall to discuss the allegations by the *Times*. George Jones was the guest of honor, and Jimmy O'Brien was also present. For hours these men gave speeches railing against the Ring and their corruption. Those present formed the nucleus of a new reform movement, its first action winning a judge's injunction against the city government raising, borrowing, or spending any money without the approval of a new board of appointment composed of reformers and called the Committee of Seventy. Shockingly, the judge who approved the order was none other than George Barnard, a bold move from a man who had to this point been in Tweed's proverbial pocket for more than a decade.

The Ring began to dissolve under the pressure. Looking to make Connelly a scapegoat, Tweed, Sweeny, and Hall began pressuring the comptroller to resign, but Connelly recognized their intentions and refused to vacate. He found unlikely support from Samuel Tilden, the high-ranking Democrat and Tweed nemesis, who wanted to prevent Hall from appointing a replacement comptroller, likely to be either August Belmont or George B. McClellan. Inspired by the *Times* articles, Tilden wanted to bring Tweed to trial for the outrageous frauds they detailed, but he needed hard evidence linking the Boss directly to the scandal. Feeling betrayed by his cohorts in the Ring, rendered politically impotent by Barnard's order, and

---

[452] Adler, 131-133; Burrows 931

under pressure from the press and the public, Connolly agreed to work with Tilden's lawyers and Committee of Seventy member William Havemeyer. On October 26, based on evidence presented to the courts by Tilden, Sheriff Matthew Brennan arrested William Tweed at his office. Bail was set at one million dollars. The Boss put up the sum and disappeared once more into his office, rarely emerging in the months to come.

As October dawned, it was clear that the once centralized power of the Tweed Ring was shattered. Peter Sweeny and other Tweed allies immediately high-tailed it out of the country, Sweeny eventually settling in Paris. Havemeyer replaced Hall as Mayor in the coming election. Connolly, who retained the legal right to name his own successor, relented to Tilden's pressure and appointed reformer (and close Tilden friend) Andrew Green as the new comptroller. Brennan arrested Connolly, his bond matching that of Tweed. Probably because Connolly was not as wealthy his boss had been and was generally believed to be less culpable in the crimes than some of the other Ring members, the sheriff (who had himself benefited for years from being the Ring's favorite lawman) showed uncommon lenience in allowing the ex-comptroller to stay under guard in a room at the New York Hotel until such a time as he could acquire the required sum from friends, provided it did not take too long. Connolly must have been desperate to stay out of jail, as he sent to John Morrissey for financial help. Morrissey saw no value for himself in financing the release of a Tweed Ring member and refused to contribute. Neither did most of the others to whom Connolly appealed, even his own wife, who told him, "Richard, go to jail." He failed to produce the required sum, and Brennan eventually hauled him out of his luxurious accommodations to prison. Judge Barnard ordered his bail lowered, allowing Connolly to exit his cell and flee to Europe.[453]

———

While Boss Tweed's friends abandoned him, the city turned on him, and his access to power and wealth dwindled, John Morrissey was at the height of his influence and prestige up in Saratoga, deserving his recognition as "the leading gamester of the Western world." His Club House was a sensation, and the annual thoroughbred races continued to best each other for receipts and acclaim year over year. In July, he oversaw that year's annual thoroughbred races, his own Defender coming in third place in an all ages, two-mile race.[454]

The month before Tweed's arrest, John oversaw the first Saratoga International Regatta, held on Saratoga Lake, a serene locale about three and a half miles out of town. "The eyes of all England, America and Canada are on this place and these races," Morrissey told a correspondent

[453] Ackerman, *Tweed*, 256
[454] *Nashville Union and American*, August 18, 1872; *New York Times* July 7 and August 9, 1871

for the *New York Herald.* He might have been embellishing a bit; he was the event's promoter, after all. However, sculling was immensely popular in the northeastern United States, and those in rowing circles recognized this international meeting as something of a world championship. Like his horse races, this event attracted the finest of New York society, "Gentlemen of leisure and high social and political status, with ladies of complexions fresh and blooming as Jersey peaches and eyes mild and softly intelligent." Thirteen crews composed of the very best of North America and England were to participate in two races, one on September 9 and one on September 11, the total prize money at stake being $5,500. Morrissey himself would act as referee. He had ordered a grandstand erected about a quarter mile from the southern end of the lake, enjoying an excellent view of the first and last miles of the course.[455]

To the disappointment of the crowds that had arrived early, strong winds forced a forty-eight-hour postponement of the first event. On the morning of Monday, September 11, the wind died down, and the boats entered the water for the first race, with the second one scheduled for the afternoon. The delay had done nothing to dissipate the size and anticipation of the crowd. Thousands cheered as the crews made their way about the four-mile course. To the delight of many, the crew helmed by the Ward brothers of Cornwall, New York came in first, winning by three lengths. They had set a new world record, completing the four miles in twenty-four minutes and forty seconds. Morrissey personally awarded them their first prize winnings, $2,000, while the Wards' supporters shouted their excitement "like demons."[456]

Following the initial race, most of the spectators stayed in their places, not wanting to lose their views for the second race, which was for sculling crews. The hundred or so people who did depart did so to return to their hotels and grab a quick bite to eat before rushing back to the lake to witness "the finest single scull race ever rowed in this country." A crew headed by one Joseph Sadler won the contest, again over four miles, with a time of thirty minutes, eighteen and a half seconds. The *Herald* acclaimed Sadler "the champion sculler of the century." However, John Morrissey was the true winner of the event. Apart from a minor controversy as to who deserved third place recognition in the first race, his debut regatta had come off as an indisputable success, thrilling the crowd, filling newspaper pages, and earning him a lot of cash.[457]

Through all this success in Saratoga, John Morrissey had certainly been reading with satisfaction the *Times* reports on Tweed and his co-conspirators and their fleecing of New York City. By October, it was clear that the Tweed Ring was no more, stripped of their power to control the

---

[455] *Daily Dispatch*, July 19, 1971, quoting *New York Herald*; *New York Herald*, September 9, 1871

[456] *New York Herald*, September 12, 1871

[457] *New York Herald*, September 12, 1871

city, exposed to the public, and fighting amongst themselves. On October 18, John returned to the City for the first time since May. Or, rather, he was just outside of town at Jerome Park in Westchester County, where his four-year-old thoroughbred Defender waited to run in the annual races there. Though his horse initially took the lead in the fourth race of the day, he wound up finishing last.

By the next month, John was back at work managing his lucrative gambling operations in New York. He brought public attention to his return by purchasing the vacant Nathan Mansion on Twenty-Third Street and announcing that he was going to turn it into a club house, a fact which garnered newspaper attention because the old building was said to be haunted. The *Charleston Daily News* joked that, "visitors may be sure they'll see no ghost – not even a ghost of a chance."[458]

As the 1871 elections proceeded, John was likely relieved that he was not on any ticket and could focus on his business interests without interruption. Meanwhile, Boss Tweed took little solace in the fact that he had been re-elected as State Senator, an affirmation of the loyalty of his largely illiterate immigrant constituents, if no one else. He was the only central Tweed Ring figure re-affirmed to at least one of his political positions. Tammany men who had once flocked to him in search of counsel or approval openly shunned him. He was re-arrested, and his various municipal positions were subsequently vacated. This time bail was set at eight million dollars, a sum the Boss reluctantly paid. Disgraced and dejected, Tweed became a virtual recluse inside his office, watching a wave of supposed reform come over the political club he once ruled. He complained that "Tammany don't amount to anything now." As if to draw out his humiliation, he would have to endure an entire year of political and social isolation while waiting for his first trial.[459]

---

[458] *Memphis Public Ledger*, December 1, 1871; *Charleston Daily News*, November 20, 1871
[459] Anbinder, 267

19.

Tammany Must Always Have a Master

"Take six feet of human stature, paid [sic] it solidly with two hundred and ten or twenty pounds avoirdupois, give it a pair of broad shoulders and hips, a steady underpinning, and a gait every motion of which is indicative of power; crown the whole with a massive head, black hair, keen, dark eyes, an immobile face and mouth, though slightly shaded by a moustache and beard, and marred by [a] broken nose, and you have as good a pantograph as I can make of the famous fighter, M.C. and millionaire," was the *Edgefield Advertiser*'s impression of John Morrissey's still impressive stature and appearance shortly after his forty-first birthday in March of 1872. The piece described the prominent personalities on or about Broadway in New York City in that period, also including brief profiles on John Heenan and Buffalo Bill Cody.[460]

One of the most noticeable traits about John Morrissey now was his voice. Though he practiced habitual silence viewed by some as anti-social and by others as idiotic, and by still others as a sign of masculine confidence, John's voice seemed muffled and forced when he did speak, as though something were stuck in his throat, or "as if he had a chronic cold." Since the early 1860s, the newspapers had chronicled reports of sporadic respiratory illnesses or allergies in John Morrissey with varying degrees of accuracy. Those with any kind of specifics usually mentioned respiratory or throat infections. Any one of these might have caused the obvious sounds of strain now present in the voice. By 1874, a writer for the *Brooklyn Daily Eagle* noticed that John, now more than a decade removed from his boxing career, was "running to flesh." This reporter felt that Morrissey looked as though he was "getting well along in years," despite having only just entered his forties. This less than complimentary assessment was by and large a rarity, greatly outnumbered by descriptions that evoked images of strength, health, and vitality.[461]

John's name was relatively absent from the newspapers through the early months of 1872. There was a lawsuit against and counter-lawsuit from an Ohio gambler, along with mentions of requests for him to referee a boxing match and officiate a boat race, both of which he declined. Once the racing season was over, most of the city focused on the continuing

---

[460] *Edgefield Advertiser,* March 21, 1872
[461] *Bismark Tribune,* September 10, 1873; *Brooklyn Daily Eagle,* September 17, 1874

revelations about the Tweed Ring fraud and the legal troubles resulting from them.

Amid this news, Morrissey realized that keeping his name out of the papers was probably a good thing, and that his expulsion from Tammany Hall had been a blessing. Morrissey's dispute with the Ohio gambler didn't amount to a drop when compared to the ocean of ink flowing across front pages throughout America of the Tweed Ring's troubles. In fact, a large number of reformers within New York City who once vilified Morrissey as a drunkard, gambler, and brawler had suddenly come to respect him as among the first Tammany insiders to defy Tweed; no matter that he had not done so out of any sense of moral offense but rather due to disputes over money, his own ambition, and a personal dislike of Tweed. Some reformers willingly embraced him as a hero for openly challenging Tweed and his cronies at a time when few had dared to do so.

––––––

Another man who found his reputation polished clean by the exposure of the Tweed Ring was one John Kelly. Like Morrissey, Kelly hailed from Irish stock. However, he had been born in New York City on April 20, 1822. Like Morrissey, he grew up poor and with a feared reputation as a street fighter. He also had little time for formal education as a child, dropping out of school as a boy following the death of his father. Like Morrissey, Kelly made up for his lack of schooling in adulthood through disciplined study; in the case of Kelly, this meant classes in night school, rather nightly tutoring from his wife. There are also stories that Kelly was a capable pugilist in his younger years. After pursuing masonry as a vocation through early adulthood, Kelly's first significant political post was as an alderman, a position he gained in 1853 and would maintain through the next couple of years. Naturally a quiet, reserved man, Kelly made few waves as an alderman, and gained a reputation as a man who would do as he was told. Tammany rewarded his apparent subservience by nominating him for the congressional seat then held by the independent Mike Walsh, "the leader of a rowdy element," in 1855. Kelly won a narrow-upset victory, garnering him more respect from his Tammany brethren as a man on the rise.[462]

A profile of Kelly in a volume of the nineteenth century *National Cyclopaedia of American Biography* says that, when young, Kelly was "a strong, heavy, raw-boned man with a firm jaw, clear and determined eyes, and awkward manners," a description certainly comparable to those of John Morrissey. As had also been the case with Morrissey, his rise to a higher stratum of society and influence seemed to smooth Kelly's rough edges. He became more diplomatic and thoughtful in his approach to politics,

[462] Myers, *Tammany*, 300-301; Ackerman, 334; Mandelbaum, 92; Golway, 123

while maintaining his reputation for being strong-willed and focused. In public, he spoke with "the quality of plain common-sense," which helped endear him to the less educated, laboring classes. Yet, Kelly could also be an eloquent orator who loved to quote Shakespeare in more enlightened company.[463]

Kelly was part of the first generation of Irish Americans to gain significant political positions within the city, and he would end up becoming the most significant Irish American politician in New York during the nineteenth century. It was his experiences in congress that developed Kelly's talents as "a born ruler of men." When fellow congressman Thomas Whitney, one of the nation's leading nativist politicians and co-founder of the Native American ("Know Nothing") Party, spoke before the house decrying "Papists" as Anti-American foreigners unworthy of citizenship, Kelly responded with what might have been the finest speech of his career, warning of the dangers of prejudice. Kelly proposed that "the rights of no class, however humble they may be, can be assailed without endangering the rights of all. The persecutor of today," argued Kelly, "when religious intolerance has fairly started on its disastrous course, will inevitably become the victim of tomorrow." Kelly, as the only congressman who was of Irish heritage at the time and the only one whose parents had been immigrants, spoke with knowledge and passion, and the speech (printed in booklets and distributed by hand) made him a hero in the Irish neighborhoods of his hometown.[464]

His eloquence in defending his Catholic constituents aside, Kelly also found other ways to use his talents for expanding his influence. His congressman's position granted him opportunities to control the distribution of federal patronage jobs in New York City, a role through which he would secure the gratitude of many men who gained lucrative incomes and political influence because of his appointments. It was around this period that he had his first noteworthy break with Tammany, angry at being passed over for a police commissioner's position. In a compromise reached with Boss Tweed, Kelly instead became sheriff, a position he held from 1858 to 1868, using his influence to enrich himself with anywhere from $150,000 to $800,000 in "fees," depending on who told the story.

Despite the compromise and his official retention of his Tammany membership, Kelly was now on the outs with Tweed and company. Perhaps because of his never quite fitting in with the Tweed crowd, Kelly somehow wound up with the enduring nickname Honest John, given to him by the *New York Herald*, but most avidly taken up by the reform crowd within the Democratic Party. These same reformers backed him in a run against A. Oakey Hall for mayor in 1868, a nomination which confirmed his opposition to the Tweed Ring. Early in the campaign, Kelly was stricken

---

[463] *National Cyclopaedia*, 416
[464] *National Cyclopaedia*, 416; Golway, 86-88.

with bronchitis. Worse yet, both his wife and daughter died of tuberculosis. Ill, grieving, and seeking rest, Kelly abandoned the race and left the country with what was left of his family. He would spend the next two years touring Europe, North Africa, and the Middle East. Many in New York wrote off his promising political career as finished.[465]

Kelly did not return to the United States until the Fall of 1871. Thus, he was not present for the dispute over the "home rule" charter, nor the Young Democracy fight. By the time of he set foot back in New York's streets, the Tweed Ring was already breaking apart under the combined pressure of political rivals, press exposure, and public outrage. As had been the case with Morrissey, his absence from Tammany Hall, initially seen as a political defeat, had instead proven to be a benefit to his reputation.

With Tweed's reign clearly ending, the Democratic Party, and Tammany in particular, was in desperate need of new leadership. The reform Democrats who had been Tweed's opponents all along, men like Samuel Tilden, Augustus Schell, and August Belmont, recognized that they had the opportunity to immediately fill the power vacuum left by the defeated Ring, and they were anxious to make Honest John the new face of Tammany. "No sooner had he reached the city than he was besieged by leading citizens, … all of whom urged him to take up the lead in a movement for the overthrow of the Tweed Ring," recorded an early Kelly biographer. Initially reluctant to return to public life, he was slowly convinced by his friends that he was the only man for the job and relented to their requests to return to the Tammany fold. In 1872, Schell (a friend of both Commodore Vanderbilt and John Morrissey) became the new Grand Sachem, replacing Tweed. Where once the names of Connolly, Sweeny, Hall, and their ilk had populated the roll of sachems beneath Tweed, the names of Samuel Tilden, Horatio Seymour, August Belmont, and John Kelly now appeared below Schell's. The *New York Herald* liked to include the marvelously mustachioed former congressman John Fox, who had been one of Morrissey's allies in the Young Democracy, alongside Morrissey and Kelly in co-leadership of Tammany, dubbing them together the "Three Johns Ring."[466]

This new roster of leadership represented a monumental shift in the politics of Tammany and the New York Democratic Party as a whole, and not simply because the leaders of the Tweed Ring no longer appeared on the rollcall. For the two decades leading up to 1872, native-born W.A.S.P. men from the working class had dominated Tammany's leadership, men like Fernando Wood and William Tweed. These were men who could relate to the masses, but made their living by politics, and thus were susceptible to bribery or at least corruption. While they posed as champions of the Irish, they were not themselves Irish, an important

---

[465] Myers, *Tammany*, 300-301; Ackerman, 334; Mandelbaum, 92; McLaughlin, 93
[466] McLaughlin, 275, 279

distinction at the time. Reformers Schell, Tilden, and Seymour may have been all native-born, but they were all born into wealth, and had few personal connections to or sympathy for the "rabble" of New York. Their real money came from other means besides politics, and they professed distain for the machinery of local politics or what they considered mob rule. Meanwhile, Kelly, Morrissey, and Fox were either first- or second-generation Irish immigrants who rose out of poverty. Their status as political leaders came directly from their ability to understand and inspire the masses. Meanwhile, aristocratic German Belmont was neither native born nor from the streets. This was an unprecedented comingling of the native and the foreign, and of the patrician and the plebian at the top of the Tammany ladder, representing both the swallowtails' recognition of a change in the demographics of the Democratic Party's constituency and the recognition by the street level politicians of the value aristocratic reformers could bring to Tammany's bruised reputation.

The attorney and railroad investor Schell might have been Grand Sachem, but the anti-Tammany leadership portrayed him as merely a figurehead installed with the consent of Kelly and Morrissey, who they saw as the true political powers behind the re-organized Tammany leadership. The ascendancy of these men to true political clout was representative of a shift happening for the Irish American community in New York City at large. The middle-to-late nineteenth century saw the establishment of an Irish middle class, a development supported in part by Tammany's decades-long cultivation of the immigrant vote and positioning of Irish Americans in government jobs. Steady incomes, a political voice, and the passage of time saw an increasing number of these people establishing permanent residences for themselves, often outside of the poorer neighborhoods like the Five Points, from which they too could now look down their noses condescendingly at the latest newcomers pouring onto the city docks. John Morrissey's unwavering popularity among the lower-class Irish of the day had been a key factor in his initial acceptance into Tammany and his obtaining a foothold in American politics. His own rise from poor immigrant to millionaire, though partly accomplished by illicit means, was in some ways a confirmation of the American dream for immigrants. His futile attempts at integration into W.A.S.P. society reflected the general ambition among many Irish immigrants for assimilation, and they could relate to the rejection he met from the clannish elites of New York's upper classes.

As devoted to him as the poor Irish might have been, the growing Irish middle class was not at all fond of Morrissey's lingering reputation as a ruffian and drunkard. They saw his image as representative the very stereotypes they were trying to overcome. Meanwhile, Kelly, despite his own impoverished, two-fisted beginnings, held greater clout among the middle class. Even with his own less-than-scrupulous rise up the political ladder, Honest John had somehow emerged with his reputation untarnished, as far as most of the public was concerned. He included Tilden, Seymour, and their wealthy swallowtail friends among his political allies; these aristocrats found him sympathetic to their desires for a fiscally responsible, efficient, and *laissez faire* government. He owned a home in the chic Murray Hill district, was a devout Catholic who had married a Cardinal's niece, and he had temporarily abandoned politics to care for his family, all things the middle-class Irish admired. In him, the first Irish American Tammany boss, they saw the culmination of their struggle for respectability and voice. Fernando Wood and William Tweed had used them, John Kelly *was* them. Thus, together, John Morrissey and John Kelly combined their constituencies, the poor and middle-class Irish respectively, to establish joint rule of Tammany Hall and re-establish its influence over city politics in the months and years following the Tweed Ring disgrace.

Not everyone was convinced that the shift in power within the Democratic Party away from the Tweed Ring and to Morrissey, Kelly, and their friends would produce any true reform. These doubters scoffed at the public's eagerness to so easily forget the past sins of such men, and felt that the presence of men like Schell, Belmont, and Tilden did nothing to mask the continued corruption in Tammany Hall. The cynical *New York Herald* expressed such sentiments. Behind this circle of gray beards and gold canes – this circle of new faces – we see our old friends," the paper mused:

> They are really old friends and have come to view every winter for years. - Fernando Wood, William F. Havemeyer, A.H. Green [the new comptroller], John Morrissey, James O'Brien and twenty more. We have had these friends in many phases. We have known them as reformers and corruptionists, opposing Tammany and serving Tammany, denounced as thieves and applauded as virtuous citizens; but we invariably found them, when reduced to their last analysis, as shrewd and audacious men, who had made money out of politics, and were anxious to make more, and who, after using the circle of gray beards and gold canes to reach power, would forget that any such men ever existed and devote themselves to amassing an honest independence at the expense of the taxpayers of New York.... New York will be infinitely worse than we can think it possible to be when she finds that reform can only come from John Morrissey, James O'Brien and Fernando Wood.[467]

Initially, if the press regarded either man as the superior over the other in terms of influence within Tammany, it was Morrissey who was thought to enjoy greater clout than Kelly, by virtue of his connection with the working men of the city's poorer wards, which meant so much to Tammany's Election Day successes. "John Morrissey is the admitted autocrat of Tammany," observed the *New York Times*, which would pride itself on remaining a thorn in Tammany's side long after the Tweed Ring

[467] *New York Herald*, September 19, 1871

had disappeared. "Whatever is done by Tammany is, in fact, done by Morrissey. Whatever morality Tammany may have is Morrissey's in reality. He has succeeded in pushing even John Kelly aside, and has stepped into Tweed's place. Tammany must always have a master, and Morrissey is the new 'boss.'"[468]

The rise of reformist politics in New York was evident in the nomination by a third party, the Liberal Republicans, of *Tribune* publisher Horace Greeley, Morrissey's old ally in the Albany fight over the Tweed Ring charter, as candidate for President of the United States. Rather than propose their own candidate, the Democratic Party also got behind Greeley, though national chairman August Belmont thought it a horrible idea to back an ex-Republican. Morrissey, eager to have a man with whom he already had ties enter the White House, encouraged strong support of Greeley from Tammany. The election results proved Belmont right. The Democratic Party's backing of another party's candidate split the Democratic vote, and Greeley's political opponents used "his hobnobbing with such characters as John Morrissey, Ben Wood, of policy-shop notoriety,... and other questionable people" as evidence of Greeley's "true character." Meanwhile, a strong national economy and continued concerns over Ku Klux Klan activity in the South bolstered the campaign of incumbent President Grant. Greeley was, in his own words, "the worst beaten man that ever ran for that high office." To the further humiliation of both the candidate and Tammany, even New York went to Grant. Greeley's health immediately went into decline and he died in a hospital three weeks after election night.[469]

Reorganization and reform or not, Tammany Hall and the Democratic Party at large were at a low point. Despite the best efforts of Kelly, Morrissey, Greeley, and their allies, New York City now existed under a Republican President (Grant), a Republican Governor (John Dix), and a Republican Mayor (William Havemeyer). As historian Terry Golway put it, "Tammany seemed destined for irrelevancy in the closing months of 1872." As the hardly objective *New York Times* preferred to put it, "This is going to be an American city once more – not simply a larger kind of Dublin."[470]

———

His enemies may have criticized him heavily in New York City, but there was one place where John Morrissey could retreat and know that he was the unassailable master: his racetrack. As he did every summer, John Morrissey presided over the racing season at Saratoga Springs between July and August of 1872, but that season proved to be especially historic for a few reasons. It was the first season where, as a result of the success of each

[468] Nicholson, 97, quoting *New York Times*
[469] Burrows, 1011 – 1012; *Horace Greeley Unmasked* pamphlet, New York 1871
[470] Golway, 113

prior year over the next, the racing program would be split into two six-day meets, the first in July and the second in August. Morrissey also got into bookmaking that year, introducing "Paris Mutual" (now called pari-mutuel) betting, or pool betting, which his staff managed from a three-story "Pool-Room" house erected behind his famous Club House. The third reason was the highly anticipated race scheduled between the two finest racehorses in America, Longfellow and Harry Bassett, a race the *New York Times* would later call "The Greatest Contest in American Turf History."[471]

Owned by John Hunter (one of the members of the Saratoga Racing Association), and named after the famed poet, Longfellow was likely the physically largest racehorse in America at the time, not quite seventeen hands high with a stride nearing twenty-six feet. He had won at both Monmouth Park and Saratoga (in a sensational come-from-behind victory over William Travers's Kingfisher) in 1871 and had emerged victorious at Monmouth again in 1872. To those who followed thoroughbred racing, Longfellow, dubbed "King of the Turf," was unbeatable.[472]

If there was a horse that could take Longfellow, many racing fans thought it would have to have been Harry Bassett, sired by Lexington and almost as tall as Longfellow. Owned by Colonel David McDaniel, Bassett had placed third in Saratoga in 1870, a remarkable finish considering he had fallen during the race. Since then, he had been winning race after race, three already in 1872 before coming to Monmouth and losing to Longfellow.[473]

Some thought that Bassett was too friendly with Longfellow, and thus had not felt the competitive drive to win at Monmouth. Thus, when the time came for a second meeting at Saratoga, Morrissey put his own horse, Defender, in as a sacrificial lamb against the two finest racehorses in America, merely there to motivate Bassett, or at least silence any excuses for a loss.

It would be a two and one quarter mile race. As Morrissey, Hunter, Travers, Belmont, and all the rest of America's thoroughbred racing crowd looked on, both horses rocketed out of the gate at the start. No one apparently noticed at first, but Longfellow hit and twisted his foot almost immediately, and Bassett came into an early but narrow lead. As turf historian Edward Hotaling would describe it, "There would never be daylight between them" through the entire race. Bassett remained in the slightest of leads until the stretch, when Longfellow suddenly pulled up neck-and-neck with Bassett as the pair passed before the stands. The audience thrilled at the sight, virtually everyone on their feet and roaring. "The men are hoarse with shouting," recorded a witness, "and the ladies shout with them." As they rounded the next turn, Bassett again took the

---

471 Hotaling, 96-97
472 Hotaling, 88-91
473 Hotaling, 93-95

lead, but only by a head's length. Then Longfellow suddenly lost his footing and lurched, causing even Morrissey to lose his famously quiet reserve. "Longfellow's beat," he shouted, likely to the astonishment of those nearby. Then, amazingly, in obvious pain, Longfellow somehow pulled even again, only to have Bassett break loose and get across the finish a shoulder-length ahead. Both horses had beaten the standing record for a two and one quarter mile race, Bassett coming in at three minutes and fifty-nine seconds. As expected, Morrissey's Defender came in well behind the other two.[474]

The crowd erupted at the narrow finish. "White-haired men are young again," marveled the writer for the *New York Times* at seeing men of every type ignore policemen and jump around fanatically in the stands; the ladies maintained their composure well enough to reserve themselves to waving parasols and handkerchiefs. The jockeys not participating "tumbled over one another" to get to the judge's stand first and hear the result.

Then everyone saw Longfellow, limping away to his stable on three legs, and the excitement disappeared almost as quickly as it had come. Astonished elation was replaced by mournful silence. When Longfellow had hit his foot at the start of the race, part of his shoe had come loose and then doubled underneath itself, digging into his foot. Thus, the 1872 Saratoga races would be historic for a fourth reason, as the final race of the great Longfellow.[475]

––––––

Likely reading of the once invincible racehorse's unexpected and sudden downfall in the New York papers while inside his prison cell, William Tweed might have felt a twinge of empathy in relating his own quick fall; that is, assuming he was not a complete sociopath. The beleaguered Boss's first trial lasted seventeen days in January 1873, and somehow ended in a hung jury, prompting accusations of bribery. While this meant that he could, for the time being, go free, prosecutors were already working on a second trial before he ever set foot outside prison. While Tweed vacationed in California, his freedom scandalized New Yorkers, further motivating the prosecutors and politicians to bring him to justice quickly.

Against the advice of his few remaining friends, Tweed voluntarily returned to New York for a second trial, which began November 19. There are some secondary sources which indicate Morrissey testified at this trial, which finally ended with Tweed's conviction on four counts of corruption. This author could find no transcript, quote, or first-person confirmation of Morrissey's supposed testimony against the defendant. The presiding judge sentenced the accused, looking utterly demoralized and helpless for the very

––––––––––

[474] Hotaling, 98-99
[475] Hotaling, 99

265

first time, to twelve years in the notorious Blackwell's Island prison. The same judge had recently handed down just four years to the murderer of Tweed's good friend Jim Fisk.

Interviewed by a reporter for the *Sun*, Morrissey was unable to resist verbally kicking his one-time antagonist while he was down. He insisted that the Tweed Ring's outrages "would not be tolerated by any other country in the world. Just look at it!" he continued. "Here is this man Tweed acknowledging under oath that every one [sic] who did legitimate work for the city from 1861 to 1870 was compelled to pay fifteen per cent of the amount of his bills to have them passed by the Board of Supervisors of which he was head; that he made seven-eighths of these men thieves by forcing them to raise their bills fifteen per cent, so that they could pay him and his band the percentage they demanded.... Tweed also acknowledges that he is the most notorious thief the world has ever seen, and that no man ever did more to make public officers thieves." He then continued to detail the rumors he had heard of multiple payouts of more than a million dollars in taxpayer money to various Tweed mistresses.[476]

———

John's pride in his victory over Tweed and ascension to the leadership of Tammany was surpassed only by that he felt for John Junior. As a boy, John Junior had worried his parents, because he seemed to have inherited his father's unruliness and distaste for schoolwork. The parents sent their only son off to a preparatory school in Montreal, where he seems to have improved in his studies well enough to gain entrance to St. John's College in Fordham, New York, the first Catholic institution for higher education to be established in the United States. The school's first headmaster had been John McCloskey, who would later become the first Cardinal to the United States and father-in-law to John Kelly. The school divided its curriculum between preparatory school and higher education. It is not clear as to which of these young John enrolled in, or if it was both. Happy to have their beloved son closer to home, they were probably still happier to find that he had gained "a refinement of manner and mental culture wholly wanting in his father." He had also acquired interests in literature and sports, being particularly skilled at shooting, baseball, and boating. His mother, an avid sports fan, never tired of boasting of her son's skills with either gun or oar. There are even stories that John Junior was a member of the Troy Haymakers, the town's local professional baseball club, of which his father was rumored to be a behind-the-scenes owner. Though the senior Morrissey did enjoy betting on the Haymakers and was seen at their

[476] Kofoed, 244-245, quoting Morrissey in the *New York Sun*

games, there is no verifiable evidence that the elder man owned the team, nor that the younger played for them.[477]

The younger John was said to be quiet by nature, and "possessing all the good qualities of which his father can boast." Despite his cultured and reserved manner, he nonetheless still possessed the carefree and irresponsible streak that had characterized him as a child, a trait which concerned his parents. The elder John intended to eventually send his son away to Europe in hopes he would gain further education and maturity.[478]

On Wednesday, September 3, 1873, John Senior was in Saratoga when word arrived that his son was badly injured. Both Susan and John Junior had been visiting with friends at Friends Lake, a little over forty miles north of Saratoga in the Adirondacks. That morning, John Junior had been outside using a three pound can of gunpowder to make "powder snakes," meaning he would pour out some of the powder from the can onto the ground in a zig-zag line and then light the snake-like shape with a burning rag. At one point, as the eighteen-year-old was pouring the powder out, some of it got too close to the rag, which he had laid still burning on the ground nearby. The powder ignited and the flame immediately carried up the strand of pouring powder into the can, which exploded in young Morrissey's hands. The sound of the explosion was reported to have been heard four miles away. When Susan and the others came to see what the matter was, they saw John unconscious and on fire. The swift thinking of a servant named Atkins in grabbing a nearby blanket and covering John's burning body prevented the young man's death right then and there.[479]

When the blanket was removed, they saw that much of John's clothes had burned away, and that his face and arms were badly burned. The worst of the damage had been done to his hands, which had not only been burned worse than any other part of his body but had also been severely lacerated by the force of the explosion and shrapnel from the can. The immediate danger over, Susan took over the care of her son, making him as safe and comfortable as possible before sending word to her husband in Saratoga. The house they were at being five miles from the nearest train station and even further from the nearest town or doctor, Susan determined that she would have to get her son home and began packing their things for a return.

Meanwhile, John Senior rushed out of his door and called upon a local doctor, who agreed to accompany him north by rail. They made a hasty stop in Troy, where the terrified father convinced another physician to join them in the journey to Friends Lake by carriage along the Adirondack Road. Mother, son, and father eventually met each other while headed in

---

[477] *Brewster Standard*, January 5, 1877; *Ithaca Daily Journal*, January 4, 1877; sabr.org/bioproj/person/eb3ffa6e, accessed 12/8/2016
[478] *Ithaca Daily Journal*, January 4, 1877; *Brewster Standard*, January 5, 1877
[479] *Troy Times*, September 13, 1873

their opposite directions, the doctors attending to the injured man as best they could before the party set a course back to Saratoga. They arrived home in the early evening on Friday and put John Junior in a bed under the anguished watch of his parents. A ten o'clock that evening, a reporter for the *Troy Times*, who had heard the news and traveled to Saratoga to get the story, found the young man burned and bandaged, but "very comfortable."[480]

———

Thankful that his son was recovering well, John was able to turn his attentions to the State Democratic Convention scheduled for October 2 in Utica. By 1873, Tammany Hall's influence and reputation in and beyond the expanding border of New York City was resurgent. The destruction of the Tweed Ring had greatly embarrassed the organization, weakened its leadership, and confirmed the suspicions of opponents as to the society's corruption. However, over the past two years, John Morrissey and John Kelly, in partnership with their swallowtail friends, had managed a remarkable revival, both for themselves as individuals, and for Tammany.

Just because the Tweed Ring had been shattered, did not mean that Thomas Nast would stop lampooning top New York Democrats in *Harper's Weekly*. In November 1873, Nast commented on the resurrection of Tammany Hall as an influence in government with a cartoon caricaturizing John Morrissey as a bearded, muscular rooster with his dukes up and a championship belt around his waist towering over the fallen Tweed. "The Tammany Phoenix is a Fighting Cock," read Nast's caption. Morrissey, Kelly, and Tilden would all remain frequent targets of the fanatically Republican and anti-immigration artist for years to come. Morrissey was almost always depictured as a bearded brute busting out of ill-fitting gentleman's attire draped in diamonds as he stared down some weaker object of disdain. Nast's illustrations were seen by thousands every week in *Harper's*, one of the most widely read periodicals in the nation, and were particularly effective because, as Boss Tweed once complained, "my constituents don't know how to read, but they can't help seeing them damned pictures."[481]

Nast may have meant to poke fun at Morrissey's pugilistic past by illustrating the champion's belt around him, but the truth was that the people of New York needed a champion. The month prior to the Utica convention, a series of simultaneous fiscal factors, compounded by bad economic policies on the part of the Republican Grant administration, had resulted in the Panic of 1873, which would lead to the near collapse of the national economy by November and the now largely forgotten first Great Depression. Thousands of businesses failed, including most of the nation's

---

[480] *Troy Times*, September 13, 1873
[481] Adler, 92-93, 265 (e-book)

railroads, compounding the crisis. New York City's unemployment rate hit twenty-five percent, the city streets becoming "absolutely blockaded with beggars." In response to this crisis, Republican Mayor Havemeyer, the esteemed reformer who had co-founded the Committee of Seventy and help bring down Tweed, stopped city public works projects which employed so many of the laboring classes. Then he put a stop to relief programs that helped to feed, clothe, and shelter the people who had been unemployed by his cuts. When the poor protested his measures, the Mayor's response was that they should save their money and not spend it drinking and carousing. Many of those left jobless, homeless, and hungry were poor Irish, and they quickly decided they had had enough of high-minded "reform," and once again looked to Tammany to give them a voice.[482]

Tammany's main rival within the Democratic Party at this point was the newly established Apollo Hall, headed by Jimmy O'Brien, the former Young Democrat. However, as the convention approached, those who followed politics got the sense that, with Tammany once again swelling in political might, O'Brien and his new organization were about to meet an embarrassing defeat.

Come October 1, just a few weeks into the Depression, Morrissey and the other Tammany delegates arrived early in the morning in Utica and had their choice of wide-open accommodations. Reporters witnessed Morrissey "working like a stag all day" for Tammany interests, while an irritable John Kelly held court in the Boggs and Butterfield houses. Bored and restless for the coming fight, Honest John had little patience for Tammany delegates filing in and out all day asking for audiences, favors, and introductions. John Fox, the third member of the so-called "Three Johns Ring," was also present, "working in a quiet way." The next day, the early predictions of an overwhelming Tammany victory proved true, with Tammany delegates and candidates swamping those of Apollo Hall and other rivals.[483]

Morrissey and Kelly returned triumphant to New York City as saviors of an organization thought utterly defeated just a year or two earlier. The *New York Times* certainly had no doubt of Tammany's resurrection. Afterward, the paper grumpily asked and answered its own questions about the shift in power represented at the convention. "Who controls the Democratic party of this State? Tammany Hall," the writer opined. "And who controls Tammany Hall? John Morrissey. And who won the elections in this city? John Morrissey and Tammany." Recognizing that Morrissey had emerged as boss in large part on his reputation as a "reformer" against the corruption personified by his enemy Tweed, the writer expressed concern that "while the change [in bosses] was easy to be seen, the reform was hard

---

[482] Golway, 115-116
[483] *New York Herald*, October 1, 1873

to discover." Recognizing that Morrissey had selected delegates with respectable reform backgrounds for the convention, men like Abram S. Hewitt, Augustus Schell, and Samuel Tilden, the *Times* nonetheless insisted that these men were but figureheads intended to distract the public from Tammany's continued thievery. The paper labeled the majority of Tammany's committee, "men who helped Tweed to make the name of Tammany infamous," men guilty of "arrogant knavery and unblushing robbery, of unquestioning obedience to a master rogue." It was clear now that, with Tweed behind bars, the *Times* had now set its sights on the destruction of his replacements.[484]

The *Times* was relentless in its coverage of every possible controversy in Morrissey's career after his rise to the "leader of the Democracy." They published an article detailing his posting bail for the two men who had previously purchased his gambling house at 818 Broadway from him, and his subsequent admission to still owning the similar establishment at 5 West Twenty-Fourth Street. They reported on his association with men who had once proposed to build a statue to Tweed. When he backed William Wickham for Mayor in 1874, they insisted that Wickham's election would bring Tweed-style corruption back to power in New York. A year later, when Morrissey sang the praises of Samuel Tilden, the *Times* painted Morrissey interchangeably as an uneducated buffoon hypnotized by Tilden's wealth and intellect, or as a political opportunist who supported anyone who could better his own prospects. As they had during his initial nomination as a congressman, they and other papers harped on his rise from prizefighter to political power as evidence of the low state of nineteenth century Western civilization.[485]

The *Times* also picked up on the first evidence of yet another split within the Tammany ranks, beginning in early May 1874. The prior month, the three Johns had worked closely at the annual election for Tammany officers, Kelly and Fox securing elections as sachems. Just as the organization was once again solidifying its hold over the Democratic Party in New York, a dispute arose between two of the "Three Johns." John Fox, now a State Senator, had felt publicly slighted by Morrissey when they ran into each other on the street and Morrissey gave him the proverbial cold shoulder. When Morrissey next ran into Fox, the ensuing quarrel ended with Fox begging Morrissey not to hurt him and being punched and head-butted anyway. Amid criticism from various New York papers, Tammany set up a committee to investigate the dispute between two of its leading figures, only to later announce its unsurprising findings that the matter was personal between the two men and not requiring the committee's interference.[486]

---

484 *New York Herald*, October 1, 1873; *New York Times*, November 8 and December 31, 1873
485 *New York Times*, December 12 and 31, 1873, November 3, 1874, and July 16, 1875
486 *Chicago Daily Tribune*, May 6, 1874

Mayor Havemeyer remained obdurate in his reform-minded crusade to shrink municipal government waste and free up the marketplace by cutting back on various city projects and relief programs in the middle of the worst economic crisis New York and the nation had seen in decades. As a result, he enjoyed powerful support from the city's financial elites, who believed the government's role was to protect the city's own treasury, not provide work and support for its citizenry; but he was also despised by the lower classes of the city, who saw him as coldly ignoring their plight. Morrissey, picking up on the discontent of Tammany's poor Irish constituency, publicly blamed the Mayor for the mess, alleging that Havemeyer's economic policies had cost New Yorkers thirty to forty thousand jobs. Havemeyer spoke plainly when it came to his opinion of Tammany's role in the mess. He published an open letter in September 1874 accusing John Kelly of being "worse than Tweed." Alleging that Kelly had acquired the specific sum of $84,482 illegally during his time as New York's Sheriff, Havemeyer mused that "Men who go about with the prefix of 'honest' to their names are often rogues." A libel suit from Kelly promptly arrived on the Mayor's desk.[487]

The insults to Kelly's reputation brought out a rare return of Morrissey's Old Smoke personality. On September 22, Morrissey attended a gathering at Collier's Ballroom on the corner of Broadway and Thirteenth Street. Also attending was the notorious alcoholic Colonel George Harris Butler, a former reporter and Civil War soldier who had recently returned from a disgraceful term as U.S. Consul General in Egypt. Butler, having attained the position thanks to the influence his uncle, General Benjamin Butler had over President Grant, had engaged in all sorts of corruption while in Alexandria, including getting drunk on the job, the auctioning off of government positions, spying on others' mail, using government money to hire nude female dancers, ordering the beating of a missionary who was investigating him, and ultimately shooting an American Army officer in a quarrel. In the end, Butler had had to flee Egypt in fear of his life. Now he was drunk at Collier's and openly referring to John Kelly as an Irish son of a bitch to John Morrissey's face. Morrissey immediately seized the smaller man by his collar with one hand and smashed Butler's hat down upon his head with the other. The room became silent and watched as the ex-boxer began cuffing the drunk about. Once he felt he had embarrassed and punished the disgraced soldier enough, Morrissey demanded that he take back the insult, which Butler promptly did, happy to escape the room with two black eyes and some swelling.

John Kelly's libel case against Mayor Havemeyer was scheduled to be the first heard by New York Supreme Court Judge Donohue on the afternoon of November 30. However, when the frigid day arrived and

---

[487] Golway, 117

most of the necessary parties came out of the cold into the courthouse, the conspicuous absence of the defendant puzzled everyone. Soon enough, word arrived that the Mayor had died in his office, only moments earlier. Havemeyer was returning from a visit to Long Island by train that morning when the train "met with an accident." With no visible injuries, the seventy-year-old Mayor exited the disabled transport and walked the remaining two and a half miles to City Hall, then died of internal hemorrhaging shortly after arriving in his office. When the news of his death reached the courthouse, the courtroom immediately broke up, with many of the politicians and reporters present setting out for City Hall in disbelief, only to have the story confirmed. In the aftermath, alderman Samuel Vance became acting Mayor, pending the election of a successor.[488]

Even before Havemeyer's death, Kelly and Morrissey had settled upon diamond merchant William Wickham as their candidate for his replacement, though Morrissey had his reservations. Wickham had been a member of the Committee of Seventy alongside Havemeyer and had since joined James O'Brien in the Apollo Hall Democracy. By backing him for Mayor, Kelly in particular intended to bring a respected reformer back into the Tammany fold, further polishing the organization's reputation, but also having that reformer grateful to them for his elevation. Morrissey was not so sure about Wickham, who he worried was nothing more than a Democrat version of the elitist Havemeyer. Only after Kelly capitulated to backing Morrissey's friend James Hayes for city register did Morrissey consent to put his weight behind Wickham.

Morrissey's worries about Wickham were likely soothed when the candidate promised a vast program of public works for the poor and to somehow simultaneously cut city expenditures. When Wickham and the majority of the Tammany ticket (including gubernatorial candidate Samuel Tilden) emerged victorious on Election Day, opponents decried him as an unquestioning servant of Boss Kelly, whom they accused of using the police as enforcers for the Tammany ticket, and crowed about a return to Tweed-era corruption.

That Tammany had won back the offices of the Governor and the Mayor from the Republicans was a clear sign of Tammany's resurgence in 1874, but it was little consolation to John Morrissey. His good friend James Hayes was one of the few New York Democrats to lose his race, a failure that Morrissey came to blame on Kelly's lack of adequate support. Morrissey had allegedly loaned Hayes the $40,000 spent on his campaign. Morrissey's later suggestion to Wickham and Kelly that they install Hayes as Fire Commissioner also never came to fruition, again infuriating Old Smoke.

———

[488] Myers, 306; *New York Times*, December 1, 1874

After taking office on January 1, 1875, new Governor Samuel Tilden announced the formation of the Committee on Organization, the stated purpose of which was to explore ways in which the taxpayers of New York State would have more control over the management of public works funded throughout the state. In practice, this meant the stripping of control over patronage jobs from New York City political bosses into the hands of the governor's statewide Committee, the membership of which was populated overwhelmingly by Tilden's wealthy swallowtail Democrat friends and fellow members of the exclusive Manhattan Club.

When Mayor Wickham betrayed the interests of the various Tammany aldermen and ward bosses by publicly supporting Tilden's Committee, Morrissey believed his initial reservations about backing Wickham for office to be confirmed. Though Kelly continued to defend Wickham, clearly intending to maintain his most powerful link to City Hall, Morrissey resented the Mayor's reformist stance and aristocratic elitism. In March of 1875, he went to City Hall to pay a visit to Wickham, only to have an aide tell him that the Mayor could not be bothered. Walking away in a huff, Morrissey told the aid to "give my compliments to His Honor Mayor William Wickham and ask him to tell Billy Wickham that when John Morrissey has times to put on French airs, he may call again."[489]

Days later, a newspaper man spotted Old Smoke, still seen by many as a rough-edged thug, parading down Madison Square in full swallowtail regalia, his muscular body stretching an impeccable dinner jacket to its limits. Even more ridiculous, the one-time illiterate openly carried a French dictionary underneath his arm. Realizing that Morrissey was waiting for someone to ask him what on Earth he thought he was doing, the reporter did just that, and the Tammany boss replied that he was off to see the new Mayor. He was hoping to win appointment to a patronage job, he said, explaining that getting an appointment with the Mayor was impossible unless one wore kid gloves and spoke French. "No Irish need apply now," he said with a smirk.[490]

When Morrissey made it to "Hotel Wickham," as he now called City Hall, and met with the astonished Mayor, Morrissey explained his reason for his outlandish dress and they both broke into a laugh together. However, there was more than just humor in Morrissey's display. He was now expressing the very real resentment of many within the Tammany ranks against Kelly and Wickham, as the organization once more headed for internal strife, pitting Honest John and the Mayor, who now courted the middle class Irish-Americans and wealthy swallowtails respectively, in public

[489] Mandelbaum, 129-132, Nicholson, 96-97
[490] Mandelbaum, 129-132; Nicholson, 97

battle against the rank-and-file members of their own party, who had long seen John Morrissey as their champion.[491]

The rift between Morrissey and Kelly was widened by Tilden, who would continue to have a long and complicated relationship with each of them. For a time, Tilden and Kelly appeared to have concurrent agendas, and Morrissey was temporarily on the outs with Tilden as a result. Despite Tilden's help in the Young Democracy fight, Morrissey, in the estimation of the *Times*, briefly became "the bitterest anti-Tilden man in New York." By 1875, however, Tilden was considering a run at the presidency the next year. This made him concerned about keeping the right people behind him – bankers, lawyers, reformers, and the wealthy elite – and distancing himself from Tammany, still tainted in the eyes of much of the general public by the stench of the Tweed scandals. Thus, when an open rivalry emerged between Kelly and comptroller Andrew Green, Tilden broke with Tammany in silently supporting Green, who had the trust of New York's business and socialite classes because of his conservative economic policies and his own role in taking down the Tweed Ring. When the animosity between Kelly and Green became open, Tilden's support of Green dealt a blow to Kelly's plans and reputation.[492]

Naturally, once Tilden and Kelly split over Green's comptrollership, Morrissey re-thought his friendship with Tilden, and Tilden was happy to partner with Kelly's rival. Caught in Saratoga by a reporter for the *World*, he was now complimenting the character of the ex-prizefighter. "I have always found Morrissey to be a man of devotion to his standards of rightfulness," he said. Tilden knew that working-class men had little enthusiasm for voting for a man of his class; he would need a man to drum up their support if he expected to become President. Despite their prominence in immigrant-supported Tammany Hall, Kelly and Wickham had little pull with the lower classes; Morrissey was undeniably the right man for the job.[493]

As had been the case in the days of the old Tweed Ring charter, many of the rank-and-file in Tammany were not happy with Kelly's centralization of power and patronage around he and a select few henchmen. As he had with Tweed, Morrissey used this resentment to gradually create a grassroots movement within Tammany against Honest John over a period of months. To these working men, he downplayed his own personal grudges against Kelly and Wickham and instead harped on the lowering of city wages amid the economic crisis. Morrissey publicly blamed the cut in pay on Kelly, his first open attacks on his Tammany co-regent. Rumors began to circulate in the halls of the Democratic Party that Morrissey was preparing a power play that would remove Kelly from Tammany's governing General Committee.

---

[491] Nicholson, 97
[492] Mandelbaum, 133–138; *New York Times*, June 27, 1876
[493] Buckman, 115

If this was Morrissey's intention, Kelly would not give him the opportunity to see his strategy play out. Kelly, who had long wanted sole power over Tammany and regarded Morrissey as an obstacle to that goal, made a preemptive strike in July. He had a resolve passed to reorganize six Democratic voting districts in the city from which Morrissey, Hayes, and their closest allies drew most of their support. The jerrymandering, passed through the General Committee, was a final confirmation of an irreconcilable split between the two Tammany bosses.[494]

Morrissey vowed revenge. In his office in Saratoga, he granted an interview to a writer with the *Tribune* on July 24. John was quick to point out that he remained loyal to the Democratic Party, saying, "they can't put me out of the party, and I don't mean to act with any other organization. After Tammany has been taught a lesson by defeat this Fall, we shall come back into the Committee and the rest will be retired into obscurity." Careful not to make personal attacks on Kelly, Morrissey said he believed his inevitable expulsion from the General Committee was because "I criticised [sic] Kelly's acts." Asked what he thought Kelly's goal to be, Morrissey replied, "John Kelly's course is a mystery to me. I can't see any purpose in it. It's the first thing in the world that ever puzzled me in this way. In most matters I can put this and that together and conclude why a man has done a thing; but I can't even guess a purpose in this." Knowing that he held greater sway than Kelly with the poor Irish that made up Tammany's base, he turned his subject to what amounted to a battle cry for the regular men of Tammany to rally around him. "Kelly was all right until success made him wild," Morrissey continued. "He has turned on every man in Tammany Hall who helped make him what he is and assisted in putting him in the front. You can't run a political organization without working men in it, and these must be taken care of if you want to keep them in it. A politician can no more ignore his organization and party than a man can snub his creditor. That's what Kelly and Wickham are doing, and there will be a foreclosure soon, you see if there isn't."[495]

As for Kelly, he insisted to an interviewer that the move against his former partner was not a matter of personal dislike for Morrissey, but a matter of political expediency, insisting that the ex-prizefighter was "a load to carry" politically. Morrissey's reputation as a fighter, drunkard, gangster, and gambler, according to Kelly, "rendered him odious to many in the Tammany organization and repelled many other good Democrats who would not affiliate with it so long as he held a prominent position and claimed to influence the action of the Tammany General Committee and had a voice in the making of nominations." Thus, Kelly indirectly revealed that the resolution of the Committee reflected not only his desire to preserve his own stature in Tammany Hall, but to court the favor of the

---

[494] *New York Tribune*, July 24 and 26, 1875
[495] *New York Tribune*, July 24, 1875

middle-class and swallowtail Democrats who had for so long been scandalized by Morrissey's position of power within their party.[496]

Morrissey remained in Saratoga while the Tammany General Committee met in New York City the next day to put an official stamp on a foregone conclusion. With his district effectively stripped from him, he was helpless to prevent his expulsion from the Committee, as were Hayes and one other friend, Thomas Ledwith, a judge and State Senator.[497]

None among the city's leading papers were sad to see Morrissey go, but neither was there much respect for Kelly's maneuvering, with some writers fearing that the city had another Boss Tweed on its hands. "The men who have been thrust out were certainly no credit to the organization," observed the *Tribune*. "The prominence of John Morrissey in politics has always been a public scandal, and however popular that eminent sport and bruiser may be among the big-pipe men on the boulevards and the gamblers at Saratoga, his reputation has cost the Democratic Party on the whole many more votes than his personal influence has ever brought it" The paper went on to separate Morrissey from men like Tweed, in that they did not view him as a thief in the manner of his now infamous predecessor, but insisted that, as a politician, he was "hardly less debasing or corrupting" to New York's politics.[498]

With his second exile made official, it was now up to Morrissey to decide his next move. The working-class men within the Tammany fold remained steadfastly loyal to him. "Rightly or wrongly they consider that Morrissey was turned out of Tammany for having tried to restore their wages to $2 a day, and to these men, for whom full pay means a bare livelihood, and short pay hunger, no stronger claim to their support can be presented," commented the *Times*. Their income and work opportunities limited, these men were also unable to pay their rents or buy anything more than essential food, which in turn had upset the landlords and merchants of the city's working-class districts; Morrissey would be sure to turn their anger against Kelly too. But he would need more than these men to fight an effective political battle against the likes of Kelly and his cronies, for the city aldermen had unanimously and publicly come out in favor of Kelly.[499]

The first important outsider to come to Morrissey's cause was the president of the German American Independent Citizens Association. Like the Irish, Germans had been flocking to American shores for decades at this point. It had been they, even more than the Irish, who had predominantly backed the rise of Fernando Wood (and with him, the Tammany Society) in New York politics during the early 1850s. However, their dominant numbers in neighborhoods like the Five Points had since

---

[496] *New York Tribune*, July 26, 1875

[497] Nicholson, 97; *New York Times*, July 29, 1875

[498] *New York Tribune*, July 26, 1875; *New York Times*, July 29, 1875

[499] *New York Times*, July 27 and 29, 1875

been swamped by the Irish fleeing the potato famine, and Tammany had largely turned its back on the Germans to favor the hordes of potential voters represented by the new immigrants. With Morrissey now ostracized from Tammany, he was free to court the Germans, and they finally had a major city politician giving them a voice again.

In time, several Republicans began to visit Morrissey, offering their aid in whatever he had planned for a confrontation with Kelly. They understood that Morrissey would never abandon the Democratic Party, but for now they had a common enemy. With a few Tammany defectors, the disgruntled German immigrants, and a host of Republicans at his back, Morrissey now found himself the face of a diverse, if unruly, coalition of Anti-Kelly crusaders eager to make a united strike against the new Boss. Before they could make their move, Morrissey knew he had to test the real power of this diverse alliance. It was imperative that the test be passed, and a plan be put into motion, before the patchwork group tore itself apart. After all, outside of their mutual hatred of the current Tammany leadership, the diverse membership could not agree on virtually any other political issue, be it worker's wages or Governor Tilden's reforms. If he was going to lead them, Morrissey wanted to do so with the firm footing that a secured government office could provide. Soon enough, an opportunity came his way.

19.

Triumph and Tragedy

Following John Kelly's coup in Tammany, John Morrissey initially returned to Saratoga and oversaw yet another successful summer racing season. He and Susan had purchased a permanent house there valued at $15,000. They, John Jr., and 87-year-old Timothy Morrissey lived there along with three live-in servants. George Wilkes, publisher of the *Spirit of the Times*, still America's leading sports magazine described Morrissey as a paragon of "the higher class of what are known as 'sporting men'" because "he dealt fairly according to the fixed laws of mathematical percentage," and ran honest gaming facilities. Since the prior season, Morrissey had renovated the accommodations at the track. The introduction of pari-mutuel betting the prior year at Saratoga and other racing venues had prompted "a new frenzy for betting on races," and Morrissey wanted his place to be ready to impress any newcomers. He had a roof installed over the second stand identical to the one already on the first, refurbished the seats, and refreshed and redesigned the groundskeeping and landscaping. Though the horse D'Artagnan set a record in the Travers stakes, the most historically interesting inclusion at the races was three-year-old General Harney, owned by President Grant, likely the only horse in Saratoga history to be entered into a race while owned by a sitting president. The most anticipated event was, as always, the Saratoga Cup, where Preakness and Springbrook recorded the first and only tie in the Cup's history by breaking Harry Bassett's 1872 record and crossing the finish line together in 3:56 1/4.[500]

There is an interesting article in the *Daily Albany Argus* intimating that someone may have attempted to burglarize the Morrissey home that racing season. It seems there had been a rash of burglaries in the resort that season, the culprits making a habit of breaking into the homes of wealthy residents while they slept. The *Argus* reported that the thieves had been "driven away in nearly every case" in early August before they could successfully pilfer any goods. "Those who visited the residences of Mrs. John Morrissey, Dr. L.B. Putnam, Albert Ott and John E. Hammond were undoubtedly convinced, from receptions received, that Saratogians should be given a wide berth after dark," noted the paper.[501]

With the crime apparently averted, his family safe, and another profitable racing season at Saratoga in the books and in his pockets, John

---

[500] Hotaling, 112-113; New York State Census for 1875, accessed at ancestry.com on 4/9/2020
[501] *Daily Albany Argus*, August 11, 1875

returned to New York City in September. He had suffered another unexpectedly terrible bout of illness that month while traveling on train from Saratoga, to the point where he had to depart from the cars at Poughkeepsie until he could recover, but he did eventually make his way back to the City. He did not have long to settle in at the Hoffman House when word arrived from Saratoga of his father's death on September 26. As of the census taken on June 7 of that year, Tim Morrissey had been living with his son, daughter-in-law, and grandson in their house in Saratoga, and was in a pleasant mood as he gave an interview to a local reporter, reminiscing about his five brothers and five uncles who all fought at the Battle of Waterloo. He had retired from a life of labor around the time of his wife's passing and had since then resided with John and Susan wherever they lived, the couple doing their best to make his later years comfortable. Following the onset of an unknown illness, he was moved to a sanitarium, even though, according to the *New York Times*, he had been in excellent health all his life, right up to the end. He was 87 years old when he passed, and buried alongside his wife in the Morrissey family plot at St. Peter's Cemetery in Troy.[502]

———

John Morrissey's return to New York City meant that the streets and public businesses surrounding the Hoffman House were daily crowded with Democrats and newspapermen looking to welcome "Old Smoke" back or talk to him about his intentions for the 1875 elections. The Hoffman House had become something of a headquarters for him over the past few years, as he had taken a particular liking to the hotel's cigar store, where those searching him out would often find him lounging against a nearby railing gazing out at the greenery of nearby Madison Park. His fellow exiles from Tammany, James Hayes and Thomas Ledwith, had been mustering their own troops for a political move against Kelly, whom many of the city newspapers now regarded as Boss Kelly, emphasizing his reputation as Tweed's successor. Hayes had made it a point to get down to the hotel to shake hands with his friend on the day he arrived, and reporters noticed that the two had a great deal to say to one another in a private conversation away from prying ears. Afterward cornered by a man from the *Times*, Morrissey declined to comment on his intentions, except to say that he would speak publicly at the impending Democratic Convention in Syracuse, meant to elect delegates for the national convention. Those who had chafed at Kelly's autocratic rule of the local Democratic Party eagerly anticipated Syracuse, elated that the man who was their best hope for

[502] *Daily Albany Argus*, May 10, 1875; *Alexandria Gazette*, September 13, 1875; *Irish American*, October 9, 1875; New York State Census, 1875, accessed at ancestry.com on 4/9/2020

ousting Kelly had returned to the fray for one more scrap and a final try for political dominance.[503]

Syracuse did not go as well for John as he had hoped. He, Hayes, Ledwith, and their delegations arrived in Syracuse in mid-September to speak their peace against Kelly's rule of Tammany and their own right to represent the party as delegates. Morrissey focused on Kelly's jerrymandering of his district, pointing out that, if Kelly could do so to Morrissey's district, "he has the right to do the same thing in any Assembly district of the State." In the end, though, the arguments were futile. Neither he nor Hayes nor Ledwith gained admission to the national convention as delegates. As testament to Tammany Hall's importance to the outcome of national elections, newspapers as far off as Nebraska carried the news of the anti-Tammany faction's defeat at the local convention, but most seemed to favor Morrissey over Kelly (with the notable exception of the *New York Tribune*, which mocked Morrissey's image as a champion of the people and considered his campaign against Kelly nothing more than a selfish vendetta). Kelly may have won the battle, but, true to his rugged reputation, Old Smoke still had plenty of fight in him.[504]

Rumors spread that Morrissey was considering a run at for the New York State Senate. Most intriguing for the gossipers was that his opponent in such a race would be none other than John Fox, the other former member of the "Three Johns." Though Morrissey had seen to Fox's brief removal from Tammany, Kelly naturally had him reinstated, and he was now the incumbent State Senator for the very district in which Morrissey expected to run.

October 16, 1875 proved a particularly busy day for Morrissey. He met with Hayes, Ledwith, Jimmy O'Brien, and other anti-Kelly men at the office of one Francis Bixbey at 23 Park Row to discuss their strategies for opposing Kelly in the coming elections. Later that day, Democratic representatives of New York's Fourth Senatorial District (composed of the first through seventh wards, along with the thirteenth and fourteenth wards) met at 80 Clinton Street and unanimously voted for a resolution to nominate John Morrissey their Senator. An appointed committee then drafted a letter to Morrissey notifying him of their request. There was one paragraph of the message, however, that clearly addressed John Kelly:

> The election involves the question whether the one-man power is to be perpetuated in the government of the Democratic Party. The assertion of that power has reached the very climax of autocracy. The nominations of Tammany Hall are all dictated by one man.

[503] *New York Herald*, September 9, 1875
[504] *New York Herald*, September 17, 1875; *New York Tribune*, September 17 and 22, 1875; *Ashtabula Telegraph*, October 1, 1875; *Nebraska Advertiser*, September 30, 1875; *Ashtabula Telegraph*, October 1, 1875; *New York Times*, September 17, 1875

The measures to be adopted by the officers elected by its votes, or appointed by its authority, are all dictated by the same one man, and your own outrageous exclusion from participation in its counsels bears striking witness to the fact that no man, however right, who disputes the will or caprice of that one man, will be tolerated in the organization. This, then, is a two-fold question which we have to meet this year – are we to be governed by one man, and that one the foe of the working classes?[505]

The letter failed to mention that Morrissey himself had made use of similar "one-man" power during his time at the head of Tammany and had seen to the exclusion of John Fox from its meetings in much the same manner as Kelly had seen to his.

Morrissey initially declined the invitation to run for office, but the move was likely a feigned show of humility, a pretense of not wanting the glory for himself. The city papers published his letter politely turning down their request on October 18. However, in stating his reasons for declining, he sounded like he was in fact campaigning for office, essentially putting into print a political manifesto for the anti-Kelly factions that had coalesced around him in the preceding months. "I remain, as I have ever been, a democrat," he explained:

I believe in the self-governing intelligence of the masses of the people, and I am a democrat because I believe the principles of the party, properly administered, are best for the people....

I differ with Tammany Hall in its policy of leaving the high salaries of [its favored] officials untouched while largely reducing the hard earned pittance of the laborer.

I differ with Tammany Hall in its policy of refusing the remunerate honest and deserving public servants simply because they refuse to be tools of a centralizing partnership.[506]

As Morrissey likely intended, passages like these in his letter only created more enthusiasm for his candidacy from those who supported him. He encountered "incessant importunities" to change his mind. Within a few days, he had done just that, admitting to a friend, "I am in for this fight. I will, unpleasant as it is, stand in the breach for Senator, not because I desire a seat in the Senate, but to aid in overthrowing a selfish and proscribing combination."[507]

On October 21, a new letter was composed and sent to the Fourth District Democratic representatives and to the city newspapers, signed with John Morrissey's name. Its closing sentence read:

---

[505] *New York Herald*, October 17, 1875; *New York Times*, October 17, 1875
[506] *New York Times*, October 18, 1875
[507] *New York Herald*, October 22, 1875

My duty to the cause which you represent demands that I should no longer refuse my active co-operation, and if, as I verily believe, the result shall be the downfall of the dictatorship which threatens to enthrall for an indefinite period the democratic votes of New York, and the vindication of the rights of free and honest labor, and, if, as part of this result, I shall be chose to the important and distinguished office of Senator, I shall endeavor so to discharge my duties as to merit in some degree the confidence which you have been pleased to express in supporting me for that office.[508]

Morrissey's official entrance into the race for office only heightened the enthusiasm among his allies for the fight with Tammany. Hayes immediately organized a base of operations for the anti-Kelly candidates, of whom Morrissey was the undisputed star, in a suite of rooms at the Anson House. His household name and notorious reputation meant that newspapers from as far afield as Washington, D.C. carried news of his candidacy for the New York State Senate. The New York papers noted that incumbent Senator Fox was himself born and raised in that very district, whereas Morrissey was a foreigner by birth. Nonetheless, on the evening of the twenty-first bets were being offered by Morrissey's supporters of one hundred dollars to seventy-five dollars that he would supplant his rival.

On October 22, Morrissey was giving the opening speech of his campaign at an outdoor meeting in Rutgers Square before a massive crowd of supporters when jeers and heckles arose from the back of the crowd. Soon enough, he was forced to rely on his old boxing instincts to dodge a series of rocks flying toward his head. Recognizing Tammany thugs when he saw them, the candidate refused to stop speaking until bricks started coming in alongside the stones, forcing him reluctantly quit the stage for his safety. When another speaker tried to take John's place, missiles and insults accosted him from multiple directions, too. Attempts by the police to stop the harassment failed and soon enough the second speaker too dove for cover. At this, the meeting fell into complete chaos until all parties eventually departed the scene.

A meeting to ratify Morrissey's candidacy, "the largest and most enthusiastic ever held in the Seventh Ward," occurred three days later at East Broadway Square. Again, a huge crowd appeared to cheer John and the other anti-Tammany Democratic candidates, thankful for no interruption by hecklers or violence. Brought to the stand to speak, Morrissey began with the same rhetoric that had characterized his prior letters. However, the language quickly became more dramatic as it progressed, promising, "if I am defeated, then you have no more voice; your necks are under the yoke and you will never be able to throw it off." Then he moved into a reference to the career that brought him fame.

---

[508] *New York Herald*, October 22, 1875

"When I was ever in a fight single handed, I always won," he said, still relying on his assertion that he had been outnumbered in his fight with Bill Poole all those years ago on the Amos Street dock. Closing the short speech with a plea for votes, John then moved on to the Fourteenth Ward, where yet another vociferous crowd greeted him nearly as large in number and briefly addressed the crowd as he had the first.[509]

On October 29, with the election only a few days away, Morrissey yet again spoke before a large, cheering crowd, this time gathered at Hibernia Hall on Prince Street. He again relied on his own record as a rebel within his own party and on the working class's concerns about wages. "I have been a democrat all my life," he told them, "and expect to die one." He then went into the details, as he saw them, of his being ostracized from Tammany Hall for opposing the lowering of workman's wages. "If this action on my part constitutes treachery I am a traitor and am willing to be so considered again. I am no candidate for office, but have been compelled to come forward and champion your rights…. This is your fight. If you do not assert yourselves now and defeat the 'one-man power,' as exemplified by John Kelly, you have nothing to hope for in the future…. You can win the fight if you will, and when the sun goes down on Tuesday next you will either be victors or slaves for the balance of your lives." With that final incitement to action, Morrissey stepped off the stage to a roar of approval. The entire audience followed him out of the building's doors to watch him get into his carriage and depart.[510]

The next day, New Yorkers picked up the *Herald* to read another letter signed by Morrissey. This one reiterated some of the things he had already said about his reasons for accepting the anti-Tammany nomination and fighting for workman's wages. However, this time Morrissey freely indulged in mudslinging, taking aim at his opponent, John Fox. He pointed out details of Fox's past as a legislator and politician which he felt made Fox "absolutely unworthy or your confidence." Fox had been a member of the notoriously greedy Board of Supervisors alongside Boss Tweed and had in fact been the chairman of the committee of "vultures and public plunderers" responsible for swindling the city and its citizens of millions of dollars, Morrissey asserted. He specifically detailed in line items a total of $2,586,756.45 paid out to contractors for city contracts, which he claimed had personally been approved by Fox; the companies to whom these payments were made had already been proven by the *Times* to be either entirely fictional or unusually friendly to Tweed, Fox, and the rest.[511]

As part of the ever-shifting political loyalties within the New York Democratic Party of the day, Governor Tilden shocked Morrissey by supporting the Tammany candidates for 1875, Fox included. Just that September, the press had been touting Morrissey as Tilden's "right-hand

<hr>

[509] *New York Herald*, October 26, 1875
[510] *New York Herald*, October 30, 1875
[511] *New York Herald*, October 30, 1875

man;" now the Governor was showing little regard for John's loyalty. Still, even with Kelly, Tilden, and Fox united, the newspapers believed that Morrissey had little to worry about at the polls. By the time they published his letter, the press almost unanimously expected Morrissey to trounce Fox at the polls. "A spirit of genuine enthusiasm in the cause of Morrissey has taken hold of the large masses of working men who inhabit this section," the *Herald* reported of the Fourth District. "Morrissey cannot be beaten by fair means," the paper concluded. Likewise, the *Times* observed that Morrissey's brief campaign had galvanized the working men of his district against Tammany more effectively than any previous man to run against the organization, adding that the working man's vote accounted for ninety percent of the electorate in the contested district. They reported that Morrissey had put money in the hands of men who were meant to distribute the cash freely in the local saloons, buying drinks for the thirsty workers there, and making sure they knew that their tab was on Morrissey. Of course, nothing was better for his campaign than making sure that the people could see their hero in person. John appeared at four separate events in a single day, one of which was at an open-air event, despite a raging thunderstorm. In the week leading up to Election Day, he personally delivered an estimated thirty total speeches.[512]

Meanwhile, Kelly, allegedly "thoroughly frightened," lashed out at Morrissey, at the Republicans, at various newspapers, and at everyone else who opposed him during a meeting at Tammany Hall on October 30. Clearly embarrassed and infuriated by what he already felt were ill prospects for his hand-selected candidates in the various races, Kelly ranted about the possibility of Tammany's destruction and with it the liberties of the Irish, the Catholics, and other minorities in the city. He accused the Republicans of reviving Know-Nothing hate rhetoric and Morrissey of betraying his own countrymen in colluding with them. He took issue with Morrissey's accusations of reducing workman's wages; he correctly pointed out that Tammany (albeit mainly in the person of Morrissey) had vigorously fought against this reduction, for which comptroller Green had been primarily responsible. He scoffed at Morrissey's claims of solidarity with the working man. "Does anyone here know of his ever doing a day's labor in his life?" he asked. Kelly also insisted that, contrary to Morrissey's statements, it was not John Fox who had voted for the fraudulent payments out of the city coffers in the days of the Tweed Ring, but that it had been Morrissey's friend James Hayes who had done so. He got the greatest applause when he accused the anti-Tammany conspirators of importing large numbers of men from out of town to vote against Tammany's ticket. To help Fox's chances, Kelly made numerous personal appearances within the Fourth Senatorial District, "taking the stump" for his beleaguered ally.[513]

---

[512] *New York Herald*, October 31, 1875; *New York Times*, November 1, 1875; *Fort Scott Daily Monitor*, September 24, 1875

[513] *New York Herald*, October 31 and November 2, 1875; *New York Times*, November 1, 1875

Kelly's defensive position did him little good; come the morning of Election Day, most in the press predicted that Morrissey and other anti-Tammany candidates would score resounding victories. Polls opened at six a.m. The Morrissey and Fox contest was the talk of the city, debated by voters waiting at the polls "as if the fate of the country depended upon the man who should be chosen to represent the Fourth district in the next State Senate." Morrissey remained ensconced in the meeting room at the Anson House for most of the day, an increasing number of visitors crowding into the room as day turned into night. Eventually well-wishers packed his room to the door.[514]

Likewise, John Kelly spent most of Election Day in the Tammany Hall committee room, awaiting the results with his compatriots. As the day progressed, huge numbers of excited Tammany faithful crowded into the room with him. As for John Fox, reports said that he and his assistants were "overbearing, confident, and even insolent," allegedly "dragging voters up to the ballot-box." Reports also circulated that Fox was putting large sums of cash in the streets of his district, hoping to buy the favor of the locals at the last minute. Morrissey and his friends had apparently predicted as much and made efforts to get groups of men to the polls "in squads of five and twenty" as soon as the polls opened, thereby getting in precious early votes before Fox's bribes had a chance to sway anyone's vote in the other direction. Though Fox seemed to have a lead at noon, any bribes obviously failed to do their intended work, for Morrissey's numbers rallied into a clear majority by the late afternoon.[515]

At a little before seven o'clock in the evening, Morrissey and Hayes emerged from the Anson House and made their way to the Central Police Office to hear the official results called out by Superintendent George Walling. Morrissey had emerged as the victor in the Fourth Senatorial District by a margin of 4,000 votes over incumbent John Fox. The anti-Tammany candidate for Recorder, John Hackett, won his race by an even larger majority, as did Republican Benjamin Phelps, who would become the next District Attorney. The *Herald* saw this as a sign of certain doom for Kelly. "Morrissey has been borne from the arena into the Senate on the shoulders of the people," the paper announced. They predicted that those men who had remained loyal to Kelly would see the victory of the anti-Tammany ticket as the go-ahead to demand his resignation. The writer then went on to proclaim, "*Le Roi est mort! Vive le Roi!* [The King is dead! Long live the King!] King Kelly dies, but the power lives in the people."[516]

After Morrissey and his friends returned from the police station to his room at the Anson House, his supporters celebrated joyously, trading speeches and cheers, but the man himself remained surprisingly sober and reserved. He eventually excused himself from the crowd to disappear into

[514] *New York Herald*, November 3, 1875
[515] *New York Herald*, November 3, 1875; *New York Times*, November 3, 1875
[516] *New York Herald*, November 3, 1875

another room, where he ate a quiet dinner, then returned to his elated friends only long enough to be polite and say his goodbyes. When he emerged onto the sidewalk, he found it overflowing with people eager to shake his hand. He slowly made his way through the crowd to his carriage, which took him away from the cheering mob to the restful quiet of the Hoffman House. He went to sleep that night not only satisfied that he had been validated in his fight against Kelly and was now a Senator of the State of New York, but with the added satisfaction that he had won an enormous sum (reported to be $200,000) in bets he had taken as to the outcomes of the various election races.[517]

Many in the press initially thought that Tammany's defeat portended doom for Kelly's brief term as that organization's undisputed master. The *Herald*, the most vociferously opposed to Kelly of all of the city's major papers, went so far as to hypothesize about his eventual successor, throwing out the names of Fernando and Benjamin Wood, Jimmy O'Brien, and William Wickham, among others. Meanwhile, the members of the Tammany General Committee convened for its monthly meeting on November 4, where they ratified several unimportant resolutions condemning their enemies and heartening their own resolve to carry on as "pure and undefiled democracy." The crowd then greeted Kelly with applause and cheers as he took the stage to deliver yet another speech lamenting the ignorance of New York's working men for how easily his enemies manipulated them. Naturally, he took the time to attack John Morrissey specifically, pointing to his gambling operations as evidence of his corruption and his willingness to corrupt others. He then called for the *New York Times* to investigate the anti-Tammany leaders and expose their sins to the public. As Kelly stepped off the stage, the crowd gave three cheers in his name. Despite the hopes of the *Herald*, John Kelly's days as leader at Tammany Hall were far from over. His speech had made it clear that his thoughts were now on the 1876 New York State Democratic Convention.[518]

————

While the two Johns fought their prolonged battle over the remains of William Tweed's political empire, the former Boss himself endured a series of triumphs and successes that shocked New York citizens through the year of 1875. In January, a judged reversed Tweed's conviction on corruption charges, setting the notorious pol free and outraging those in the press and politics who had fought so hard for his conviction. Years of legal battles had left him broke and his name was now an anathema to the same men who had once flocked to him in search of favor. The humiliation and trials of the past few years had aged him considerably, draining his legendary

---

[517] *New York Herald*, November 5, 1875
[518] *New York Herald*, November 5, 1875

energy, turning his hair white, arching his back, and adding even more girth to his much-lampooned waistline. With the state and national election campaigns going strong, Tweed proved an easy of a target for politicians wishing to improve their credentials as reformers. A coterie of Tweed enemies saw to it that the City of New York brought a six-million-dollar civil suit against him for the money he had swindled during the heyday of the Tweed Ring. Police again arrested Tweed on charges stemming from the new revelations this case brought, and bail was set at three million dollars, much more than the ruined man could hope to produce. While he sat in the Ludlow Street Jail, yet another civil suit, this one for one million dollars, fell into the pile of trials awaiting him. A judge subsequently raised his bail to four million dollars.

The Ludlow Street Jail was far from the desolate dungeon that was the Tombs. Its accommodations were so luxurious by comparison, that free individuals often rented out rooms in Ludlow as a place to get inexpensive but decent shelter, meals, and facilities. Tweed got chummy enough with the warden to convince him to let the beleaguered inmate outside on at least four occasions during the summer and fall of 1875. Accompanied by guards, he usually took a carriage ride through Central Park and then dined with his family at home before heading back to the jail. He enjoyed a Thanksgiving dinner at his son William's house.

On December 4, Tweed convinced the warden to allow William to pick him up for yet another afternoon outing. This time the warden himself would ride along, with a single guard in tow. After the usual trip through the park and a few other stops, the group paid a visit to the home of Tweed's other son, Richard, on Madison Avenue. Tweed's wife Jane, who had been staying with Richard, had been sick, and he wanted to visit her bedside. After dinner, he asked for privacy while he visited Jane, who was in an upstairs bedroom. After night fell, the prisoner had still not emerged from Jane's room, and the warden grew restless. He sent William Junior up to retrieve his father and prepare him for the return trip to the prison. However, when he entered his mother's room, William found no sign of his father.

Tweed had never gone upstairs to visit his ailing wife. Instead, he had stepped out of the front door and hid until a carriage arrived, according to a pre-arranged plan. He spent the next few hours traveling under cover of darkness by carriage, boat, and wagon until he made his way to a shack in the New Jersey woods, where he would spend the next several days perfecting a new identity. While carefully monitoring the news of his escape in the newspapers, he shaved his famous beard and adopted a wig and glasses, as well as a new name, John Secor.

The story of Tweed's escape became the obsession of the New York press and its readers, a thrilling distraction from the animosity engendered by the recent elections. Some papers demanded the fugitive's immediate arrest and return to justice, others celebrated his escape, if only because it meant the notorious swindler could never play a part in New York public life again. Reporters, law enforcement, and citizens alike enjoyed trading conspiracy theories as to how Tweed had pulled it off, and who had plotted the escape with him.

———

Though he and Tweed had not spoken to one another since 1868, John Morrissey was not immune to the excitement over the news. Despite their long-held animosity toward one another, he could not help feeling some admiration and sympathy for Tweed and his brazen dash for freedom.

"I'm glad that Tweed got away," he told a group of friends while visiting Governor Tilden, who had been one of his allies in the fight against the Tweed Ring.

"Why do you say that?" asked the Governor.

"Because, I think he has suffered enough for his crimes," replied Morrissey, to the utter surprise of every man in the room.

As astonished as the rest of them, Tilden cast a stern glare in Old Smoke's direction. "Morrissey, you don't dare express that opinion publicly," he ordered. Tweed's name was now synonymous with civic corruption throughout the nation. Any politician wanting to paint himself as a reformer still brought up his name as a boogeyman against which to contrast himself. Publicly saying that the country's most famous swindler had endured enough punishment for his crime was tantamount to political suicide.

"Oh, yes, I dare," Morrissey shot back with equal severity. "I cut loose from Tweed in 1868, before it was known that he did anything wrong. But you stuck to him until 1871."

Tilden made no reply, but could not remove the scowl from his face, even as the conversation continued awkwardly on to other subjects.[519]

While the defendant remained in hiding, a jury found Tweed guilty in his civil trial, prompting his final resolution to flee the country. He made a dash for Florida and from there to Cuba, where he found work as a common deckhand aboard a boat bound for Spain. He made it to Europe, but Spanish authorities immediately discovered and arrested him. An American warship returned the prisoner to New York and the Ludlow Street Jail. His defeat and humiliation now complete, the former Boss offered to tell all he knew about the Tweed Ring, its actions, and its confederates in exchange for leniency in sentencing. Transcripts of his confessions, among them his descriptions of Morrissey's work as a Tammany ballot stuffer and payoff man, made headlines across the nation. However, the Tweed Ring was old news to many as 1875 became 1876.

---

[519] *New York Times*, September 4, 1876

Tweed's testimony did little to satisfy reformers that he had served the cause of justice or changed his ways, and, anyway, 1876 was to be an election year, and a deal with the most notoriously corrupt man in America would not serve anyone's political goals. Tilden refused a pardon, and few criticized his decision. Tweed continued to waste away spiritually and physically in prison until his penniless and friendless death on April 12, 1878.

There is no record that Morrissey ever did bring his opinions about Tweed's escape to the public's attention. More than anything, his threat to do so was likely part of the widening gap between he and Tilden. They remained political allies as Democrats, and they needed one another. Morrissey, who regarded Tilden as "one of his discoveries," needed the swallowtail's image as a reformer to help clean his own. Having access to the Governor of New York was not a bad perk either. Meanwhile, Tilden required Morrissey's image as a man of the people with the working classes at the polls; and now that Morrissey was a State Senator, he could be of additional use, especially in light of the rumor that Kelly was going to withdraw Tammany's support from the Governor. Still, Tilden resented that Morrissey's reputation as the country's most notorious gambling kingpin tarnished his own respectable image, just as Morrissey had little patience for Tilden's swallowtail pretensions. Their backgrounds, constituencies, and means to getting things done were vastly different, and this put a strain on working relationship.[520]

———

Senator Morrissey was in Albany shortly after the New Year to attend his first session there on January 4, 1876. In general, he was much more active in his role as State Senator than he had been as a Congressman in the prior decade. He was the first to present a new bill to the legislature on January 5, one that demonstrated to those who had voted for him that he was true to his word. It provided "that all persons employed as laborers by the Mayor, Aldermen, and Commonality of the City of New York, or by any of the departments, shall be paid at a uniform rate for each day of service, such rate to be fixed from time to time by the Common Council; provided, however, that the rate shall not exceed $2 a day." The Senate batted the bill back and forth between its supporters and detractors for weeks, the main controversy being whether the power to set workers' rates should belong to the Common Council. On February 4, the Senate passed the bill and delivered it to the State Assembly. On March 7, Morrissey was convinced to take the floor and deliver a speech before the Assembly Committee on Cities in defense of his pet project. He accused Mayor Wickham and Tammany Hall of colluding to prevent the bill's passing, at which point the Committee Chairman produced and read aloud a letter he

———

[520] *New York Herald*, May 2, 1878

had personally received from the Mayor which proved Morrissey's allegations. Senator Morrissey thereafter had the satisfaction of seeing his law ratified, yet another victory over his enemies.[521]

In this same period, the famed German composer Jacques Offenbach was touring the United States and was impressed enough by his meeting with John Morrissey during his time in New York to include a description of him in a book later published under the title *America and Americans*. Offenbach described John as "a young man, very big and admirably proportioned." He noticed the ex-fighter's "slightly smashed" nose and explained that the Senator considered it a "glorious souvenir" of his boxing career. "In reading this story, it may perhaps be thought that the Senator has some roughness, if not absolute brutality in his manner" remarked the composer. "But this is quite an error. He is a very mild and courteous gentleman, speaking to everybody with much taste and tact." Offenbach also marveled at just how far Morrissey had raised himself in wealth and social standing during his relatively short lifetime.[522]

———

As the Democratic Party prepared for its national convention scheduled for that June in St. Louis, Missouri, the deeply divided New York Democrats converged upon Utica, New York for their state convention on April 26. Important members of the Tammany and anti-Tammany factions both attended, including both Kelly and Morrissey, which naturally kicked off a confrontation that a reporter for the *Times* would describe as "dramatic in the extreme." On April 27, while Kelly delivered a speech in praise of himself and Tammany Hall before the assembled convention, he stood just a few feet away from Morrissey, whose anger at his rival's audacity was obvious to all. As soon as Kelly finished and returned to his chair, Morrissey could not resist the opportunity to reply, and he demanded the floor "in much stronger tones." Recognized by the chair, Morrissey rose and made a point of walking to stand even closer to Kelly than the Tammany Boss had stood to him. He then "proceeded to beard Tammany in its den in a fashion never before seen." Normally noted for his reserved manner when sober and in respectable company, Morrissey suddenly seemed overcome by the quick-tempered, passionate violence of his youth. His eyes burned with an anger matched only by the sincere outrage in his croaking voice. He swung his arms about as if back in the ring with Heenan, and his words bled with pure, undisguised hatred in for John Kelly and his followers. He plainly called them frauds, insisting that they cared nothing for the average, working Democrat, only for their wealthy benefactors in the city's brownstone neighborhoods. The *Times* called it

---

[521] *New York Times*, January 6 and March 8, 1876; *Journal of the Senate of the State of New York*, 56, 160-161
[522] Offenbach, 65

"the best speech Morrissey ever made," and the *Albany Evening Journal* dubbed it the best made at the convention. Once Morrissey had finished, another inspired Anti-Tammany took the floor and concurred with Morrissey's accusations. Naturally, Kelly then jumped up to defend his organization, and a conflagration of bickering and insults spread through the hall, threatening a riot.[523]

Recognizing the necessity of restoring peace, the convention chairman called for a vote as to which faction would remain. Following the vote, the entire Tammany roster remained, while the anti-Tammany partisans were ousted. A great many cheers arose through the hall at the result while Morrissey and his followers, each one grinning mysteriously, rose from their chairs and made their way in procession toward the exit doors. Just then, Augustus Schell stood and loudly proposed above the din that all parties stay and participate in the convention to prevent a calamitous division in the party. The exiled men paused at the door, awaiting the result. The chairman called for a vote on Schell's proposition and the result effectively welcomed the Morrissey crowd back in. At this, Morrissey looked back at the members of the hall with a huge smile and led his men out of the convention anyway.

In their absence, the Convention confirmed Governor Tilden as the New York State Democratic Party's nominee for President of the United States, pending confirmation at the National Convention to come in St. Louis. Proving the rumors true, Kelly had not personally supported Tilden, labeling the swallowtail incapable of carrying the national ticket.

Tilden's victory aside, Kelly likely regarded the Utica convention's outcome as a victory. Embarrassed by the successes of his enemies in the state elections just a few months earlier, his reputation as the master of Tammany and a powerful figure in state politics had been rescued by Tammany's successful ousting of his enemies, particular Morrissey, from the convention.

In anticipation of the National Convention a month later, Morrissey made a week-long trip to Louisville, Kentucky to take to the stump in the South on Governor Tilden's behalf. The locals who came out to see him speak found him to be "One of the best talkers, though of reserved and quiet habits." He then made a brief return to New York to organize a contingency of anti-Tammany cohorts to take to St. Louis with him to back Tilden. The scene at Utica denied Morrissey official status as a delegate to the convention, but he would be there, if only to get revenge on Kelly. John left New York City aboard the New York Central and Hudson River Railroad in the evening hours of June 14. His assembled team of anti-Tammany men left together the next day.[524]

---

[523] *New York Times*, April 28, 1876
[524] *Ogdensburg Journal*, May 25, 1876, quoting *Courier-Journal*; *New York Times*, June 23, 1876

They arrived in St. Louis on June 24 to find the city a crowded nightmare of confused humanity seething with political animosity. Despite plenty of notice that their city was to be the site of that year's Democratic National Convention, the city and its businesses looked as though the event had somehow caught them off guard. The place was sorely lacking in accommodations for the 30,000 or more men who now milled aimlessly about in massive crowds through their streets, meeting halls, and drinking establishments, debating the merits of Samuel Tilden with varying degrees of civility. Trains continued to pull in all day, each unloading still more out-of-towners into the unprepared city. When it came time for the invaders to finally sleep off the strains of the day's travels, drinking, and arguments, they found themselves contesting each other for the limited number of cots stuffed into the hotel rooms, halls, lobbies, and bathrooms; those unable to claim such luxuries as their own had to content themselves with the floors of these areas.[465]

The *New York Times* writer present captured the tumult in St. Louis on the night before the convention:

> To-night St. Louis is in such a blaze of excitement as has seldom been witnessed in this continent. All the dwellings, saloons, and beer gardens are filled with delegates and their friends. The streets are crowded with people from all parts of the country, the hotels are illuminated, and the Tammany men and others, with bands of music at their head, are continually marching from one place to another. In all the places of resort the scenes which characterized the early evening were enacted over again. There were three or four more knock-down fights, and the war of the Tilden and anti-Tilden factions went on with quite as much bitterness as during the heat of the day.[525]

The National Convention quickly succumbed to the same divisive hatred that had threatened the caucus in Utica. *The Times* man felt that the two factions were at each other's throats with "a vehemence, heat, and bitterness which has already produced much bad blood," and that there was a real possibility that this convention would shatter the Democratic Party as a whole. Likewise, the man for the *New York Tribune* found the anger between the various factions of Democrats to be "deep and powerful." From the start, Governor Tilden was regarded as the party's presumptive nominee for President, as those against him, plentiful enough to be dangerous if united, were dividing their support between the five other candidates, the most prominent of which were Governor Thomas Hendricks of Indiana and Major General Winfield Scott. The divided loyalties of the anti-Tilden men did nothing to abate their unity in their

[525] *New York Times*, June 27, 1876

hatred for the Northern swallowtail, which was matched only by the passion for which pro-Tilden men supported their candidate.[526]

Kelly, despite leading many at Utica to believe that he would not be attending the National Convention, arrived in town with several other high-ranking Tammany figures about a week before the Convention. He took up residence at the Lindell House, where they began strategizing Tilden's defeat. As soon as the Convention began, he dispersed a team of underlings throughout the city to visit the various state delegations and chip away at the Governor's support. They focused on the Southern states, where enthusiasm for a politician from the North would be the easiest to discourage. Kelly himself was on the convention floor, insisting to all that would listen that the Democrats would regret nominating Tilden, whom he apparently felt did not have a chance of winning the general election. Swallowtail power players August Belmont and Augustus Schell were also in evidence. These men had once been Morrissey's friends. However, they sided with Kelly in the fight against Tilden, as had Cornelius Vanderbilt, to Morrissey's disgust. Though these men all socialized in the same societal circle as Tilden, they viewed him as too ambitious, too divisive, and traitorous against his own class in pandering to the immigrant rabble Morrissey represented. They also agreed with Kelly that, if nominated, Tilden could not win the national election. Undeterred, Morrissey strode about the convention floor, "working desperately" on Tilden's behalf, despite his own personal differences with the Governor.[527]

Kelly and Morrissey were now the two most conspicuous figures at work in the Convention, their personal rivalry having opened a rift in the Democratic Party on a national level. They fought their way back and forth across the convention floor as though it were a gladiatorial arena and delegates were their weapons and armor, each man with followers cheering him fanatically. One writer described Kelly's followers as "yelping bands of scalp-taking Tammany Indians," while Morrissey was capable of organizing a "circus" at the slightest gesture. At some point, John wound up in an argument with a Democrat from the West, who asserted that Morrissey did not truly believe that Tilden had any chance of winning the general election. If Morrissey honestly believed so, asserted the other gentleman, he would put his money where his mouth was. When Morrissey asked the westerner what he proposed, the man put down fifty dollars, betting that Morrissey was not willing to put up a $10,000 bet on Tilden becoming U.S. President. As always, Morrissey could not resist the challenge. He immediately went through the halls offering a $10,000 bet that Tilden would win the Democratic nomination, and another $10,000 that Tilden would win the national election. He eventually found a taker, albeit for a smaller sum, and

[526] *New York Tribune*, June 27, 1876; *New York Times*, June 27, 1876
[527] *New York Times*, June 27, 1876; *New York Tribune*, June 27, 1876; *New York Herald*, July 2, 1876; Mendelbaum, 137

each party placed $5,000 down with a trusted stakeholder, pending the results of the convention and the national election.[528]

Kelly was incensed when, once they got to the convention, otherwise loyal Tammany men openly defied him in supporting Tilden for the nomination. Even Wickham was vocally joining John Morrissey's cries of support for the Governor. The press thought it nothing less than an "open revolt" against Kelly's leadership, and predicted dire consequences for his future within the party, particularly should he fail in preventing Tilden's nomination. Should Tilden enter the White House, they surmised, Kelly's refusal to back him meant that the new President's ears would be closed to Kelly's influence.[529]

Ultimately, Samuel Tilden did indeed win the Democratic Party's nomination for President, in no small part thanks to John Morrissey's support. "[Tilden's mouthpiece] The *New York Sun* thanks God for the nomination," commented the *New Orleans Republican*, "Tilden thanks John Morrissey." The *Chicago Daily Tribune* mused, "When Tilden becomes President, Morrissey will be our Secretary of Stakes, - he has held a good many in his times." As a cacophonous fireworks display appropriately brought a close to the Democratic National Convention that year, New York newspapers predicted that the animosity between Morrissey and Kelly would only be exacerbated by their battle in St. Louis, and that the pair of political bosses could be expected to continue their rivalry with more vicious gusto upon their inevitable return to Gotham.[530]

———

Rather than head straight home to Saratoga and Susie, John decided to bask in his victory by stopping in New York City before proceeding upstate. Many of the working men and anti-Tammany leaders greeted him with enthusiastic congratulations upon his return to the Hoffman House. The next day, the *Herald* urged him to press his advantage and completely take over Tammany from its current boss. When Tilden procrastinated for more than a month in producing an acceptance letter, the *Times* sarcastically proposed that, if Tilden made it to the White House, he should take Morrissey with him "to spur him up or write his Messages for him."[531]

John stayed on long enough in New York City to witness the grand Fourth of July festivities celebrating the nation's centennial before he returned to Saratoga to organize an anniversary celebration that had more personal relevance. On August 6, John Junior would turn twenty-one years of age. The birthday was especially important because there had been some

[528] *New York Tribune*, June 27, 1876

[529] *New York Times*, June 25, 1876; *New York Tribune*, June 27, 1876

[530] *New York Herald*, June 28, 1876; *New Orleans Republican*, July 4, 1876; *Chicago Daily Tribune*, July 2, 1876

[531] *New York Herald*, June 29, 1876; *New York Times*, August 4, 1876

doubt as to whether the young man would see it. There had been the nearly lethal fireworks accident of three years prior. However, as recently as the prior winter, the young man had contracted tuberculosis and pneumonia simultaneously, requiring that he travel south to the warmer climes of Florida to recover. He had returned in improved health and fifteen pounds heavier, but as symptoms of serious illness were returning. The Morrisseys' physician, Doctor E. Bradley recommended that he again travel south for his health, but this time Susan refused. If the first trip had not cured him, she saw no reason why he should not stay in Saratoga; after all, who could give a boy better care than his mother? Once he recovered, John Senior intended to send his son back to school to complete the education his illness had interrupted.

On the evening of the sixth, the proud mother and father played host to more than a hundred guests in their home on Matilda Street. The celebration lasted for an hour and a half and featured two tables worth of food. Several people toasted the birthday boy, his mother's loving words bringing tears to the eyes of some present. John Junior opened many fine gifts that evening, some of them made of silver which one observer estimated to be worth a total of about $1,000. Susan gave him a gold locket encrusted with diamonds in the shape of an 'M.' The most astonishing gift was revealed when the birthday boy came to a simple envelope with his father's handwriting on it. Curious, the young man opened the envelope and pulled out a deed to land valued at $10,000. John Senior was finally able to give his son the start in life that he had always intended.[532]

Having spent months away in political fights in New York City, Utica, and St. Louis, John was thankful for the opportunity to enjoy the company of his family in Saratoga for a few weeks, as that year's second State Convention of the Democratic Party was to be held in Saratoga. With the national election coming up, it was important that Democrats unite behind their presidential candidate, and the bitter, longstanding feud he had with Kelly now required an attempt at a truce, or at the very least that Morrissey appear to be the one promoting party unity. However, John could not help but worry if the hardcore anti-Tammany men would understand the need for reconciliation.[533]

By August 27, most of the prominent Democratic politicians in the state were joining Morrissey at the Town Hall in Saratoga. John Kelly, John Hoffman, Augustus Schell, Jimmy O'Brien, Benjamin Wood, Andrew Green, Senator Francis Bixby, and Mayor Wickham were just a few of the well-known names finding accommodations in the resort's many hotels. Though this convention was meant to choose candidates for the state-level offices, its true test was whether the state Democrats could find any kind of unity behind their Presidential candidate. The opening session took place

---

[532] *New York Times*, August 11, 1876
[533] *Ogdensburg Journal*, August 23, 1876

on August 31, called to order at 10:40 a.m. and almost immediately generated into a scene that was disgraceful beyond words, at least in the estimation of the *New York Times*. The large crowd of delegates had been waiting for entry for more than half an hour outside of the main room while the State Committee deliberated. Jam-packed in cramped stairways and hallways, the delegates of various factions argued with one another, the close quarters and delay only exacerbating their irritation with one another. Despite his governorship of the state and his selection at the National Convention in St. Louis, most of those attending vehemently objected to Tilden. Almost as soon as the doors finally opened, it became clear to John that he would not change their mind. Tilden's detractors were openly spitting in the faces of his supporters, resulting in brawls on the convention floor. In the interest of not splitting the party ticket, Kelly had by now agreed to support Tilden in the national election. However, the crowd shouted Kelly down when he was but a few sentences into a speech to that effect on August 30. Few who attended left confident of either party unity or the Governor's chances of winning even his own state.[534]

"The Democratic 'happy family' of this City have never been more divided than they are at present," the Republican-leaning *Times* reported with just a hint of satisfaction. For John Morrissey, who, as the most prominent Democrat residing in Saratoga, had been the unofficial host of the convention, the event had been an embarrassment. Though Morrissey's followers had cheered their man's name, it was Kelly, previously thought to be about to fall, who emerged looking the stronger man politically, the "head and front of the Democratic Party, its dictator and guide." Members of the crowd may have booed Honest John's words in support of Tilden, but the chaos in Saratoga had been bad for John Morrissey, and that what was bad for Morrissey was good for Kelly. The Convention reconvened in Saratoga on September 12, but both attendance and enthusiasm had noticeably dwindled, and little happened to repair the divisions within the party.[535]

Attempting to put on a united front for the sake of the national campaign, Morrissey and Kelly attended a conference held at the Young Men's Democratic Club in New York's Union Square on October 2. Before their respective followers, Morrissey and Kelly surprised many by delivering speeches in favor of amity. However, when it came down to the nitty gritty of how the two groups would split their representatives to future meetings and share the political appointments of the city, they made little progress. A follow-up conference later in the afternoon provided little resolution, with Morrissey agreeing to Tammany's offer of allowing the anti-Tammany Democrats to select roughly one third of the city appointments, the rest going to Kelly and Tammany. However, few among

---

[534] *New York Times*, August 27 and September 1, 1876
[535] *New York Times*, August 27, 1876, September 1, 12 and 13, 1876

the rank and file anti-Tammany men supported this concession, which they saw a submission to the rule of John Kelly.[536]

Morrissey made yet another plea for unity when the anti-Tammany leadership convened at Irving Hall, the old Young Democracy headquarters and current base of operations for Jimmy O'Brien, twelve days later. Tensions were high enough that a contingent of police was on hand to quell any violence that might arise. Men packed the Hall to capacity, and every major anti-Tammany Democrat was on hand, from O'Brien to James Hayes. Morrissey was the leader of the minority's calls to stand by the peace agreement made with Tammany, but O'Brien and others vociferously objected, rousing the crowd into a frenzy. Amid the chaos, Morrissey once again took the floor. He insisted that he continued to stand against Tammany for the long term, then said directly to his opponents, "You don't look like a convention. You look like a mob. Let those who choose to, hoot and yell." At this, O'Brien and his cohorts rose as one, and it seemed violence was imminent. The chairman called for the police on hand, who stepped in to restore order.[537]

Once his opponents had returned to their seats, Morrissey continued with a final plea. "While you differ from me that is your right, and I claim the same right," he said. "In the manner in which Tammany is now organized, under no inducement would I go into it. Time will tell whether I speak the truth. I have no right to bring my personal feelings into a campaign so important as the present one. I ask you, as sensible men, to act without passion and reflect. There need be no disbandment of this organization in making a combination with Tammany Hall. You will get more by such a coalition than in any other way. Don't let it go abroad that the Democracy of this City is divided in so important an election as the coming one. Don't be hasty. Don't be passionate about it. Think, if you reject Tammany's offer, what will you get?"[538]

An intense argument then broke out directly between Morrissey and O'Brien which was so passionate and hateful that it left the rest of the crowd in a shocked silence. An official vote followed and confirmed the resolution to reject Tammany's offer. The meeting adjourned, John was among the first to exit the building, clearly dejected by his inability to persuade the crowd to see his way. He told reporters that he still maintained hope of a unified Democratic Party in New York City, at least for the purpose of the election.[539]

Two more meetings occurred over the next week, and many of those present complained that Morrissey was attempting to "sell out the party to

---

[536] *New York Times*, October 3, 1876
[537] *New York Times*, October 15, 1876
[538] *New York Times*, October 15, 1876
[539] *New York Times*, October 15, 1876

John Kelly." Morrissey was not present, but he sent a letter to the meeting, which someone read aloud before all:

HOFFMAN HOUSE, NEW YORK. OCT. 18, 1876.

Hon. Emanuel B. Hart, Chairman of the Executive Committee New-York County Democracy:

DEAR SIR: In consideration of the action of the County Convention of your body in rejecting the proposition for a union of the Democratic Party, as proffered by the organization known as Tammany Hall, I hereby tender my resignation as a member of your Executive and Conference Committees, and notify you of my withdrawal from every connection with your political body. I esteem the success of the Democratic ticket at the coming election as of infinitely greater importance than the success of any mere office-seekers, and cannot but regard the action of your convention upon Saturday last as [contrary] to the interests and principles of the Democratic Party. Respectfully,

JOHN MORRISSEY[540]

Those present responded to the letter with applause, some even calling out that resignation was too good for Morrissey, that they should bar him as a traitor. Members composed a response letter later approved by the meeting as a whole. The committee accepted the resignation "with great pleasure," it said, for they were "happy to be rid of one who… has been mainly engaged in conspiring against our interests…. Your profession of interest in the Democratic ticket is appreciated by those of our organization who understand the treacherous course you have been pursuing," closed the letter, "solely for the purposes of promoting your personal ends."[541]

In an interview with the *Times* the same day, Morrissey expressed his disappointment that, despite his best efforts, the Democratic Party of New York could not be unified. He again defended his choice to accept Tammany's offers of a deal, because "it was better to accept it than to have any division in the party." He accused Jimmy O'Brien and his "band of assassins" of manipulating the anti-Tammany men against unity for selfish purposes.[542]

Come the November election, Tilden did in fact take New York State, but, after great controversy, Republican candidate Rutherford B. Hayes, Governor of Ohio, ultimately won the national election by a margin of a single electoral vote. There were accusations on both sides of election fraud, some Republicans implicating Morrissey in buying votes for Tilden. Morrissey denied these claims of course, though he did admit to fellow Democrat Jeremiah Maguire that two Southern members of the Electoral

[540] *New York Times*, October 19, 1876
[541] *New York Times*, October 19, 1876
[542] *New York Times*, October 19, 1876

College had visited him offering to sell him their votes for a tidy sum. He told Maguire that he sent the men away unsatisfied because "I wouldn't cross the street to make Tilden president that way. He's ungrateful and deceiving, and if it had come out he would have denied all knowledge of it, and thrown all the odium on me." Maguire admitted that he was surprised to hear Morrissey say such a thing, because he had always seen John as an especial champion of the Governor, an impression Morrissey was quick to deny, saying he had only joined forces with Tilden as a means of defeating John Kelly. Clearly, with the election now over and Tilden not headed for the White House, Morrissey was free to speak his mind on the Governor once more.[543]

Two years later, a John Ray, who had been the attorney for the Louisiana Returning Board for the 1876 Presidential election, confirmed to a *New York Times* reporter that he had indeed been approached by a New Orleans gambler who identified himself as being partnered with John Morrissey in some New York gambling ventures. Following the general election, there was considerable controversy as to whether Democrats had suppressed Republican votes in several Southern states, Louisiana one of them. The Returning Board's job was to determine which candidate would receive Louisiana's electoral votes considering the various Democratic frauds proven and alleged. The gambler, according to Ray, bluntly offered $250,000 to the lawyer if the Returning Board would find for Tilden. When Ray replied that not even a million dollars would suffice, the gambler returned a short while later and asked Ray to approach the members of the board as to what sum would truly be acceptable to announce Tilden the victor. Ray again refused and the gambler disappeared, never to approach him again.[544]

Regardless of what methods he may or may not have used, John's gamble on backing Tilden against Kelly had clearly backfired, and he was now on the proverbial outs with both men as well as both Tammany and the anti-Tammany Democrats.

The political and business trials of 1876 did nothing to prepare John Morrissey for the greatest tragedy of his lifetime, which came just two days before the end of the year. The Morrissey family celebrated Christmas together at home in Saratoga, but they feared it might be their last as a family. Susan had been helpless to stop the decline of her son's health, but he was young and both parents still held hope for a full recovery right up until his passing on the evening of December 30. He had been just twenty-one years old. Both parents were at his bedside when he died. Still, his death of their idolized son traumatized them both. John, Jr. had been the

[543] *New York Times*, December 7, 1878, quoting Jeremiah Maguire
[544] *New York Times*, October 18, 1878

stated motivation for his father's transformation from violent thug into a millionaire businessman and State Senator. Later that night, a crowd of young people "who loved young Morrissey" arrived at the Morrissey home in disbelief. Seeing the rumors confirmed, some among them began weeping. John and Susan did not even seem to notice the visitors, distracted as they were with their own grief.[545]

The various newspapers of the day listed the cause of John Junior's early death as anything from consumption to Bright's Disease. The bereaved parents spent New Year's Eve and New Year's Day preparing their only son's funeral. His remains were transported the roughly thirty miles from Saratoga to Troy, where his funeral took place on the morning of Saturday, January 2, 1877 at St. Peter's Church. Members of Saratoga's Morrissey Hose Company carried the remains in a casket to their final resting place, over which loomed a towering headstone intended for the entire family. The casket was resplendent with a solid silver frame and the deceased's name in gold plate along the exterior. Priests from both Saratoga and Troy were present, as well as members of the Solitaire Social Club, which the deceased had founded. A vast and varied collection of floral arrangements were laid about the grave site. On the tombstone, under large letters declaring the family name, was the following inscription:

> Weep not dear parents but be content
>
> For unto you I was but lent;
>
> In love we lived, in peace I died,
>
> You asked my life, but twas denied[546]

John Morrissey Senior would never make any public statement about the death of his beloved son, but Susan would later confide to a reporter that John found it too painful to ever visit his dead son's grave.[547]

---

[545] *Brewster Standard*, January 5, 1877; findagrave.com, accessed February 3, 2017; Nicholson, 103

[546] *Brooklyn Daily Eagle*, January 6, 1877; Findagrave.com, accessed 2/3/2017

[547] *Russellville Democrat*, November 27, 1879, quoting *Philadelphia Record*

20.

The Sweet Bye and Bye

Just two days after John Junior's death, New York City newspaper headlines announced the death of Cornelius Vanderbilt. Morrissey and Vanderbilt had been on the outs at least since the St. Louis Convention, possibly before. There is little record of their spending much time with each other or investing in any shared business ventures together since Black Friday of 1869. Thus, it should have come as no surprise to those who knew them that Morrissey, still mourning his son, considered the passing of his former friend of little consequence. "Well, he died without making a bad debt or leaving a friend," was John's only public comment on the matter at the time. Later in the day, while John was visiting some friends at the Fifth Avenue Hotel, the Commodore's demise came up. Again, John's bitterness was clear to all. "Vanderbilt destroyed everything that came near him except a bug," he grumbled; "nothing could live near or with him, except only one man." Sometime later, when Vanderbilt's name came up, Morrissey was even less complimentary. "I have known in the course of my life burglars, fighting men, and loafers, but never have I known such a bad fellow as Commodore Vanderbilt." It should be noted that John was far from alone in his detest for the late railroad tycoon; many people who knew the deceased expressed similar sentiments about the cold, calculating, and unscrupulous Commodore before and after his death. John did not attend the millionaire's funeral.[548]

In the months immediately following the loss of his son, Morrissey was relatively quiet as a public figure. He occasionally returned to both Albany and New York City for various political and business engagements, but he remained a noticeably sullen bystander at them. At a meeting to discuss the municipal budget of New York City he was temperamental and impatient, speaking bluntly in proposing that half of the men at the table with him be struck from the city payroll and their departments eliminated. His forty-sixth birthday on February 12 found him with little to celebrate. He had lost his precious only child a little more than a month earlier. Politically, he had been ostracized by the two main Democratic organizations in the state, and his senate term would be over at the end of the year. Compounding these concerns, the chronic respiratory problems which had plagued him for more than a decade were once again resurfacing, leaving him weak and at times unable to speak.[549]

---

[548] Stiles, 566; *New York Herald*, May 2, 1878
[549] *Irish World*, February 24, 1877

The summer racing season provided welcome distractions. Horse racing continued to increase in popularity with all levels of society in the United States, and he was profiting handsomely. Still, even in this pursuit he seemed to be getting irritable and strict. He instituted high penalties for horse teams whose animal did not perform acceptably in his races. When owners and riders complained, Morrissey dismissed their concerns by insisting that owners were entering their famous horses in the Saratoga races too soon after running them in a previous event, which resulted in disappointing showings for his paying customers.

A Catholic Mass occurred at St. Peter's Church in Saratoga on August 6, 1877 celebrating the occasion of what would have been John Junior's twenty-second birthday. Father McMenomy, the longtime family friend who had watch the deceased grow up, attempted to soothe the pains of his parents by speaking of the happiness of the Christian afterlife. "During the delivery of the address it was heart rending to witness the great grief that was oisible [sic] in the appearance of the parents of the deceased," noted a writer for New York City's *Irish American*, "especially that of the mother, whose anguish at her loss seemed as keen and fresh as when death deprived her of her only child."[550]

As the year progressed, Morrissey's passion for political fights seemed to slowly resurface and he began to publicly and privately voice his displeasure for Tammany Hall once more. Anti-Tammany crusaders who had criticized him only months earlier began to see in him a potential ally again. As a Senator, he was the most prominent opponent to a bill put forth that Spring by Kelly and his cohorts concerning the charter by the city's latest mayor, Smith Ely. In the Autumn, he took the time to defend himself against Tweed's confessions, which implicated him in election rigging and bribery. Kelly was using these as political weapons against Morrissey, and Morrissey eagerly fired back in the press. He accused Tweed of wanting to get back in Tammany's good graces, pointed out that Tweed's confessions had thus far only implicated men who were either enemies of Tammany or dead, and estimated that fifty of Tweed's underlings remained on the Tammany General Committee. Before long, the Irving Hall rebels welcomed Morrissey back into the fold.

"I have nothing to live for," John told an interviewer around this period, "except my wife. We have no living children. My son is gone. I would like to be respected – to be considered honorable – for my poor, meagre opportunities. I like the respect of Americans. Every word I hear kind to me from these great republican people goes to my heart."[551]

A short time later, Morrissey would hear plenty of kind words at an anti-Tammany assembly at Brookes' Academy on Broome Street in the city's Third District. Initially, the meeting began as a heated remonstration of

---

[550] *Irish American*, August 18, 1877
[551] *New York Herald*, May 2, 1878

John Kelly's control over Tammany. Not long into the discussion, a cry went up for John to appear, and he went to the stage and took a seat, not speaking. The committee resolved to thank him for his efforts in the state legislature to securing funds for the district's streets, parks, and waterworks, and he was named their delegate to that year's State Democratic Convention to be held in Albany. As the crowd cheered and shouted his name, Morrissey rose to speak. In his first important public address since the death of his son, John said that he had not come intending to speak, explaining that his health was not good, but that he would be happy to answer any questions his audience might have. He reviewed his record in the State Senate, which was set to end at the close of the year. He insisted that he remained against Tammany Hall, especially John Kelly's dominance of the organization, for, he said, "there is nothing in it but him. If there is, no one dares say so." As to his critics, including Kelly and Tweed, he said, "They tell you stories about who and what I am – John Morrissey. There is not one act in my whole life that I am not willing to tell you of here to-night. There are many things in it I might regret. But they never could tell you that I stole the public funds or betrayed a public trust." After expressing thanks for his nomination as delegate, the meeting adjourned with three cheers for Morrissey.[552]

On Monday, October 8, John's breathing problems made it difficult for him to get out of bed. He managed to do so and dress and made his way downtown to attend to his political and business interests. By the time he returned home at six o'clock that evening, he went straight to bed, telling Susan he had a bad cold. As the evening progressed, his breathing became even more labored, a loud wheezing sound emanating from each breath. He could barely speak now. Susan called for the doctor and notified friends, all of whom arrived in short order. Diagnosing the patient with severe pneumonia, the doctor managed to alleviate some of John's suffering, while his friends agreed to visit in shifts and help Susan care for her husband. On Tuesday, the symptoms worsened again, and he was obviously in great pain, but unable to speak. That evening, news spread around New York City that John Morrissey had died of pneumonia. However, by the time the news of his death had circulated, the supposed corpse was miraculously on the mend. His doctor predicted a return to full health in a matter of days.

The illness created some concern for John's chances for a second term in the State Senate. He decided not to run for re-nomination in the Fourth District, where he was the incumbent, feeling that the work of canvasing the district, shaking hands and talking to the residents, would not bode well for his health. However, he ultimately consented to pursue the Seventh District's nomination, as he felt he stood a better chance of winning in this district with less physical effort, due to the anti-Tammany leanings of its residents. The Seventh District had historically voted against Tammany

---

[552] *New York Times*, September 27, 1877

(Jimmy O'Brien had formerly been the Senator here). However, there was an added personal incentive to win here; the Seventh District was home to posh, aristocratic Murray Hill, home of John Kelly and many of his swallowtail friends. To beat John Kelly's forces in Kelly's district would be a sweet victory, indeed.

Overall, the strength of the various anti-Tammany factions within the city was reaching a peak as Election Day 1877 approached. As late as October 26, Tammany Hall had yet to settle upon a candidate to oppose Morrissey for the Seventh District seat. Reporters noticed that Morrissey was in excellent spirits when meeting with both Democratic and Republican allies at his headquarters in the Ashland House on the corner of Twenty-Fourth Street and Fourth Avenue. He was not only a candidate, but the central strategist of the anti-Tammany campaign. Reporters noticed him giving orders to friends and subordinates with the zeal of old and making sure that word got out to the public as to which candidates he approved. The fact that he remained mostly indoors, still taking care to prevent a relapse of his illness proved to be of little consequence to his chances for election. Important members of both parties were perfectly willing to pack shoulder to shoulder into his room almost every day. When he was not meeting with allies in person, he sat at his desk producing letter after letter of instructions, promises, and requests.

Finally, on the afternoon of October 26, the Tammany leaders "grasped at a straw" and chose Morrissey's former friend Augustus Schell, their own Grand Sachem, as Morrissey's opponent in the Seventh District. On a state and national level, Schell was a formidable politician. He was, as one paper put it, "one of the bluest bloods, coming from an old Knickerbocker family, and as rich as Croesus." In addition to enjoying a second term as Tammany's Grand Sachem, he had only recently ended a long tenure as Chairman of the Democratic National Committee. He was a wealthy and well-respected reformer, had been Commodore Vanderbilt's most trusted attorney, was on the board of directors for several railroads, and included nearly all the prominent swallowtail Democrats among his allies. However, Schell's associating with historically corrupt Tammany Hall did not sit well with his fellow aristocrats of the Seventh District. By contrast, Morrissey, despite being an immigrant from humble beginnings, had opposed Tammany in the past and was now doing it again, a fact which just might endear him to the upper-class voters in places like Murray Hill. This, combined with the fact that Schell had entered the race so late, had many predicting an easy win for Morrissey, who was now referring to Schell as "a white headed old fool." Seeing a poster for Schell up, an Anti-Tammany Democrat tore the poster down and brought it to Morrissey at the Ashland House. It was the first confirmation John had received as to whom the Tammany leaders had settled upon to face him. Grinning, he personally secured the poster to the wall of his own office and told his men to make sure that as many people as possible knew that Tammany's candidate was

Augustus Schell. "The best fighters in the world couldn't beat me," Morrissey bragged to a reporter, "and Augustus Schell, who couldn't lick his weight in Tabby cats, ain't going to start now!"[553]

The best offense Schell and Tammany could mount was to once again bring up Morrissey's disreputable past, focusing mostly on his time aiding the corruption of the Tweed Ring. John was more than used to such criticism from political opponents by now and knew they posed little threat to his success. "Of course, I did," he confidently responded. "Every man wants to feather his nest. There ain't a person within the sound of my voice that wouldn't have done the same. I'm no angel, but the things that gang did turned my stomach. I'm fighting them now as hard as I fought for them. That's to your advantage. They haven't changed any. You all know that I never struck a foul blow or turned a card. My word is as good as my bond... I'm not afraid of any man or every man in Tammany Hall."[554]

As October became November, John experienced a relapse of his illness that once again left him bedridden. His physician, Dr. Bradley, made the trip down from Saratoga to attend to him. Nevertheless, on the evening of November 1, he rose and dressed to keep a promise to make a public address at the Germania Assembly Hall on the corner of Twenty-Sixth Street and Seventh Avenue. In anticipation of his now rare public appearance, people mobbed the streets surrounding the hall. By the time the meeting came to order at eight o'clock, there was standing room only inside, while those disappointed to not gain admission encircled the building, their numbers even greater than the large crowd inside. By the time the guest of honor's carriage arrived, he had difficulty getting out of his car for the mass of people that crowded around the door. One man described the cheers that greeted Morrissey as he plodded through the mass of bodies as "deafening." They chanted John's name throughout his slow progress through the mob outside and into the hall, where the audience inside took it up until he reached the stage. They quieted to hear his weakened voice croak out surprisingly respectful words for his opponent, Augustus Schell, though he made a point of recognizing him as a puppet of Kelly. After once more going over the history of his feud with Kelly and break with Tammany, and reiterating his support for the working man, John made a reference to the fighting career that had brought him fame. He had won many fights for himself, he told the crowd, but now he was relying upon them to win this fight. With that, John took his seat to a chorus of applause. After listening to a few other men speak, he departed.[555]

Though he still felt sick and weak, John neglected to return home and instead accepted an invitation to speak to another gathering on Third

[553] *Winnsboro News and Herald*, May 4, 1878; *New York Times*, October 27, 1877; Bouyea, 175 (e-book)
[554] Bouyea, 176 (e-book)
[555] *New York Times*, November 2, 1877

Avenue. He was brief, emphasizing that Kelly and Tammany were enemies of the poor. Once finished, he ordered his driver to head back to the Ashland House. John's worn and sickly appearance upon entering his suite alarmed Bradley, who ordered his patient to bed immediately.

There were more meetings scheduled for the next day, and John insisted that he felt well enough to attend them. Ignoring his doctor's orders, left the Ashland House for Jefferson Hall at eight o'clock in the evening. The place was "crammed almost to suffocation" with people. Once again, he had to press his way slowly through the mass of people in the street to make his way to the door. He kept his speech to just fifteen minutes before making his departure back through the cheering crowd and heading for an unscheduled appearance at Welsh's Hall. Here, his surprise appearance and brief words received boisterous approval from the crowd. Then it was on to a third large gathering of supporters at the corner of Twenty-Second Street and Second Avenue. The biggest crowd was at his fourth meeting for the night, where as many as 3,000 people lined the sidewalks when his carriage pulled up at the corner of Eighth Avenue and Thirty-Fourth Street. The chants from the crowd matched those of the people shouting from the windows of the hall above, and again they cheered him until he reached the stage. After some opening speeches from others, John rose at ten o'clock to talk briefly to the audience, opening with an apology for the weakened state of his voice. He then proceeded on a speech not dissimilar to the one made at Jefferson Hall the prior evening. Once finished, he and his friends found the door blocked by such a mass of people that they could not escape and had to sneak off to a back exit. He was able to get out of the building, where the crowd there recognized his weakened state and allowed him to pass and get into his carriage for his return to his room. There, he told his friends, "Kelly must beat me or I will beat him," he promised them. "If he lets me get back to the Legislature for two years, I will have him out of the Controller's office before the last of May. Don't you make any mistake about it." He then followed his doctor's orders to get back into bed.[556]

The campaign continued through the next few days in predictable fashion. Morrissey remained popular among the working classes, prompting Schell and other Tammany loyalists to dredge up the age-old accusations regarding his criminal record, his reputation as a brawler and a drunk, his gambling interests, and his conspiring with Republicans. These tired attacks were no more effective at counteracting Morrissey's popularity than they had been in the past. On November 5, the day before Election Day, the attacks on his reputation compelled him to publish an address to the people of New York that accused Kelly of conspiring against him for Tweed while Morrissey lay in bed sick. He pointed out that the insults and accusations Tammany had made against him were all events in the distant past and had not prevented the public's trusting him as their representative

[556] *New York Times*, November 3, 1877

both in Congress and the New York Senate, and he did not expect these same criticisms to prevent a second term as Senator.

———

The next morning, the sun rose in a clear sky to light a surprisingly quiet city on Election Day. The chilly November air ensured that early voters made their trips to and from the polls quickly and generally without incident. There were a few minor squabbles along Second and First Avenues, but even these failed to warrant police response. Most voters had done their duty and made it home or to work peacefully by noon.

Beginning as early as 6:30 that morning and continuing until well after sundown, John Morrissey's rooms at the Ashland House were the scene of a constant flow of anti-Tammany partisans. The man himself never left his bed and his physician remained vigilant at his side, pleading with him not to talk too much. His doctor permitted only his closest friends at his bedside. Despite the nervousness of his friends over the pending results, and despite his infirmity, John maintained a calm, confident demeanor. News of the poll results began coming in around 5:30. The results of the Seventh District senate race were among the first to come in. By seven o'clock, the Ashland House was echoing with a steady flow of cheers as the district results began pouring in more frequently, showing a certain victory for Morrissey. "The sun goes down," reported the *Irish World*. "Down, too, go Schell and Kelly." He defeated Schell by between 2,000 and 4,000 votes.[557]

After the results came out, Dr. Bradley permitted a reporter from the *Times* to enter the victor's room for an interview. The writer found his subject still in bed but sitting up. He was sweating profusely and had a checkered shawl wrapped around his shoulders. With great effort, John greeted the reporter with a smile and the words, "Didn't I tell you I'd carry Kelly's own district? I have, and by more than a hundred majority. If I had another week I would have carried it by a 1,200 majority." After these triumphant words passed his lips, the energy seemed to go immediately out of the Senator's body, but he continued on laboriously, his gravelly voice quaking. "I have been sick for 23 days in the campaign, and was about at work when I ought not to have been. I laid the work out all myself, and ran the district from my tent." He went on to accuse Kelly of being "unmanly" in his campaign tactics and promised to expose the true Honest John and his cronies to the public. "I wouldn't take a certificate of election as President for this victory to-night in Kelly's own district," he said proudly.[558]

[557] *New York Times*, November 7, 1877; *Irish World*, November 17, 1877
[558] *New York Times*, November 7, 1877

John awoke the next morning feeling so invigorated by the previous evening's success that he got himself out of bed at nine o'clock and, avoiding Dr. Bradley, made his way out of the Ashland House and over to the Hoffman House (also on Twenty-forth Street) for breakfast. By the time he arrived at his table, he was on the verge of collapse and regretting his decision. He ate only a small amount before Bradley entered, chastising his patient for risking his health in such a way. The doctor called for a carriage. Leaning on Bradley for support, Morrissey made his way with difficulty into the car, where the doctor wrapped him in blankets. He refused the doctor's advice to return home and instead insisted on making a trip to Central Park. However, by the time the carriage arrived at the entrance, he had changed his mind and they returned to home and bed.

After several hours of sleep, he awoke at nine o'clock in the evening to the sound of a brass band outside of his window. A local alderman was on the street outside with the band and a crowd of admirers, who embarked upon a congratulatory serenade. In short order, as many as 5,000 people gathered around the band on the street. Above, Susan and several female friends enjoyed the music from a balcony, and someone opened the windows of the Ashland House so that John and other guests could enjoy the music. When the band finished, a call went out for the Senator to appear. Instead, one of the many friends who were constantly stopping by to check on John, an Ira Shafer, appeared on his balcony to apologize on John's behalf. The Senator was so sick, Shafer explained, that something as simple as exposure to the chill of the night air could endanger his life. Shafer expressed Morrissey's gratitude and regret. Once Shafer bid them farewell, the band broke into "The Sweet Bye and Bye" and the crowd began to disperse, leaving the ailing man to his rest.

Despite the joy which his political victory had brought him, John was not able to rise from his bed again for a week. Even then, Dr. Bradley considered his health too fragile to risk going out of doors, and the doctor made arrangements for his patient to take a trip to the South in order to escape the chill of New York's winter, not to mention the stresses of a political life in a political city. A ticket was purchased for John aboard the steamship *San Jacinto*, which would take him to the warmer climes of Savannah, Georgia. With this settled, John took the time to file a will written for him by his friend Harry Ford. In it he bequeathed his estate to Susannah of course, except for $10,000 each going to three of his sisters, and he named William Travers and Troy Mayor Edward Murphy, Jr. his executors. Only Dr. Bradley, Susan Morrissey, Jimmy Hayes, and another friend knew of the plans, and in the early morning hours of November 16, he quietly got on board with only these chosen few to bid him farewell. Only Bradley and a single servant would accompany him for the journey; Susan would follow a short time later. Hayes and the other friend helped to support him on the journey up to the deck, where they then shook his hand and said their goodbyes. A reporter for the *Times* happened to be on the dock to cover a non-related story. Recognizing Morrissey, he asked him if he planned to be back before the legislature convened. "Oh, I'll be there," the Senator replied, "if I am alive."[559]

Apparently, Savannah was not as beneficial for John's health as the good doctor had surmised; Morrissey relocated to Jacksonville, Florida in December. He didn't like Florida any better. January brought erratic shifts in his condition for a week. After four days in critical condition, he suddenly seemed to recover, but then another couple of days saw his health falter enough that Susan was reported to have "given up hope," and was seen working to get her husband's affairs in order. Dr. Bradley informed reporters that he had diagnosed the patient with both Bright's Disease and heart disease.[560]

On January 21, a correspondent from the *Savannah News* sent the following description of Morrissey's latest condition and state of mind:

> While the cough is yet troublesome and breathing somewhat labored, there is less oedema [sic] of the lower limbs, and rest can be obtained in a horizontal position. Mr. Morrissey is now again able to walk from room to room and enjoy a fair appetite. His morale is excellent, and in all respects he is a model patient, carrying out implicitly and cheerfully the instructions of his physicians to the minutest details. Although perfectly conversant with the nature of his disease and of its probably fatal issue, he surveys the field with characteristic fortitude and composure, and displays remarkable equanimity and resignation. During the recent crisis he expressed great satisfaction with the visits of the venerable Father Dufau, Pastor of the Church of the Immaculate Conception, declaring himself a true son of the Roman Catholic Church and warmly devoted to its ancient rites and usages. His confinement is cheered by the presence of his wife and Mr. Lamb, an intimate friend.[561]

The frustrating cycle of relapses and recoveries continued through the next several weeks. He celebrated his forty-seventh birthday on February 12 in Jacksonville fully aware that it would likely be his last, according to the above article. He had also apparently converted to the Catholic faith of his wife and most of his constituents. Susan's presence gave him comfort, and she and one of his sisters spent most of their day nursing him. They had come down during his final days in Savannah. In Florida, the couple had two beds, John's much larger than Susan's, so that he had room to lay in whatever position allowed him to breathe and sleep easiest without worrying about disturbing her. He came to affectionately call her smaller

---

[559] *New York Times*, November 16, 1877 and May 3, 1878; New York Wills and Probate Records, 1659-1999, accessed at ancestry.com on 4/9/2020
[560] *New York Times*, January 15, 16, 17, and 18, 1878; Hotaling, 121
[561] *New York Times*, January 28, 1878

bed, "the pony." Susan had a habit of going to bed earlier than anyone else in their party and, as long as they had been together John had always had the habit of kissing her goodnight before he himself came to bed and went to sleep. Even in Florida, as sick as he was, he maintained this tradition, asking to be carried to "the pony," where he would sit on the side of her bed and watch her sleep before kissing her and being helped to his own. During the day, in pity for her constantly slaving over her invalid husband, John would affectionately call Susan "Poor Hard Knocks" and "Poor Little Hard Times."[562]

With the weather in New York warming that March, and with Morrissey's condition apparently stabilizing, Dr. Bradley agreed to allow his patient to begin his trip home. The small party traveled by carriage to Charleston, South Carolina, where they boarded the steamship *Charleston*. The trip to New York City took just sixty hours, unusually fast for the period. When the Senator disembarked at 6:30 in the evening, a reporter who caught sight of him recorded that he "appears somewhat worn, but... able to walk smartly from the steamer along the pier to a coach that was in waiting, and, though he carried a stout cane, did not use to it to aid or support himself." Another noticed that he had lost a good deal of weight, but that he remained energetic, lucid, and conversant. The press reported that Morrissey felt a good deal better, but not yet well enough to take his seat in the legislature. He spent a restless night at the Ashland House, refusing all visitors and cards. Rising early the next day, he left at nine in the morning for business meetings at the Hoffman House and Astor House, which lasted until the afternoon. Exhausted and complaining of heart palpitations, he made his way down to the docks at the end of Canal Street, where he boarded the steamship *St. John*. Booking a double stateroom, he sent for his wife and went immediately to bed, where he finally slept. Once Susan arrived, he passed along word that he intended to travel home to Saratoga, possibly with a stop-over at Albany to be sworn in, if he felt up to it.[563]

Ultimately, he went to neither Albany nor Saratoga, at least not immediately. Instead, he and Susan made it no further than their old hometown, Troy, one of the *St. John*'s stops along the Hudson. Though there were relapses, he seemed to be on the mend overall and, by late April, his physicians felt confident enough to allow a return to Saratoga. The patient himself expressed doubts that he would live any longer than a few more weeks, but his doctors and wife maintained hope. It was not long after his arrival in Saratoga that he suffered a stroke on Monday, April 28. This left him partially paralyzed on his right side and greatly limited his ability to speak, though his physician, a Dr. Grant, was relieved that he could still recognize people and commands. The difficulty of his breathing intensified almost to the point of suffocation, but the horse race man in

[562] *New York Times*, January 28, 1878; *Irish American*, March 23, 1878
[563] *Irish American*, April 6, 1878

him was able to string together a metaphor to those at his bedside on Tuesday. "I am running neck and neck with death, and rapidly tiring," he confessed. Later the same day, he spoke the single word, "Mother," recognizing his mother-in-law when she entered his room. It would be the last word he would find the strength to utter. Newspapers from as far away as Tennessee and Nebraska now carried daily updates on his condition.[564]

Susan Morrissey continued to maintain to the press that her husband would recover, her hopes buoyed by Dr. Grant's insistence that "there is hope as long as there is life." When she was not attending to her husband's medical needs, she was reading to him the letters from well-wishers as far away as Jacksonville, Florida. She and his physicians were encouraged by the fact that the sound of his wife's voice seemed to enliven him and allow him to breathe easier, though he remained mute.[565]

On the evening of April 30, a correspondent from the *Herald* managed to corner Dr. Grant and ask him about Morrissey's condition. The doctor admitted that he held little hope for the Senator's recovery, but he assured the reporter that the patient was resting well and comfortable. The paralysis had greatly weakened him, said the doctor. However, John Morrissey's reputation for endurance as a prize-fighter followed him even to his struggle against death decades later. "Where an ordinary man would be considered at the point of death Senator Morrissey is still good for a long struggle," Dr. Grant said, before leaving the reporter to compose his story.

The struggle would not last as long as the doctor surmised. Early the next morning, John awoke in a clearly agitated mood, and mutely conveyed a bizarre request for bananas. Someone sent for the fruit, and the ailing man devoured a banana before his usual meal of crackers, beef broth, and buttermilk. Having eaten, he set his wife and doctors at ease by indicating that he recognized them all and understood them. He did not speak but communicated clearly with hand signs. His breathing seemed easy and, once given his glasses, he seemed to read through an early edition the *Herald* without any problem. Later that morning, members of the Sisters of Mercy came to see him, and he calmly communicated to them that he did not think he would make it through the day. He grabbed one of their crucifixes and would not let go of it until Susan arrived and placed his hand in her own.

"Are you ready to go," one of the nuns asked him, to which he nodded in the affirmative.

"Will you be glad to go and be with Johnny," they asked. He again replied with a nod. The Sisters of Mercy left with the feeling that John Morrissey was at peace with the world, and at peace with death. Even

---

564 *New York Times*, April 2, 12, 30, and May 3, 1878; New *York Sun*, May 2, 1878; Hotaling, 121
565 *New York Herald*, May 1, 1878

Susan admitted to herself that, for the first time, she saw death in his eyes. Word was sent to his friends that John Morrissey would likely not survive the evening.[566]

By four thirty in the afternoon, the patient's condition had deteriorated so rapidly that Dr. Grant left his bedside, feeling utterly useless. "I have never seen a man sink so rapidly as he has done in the last two hours," the doctor muttered upon leaving. John sat propped up on pillows in his bed to ease his now labored breathing. Someone had opened a window in hopes of aiding his respiration. Two of his friends stood nearby, fanning him. His longtime friend Father McMenomy performed last communion for John. After doing so, the priest saw that John's "large eyes had an unwonted lustre and... his whole countenance expressed not merely peace but triumph in death."[567]

While a group of John's friends solemnly surrounded his bed at seven in the evening, his beloved Susie held her dying husband's hand. Father McMenomy's fervent prayers were the only sound in the room aside from John's wheezing breath and the occasional sob of a helpless loved one. At about seven thirty that night, the effort to breathe became violent as John's body changed color and writhed with the agony of not being able to fill his desperate lungs. Finally, his head fell silently against his pillow, the struggle now clearly over. The priest, who had been holding one of John's hands at that moment, bent over the body for close inspection and rose with the words "He is gone."

Susan cried out and fell over her dead husband's body. "Oh, I'm left all alone," she sobbed, "all alone." After a time, some friends tried to take her away and comfort her until she stood up on her own and, raising her hands into the air, wailed, "He has gone to be with Johnny, and left me all alone."[568]

———

News of John Morrissey's passing, sent from Saratoga by friends who had been at his home and watched him go, reached New York in extraordinary time. "A gloom overspread the public centres most frequented during life by the deceased," recorded the *Herald*. Soon enough, the late man's friends had gathered at the Hoffman House, where so many of them had spent many a day and evening planning and strategizing with Morrissey. They told stories and talked of the struggles of his final days.[569]

"It cost John Morrissey $500 every time he went to Troy," a former official from Morrissey's hometown remembered. "Old foundrymen who

[566] *New York Herald,* May 2, 1878
[567] *New York Herald,* May 5, 1878
[568] *New York Sun,* May 2, 1878
[569] *New York Herald,* May 2, 1878; *New York Sun,* May 2, 1878

had worked with him in his early days came to him with stories of hardship, and every gambler that was out of luck wanted a stake. A Trojan, he always fancied, had a peculiar claim on him." Following this, others gave their own recollection of the famed man's generosity and soft spot for the working man. James Hayes, who had been so instrumental in helping John win his first election to Congress, would later go so far as to call him "the most generous and most charitable man I ever knew."[570]

The news reached Albany by eight o'clock. It was the responsibility of a Senator Harris to announce the news to the House, at which point the session was adjourned. When they returned the next day, they found Morrissey's long vacant desk covered with a pyramid and a cross of flowers. The session opened with a series of eulogies from fellow senators, some of whom knew him well and others who did not. Virtually all of the speeches, which came from both Republicans and Democrats, praised the deceased for "those qualities with which his memory will always be associated – sterling integrity and stalwart manliness." His good friend, Assemblyman James Hayes spoke only briefly, but praised him as "not a self-made man, but a God-made man." Surprisingly, the Senators with the most complimentary accolades for John Morrissey were those who had been his most adamant opponents when he was alive.[571]

In true bureaucratic fashion, the Senate went about recording their grief through official resolutions:

> Resolved, That the Senate has heard with profound emotion of the death of our late associate, Hon. John Morrissey.
>
> Resolved, That we wish to testify our respect for the remarkable qualities of the deceased; for his individuality of character; for his great moral courage; for his devotion to principle and to his friends; for the persistent energy which marked his life-long struggle against the most formidable obstacles, and above all, for his rare and unquestioned integrity.
>
> Resolved, That we tender our deepest sympathy in the hour of their bereavement to his afflicted widow and family, and that, as a further mark of respect to his memory, the Senate will attend his funeral in a body.[572]

On May 2, the citizens of New York City woke to find the flags at half-mast. Nearly all the major newspapers in America carried the story of John Morrissey's death that day, many of their announcements followed by extensive summaries of his extraordinary life and careers as a prize-fighter, gambler, investor, and politician. His birth in Ireland; his impoverished, rowdy youth in Troy; coming to New York and stowing away to California;

---

570 *New York Sun*, May 2, 1878; *Evening World*, February 6, 1891
571 *New York Sun*, May 2, 1878; *New York Herald*, May 3, 1878
572 *New York Herald*, May 3, 1878

the ring battles with Thompson, Sullivan, and Heenan; becoming the most notorious millionaire in Saratoga; his successes and failures in the stock-market; his elections to Congress and the New York Senate; his rivalries with Poole, Tweed, and Kelly. As is the case when so many controversial men pass, many of the newspapers were quick to point out his redeeming qualities and downplay the allegations of corruption and criminality that followed him all his life; only a very few took a critical view of his life.[573]

A writer for the *New York Herald* gave as complimentary and well-written of a eulogy as any the deceased could receive:

> The death of John Morrissey marks the close of a unique career. America is emphatically the country of self-made men; but of all those who in one way or another during the past quarter of a century have kept themselves before the public eye not one can be pointed to who, from such beginnings as his, struggled up through so many vicissitudes of fortune to a position of honor, and, we may say, respect. Born of the poorest, bred among the roughest and rougher than any of them…. In truth the rugged strength and vital force of his body were only equalled [sic] by the strength and force of his mind. If his mind had been as cultured as his fist what a man he might have been! For there was a natural grasp of affairs in him, a keenness of perception, a directness and immutability of purpose, and… an unflinching fidelity to any obligation he assumed. He was a man of action and a man of his word. Add to this a large-hearted generosity, and the man may be fairly judged.[574]

Despite often showing bias against Morrissey during his lifetime, the *New York Times* was complimentary to the point of hysterics after his death, their writer washing away the deceased's sins with his tearful words, "The ex-prizefighter and gambler is remembered only as a true friend, the honest, clear headed, right minded legislator, the loyal, whole souled, generous man."[575]

Not all of the papers were complimentary, of course. The *New York Ledger* recognized that John had risen out of impoverished circumstances to better himself to a degree, but they questioned whether that betterment qualified him for hero worship and election to office. "Reforming from a pugilist into a gambler strikes us as a very doubtful kind of reform," quipped the writer. "We have no idea that a better gambler ever represented us in Congress or in the State Senate than John Morrissey; but we hope no professional gambler will ever represent us again."[576]

---

[573] *New York Herald*, May 2, 1878; *New York Times*, May 2, 1878; *New York Sun*, May 2, 1878; *Evening Star*, May 4, 1878; *Winnsboro News and Herald*, May 4, 1878
[574] *New York Herald*, May 2, 1878
[575] Redmond, 117, quoting *New York Times*
[576] *Vancouver Independent*, quoting *New York Ledger*, July 25, 1878

As had been the case with his son, most of the papers listed Bright's Disease as the medical cause of John Morrissey's demise; though almost all acknowledged that it was the stress of the campaign which truly killed him. The *Daily Globe* in St. Paul, Minnesota put it bluntly, "Morrissey defeated Kelly and killed himself."[577]

In Washington D.C., word of his demise greatly saddened many of his fellow politicians, who had come to admire his confrontational bluntness as refreshing and honest during his time there as a reluctant congressman. On the afternoon of May 4, several politicians, among them former Secretary of War Simon Cameron of the Lincoln Administration, gathered together at a leading hotel in the capital where they fell into a prolonged conversation about the deceased, sharing their favorite stories about the boxer-turned-congressman into the night, until the late hour and the need for sleep forced them to stop. Unlike the rest of the men present, Cameron had only a passing acquaintance with Morrissey, but contributed perhaps the most moving and telling story about John of them all, which had come to him second-hand:

> When Morrissey first came to Washington I must confess I was not very favorably impressed with him. He had a bad record, of course, and somehow or other most people in this world have a mean habit of remembering all the bad things a man does and forgetting all the good ones. At all events, I had never heard anything good about Morrissey. For this reason I was very much surprised one day to hear my friend – (Senator Cameron named one of the best known Republican leaders in New York) – speak in terms of great kindness of him. I gave expression to this surprise, when my friend told me that I was very much mistaken in Morrissey's character, and to prove what he said related the story to which I alluded. It was to the effect that a young man of great promise, a resident of New York City, and a clerk in a large business house, had found his way into Morrissey's gambling saloon, and while there had lost in play $12,000, which was for the moment in his possession, but which belonged to the firm in whose employ he was. The next morning, the young man, fully realizing his position, went to his mother and told her the whole story. She, almost wild with grief, went to her husband and repeated it to him. The old man was so stunned by the information of his boy's dishonor that he could suggest no plan by which he might escape public disgrace and punishment. In fact... they were all in a mighty bad way, but, as usual, the old woman was the first to get her wits about her, and she suggested to the boy's father to go to his friend, - (the Republican leader already alluded to,) and to get him to go to Morrissey and see if he would not help them out of their trouble. The friend, consented, much against his

577 *Daily Globe*, May 4, 1878

will. He went to the gambler, told him the whole story, and assured him that disgrace and ruin would be brought upon an estimable family if the money lost by the young man was not returned. Morrissey listened quietly to all that was told him, and then said: 'Well, that's all very well, but the young fellow lost the money fair; and as for him bein' a poor innocent young dove that didn't know nothing of the world, that's all stuff; he's been in our place often, and won many a pile, but for the old woman's sake I'll see what I can do. Come to my house to-morrow morning, and like as not I can make the thing all right.' The next morning the gentleman came as he was directed, and with the simple words: 'Tell the old woman to keep her boy away from sportin' houses,' Morrissey handed him the exact sum the young clerk had lost. If such an action... does not cover a multitude of sins, my 79 years of life have taught me no lessons and brought me no knowledge.[578]

Back in Saratoga, Morrissey's remains were placed inside a large casket made of varnished black walnut with a white interior and transported to the second-floor parlor of the Adelphi Hotel by May 3. "There he lies," observed a correspondent for the *Herald*, "his hair brushed back from his forehead, the eyes peacefully closed, his right hand laid across his chest. Neither his features nor his frame are wasted. His mouth wears a sweet and tranquil smile." Even after his death, Susan remained almost constantly by her late husband's side, "absorbed by her affliction and unwilling for a moment to quit the neighborhood of the dead, to whom in life she was bravely, incessantly devoted." By this point, hundreds of telegrams of sympathy for Mrs. Morrissey had poured into the house from around the country, but she could not yet bring herself to separate from her late husband long enough to respond to one. The room was open to the public that morning, and people of all classes and backgrounds entered to pay their respects.[579]

One of Susan's brothers handled the funeral arrangements, organizing transport for the casket from Saratoga to Troy at noon for a funeral scheduled for the next day. As the train carrying the deceased passed through each station along the way, crowds gathered to catch a glimpse, the men removing their hats in mourning respect. The coffin was brought into the back parlor of the same house in which John and Susan had been married twenty-four years earlier. On the eve of the funeral, when a writer for the *New York Herald* arrived to interview some of the close friends in the house, Susan pleaded from the stairs above for the reporter to come and visit her. "I am so lonely," she cried. Upstairs, the reporter sat with Susan and asked what her late husband had been like away from the public eye. She lamented that many considered her husband to be of rough character, when to her he was always "sweet and kind and good and noble and

---

[578] *New York Times* May 6, 1878
[579] *New York Herald*, May 4, 1878; *New York Times*, May 5, 1878

tender." Friends and family surrounded her in Troy, and said she dreaded returning alone to their empty house in Saratoga.[580]

The next morning, the doors of the house were opened for the citizens of Troy to file through and view the body, many of whom did so before leaving to join the crowds which lined the sidewalks along the route to the church. One man present estimated the number of people who came to view the late Senator's body in the house that day at 5,000. During the nine o'clock hour, as the widow and her family gathered around the casket, the last stragglers of the public began to file out of the house. Shortly before ten o'clock, the pallbearers, composed of New York Lieutenant Governor William Dorsheimer and nine state senators, arrived. A well-known local singer then sang a hymn while the veiled widow bent over her husband crying, letting her tears drip upon his face.[581]

A hearse then carried the casket through the streets, which were "filled without being blockaded by crowds of men, women, and children" numbering an estimated 15,000 to 20,000 people, the most-attended funeral in Troy's history. The family and very close friends walked behind the hearse; behind them were the pallbearers and other high-placed members of New York's state government. The correspondent for the *New York Times* noticed John Lawrence and Nelson Parker, both Troy natives, among this group. Both men, noted the writer, had known John since his days as a deckhand in Captain Smith's employ, Lawrence having worked as a fireman and Parker a waiter aboard the same vessel. Lawrence went on to become John's most frequent training assistant during his prize-fighting career. He also owed his current job as a detective for the New York Central Railroad to his friendship with John, as did Parker his job as a waiter in a drawing room car of the same line. When the hearse reached the St. Peter's Roman Catholic Church on Fifth Avenue, the family found the building itself surrounded by thousands of people, one reporter estimating as many as 5,000. The *Times* correspondent described the scene:

> Troy never saw such a funeral as that of to-day. There have been more pompous ceremonies; funerals accompanied with much more of the outward show than that of to-day, but no burial ever evoked so many expressions of sorrow from the mass of the people – the hard, rough workingmen and women in the class out of which Morrissey sprang, and which he always claimed as his, for sympathy and support. They turned out en masse to-day, in their working clothes, and with the grit upon their faces, to watch with tears in their eyes, the passage of the funeral procession.[582]

[580] *New York Herald*, May 5, 1878; *New York Times*, May 3, 1878; *New York Times*, May 4, 1878
[581] *New York Herald*, May 5, 1878; *New York Times*, May 5, 1878; Redmond, 117
[582] *New York Times*, May 4 and 5, 1878; *New York Herald* May 5, 1878; Redmond, 117; Fox, 61

Among the first to enter the church were the Mayor of Troy, the Troy Chief of Police, those members of the New York State Senate who were not bearers, even more members of the State Assembly, members of the Governor's staff, the New York Attorney General and the state comptroller, along with several other officials and politicians from New York City, Albany, Saratoga, and other cities. These men took the reserved pews in front of the altar. The remaining seats stayed open to friends and family not in the procession, hundreds from "every class of his business, political, and personal associates." Then the pallbearers brought in the casket, Susan and other mourners behind them. Once the priests entered, the ceremony and mass were traditional and simple.

The burial was equally humble and without event, notable only for the despair of those present and the fact that both Catholic (the religion of the widow, and the religion to which the deceased had converted) and Protestant (the religion of the deceased's parents) ceremonies were delivered. In the Catholic Oakwood Cemetery, Father McMenomy, in saying his words over the casket, became unusually emotional, for Morrissey was said to be like a son to him. His evident struggle to maintain a calm demeanor spread through the mourners. Susan was understandably the first, moaning without restraint as she rocked back and forth in her chair. When the Father described John as a dutiful husband, Susan cried out, "Oh, that he was, indeed; that he was; a savior; where lives another like him!" At this, other women present began to sob as well, and soon after Morrissey's government colleagues did the same. After Father McMenomy finished praising and saying goodbye to his friend, a Father Hughes pronounced the absolution and the Catholic mourners began to leave the cemetery. The casket was brought to its resting place atop a hill in St. Peter's Cemetery, the Protestant cemetery adjoining Oakwood. He was laid to rest between his father and his son (a request he had specified shortly after John Junior's death) beneath the towering granite monument he had had erected for his family twelve years previous. Following a Protestant service, these mourners too departed.[583]

[583] *New York Herald*, May 5, 1878; *New York Times*, May 5, 1878

Epilogue:
Friends and Foes

In his will, John left the majority of what remained of his fortune to his widow, though he allotted smaller portions to three of his sisters, two of whom lived in Troy, while the other resided in Chicago. Estimates of Morrissey's wealth made in the days immediately following his demise ranged a great deal, between $30,000 to $200,000. Clearly, he was no longer the millionaire the newspapers had once purported him to be. One reporter later surmised that the depletion of his wealth was the result of bad business investments made on his own after his break with Vanderbilt. He had sold off most of his gambling interests in New York City over the last years of his life, seeing them as obstacles to the legitimacy he was chasing through his political career. By 1877, only his gambling interests in Saratoga remained. The last New York City gambling house to go was his famous house on West Twenty-fourth Street in New York, which he sold for $80,000 to his one-time partners Charles Reed and Albert Spencer. Chronic health problems, travel, campaigning, generosity, and a love of the finer things had chipped away at his savings in the same period, leaving behind a much smaller estate than the general public had assumed. *The Herald* reported that his assets consisted of his percentages in the racetrack and a share of the Club House at Saratoga, along with shares in ferry and railroad stocks. They also reported the shocking detail that Morrissey had neglected to open a life insurance policy on himself.[584]

Morrissey had bequeathed $10,000 each to three of his sisters, with the remainder, after debts were paid, going to Susan. William Travers, John's old partner in the Saratoga Racing Association, along with Edward Murphy, Jr., Mayor of Troy, were the executors of the deceased's estate. Travers and Murphy made an accounting of the estate's funds at $14,750 against moneys owed to creditors at $54,535.19. As shocked as everyone else at the relatively dismal valuation, the creditors immediately filed objections to the executors' valuation of the estate. In 1861, having received none of her inheritance, John's sister Margret would later charge both Travers and Murphy with neglect and successfully gained injunctions against either settling his will. This author has not been able to discover the results of the charges against Travers and Murphy, and the ultimate distribution of the estate.[585]

---

[584] *New York Herald*, May 2, 1878; *Redwood Gazette*, May 9, 1878; *Seattle Post-Intelligencer*, January 1, 1893
[585] *Chicago Daily Tribune*, July 29, 1880; *National Republican*, January 6, 1881

As for the gambling empire over which Morrissey once ruled, like the empire of Alexander, it broke apart amongst his closest subordinates and rivals. He sold his interest in the house at 8 Barclay Street, which would go on to become the longest-lived gambling business in the city, to his longtime business partner Matt Danser in the 1860s. Danser would go on to become one of the most prominent gambling impresarios in the city's history. Though he officially retired a millionaire in 1872, some believed he was he a silent partner in a combination of businessmen who purchased the luxurious operation at 818 Broadway from Morrissey in 1877. Two years later, this business was operated by Ferdinand Abell and was named the Central Club before it finally closed in 1890.

Despite Danser's successes, the man who would truly inherit Morrissey's status as the premier gambling operator in New York and throughout the nation was Richard Canfield. Canfield purchased Morrissey's famed Saratoga Club House from Morrissey's partners Reed and Spencer, who had themselves purchased Morrissey's share in the place from his widow. Born in Massachusetts in 1855, Canfield had been a small-time operator until he took a trip to Europe and visited Monte Carlo, making observations which inspired him upon his return to the States. Moving to New York City, he experienced many setbacks until finally hitting success in 1888 with the Madison Square Club on West Twenty-sixth Street. His success there and at other enterprises in Manhattan earned him a reputation as the Prince of Gamblers. After expanding into Saratoga and taking over the racecourse and Club House that had once been Morrissey's in 1894, he found these to be even more successful than his New York City interests and focused mainly on the resort. Expanding the Club House and other investments, he dominated New York gambling for decades before several costly raids in the early twentieth century forced him to withdraw and focus on his other passion, art collecting. Today the old Club House building is the Saratoga Springs History Museum and is rumored to be haunted by the spirit of its original owner.[586]

———

Despite his death at a relatively young age, few of Morrissey's closest friends and fiercest rivals survived him. James "Yankee" Sullivan, from whom John won his boxing championship in 1853, died under suspicious circumstances in California the next year. Bill "The Butcher" Poole, of course, was murdered by Morrissey's obsessive lackey Lew Baker in 1855. Street thug Patrick "Paudeen" McLaughlin was shot down by Morrissey's close friend Daniel "Dad" Cunningham in 1858. Former boxing champion Tom Hyer died a penniless invalid in 1864. Railroad magnate James Fisk, the man most responsible for the Black Friday stock market crash that

[586]https://saratogatodaynewspaper.com/history/item/10542-haunted-saratoga-ghosts-john-morrissey-katrina-trask-angelina-witch-of-saratoga, accessed 4/4/2020

almost ruined Morrissey financially, was shot to death by his wife's lover at age 36 on January 7, 1872. John "The Benicia Boy" Heenan, who gave Morrissey such a fierce fight in 1858 and fought to a draw with the English champion Tom Sayers in 1860, fought once more, losing to England's Tom King. Retiring from the ring, he had brief success as a gambling empresario in the Morrissey mold, but eventually lost his money before dying of tuberculosis in Colorado at just 39 years of age in 1873. Heenan's ex-wife, the famed beauty Adah Menken, fell ill of an unspecified affliction on a European tour and preceded him to the grave in 1868 at age 33. Cornelius Vanderbilt died an obscenely wealthy man at the age of 83 on January 4, 1877, his fortune split between his widow and children. The once indomitable William "Boss" Tweed met an inglorious end in prison in 1878, just weeks before Morrissey himself passed. The fate of Dad Cunningham, perhaps the man most worthy of being called Morrissey's best friend in his younger years, seems to have been lost to history, his last appearance in New York City newspapers being an arrest for running a gambling house in 1862. The fates of brothel-keeper Alexander Hamilton, gambler John Petrie, madame Kate Ridgely, and boxer George Thompson are also unknown.

As for those allies and enemies who did survive Morrissey, Bill Poole's killer, Lew Baker, made haste for Europe after his acquittal on murder charges and died in Paris in 1878 in his early fifties. Slippery Dick Connolly, who cooked the books for the Tweed Ring, lived in exile until his death in France of Bright's Disease in 1880 at about age 70. Fernando Wood, the ex-Mayor of New York and one-time master of Tammany Hall, became a prominent figure in national politics and would ultimately serve five terms in Congress between 1841 and his 1881 death at the age of 68 on a visit to Hot Springs, Arkansas. Augustus Schell, Morrissey's swallowtail rival for the New York Senate, ran unsuccessfully for mayor the next year and passed away a multi-millionaire from Bright's Disease in 1884 at age 71. Isaiah Rynders, the political weathercock who was once the master of corruption in New York's Five Points neighborhood, was essentially supplanted in that role by Morrissey and others after the Civil War. Though he remained active in politics for some time, his influence waned quickly, and the one-time knife-fighter surprised many by living into his early eighties, passing away on January 3, 1885. After a long career in politics, Samuel Tilden, one of the most admired New Yorkers of his day, died a millionaire in his home on August 4, 1886 at the age of 72, part of his fortune going to found what would become the New York Public Library. Charles "Dutch Charley" Duane remained violently embroiled in California politics and crime until his death in San Francisco on May 13, 1887 at age 60. He is one of the few men who personally knew the young Morrissey to leave behind a substantial written first-person account of the man and his era in his memoirs. James Hayes, Morrissey's most loyal political ally, seems to have seen his political career stall after Morrissey's death. He died in New York City on March 14, 1897 at about 70 years of age. After a series of trials, ex-mayor A. Oakey Hall was acquitted of all wrongdoing as one of the leaders of the nefarious Tweed Ring in 1873 and disappeared to England, where he lived under an assumed name for years. After returning to New York in 1892, he died there six years later at age 72. Cartoonist Thomas Nast remained a thorn in the side of New York Democrats for years to come, staying on at *Harper's Weekly* until 1886. After failing with his own newspaper, he accepted a position from his admirer President Theodore Roosevelt as a United States Consul General in Ecuador but died there of Yellow Fever on December 7, 1902 at age 62. His artistic style and creations remain profoundly influential in popular culture to this day. Remaining obdurately opposed to Tammany Hall, James O'Brien, John's old partner in the Young Democracy, won a seat in Congress as an independent Democrat in 1878. After serving one term, he retired from politics to become a stockbroker, dying in New York City on March 5, 1907 at age 65. Peter Sweeny, the so-called "Brains" of the Tweed Ring eventually returned to New York from Paris, but essentially remained in hiding from the public eye until his death in 1911 at age 86.

Morrissey's death removed Honest John Kelly's most obstinate obstacle for domination of the Democratic Party in New York City and much of the rest of the state. He did come up against Tilden on repeated occasions, but the swallowtail reformer was not able to prevent Kelly's controlling most of the New York City and state elections, nor his appointment to the position of New York City comptroller, giving him access to the city funds. Despite ever-present depictions as the successor to that icon of embezzlement Boss Tweed, Kelly handled the municipal funds conservatively and greatly reduced the city's deficit, a fact which his swallowtail friends appreciated but much of the working class resented as it often left them out in the cold, literally. Retiring in 1884, Kelly died wealthy and respected two years later at age 64.

Kelly's successor in dominance over Tammany Hall fell to one of his most loyal lieutenants, Richard Croker. Under the guidance of men like Croker and "Big Tim" Sullivan, the organization would remain at the center of New York State politics well into the twentieth century. As it had been the case during Morrissey's day, Tammany continued to rely heavily on the immigrant vote and was constantly under attack by reformers accusing the organization of rampant corruption. During the 1940s and 1950s, the combined efforts of Democratic U.S. President Franklin Roosevelt and Republican New York Mayor Fiorello La Guardia saw to the weakening of its grip. By the close of the 1960s, Tammany Hall was no more.

––––––

After John's death, Susannah Morrissey returned to their home on Matlida Street in Saratoga and lived there for several years before returning to Troy to live her remaining years in the house in which she and John were married. Susan kept a portrait of her late husband in her room and surrounded it with flowers. She never remarried and inherited little if anything from her late husband's estate. Though she felt cheated of her inheritance by those who had handled the estate and swindled by those to whom her husband had loaned money, she declined to take legal action, wanting to avoid "the shame of a public contest." When a reporter confronted Morrissey's executor Edward Murphy about the widow's financial woes, Murphy replied, "She must have had $25,000 to $30,000 worth of jewelry alone. That woman was a poor, silly fool. She was crazy for the admiration of men."[587]

Once one of the most visible and ostentatious women in New York, Susan disappeared from public view, excepting for the very rare interview about her youth at John's side. In one of these, she alluded to there being more children born to them than John, Jr and a second, short-lived baby boy. "We had ten children," she tearfully told a reporter. "I sit here alone to-day. There are ten little graves and one large one, where all my ambition for my own lies buried." Adhering to a request he had made in life, Susan rarely visited her husband's grave.[588]

At some point, Susan adopted a son who sent her small sums of money on which to live after he moved to California. Her health began to decline in her fifties. In 1893, the *Seattle Post-Intelligencer* reported that Susan, "at one time one of the most beautiful women in America, gentle, accomplished, refined, is now eking out a bare subsistence in a collar factory at Troy, N.Y., the former home of her dead husband. She earns about $1 a day at her wearisome labor, a sum which she dispensed at least a dozen times a day in charity during the era of her husband's prosperity. Once she wore $300,000 worth of diamonds; now, poor woman, she must be content with food and shelter." Three years later, she was blind and paralyzed and complaining of being "robbed of her fortune by her enemies." Eventually one of John's old friends took up a collection for her. Susannah Morrissey, or "Baby," as John affectionately called his wife, would outlive her son and husband by two decades, passing away in Troy on September 22, 1898. She was 62 old.[589]

[587] *Salt Lake Herald*, July 30, 1889; *Daily Inter Ocean*, November 11, 1878
[588] *Russellville Democrat*, November 27, 1879, quoting *Philadelphia Record*; *Salt Lake Herald*, July 30, 1889
[589] *Seattle Post-Intelligencer*, January 1, 1893; *San Francisco Call*, January 25, 1896; *Madison Daily Leader*, January 24, 1896; *Burr Oak Herald*, August 6, 1896

Afterward:
For Better or Worse

So much was written about John Morrissey in his time, and his life encompassed such a wide range of adventure, activity, mistakes, and controversies, that arriving at a summation that is both original and adequate is beyond the capabilities of this author. There will be no attempt here to place a final moral judgement on a man or his dramatic and complicated life and times. However, it is perhaps important to reflect upon the facts of his legacy and the different ways his life shaped, for better or worse, the America and Americans that came after him.

When John Morrissey entered life as a prize-fighter in the early 1850s, the sport was legal in only the most lawless states and territories, ignored as a side-show oddity by the public at large, and completely abhorred as disgusting and immoral by several sections of society. Though it remained widely illegal and scandalous during and after their careers, John Morrissey and John Heenan were the first athletes to become household names throughout America, and that sort of fame inevitably raised boxing to a more prominent place in the American consciousness, even if that consciousness did not yet approve of its own fascination with the sport. Born five days before Morrissey and Heenan engaged in their incredible battle, John L. Sullivan doubtless grew up hearing about and emulating them as so many other working class Irish-American boys did; as an adult, he cited Morrissey as one of his inspirations. When Sullivan, a bold and rugged bare-knuckle boxing champion of Irish heritage, became arguably the most famous (and infamous) American celebrity of his generation and made boxing a mainstream American sport during the 1880s, he did so with the spirit of John Morrissey in his corner.[590]

For his role as an early American practitioner of the sport and for his reputation as the toughest pugilist of his era, John Morrissey would be posthumously inducted into *The Ring* magazine Hall of Fame in 1954 and the International Boxing Hall of Fame in the Pioneers category in 1996. Enshrined alongside him are Young Barney Aaron, John Heenan, Tom Hyer, Jem Mace, and Tom Sayers, all fighters he knew well. Interestingly enough, Yankee Sullivan, once considered the indominitable master of the ring, has yet to be inducted. The International Boxing Hall of Fame museum can be found in Canastota, New York.

A little over 100 miles east of Canastota is another museum, the Saratoga Springs History Museum. Though few who stroll through the

---

[590] Isenberg, 149

well-groomed park outside realize it, the large, three-story brick edifice in which that institution is appropriately housed was once the most resplendent and notorious gambling hall in the western hemisphere, Morrissey's Club House. Though America has largely forgotten John Morrissey's name through the generations, the people of Saratoga Springs remember better than most. Before he came to town, Saratoga Springs was already a spa resort for the wealthiest families in the North, and gambling and harnessed horse racing already existed there. But it was John Morrissey whose work, money, vision, and presence turned Saratoga Springs into one of the most successful horse racing venues in the United States, not to mention (for a long time, anyway) the most popular resort destination in the country as well. Thoroughbred racing's continued popularity in this country stems directly from John Morrissey's promotions in the 1860s and 1870s. The racetrack he built there still stands and still hosts one of the most important racing seasons in America every year, where one of the annual races is dubbed the Morrissey Stakes.

For starting thoroughbred racing in Saratoga Springs and for turning it into the most popular sport in the nation for generations to come after him, John Morrissey was posthumously inducted into National Museum of Racing's Hall of Fame in the Pillars of the Turf category in 2018. Several of the horses who ran at Morrissey's track during his management at Saratoga, including Longfellow, Harry Bassett, and Preakness, are also enshrined there. Not surprisingly, this museum also resides in Saratoga Springs, New York.

The National Museum of Racing was founded by Cornelius Vanderbilt Whitney, the great-grandson of John Morrissey's friend and benefactor, the original Wall Street tycoon, Cornelius Vanderbilt. His association with Vanderbilt and other men of the world of high-finance, as well as his close relationships with aristocrats like August Belmont and Samuel Tilden points to another unique aspect of John Morrissey's life, his being the first Irish immigrant to achieve such a social standing in America, and thereby opening doors for a whole swath of the American populace to achieve greater things in this country. Though W.A.S.P. society would never fully accept him as their own (to his great resentment), that they allowed him in their circles and courted him as a friend and ally was unprecedented. He was part of the first generation of Irish Americans to attain national political office, and he joined John Kelly as the first two Irish American bosses of the dominant political machine in New York State, Tammany Hall. He may have also been the first person of Irish birth to become a millionaire in the United States of America.

Morrissey doubtless attained a significant portion of his wealth and influence through means that were illegal. Because he was the alleged leader of the feared (and possibly fictional) Dead Rabbits street gang, because he certainly participated in his share of political corruption, and because he was the undisputed czar of New York gambling for over a decade, Morrissey has been characterized as the "first true Irish Mob boss in American history," and with good reason.[591]

Many of the political and social issues surrounding Morrissey a century and a half ago continue to stir passionate debate to this day. America's ceaseless battles over immigration, big government or local government, political corruption, corporate corruption, the popular vote and the electoral college, privatization or regulation, nationalism, impeachment, refugees, foreign influence, xenophobia, and demagoguery were all matters of heated and often violent arguments in which Morrissey was either personally or professional embroiled, and remain important to us today as the United States continues on its constant cycle of self-evaluation and re-definition.

More than anyone else, John Morrissey personified the links between sports, gambling, high-finance, politics, and crime in nineteenth century America. In some ways, these links still exist, though there certainly is no American today who has juggled all of those compelling but dangerous facets of society with as much skill, bravado, and ambition as did John Morrissey, for better or worse.

---

[591] English, 68

Bibliography & Sources

Books Referenced:

Ackerman, K. (2005). *Boss Tweed: The Rise and Fall of the Corrupt Pol Who Conceived the Soul of Modern New York.* New York: Carroll & Graf.

Adams, P. (2005). *The Bowery Boys: Street Corner Radicals and the Politics of Rebellion.* Westport: Prager.

Adler, J. and Hill, D. (2008). *Doomed by Cartoon: How Cartoonist Thomas Nast and the New York Times Brought Down Boss Tweed and His Ring of Thieves.* Garden City: Morgan James.

Anbinder, T. (2001). *Five Points: The 19th Century New York Neighborhood that Invented Tap Dance, Stole Elections, and Became the World's Most Notorious Slum.* New York: Plume.

Asbury, H. (1928). *The Gangs of New York: An Informal History of the Underworld.* New York: Thunder's Mouth.

Asbury, H. (1938). *Sucker's Progress: An Informal History of Gambling in America.* New York: Thunder's Mouth.

Bartels, J. (2007). *Saratoga Stories.* Lexington: Eclipse.

Bassett, G. (1889). *The Book of County Tipperary.* Dublin: Sealy, Byers & Walker.

Bergeron, P., editor. (1997). *The Papers of Andrew Johnson.* Knoxville: University of Tennessee.

Boddy, K. (2008). *Boxing: A Cultural History.* London: Reaktion.

Boessnecker, J. (1999). *Gold Dust and Gunsmoke: Tales of Gold Rush Outlaws, Gunfighters, Lawmen, and Vigilantes.* New York: John Wiley & Sons.

Bouyea, B. (2016). *Bare Knuckles & Saratoga Racing: The Remarkable Life of John Morrissey* Charleston: History Press.

Breen, M.P. (1899). *Thirty Years of New York Politics Up-to-date.* New York: Breen.

Browne, J.H. (1869). *The Great Metropolis: A Mirror of New York.* Hartford: American.

Buckman, B. (1876). *Samuel J. Tilden Unmasked!* New York: Benjamin E. Buckman.

Burrows, E.G. and Wallace, M. (1999). *Gotham: A History of New York Until 1898.* New York: Oxford University.

Caliendo, R.J. (2010). *New York City Mayors, Part I.* Xlibris.

Cliff, N. (2007). *The Shakespeare Riots: Revenge, Drama, and Death in Nineteenth-Century America.* New York: Random House.

Duane, D.C. (1999). *Against the Vigilantes: The Recollections of Dutch Charley Duane.* Norman: University of Oklahoma.

Duke, T.S. (1910). *Celebrated Criminal Cases of America*. San Francisco James H. Barry Co.

English, T. (2005). *Paddy Whacked: The Untold Story of the Irish-American Gangster*. New York: Regan.

Fox, R.K. (1889). *Prize Ring Heroes: Life and Battles of Tom Hyer, Yankee Sullivan, John Morrissey, Tom King*. New York: Richard K. Fox.

Gammie, P. (July, 1994). 'Pugilists and Politicians in Antebellum New York: The Life and Times of Tom Hyer.' *New York History*.

Gilfoyle, T.J. (1992). *City of Eros: New York City, Prostitution, and the Commercialization of Sex, 1790-1920*. New York: W.W. Norton & Co.

Ginsburg, D.E. (2004). *The Fix is In: A History of Baseball Gambling and Game Fixing Scandals*. Jefferson: McFarland.

Gipe, G.A. (1974, September 30). 'run, Sullivan! Run!' *Sports Illustrated*, p. 101.

Golway, T. (2014). *Machine Made: Tammany Hall and the Creation of Modern American Politics*. New York: W.W. Norton & Co.

Gorn, E.J. (1986). *The Manly Art: Bare-Knuckle Prize Fighting in America*. Ithaca: Cornell.

Gorn, E.J. (1987). "'Good-Bye Boys, I Die a True American': Homicide, Nativism, and Working-Class Culture in Antebellum New York City." *The Journal of American History*.

Gover, W.C. (1875). *The Tammany Hall Democracy of the City of New York*. New York: Martin Brown.

Graysmith, R. (2012). *Black Fire: The True-Story of the Original Tom Sawyer – And of the Mysterious Fires that Baptized Gold Rush-Era San Francisco*. New York: Crown.

Grayson, R. (2012). *California's Gold Rush*. Minneapolis: ABDO.

Haswell, C.H. (1896). *Reminiscences of an Octogenarian of the City of New York*. New York: Harper.

Holmes, T. (2008). *Saratoga Springs, New York: A Brief History*. Charleston: History Press.

Hotaling, E. (1995). *They're Off! Horse Racing at Saratoga*. Syracuse: Syracuse University.

Howell, J. (2012). *Gangs in America's Communities*. SAGE: Los Angeles.

Isenberg, M. (1994). *John L. Sullivan and His America*. Urbana; University of Illinois.

Jacob, K.A. (2010). *King of the Lobby: The Life and Times of Sam Ward, Man-About Washington in the Gilded Age*. Baltimore: Johns Hopkins University.

James, E. (1880). *The Life and Battles of Tom Hyer*. New York: Ed James.

James, E. (1880). *The Life and Battles of Yankee Sullivan*. New York: Ed James.

James, E. (1878). *Practical Training for Running, Walking, Rowing, Westling, Boxing, Jumping, and All Kinds of Athletic Feats*. New York: Ed James.

Kofoed, J. (1938). *Brandy for Heroes: A Biography of the Honorable John Morrissey, Champion Heavyweight of America and State Senator.* New York: E.P. Dutton.

Laing, J.M. (2015). *The Haymakers, Unions and Trojans of Troy, New York: Big-Time Baseball in the Collar City, 1860-1883.* Jefferson: McFarland.

Lewis, A.H. (1912). *Nation-Famous New York Murders.* Chicago: M.A. Donohue.

Lloyd, A. (1977). *The Great Prize-Fight.* London: Souvenir.

Maguire, J. (1868). *The Irish in America: A History of Nineteenth Century Immigration.* New York: D. & J. Sadlier.

Mandelbaum, S.J. (1965). *Boss Tweed's New York.* Chicago: Elephant.

McAlpine, R.W. (1872). *The Life and Times of Col. James Fisk, Jr.* New York: New York Book Co.

McClure, J.B. (1896). *Abraham Lincoln.* Chicago: Rhodes & McClure.

McClure, A. (1901). *Abraham Lincoln's Yarns and Stories.* New York: Western W. Wilson.

McLaughlin, J. (1885). *The Life and Times of John Kelly.* New York: American News Co.

Medbery, J. (1870). *Men and Mysteries of Wall Street.* Boston: Fields, Osgood, & Co.

Mee, B. (2001). *Bare Fists: The History of Bare Knuckle Prize Fighting* New York: Overlook.

Merritt, E.A. (1911). *Recollections, 1828-1911.* Albany: J.B. Lyon Co.

Mooney, C. (2014). *Race Horse Men: How Slavery and Freedom Were Made at the Racetrack.* Cambridge: Harvard.

Myers, A. (1973, April 2). "The Brawls at Boston Corners." *Sports Illustrated.* p. 114.

Myers, G. (1901). *The History of Tammany Hall.* New York: Gustavus Myers.

Mushkat, J. (1990). *Fernando Wood: A Political Biography.* Kent: Kent State University Press.

Nichols, T.J. (1874). *Forty Years of American Life.* London: Longmans, Green, & Co.

Nicholson, J.C. (2016). *The Notorious John Morrissey: How a Bare-Knuckle Brawler Became a Congressman and Founded Saratoga Race Course.* Lexington: University Press of Kentucky.

Offenbach, Jacques. (1877). *America and the Americans.* London: W. Reeves.

Pafford, J.M. (2019). *Chester A. Arthur: The Accidental President.* Washington D.C.: Regnery.

Redmond, Patrick R. (2014). *The Irish and the Making of American Sport.* Jefferson: Mcfarland.

Reiss, S. (2011). *The Sport Kings and the Kings of Crime: Horse Racing, Politics, and Organized Crime in New York.* Syracuse: Syracuse University.

Renehan, E. (2009). *Commodore: The Life of Cornelius Vanderbilt*. New York: Basic.

Rittner, D. (2002). *Troy*. Charleston: Arcadia.

Sage, M.R. (1898). *Emma Willard and Her Pupils*. Troy: Sage.

Schwartz, D.G. (2006). *Roll the Bones: The History of Gambling*. New York: Gotham.

Smith, M.H. (1874). *Bulls and Bears of New York*. Hartford: J.B. Burr.

Stewart, D. (2009). *Impeached: The Trial of President Andrew Johnson and the Fight for Lincoln's Legacy*. New York: Simon & Schuster.

Stanway, E. (2020). *Bill the Butcher: The Life and Death of William Poole*. Fitzwilliam: EMU.

Stiles, T. (2009). *The First Tycoon: The Epic Life of Cornelius Vanderbilt*. New York: Vintage.

Stott, R. (2009). *Jolly Fellows: Male Milieus in Nineteenth-Century America*. Baltimore: Johns Hopkins University.

Strausbaugh, J. (2016). *City of Sedition: The History of New York City During the Civil War*. New York: Hachette.

Sutton, C. (1874). *The New York Tombs: Its Secrets and Its Mysteries: Being a History of Noted Criminals, with Narratives of Their Crimes*. San Francisco: A. Roman & Co.

Timony, P. (1849). *American Fistiana, Containing a History of Prize Fighting in the United States, With All the Principle Battles for the Last Forty Years*. New York: H. Johnson.

Unknown. (1852). *San Francisco Directory for the Year 1852-53*. San Francisco.

Unknown (1876). *Journals of the Senate of the State of New York: At the Ninety-Ninth Session*. Albany: Weed, Parsons & Co.

Walling, G.W. (1887). *Recollections of a New York Chief of Police*. New York: Caxton Book Concern.

Weise, A.J. (1886). *The City of Troy and its Vicinity*. Troy: Edward Green.

Werner, M.R. (1968). *Tammany Hall*. New York: Greenwood Press.

Wingate, C.F. (1875, January). 'An Episode in Municipal Government.' *North American Review*. p. 119.

Zimmerman, K. (2015). *Morrissey v. Poole: Politics, Prizefighting and the Murder of Bill the Butcher*. St. Louis: Zimmerman

Periodicals Referenced:

Albany Evening Journal; Alexandria Gazette; Amsterdam Evening Recorder; Ashtabula Telegraph; Atlas; Baltimore Sun; Bell's Life in London; Birmingham Daily Post; Bismark Tribune; Brewster Standard; Brockport Republic; Brooklyn Daily Eagle; Burlington Daily Times; Burr Oak Herald; Cazenovia Republican; Charleston Daily News; Chicago Daily Tribune; Cleveland Daily Reader; Cleveland Plain Dealer; Commercial Advertiser; Daily Albany Argus; Daily Alta California; Daily Dispatch; Daily Empire; Daily Globe; Daily Inter Ocean; Daily Journal; Daily Ledger; Daily

Milwaukee News; Daily National Era; Daily Telegraph; Daily True Delta; Danville Express; Edgefield Advertiser; Era; Evening Journal; Evening Post; Evening Star; Fort Edward Ledger; For Scott Daily Advertiser; Frank Leslie's Illustrated Newspaper; Helena Independent; Holt County Sentinel; Indiana Herald; Irish American; Irish World; Ithaca Daily Journal; Ithaca Journal; Jackson Standard; Jeffersonian; Journal of American History; Lancaster Ledger; London Evening Standard; Louisville Daily Courier; Manawatu Times; Manhattan Nationalist; Manchester Journal; Maryland Free Press; Memphis Daily Appeal; Memphis Public Ledger; Middlebury Register; Morning News; Nashville Union and American; National Police Gazette; National Republican; New Orleans Crescent; New Orleans Democrat; New York Clipper; New York Daily Tribune; New York Herald; New York History; New York Semi-Weekly Express; New York Sun; New York Times; North American Review; Ogdensburg Journal; Pittsfield Sun; Public Ledger; Nashville Union and American; Nebraska Advertiser; New Orleans Republican; Northern New York Journal; Pilot; Raftsman's Journal; Redwood Gazette; Richmond Enquirer; Russelville Democrat; Rutland Weekly Herald; Sacramento Transcript; San Francisco Call; Schenectady Cabinet; Seattle Post-Intelligencer; Spirit of Democracy; Sports Illustrated; Sunday Star; Times-Picayune; Troy Weekly Times; Urbana Union; Vancouver Independent; Waterford News; Watertown Re-union; Watertown Times; Wheeling Daily Intelligencer; Wide West; Winnsboro News and Herald

Websites Referenced:

allthatsinsteresting.com; ancestry.com; books.google.com; britishnewspaperarchive.co.uk; cdnc.ucr.edu; chroniclingamerica.loc.gov; cityofsmoke.com; cyberboxingzone.com; geneaologybank.com; govtrack.us; gwu.edu; healthline.com; ibhof.com; irishstudies.sunygenesoenglish.org; jstor.org; legendsofamerica.com; loc.gov; malakoff.com; meritimeheritage.org; newspapers.com; newspapers.bc.edu; noehill.com; nyshistoricnewspapers.org; nysun.com; nytimes.com; rootsweb.ancestry.com; sabr.org; sfcityguides.org; shu.edu; theirishmob.com; vancouverisland.com

Index

www.ingramcontent.com/pod-product-compliance
Lightning Source LLC
Chambersburg PA
CBHW020455270326
41926CB00008B/619

9 781949 783025